W9-AWC-634

PROPERTY OF FULTON COUNTY
SCHOOL SYSTEM

Milton High School
86 School Drive
Alpharetta, GA 30004
770-740-7000

A Guide to
Programming in C++

Tim Corica
Beth Brown
Bruce Presley

Copyright © 1997
by

Lawrenceville Press

First Edition

ISBN   1-879233-90-8   (softcover)
ISBN   1-879233-91-6   (hardcover)

All rights reserved. No part of this work covered by the copyright may be reproduced or used in any form or by any means — graphic, electronic, or mechanical, including photocopying, recording, taping, or information storage and retrieval systems — without the written permission of the publisher, with the exception of programs, which may be entered, stored, and executed in a computer system, but not reprinted for publication or resold in any other form.

Printed in the United States of America

All orders including educational, Canadian, foreign, FPO, and APO may be placed by contacting:

Lawrenceville Press, Inc.
P.O. Box 704
Pennington, NJ 08534-0704
(609) 737-1148
(609) 737-8564 fax

This text is available in hardcover and softcover editions.

16 15 14 13 12 11 10 9 8 7 6 5 4 3

The text is written and published by Lawrenceville Press, Inc. and is in no way connected with Borland, Inc. or the Microsoft® Corporation.

Borland screen captures are copyrighted by and reprinted with permission of Borland International, Inc., 1995. All rights reserved.

Microsoft is a registered trademark of the Microsoft Corporation. Screen shots reprinted by permission from Microsoft Corporation.

P | Preface

We have strived to make this the clearest, most comprehensible C++ text available. Our primary objective in this text is to present material in clear language with easy to follow examples. To meet this objective, we and our reviewers have thoroughly classroom tested the text.

We believe that students must be instructed in what constitutes good programming style so that their programs are easy to understand, modify, and debug. Good programming techniques are presented throughout the text.

As programming teachers, we have reviewed most of the currently available C++ texts and have found them too often lacking the clarity required to explain difficult concepts. Also, we have discovered that the teacher support material provided with these texts is both limited and inadequate. This text and its comprehensive Teacher's Resource Package are our answer to the problem.

It is our belief that learning to program offers the student an invaluable opportunity to develop problem-solving skills. The process of defining a problem, breaking it down into a series of smaller problems and finally writing a computer program to solve it is an exercise in learning to think logically. In addition, the student is made aware of the capabilities and limitations of the computer and soon realizes that the programmer—the human element—is more important than the machine.

A Guide to Programming in C++ is written for a one or two-term course. No previous programming experience is required or assumed. It is the goal of this text to provide the best possible introduction for students learning C++, whether they will continue on to more advanced computer science courses or end their computer education with this introductory course.

Topic Organization

Chapter One presents a brief history of computing and introduces the student to computer and programming terminology.

In Chapter Two students learn what an object-oriented language is and are introduced to C++ programming structure. From the beginning the importance of employing good programming style is emphasized.

Chapter Three presents variable assignment, data types, and string types. The first Case Study is presented where students are taught the process of specification, design, coding, and debugging and testing.

Chapter Four introduces the if statement, the looping statements do-while and for, and Boolean variables. The Case Study that ends the chapter produces a guessing game program.

The emphasis of Chapter Five is on the user-defined function. Concepts presented include using default parameters, passing values, and using pre and post conditions. Students are shown how to build a library and how to use top-down design in constructing large programs. In the Case Study a program to play a game of 21 is created.

Chapter Six presents classes and objects including the concept of instantiation and member functions. Students are taught how to solve the towers of Hanoi puzzle. In the Case Study, data storing a college database is displayed.

Mathematical functions, rounding values, recursion, and enumerated types are discussed in Chapter Seven. In the Case Study a program is written to perform numerical integration for several mathematical functions.

Using arrays including storing values, searching, and manipulating a string object is explained in Chapter Eight. Both two and three dimensional arrays are presented. A vote analysis program is written in the Case Study.

Chapter Nine explains how a stream processes characters. The fstream library is used. Students are taught how to read numeric and character data and how to pass and return stream objects as parameters. Random access files are also presented.

Chapter Ten explains how to create classes. Topics such as defining member functions, building utility classes, and using special member functions are presented. The fundamental concepts of object-oriented programming and object-oriented design are discussed. The Case Study improves upon the AccountClass developed in the chapter.

Chapter Eleven explains event-driven programming. Students create GUI-based programs using libraries included with this text.

Sorting a list using a selective sort or a merge sort as well as measuring the efficiency of a sorting algorithm are discussed in Chapter Twelve. Searching a list using a binary search or a depth-first search is also discussed.

Chapter Thirteen introduced advanced data structures including stacks, queues, and linked lists. Dynamic memory and binary search trees are also explained.

Design and Features

Classroom Tested

This text has been written based upon the author's more than thirty years of experience in teaching programming. All of the material in this text has been tested and developed in their classrooms. The text has also been reviewed as it was being written by more than thirty experienced computer educators.

Problem Solving

From the very beginning, students are taught to solve problems using proper programming techniques.

Programming Style

Throughout the text separate sections are devoted to explaining in detail the concepts of proper programming style so that students will make their programs easy to read, modify, and debug.

P

Demonstration Programs and Runs	Many demonstration programs are included, complete with sample runs, so that students are shown both proper programming techniques and the output actually produced by their computer.
Format	Each C++ statement is given a clear definition, shown in a single program line and then demonstrated in a program body.
Case Studies	Beginning in Chapter Three, most chapters end by stating a problem and then developing the appropriate algorithm. The process of specification, design, coding, and debugging and testing is clearly outlined for producing the problem's solution.
Reviews	Numerous reviews are presented throughout each chapter which provide immediate reinforcement to newly learned concepts. Solutions to the reviews are given in the Teacher's Resource Package.
Chapter Summaries	A summary appears at the end of each chapter. These summaries offer the student a review of the important concepts presented in the chapter.
Vocabulary	Newly introduced terms are defined at the end of each chapter.
C++	A review of new symbols, keywords, and libraries is presented at the chapter's end.
Exercises	Each chapter includes a large set of exercises of varying difficulty, making them appropriate for students with a range of abilities. Many of the exercises contain a demonstration run to help make clear what output is expected from the student's program. Exercises based on previous work are marked with a ☼ symbol. Advanced exercises are indicated as such, and require a carefully thought-out algorithm and stepwise refinement as part of its solution, similar in form to that used in solving the Case Study. Answers to the exercises are included on diskette.
Illustrations	Considerable care has been taken to make the many illustrations in this text meaningful so that they serve to increase the student's understanding of topics being discussed.
Indexes	In addition to the standard index an index of the major programs in the text is included.
Software Appendices	Separate appendices for Turbo C++ and Microsoft Visual C++ are included to cover the unique features of each software package.

Teacher's Resource Package and Diskette

When used with this text, the Lawrenceville Press Teacher's Resource Package provides all the additional material required to offer students an excellent introductory programming course. These materials place a strong emphasis on developing the student's problem-solving skills. The Package divides each of the chapters in the text into lessons that contain the following features:

Assignments - Suggested reading and problem assignments.

Teaching Notes - Helpful information that we and our reviewers have learned from classroom experience.

Transparency Masters - Diagrams of the different topics that can be copied onto film.

In addition to the material in the lessons, other features are included for each chapter:

Tests - A comprehensive test for each chapter as well as a midterm and final examination. Each test consists of multiple choice questions and problems that are solved on the computer by writing a C++ program. A full set of answers and a grading key are also included.

Answers - Complete answers for the reviews and exercises presented in the text.

A master diskette, included with the Package contains the following files:

Program files - All major programs including all programs in the program index, the Case Studies, and the Lawrenceville Press libraries are included on the diskette.

Tests - The tests are also provided in text files so that they can be edited.

Answer files - Answers to the reviews, exercises, and tests.

Student diskettes containing many of the example programs, Case Studies, and the Lawrenceville Press libraries can be easily made by following the directions included in the Teacher's Resource Package. Student diskettes are also available in packs of 10.

As an added feature, the Package is contained in a 3-ring binder. This not only enables pages to be removed for duplication, but also allows you to keep your own notes in the Package.

A Guide to Programming in C++

Previous editions of our programming texts have established them as leaders in their field, with more than two million students having been introduced to computing using one of our texts. With this new C++ text, we have made significant improvements over our earlier programming texts. These improvements are based on the many comments we received, a survey of instructors who are teaching the text, and our own classroom experience.

A Guide to Programming in C++ is available in softcover and hardcover editions. As an additional feature the softcover edition has an improved sewn lay-flat binding which keeps the text open at any page and gives the book additional strength.

As classroom instructors, we know the importance of using a well written and logically organized text. With this edition we believe that we have produced the finest introductory C++ programming text and Teacher's Resource Package available.

Lawrenceville Press Libraries

The libraries supplied by Lawrenceville Press are based on the classes defined for use in the AP Computer Science courses. Inclusion of the C++ classes defined for use in the Advanced Placement Computer Science courses does not constitute endorsement of the other material in *A Guide*

P

to Programming in C++ (Lawrenceville Press, June 1997) by the College Board, Educational Testing Service, or the AP Computer Science Development Committee.

Acknowledgments

The authors are especially grateful to the following instructors and their students who classroom tested this text as it was being written. Their comments and suggestions have been invaluable:

Neil Ascione, Madison, NJ
Betty Badgett, Abington, PA
Bob Britten, Victoria, BC Canada
Fran Bucci, Pennellville, NY
Gerald Chung, Sherwood Park, AB Canada
David Coad, Campbell River, BC Canada
Judith Conway, Bear, DE
M.G. Corcoran, Suffield, CT
Mike Dubin, Euclid, OH
Gary Farbman, Pine Bush, NY
Jim Fraser, Hebron, NE
William Freitas, Claremont, CA
Kyle Gillett, Denver, CO
Bev Hall, Farmington, CT
Robert Hare, Ardmore, OK
Edwin Hensley, Round Rock, TX
Nan Hert, Boca Raton, FL
Nancy Hudanich, Cape May, NJ
John Junell, Sequim, WA
Roger Kiel, Annandale, NJ
Deborah Klipp, Linwodd, NJ
Helen Koch, Calgary, AB Canada
Kathleen Larson, Kingston, NY
Carol Martin, Marietta, GA
Sue Michaels, New Milford, NJ
Dan Minsart, Chico, CA
Meezie Pierce, West Palm Beach, FL
Dennis Pieretti, Toms River, NJ
Joel Tomski, Des Plaines, IL
Evelyn Torres-Rangel, San Gabriel, CA
Conrad Trapp, New Ulm, MN
Joel Wagnor, Englewood, NJ
John Wieja, Wassenaar, Netherlands

A special thanks is due Helen Koch, Calgary, AB Canada. She has provided many helpful comments and suggestions from her review of the text. We also wish to thank her students.

We thank Courier Book Companies, Inc. who supervised the printing of this text.

The success of this and all of our texts is due to the efforts of Heidi Crane, Vice President of Marketing at Lawrenceville Press. Joseph Dupree and Robin Van Ness run our Customer Relations Department and handle the many thousands of orders we receive in a friendly and efficient manner. Rich Guarascio and Michael Porter are responsible for the excellent service Lawrenceville Press offers in shipping orders.

Vickie Grassman, a member of the Lawrenceville Press staff, edited Chapters One and Eleven, authored both appendices, and reviewed much of the text. Marie Gann, a student at Florida Atlantic University, reviewed the text and tested much of the code. Jeff Dytko, a student at the University of Dayton, is responsible for the table of contents and comprehensive index. We appreciate their efficiency and thoroughness.

The graphics in this text were produced by Elaine Malfas, director of computer graphics at Lawrenceville Press, and John Gandour. Elaine also produced the cover. Her artistic ability and professionalism are greatly appreciated.

A note of appreciation is due our colleague Nanette Hert. She helped test this text in her class and has offered valuable suggestions on ways in which it could be improved.

Finally, we would like to thank our students, for whom and with whom this text was written. Their candid evaluation of each lesson and their refusal to accept anything less than perfect clarity in explanation have been the driving forces behind the creation of *A Guide to Programming in C++*.

Mr. Corica wishes to express his appreciation for the support and sacrifices made by his family, Maryanne, Matthew, and Daniel during the writing of this text. He also promises to return the dining room to its originally intended use.

About the Authors

Tim Corica earned both his A.B. degree and M.S. degree in computer science from Princeton University. Mr. Corica has been teaching computer programming for nearly twenty years. He served on the development committee of the Advanced Placement Computer Science Examination and as examination leader at the Advanced Placement grading. Mr. Corica, who co-authored *A Guide to Programming in Turbo Pascal* for Lawrenceville Press, is currently teaching computer science.

Beth A. Brown, a graduate in computer science of Florida Atlantic University, is director of development at Lawrenceville Press where she has co-authored a number of programming and applications texts and their Teacher's Resource Packages. Ms. Brown currently teaches computer programming and computer applications.

Bruce W. Presley, a graduate of Yale University, taught computer science and physics and served as the director of the Karl Corby Computer and Mathematics Center located in Lawrenceville, New Jersey. Mr. Presley was a member of the founding committee of the Advanced Placement Computer Science examination and served as a consultant to the College Entrance Examination Board. Presently Mr. Presley, author of more than twenty computer textbooks, is president of Lawrenceville Press and teaches computer programming and computer applications.

T | Table of Contents

Chapter Three - Variables and Constants

Chapter Four - Controlling Program Flow

A Guide to Programming in C++

T

Chapter Five - Functions

Chapter Six - Classes and Objects

Chapter Seven - Mathematics, Recursion, and enum

Chapter Eight - Arrays and structs

T

Chapter Nine - Streams and Files

Chapter Ten - Building Classes

Chapter Eleven - Graphics and Event-Driven Programming

Chapter Twelve - Advanced Algorithms and Recursion

Chapter Thirteen - Data Structures

T

Appendix A - Turbo C++

Appendix B - Microsoft Visual C++

Appendix C - Keywords in C++

Index

T

A Guide to Programming in C++

Chapter One
An Introduction to Computers

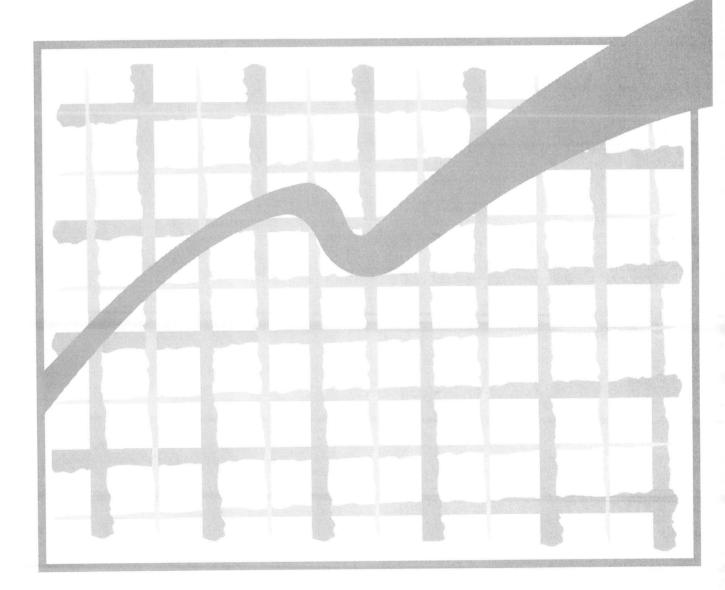

Objectives

After completing this chapter you will be able to:

1. Discuss the history of computers.

2. Understand how the microcomputer works.

3. Understand the binary number system.

4. Understand how data is stored in memory.

5. Understand the ethical responsibilities of the programmer.

1

In this chapter you will learn about computers, their history, and how they process and store data. Important issues relating to computers is also discussed.

There are three reasons for learning how to use a computer. The first and most important is to develop problem-solving skills. This is done by learning how to analyze a problem carefully, develop a step-by-step solution, and then use the computer as a tool to produce a solution.

A second reason for learning about computers is to become acquainted with their capabilities and limitations. Because you are a part of a computerized society, learning to use a computer is probably the best way to become familiar with one.

Finally, using a computer can be fun. The intellectual challenge of controlling the operations of a computer is not only rewarding but also an invaluable skill. The techniques learned in this class can be used both at home and on the job.

1.1 What is a Computer?

A *computer* is an electronic machine that accepts information (called *data*), processes it according to specific instructions, and provides the results as new information. The computer can store and manipulate large quantities of data at a very high speed and, even though it cannot think, it can make simple decisions and comparisons. For example, a computer can determine which of two numbers is larger or which of two names comes first alphabetically and then act upon that decision.

Although the computer can help to solve a wide variety of problems, it is merely a machine and cannot solve problems on its own. It must be provided with instructions in the form of a computer program. A *program* is a list of instructions written in a special language that the computer understands. It tells the computer which operations to perform and in what sequence to perform them. You will use the C++ language to create programs.

The History of Computers

Many of the advances made by science and technology are dependent upon the ability to perform complex mathematical calculations and to process large amounts of data. It is therefore not surprising that for thousands of years mathematicians, scientists, and business people have searched for computing machines that could perform calculations and analyze data quickly and accurately.

1.2 Ancient Counting Machines

As civilizations began to develop, they created both written languages and number systems. These number systems were not originally meant to be used in mathematical calculations, but rather were designed to record measurements like the number of sheep in a flock. Roman numerals are a good example of these early number systems. Few of us would want to carry out even the simplest arithmetic operations using Roman numerals. How then were calculations performed thousands of years ago?

Calculations were carried out with a device known as an *abacus* which was used in ancient Babylon, China, and throughout Europe until the late middle-ages. Many parts of the world, especially in the Orient, still make use of the abacus. The abacus works by sliding beads on a frame with the beads on the top of the frame representing fives and the beads on the bottom of the frame representing ones. After a calculation is made the result is written down.

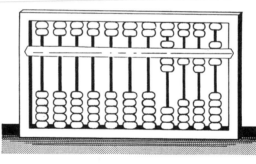

The abacus is a calculating device used throughout the Orient

1.3 Arabic Numerals

Toward the end of the middle ages, Roman numerals were replaced by a new number system borrowed from the Arabs, therefore called Arabic numerals. This system uses ten digits and is the system we still use today. Because the Arabic system made calculations with pencil and paper easier, the abacus and other such counting devices became less common. Although calculations were now easier to perform, operations such as multiplication and division were able to be done by only those few mathematicians who were well educated.

1 1.4 The Pascaline

One of the earliest mechanical devices for calculating was the *Pascaline*, invented by the French philosopher and mathematician Blaise Pascal in 1642. At that time Pascal was employed in the recording of taxes for the French government. The task was tedious and kept him up until the early hours of the morning day after day. Being a gifted thinker, Pascal thought that the task of adding numbers should be able to be done by a mechanism that operated similarly to the way that a clock keeps time.

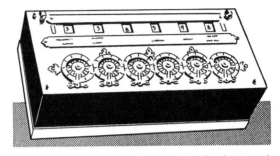

The Pascaline was a mechanical calculating device invented by Blaise Pascal in 1642

The Pascaline he invented was a complicated set of gears which could only be used to perform addition and not for multiplication or division. Unfortunately, due to manufacturing problems, Pascal never got the device to work properly.

1.5 The Stepped Reckoner

Later in the 17th century Gottfried Wilhelm von Leibniz, a famous mathematician credited with being one of the developers of calculus, invented a device that was supposed to be able to add and subtract, as well as multiply, divide, and calculate square roots. His device, the *Stepped Reckoner*, included a cylindrical wheel called the *Leibniz wheel* and a moveable carriage that was used to enter the number of digits in the multiplicand.

Though both Pascal's and Leibniz's machines held great promise, they did not work well because the craftsmen of their time were unable to make machined parts that were accurate enough to carry out the inventor's design. Because of the mechanically unreliable parts, the devices tended to jam and malfunction.

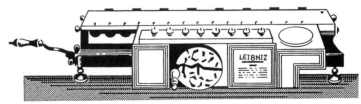

The Stepped Reckoner was another early attempt at creating a mechanical calculating device

1.6 The Punched Card

In 1810 Joseph Jacquard, a French weaver, made a revolutionary discovery. He realized that the weaving instructions for his looms could be stored on cards with holes punched in them. As the cards passed through the loom in sequence, needles passed through the holes and then picked up threads of the correct color or texture. By rearranging the cards, a weaver could change the pattern being woven without stopping the machine to change threads.

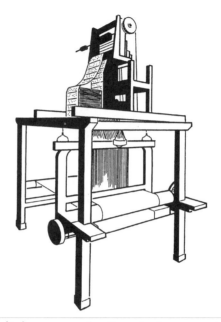

Jacquard's loom was the first device to make use of punched cards to store information

The weaving industry would seem to have little in common with the computer industry, but the idea that information could be stored by punching holes on a card was to be of great use in the later development of the computer.

1.7 Babbage's Difference and Analytical Engines

In 1822 Charles Babbage began work on the *Difference Engine*. His hope was that this device would calculate numbers to the 20th place and then print them at 44 digits per minute. The original purpose of this machine was to produce tables of numbers that would be used by ship's navigators. At the time navigation tables were often highly inaccurate due to calculation errors. In fact, several ships were known to have been lost at sea because of these errors. However, because of mechanical problems similar to those that plagued Pascal and Leibniz, the Difference Engine never worked properly.

Undaunted, Babbage later planned and began work on a considerably more advanced machine called the *Analytical Engine*. This machine was to perform a variety of calculations by following a set of instructions, or *program*, entered into it using punched cards similar to the ones used by

Joseph Jacquard. During processing, the Analytical Engine was to store information in a memory unit that would allow it to make decisions and then carry out instructions based on those decisions. For example, for comparing two numbers it could be programmed to determine which was larger and then follow different sets of instructions. The Analytical Engine was no more successful than its predecessors, but its design was to serve as a model for the modern computer.

Babbage's Analytical Engine was a calculating machine that used punched cards to store information

Babbage's chief collaborator on the Analytical Engine was Ada, Countess of Lovelace, the daughter of Lord Byron. Interested in mathematics, Lady Lovelace was a sponsor of the Engine and one of the first people to realize its power and significance. She also tested the device and wrote of its achievements in order to gain support for it. Because of her involvement she is often called the first programmer.

Babbage had hoped that the Analytical Engine would be able to think. Lady Lovelace, however, said that the Engine could never "originate anything," meaning that she did not believe that a machine, no matter how powerful, could think. To this day her statement about computing machines remains true.

1.8 The Electronic Tabulating Machine

By the end of the 19th century, U.S. Census officials were concerned about the time it took to tabulate the continuously increasing number of Americans. This counting was done every 10 years, as required by the Constitution. However, the Census of 1880 took 9 years to compile which made the figures highly inaccurate by the time they were published.

To solve the problem, Herman Hollerith invented a calculating machine that used electricity rather than mechanical gears. Holes representing information to be tabulated were punched in cards similar to those used in Jacquard's loom, with the location of each hole representing a specific piece of information (male, female, age, etc.). The cards were then inserted into the machine and metal pins used to open and close electrical circuits. If a circuit was closed, a counter was increased by one.

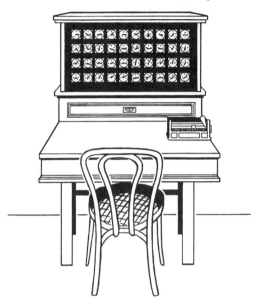

Herman Hollerith's tabulating machine, invented for the Census of 1880, used electricity instead of gears to perform calculations

Hollerith's machine was immensely successful. The general count of the population, then 63 million, took only six weeks to calculate, while full statistical analysis took seven years. This may not sound like much of an improvement over the nine years of the previous census, but Hollerith's machine enabled the Census Bureau to make a far more detailed and useful study of the population than had previously been possible. Based on the success of his invention, Hollerith and some friends formed a company that sold his invention all over the world. The company eventually became known as International Business Machines (IBM).

1.9 The Mark I

By the 1930s, key-operated mechanical adding machines had been developed which used a complicated assortment of gears and levers. Scientists, engineers, and business people, however, needed machines more powerful than adding machines; machines capable of making simple decisions such as determining which of two numbers was larger and then acting upon the decision. A machine with this capability is called a computer rather than a calculator. A calculator is not a true computer because, while it can perform calculations, it cannot make decisions.

The first computer-like machine is generally thought to be the *Mark I*, which was built by a team from IBM and Harvard University under the leadership of Howard Aiken. The Mark I used mechanical telephone relay switches to store information and accepted data on punched cards, processed it and then output the new data. Because it could not make decisions about the data it processed, the Mark I was not a real computer but was instead a highly sophisticated calculator. Nevertheless, it was impressive in size, measuring over 51 feet in length and weighing 5 tons!

It also had over 750,000 parts, many of them moving mechanical parts which made the Mark I not only huge but unreliable.

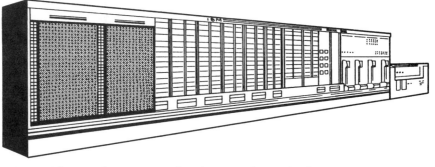

The Mark 1 was 51 feet long and weighed over 5 tons

1.10 ENIAC: The First Electronic Computer

In June 1943, John Mauchly and J. Presper Eckert began work on the Electronic Numerical Integration and Calculator, or *ENIAC*. It was originally a secret military project which began during World War II to calculate the trajectory of artillery shells. Built at the University of Pennsylvania, it was not finished until 1946, after the war had ended. But the great effort put into the ENIAC was not wasted. In one of its first demonstrations ENIAC was given a problem that would have taken a team of mathematicians three days to solve. It solved the problem in twenty seconds.

ENIAC was different from the Mark I in several important ways. First, it occupied 1500 square feet, which is the same area taken up by the average three bedroom house and it weighed 30 tons. Second, it used vacuum tubes instead of relay switches. It contained over 17,000 of these tubes, which were the same kind used in radios. Because the tubes consumed huge amounts of electricity the computer produced a tremendous amount of heat and required special fans to cool the room where it was installed. Most importantly, because it was able to make decisions, it was the first true computer.

Because it could make decisions, ENIAC was the first true computer

ENIAC had two major weaknesses. First, it was difficult to change its instructions to have the computer solve different problems. It had originally been designed to compute artillery trajectory tables, but when it needed to work on another problem it could take up to three days of wire pulling, replugging, and switch-flipping to change instructions. Second, the ENIAC was unreliable because the tubes it contained were constantly burning out.

Today, much of the credit for the original design of the electronic computer is given to John Atanasoff, a math and physics professor at Iowa State University. Between 1939 and 1942, Atanasoff, working with graduate student Clifford Berry, developed a working digital computer on the campus at Iowa State. Unfortunately, their patent application was not handled properly, and it was not until almost 50 years later that Atanasoff received full credit for his invention, the *Atanasoff Berry Computer* (ABC). In 1990, he was awarded the Presidential Medal of Technology for his pioneering work, and some of his early devices were exhibited at the Smithsonian.

1.11 The Stored Program Computer

In the mid 1940s, John von Neumann developed the idea of storing computer instructions in a central processing unit, or *CPU*. This unit consisted of different elements to control all the functions of the computer electronically so that it would not be necessary to flip switches or pull wires to change the instructions. Now it would be possible to solve many different problems by simply typing in new instructions at a keyboard. Together with Mauchly and Eckert, von Neumann designed and built the *EDVAC* (Electronic Discrete Variable Automatic Computer) and the *EDSAC* (Electronic Delay Storage Automatic Computer).

With the development of the concept of stored instructions, or programs, the modern computer age was ready to begin. Since then, the development of new computers has progressed rapidly, but von Neumann's concept has remained, for the most part, unchanged.

Based on von Neumann's concept, all computers process information, or *data* by carrying out four specific activities:

1. Input data
2. Store data while it is being processed
3. Process data according to specific instructions
4. Output the results in the form of new data.

The next computer to employ von Neumann's concepts was the UNIVersal Automatic Computer, or *UNIVAC*, built by Mauchly and Eckert. The first one was sold to the U.S. Census Bureau in 1951.

Computers continued to use many vacuum tubes which made them large and expensive. UNIVAC weighed 35 tons. These computers were so expensive to purchase and run that only the largest corporations and the U.S. government could afford them. Their ability to perform up to 1,000 calculations per second, however, made them popular.

1.12 The Transistor

It was the invention of the *transistor* that made smaller and less expensive computers possible, with increased calculating speeds of up to 10,000 calculations per second. Although the size of the computers shrank, they were still large and expensive. In the early 1960s, IBM, using ideas it had learned while working on projects for the military, introduced the first medium-sized computer named the model 650. It was still expensive, but it was capable of handling the flood of paper work produced by many government agencies and businesses. Such organizations provided a ready market for the 650, making it popular in spite of its cost.

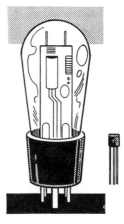

One transistor replaced many tubes, making computers smaller, less expensive, and more reliable

These new computers also saw a change in the way data was stored. Punched cards were replaced by magnetic tape and high speed reel-to-reel tape machines. Using magnetic tape gave computers the ability to read (access) and write (store) data quickly and reliably.

1.13 Integrated Circuits

The next major technological advancement was the replacement of transistors by tiny integrated circuits or *chips*. Chips are blocks of silicon with logic circuits etched into their surfaces. They are smaller and cheaper than transistors and can contain thousands of circuits on a single chip. Integrated circuits also give computers tremendous speed allowing them to process information at a rate of millions of calculations per second.

Chips are covered by intricate circuits that have been etched into their surfaces and then coated with a metallic oxide that fills in the etched circuit patterns. This enables the chips to conduct electricity along the many paths of their circuits. Because there are as many as millions of circuits on a single chip, the chips are called integrated circuits.

Integrated circuits are so small that they must be housed in special plastic cases that have metal pins coming out of them. The pins allow the chips to be plugged into circuit boards that have wiring printed on them.

A typical integrated circuit chip (approximately half an inch wide and 1.5 inches long)

One of the most important benefits of using integrated circuits is to decrease the cost and size of computers. The IBM System 360 was one of the first computers to use integrated circuits and was so popular with businesses that IBM had difficulty keeping up with the demand. Computers had come down in size and price to such a point that smaller organizations such as universities and hospitals could now afford them.

1.14 Mainframes

Mainframe computers are large computer systems that cost many hundreds of thousands, if not millions, of dollars. Mainframes can carry out many different tasks at the same time. They are used by large corporations, banks, government agencies, and universities. Mainframes can calculate a large payroll, keep the records for a bank, handle the reservations for an airline, or store student information for a university—tasks that require the storage and processing of huge amounts of information.

Mainframe computers are large, often requiring their own rooms

Most people using mainframes communicate with them using *terminals*. A terminal consists of a keyboard for data input, and a monitor for viewing output. The terminal is connected by wires to the computer, which may be located on a different floor or a building a few blocks away. Some mainframe computers have hundreds of terminals attached and working at the same time.

1 The Modern Computer

Even though the field of computer science is a relatively young one, a great many advances have been made in its first 45 years. The previous sections on the history of computers introduced the different generations of computers that lead to the modern computer. Computers developed between 1951-1958, such as ENIAC, used vacuum tubes and are often called *First Generation* computers. *Second Generation* computers were developed between 1959-1964 and used transistors instead of vacuum tubes to process information. Because of transistors, computers like the IBM model 650 were smaller, faster, and could process larger amounts of information than their predecessors. The next generation of computers used integrated circuits, reducing size and cost while increasing speed and reliability. These *Third Generation* computers were developed between 1965-1970, with the IBM System 360 being the most popular. *Fourth Generation* computers, which began development in the early 1970s, include large-scale integrated circuits and microprocessors. Today's desktop personal computer is an example of a Fourth Generation computer.

1.15 The Microprocessor and the Microcomputer

The most important advancement to occur in the early 70s was the invention of the *microprocessor*, an entire CPU on a single chip. In 1970, Marcian Hoff, an engineer at Intel Corporation, designed the first of these chips.

The small microprocessor made it possible to build a computer called a *microcomputer* that fit on a desktop. The first of these was the ALTAIR in 1975. In 1977, working originally out of a garage, Stephen Wozniak and Steven Jobs designed and built the Apple computer.

Fast advances in technology made microcomputers inexpensive and therefore available to many people. Because of these advances almost anyone could own a machine that had more computing power and was faster and more reliable than either the ENIAC or UNIVAC. As a comparison, if the cost of a sports car had dropped as quickly as that of a computer, a new Porsche would now cost about one dollar.

1.16 The Personal Computer

Microcomputers, often called *personal computers* (PCs), can cost as little as a few hundred dollars and fit on a desk. During the past few years their processing speed and their ability to store large amounts of data have increased to the point where some microcomputers now rival older mainframe computers. The computer you will use is a microcomputer.

A microcomputer consists of several *hardware* components:

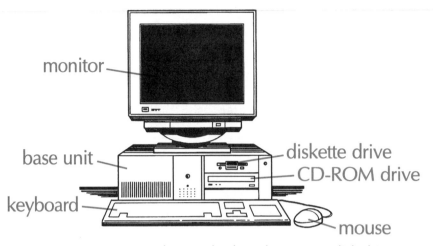

monitor

base unit

keyboard

diskette drive

CD-ROM drive

mouse

A microcomputer combines a keyboard, monitor, disk drives, and a mouse in a desktop-sized package

The base unit of a microcomputer contains the CPU and data storage devices such as a diskette drive, a CD-ROM drive, and a *hard disk* which is a disk drive completely contained inside the base unit. The keyboard, mouse, and disk drives are used to input data, and the monitor is used to view input and output. A microcomputer also has *software* which are programs that tell a computer what to do.

Many businesses and schools have *networked* their microcomputers. In a network, microcomputers are connected so that data can be transmitted between them. Because a network can include a large number of computers, it can perform many of the functions of a mainframe. As network technology progresses, the distinction between a mainframe computer and networked microcomputers is rapidly becoming blurred.

1.17 Computer Architecture

Computer architecture deals with the hardware components of a computer system. Computer systems contain four subsystems:

1. **Input Devices:** tools from which the computer can accept data from the user. A keyboard, scanner, and a mouse are all examples of input devices.

2. **Memory:** the electronic storage of instructions and data.

3. **Central Processing Unit (CPU):** a chip inside the computer that processes data and controls the flow of data between the computer's other units. It is here that the computer makes decisions.

4. **Output Devices:** tools from which the computer can display data to the user. Monitors and printers are the most common visual output devices.

A Guide to Programming in C++

This diagram illustrates the direction in which data flows between a computer's subsystems:

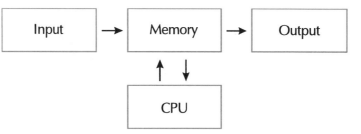

memory

There are different types of memory in a computer system. *Read Only Memory*, or *ROM*, contains the most basic operating instructions for the computer. It is a permanent part of the computer and cannot be changed. The instructions in ROM enable the computer to complete simple jobs such as placing a character on the screen or checking the keyboard to see if any keys have been pressed.

Three additional memory components are *Random Access Memory* (*RAM*), registers, and auxiliary memory. RAM, also called *main memory*, is where data and instructions are stored temporarily. Data stored in RAM can be changed or erased. When the computer is first turned on, this part of memory is empty and, when turned off, any data it stores is lost. *Registers* are temporary memory locations within the CPU that are involved in the execution of every instruction. The information stored in registers can be retrieved at very high speeds. Because RAM and register storage is temporary, computers use *auxiliary memory* storage for long term storage of programs and data. Auxiliary memory devices are discussed later.

The computer's memory components work together by first accessing a program and necessary data stored in the auxiliary memory and then copying it into RAM. Data is copied into a register when instructions are performed. The results are copied back to RAM and eventually stored for later use in auxiliary memory. During this process, data can be received from input devices and results sent to output devices.

CPU

The *Central Processing Unit*, or *CPU* directs all the activities of the computer, and all information flows through the CPU. Because one of the tasks of the CPU is to control the order in which tasks are completed, it is often referred to as the "brain" of the computer. However, this comparison with the human brain has an important flaw. The CPU only executes tasks according to the instructions it has been given; it cannot think for itself. It can only follow instructions that it gets from ROM or from a program in RAM.

A CPU chip many times more powerful than the Mark I measures about 2 inches by 2 inches

The *Arithmetic Logic Unit*, or *ALU*, is the part of the CPU where the "intelligence" of the computer is located. It can perform only two operations: adding numbers and comparing numbers. How does the computer subtract, multiply, or divide numbers if the ALU can only add and compare numbers? The ALU does this by turning problems like multiplication and division into addition problems. This would seem to be a very inefficient way of doing things, but it works because the ALU is so fast. For example, to solve the problem 5×2, the computer adds five twos, $2 + 2 + 2 + 2 + 2$, to calculate the answer, 10. The ALU is so fast that the time needed to carry out a single addition of this type is measured in *nanoseconds* (billionths of a second). The other job of the ALU is to compare numbers and then determine whether a number is greater than, less than, or equal to another number. This ability is the basis of the computer's decision-making power.

1.18 Auxiliary Memory

Most microcomputers have auxiliary memory devices that may include: a diskette drive, a CD-ROM drive, and a hard disk drive. The diskette drive and CD-ROM drive are accessible from outside the base unit, and the hard disk is completely contained inside the base unit. All three types of disks are used to store data so that they can be reused:

diskette   CD-ROM   hard disk

Data can be stored on a diskette, a CD-ROM, or a hard disk

Sometimes called a floppy disk, *diskettes* are made of a mylar (thin polyester film) disk that is coated with a magnetic material and then loosely encased in hard plastic. Each diskette has a capacity of 1.44 MB. The CD-ROM drive reads data from *CD-ROMs* (an acronym for compact disc, read-only memory). The discs are made of mylar with a reflective coating that is sealed in clear, hard plastic. Each CD-ROM can store over 600 megabytes of data, equal to the storage capacity of over 430 diskettes. Hard disks are made of an aluminum disk coated with a magnetic material. Unlike diskettes and CD-ROMs, hard disks are permanently installed inside the hard disk drive. Each hard drive may have multiple disks inside, and therefore have large storage capacities of 1 GB or more.

Although the files on a CD-ROM are permanent and cannot be changed, the files stored on diskettes and hard disks can be added to, deleted, and modified.

1.19 Number Systems

The electrical circuits on a chip have one of two states, OFF or ON. Therefore, a system was developed that uses two numbers to represent the states: 0 for OFF and 1 for ON. A light switch is similar to a single computer circuit. If the light is off, it represents a 0, and if on, a 1. This number system, which uses only two digits, is called the *binary* (base 2) number system.

base 10

Our most familiar number system is the decimal, or *base 10*, system. It uses ten digits: 0 through 9. Each place represents a power of ten, with the first place to the left of the decimal point representing 10^0, the next place representing 10^1, the next 10^2, and so on (remember that any number raised to the zero power is 1). In the decimal number 485, the 4 represents 4×10^2, the 8 represents 8×10^1 and the 5 represents 5×10^0. The number 485 represents the sum: $4\times100 + 8\times10 + 5\times1$ (400 + 80 + 5) as shown below:

Decimal Number	Base 10 Equivalent
485	$4\times10^2 + 8\times10^1 + 5\times10^0 = 400 + 80 + 5$

base 2

The binary, or *base 2*, system works identically except that each place represents a power of two instead of a power of ten. For example, the binary number 101 represents the sum $1\times2^2 + 0\times2^1 + 1\times2^0$ or 5 in base ten. Some decimal numbers and their binary equivalents are shown below:

Decimal Number	Binary Number	Base 2 Equivalent		
0	00	$= 0\times2^1 + 0\times2^0$	$= 0\times2 + 0\times1$	$= 0 + 0$
1	01	$= 0\times2^1 + 1\times2^0$	$= 0\times2 + 1\times1$	$= 0 + 1$
2	10	$= 1\times2^1 + 0\times2^0$	$= 1\times2 + 0\times1$	$= 2 + 0$
3	11	$= 1\times2^1 + 1\times2^0$	$= 1\times2 + 1\times1$	$= 2 + 1$
4	100	$= 1\times2^2 + 0\times2^1 + 0\times2^0$	$= 1\times4 + 0\times2 + 0\times1$	$= 4 + 0 + 0$

base 16

The *hexadecimal*, or *base 16*, system is based on 16 digits: 0 through 9, and the letters A through F representing 10 through 15 respectively. Each place represents a power of sixteen. For example, the hexadecimal number 1F represents the sum $1\times16^1 + 15\times16^0$. Some decimal numbers and their hexadecimal equivalents are shown below:

Decimal Number	Hexadecimal Number	Base 16 Equivalent		
0	0	$= 0\times16^0$	$= 0\times1$	$= 0$
10	A	$= 10\times16^0$	$= 10\times1$	$= 10$
15	F	$= 15\times16^0$	$= 15\times1$	$= 15$
20	14	$= 1\times16^1 + 4\times16^0$	$= 1\times16 + 4\times1$	$= 16 + 4$
25	19	$= 1\times16^1 + 9\times16^0$	$= 1\times16 + 9\times1$	$= 16 + 9$
30	1E	$= 1\times16^1 + 14\times16^0$	$= 1\times16 + 14\times1$	$= 16 + 14$

For clarity, a non-base 10 number should have the base subscripted after the number. For example, to tell the difference between 100 in base 10 and 100 in base 2 (representing 4), the base 2 number should be written as 100_2.

1.20 Storing Data in Memory

Both numeric and character data are stored in memory using the binary number system discussed previously. Each 0 or 1 in the binary code is called a *bit* (BInary digiT) and these bits are grouped by the computer into 8-bit units called *bytes*.

The size of the RAM memory in a computer is also measured in bytes. For example, a computer might have 8 MB of RAM. In computers and electronics *MB* stands for *megabytes* where mega represents 2^{20} or 1,048,576 bytes and *GB* stands for *gigabytes*, which is 2^{30} bytes. Bytes are sometimes described as *kilobytes*, for example 256K. The *K* comes from the word kilo and represents 2^{10} or 1,024. Therefore, 64K of memory is really 64×2^{10} which equals 65,536 bytes.

ASCII code

The computer uses binary digits to express not only numbers, but all information, including letters of the alphabet. Because of this, a special code had to be established to translate numbers, letters and characters into binary digits. This code has been standardized for computers as the American Standard Code for Information Interchange, or *ASCII*. In this code, each letter of the alphabet, both uppercase and lowercase, and each symbol, digit, and special control function used by the computer is represented by a number. The name JIM, for example, is represented by the ASCII numbers 74, 73, 77. In turn, these numbers are then stored by the computer in binary code:

Letter	ASCII	Binary Code
J	74	01001010
I	73	01001001
M	77	01001101

Each ASCII code is translated into one byte (8-bits) and stored in memory. Note how eight 0s and 1s are used to represent each letter in JIM in binary code.

ASCII codes 0 through 31 are reserved for use by the computer. Code 32 is the space character. Codes 33 through 126 are symbols, numbers, and letters. Codes above 126 are either unused, or may differ from system to system.

memory address

Data stored in memory is referred to by an address. An *address* is a unique binary representation of its location in memory. Therefore, data can be stored, accessed, and retrieved from memory by its address. For data to be addressable in memory, it must usually be at least one byte. For example, to store JIM in memory each character can be stored in binary code in a separate location in memory designated by its address:

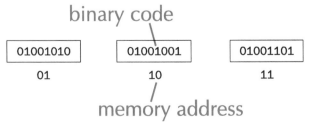

A Guide to Programming in C++

Because JIM is a character string, it will probably be stored in adjacent addresses.

Bits grouped in units of 8 to 64 bits or more are called *words*. Data stored in a word is also located by an address. The size of a word depends on the computer system.

integers

The binary representation of an integer number is usually stored in one word of memory. Because an integer is stored in one word, the size of the word determines the range of integers that can be stored. An *overflow error* occurs when the number of bits that represent the integer is greater than the size of the word.

real numbers

Real numbers, also called *floating point numbers*, are numbers that contain decimal points. The binary representation of a real number is also stored in one word of memory. The binary number 111.10 is equivalent to the real decimal number 7.5 and is stored in memory as the binary number 0.11110×2^3. In this form, the bits that represent the *mantissa* (fractional part) are stored in one section of a word and the *exponent*, in this example 3 (11_2), is stored in another section of the word:

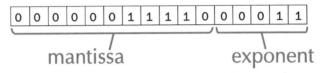

The overflow problem discussed for integers can also occur in real numbers if the part of the word storing the exponent is not large enough. A *roundoff error* occurs when there are not enough bits to hold the mantissa.

roundoff error

1.21 Operating Systems

All microcomputers run software that allow the user to communicate with the computer using the keyboard and mouse. This software is called the *disk operating system* (DOS). Popular operating systems include Windows 95, MS-DOS (Microsoft Disk Operating System) and Unix. When the computer is turned on, the operating system software is automatically loaded into the computer's memory from the computer's hard disk in a process called *booting*.

The Windows 95 operating system is a special kind of program known as a *graphical user interface*, or GUI (pronounced "gooey"). When the Windows 95 GUI is running it provides the user with pictures called *icons* to create a user-friendly environment. Windows 95 also supplies applications and tools that allow you to easily work with the software.

Windows 95 is an object-based operating system. This means that each item that appears on the screen is an *object*, such as a window or dialog box. A *window* is the area on the screen that contains an open program or file. A *dialog box* allows the user to choose and enter information that is needed to complete an action. Through the use of windows, multitasking is possible. *Multitasking* is where the user can have more than one application running at a time. This allows you to switch between the two applications.

An important advance occurring in the 1960s was the development of programming languages. Previously, computers had to be programmed by rewiring different switches to their ON or OFF positions. The first programming languages, referred to as low-level languages, used 0s and 1s to represent the status of the switches (0 for OFF and 1 for ON). The lowest-level language was called *machine language* and consisted of directly typing in 0s and 1s, eliminating the time-consuming task of rewiring. However, accurately typing instructions consisting of only 0s and 1s is extremely difficult to do, therefore high-level languages were developed that allowed programmers to write in English-like instructions.

One of the first popular high-level languages was FORTRAN (FORmula TRANslator) which had intuitive commands such as READ and WRITE. Fortran was developed in 1956 by John Backus and a team of programmers.

A widely used high-level programming languages has been COBOL. COBOL was first developed by the Department of Defense in 1959 to provide a common language for use on all computers. In fact, COBOL stands for COmmon Business Oriented Language. The designer of COBOL was Grace Murray Hopper, a commodore in the Navy at the time. Commodore Hopper was the first person to apply the term *debug* to the computer. While working on the Mark I computer in the 1940s, a moth flew into the circuitry, causing an electrical short which halted the computer. While removing the dead moth, she said that the program would be running again after the computer had been "debugged." Today, the process of removing errors from programs is still called debugging.

A number of high-level languages have been developed since that time. Pascal was developed in 1971 by the Swiss computer scientist Niklaus Wirth to teach the fundamentals of programming. C is a popular programming language designed by Bell Laboratories in 1978 and was later extended into C++ in the early 1980s. The Department of Defense developed Ada in 1979 named after the first programmer, Ada Augusta, the Countess of Lovelace.

A program written in a high-level language is called the *source program*. After the source program is written, it is translated into machine language in a process called *compiling*. The translated program is called the *object program*. In this text you will use the C++ language to write programs.

1 | Computer Issues

Although computers cannot think, they do have some advantages over the human brain. For example, suppose you were given a list of ten numbers (input) and were asked to first, remember them (memory), second, calculate their average (process), and third, write down the average (output). In so doing, you would perform the same four tasks as a computer. Now suppose you were given 100 or 1,000 numbers and asked to calculate the average. Chances are you would get confused and tired performing all the calculations. The computer would have none of these problems. It would accurately remember all of the data and be able to quickly calculate the answers. The computer, therefore, has three important advantages over the human brain:

1. Reliable memory, with the ability to store and recall large amounts of data over long periods of time.
2. Speed, which enables it to process data quickly.
3. The ability to work 24 hours a day without rest.

Remember that as reliable and fast as a computer is, it is only as smart as the instructions it is given by a program.

1.23 The Ethical Responsibilities of the Programmer

It is extremely difficult, if not impossible, for a computer programmer to guarantee that a program will *always* operate properly. The programs used to control complicated devices contain millions of instructions, and as programs grow longer the likelihood of errors increases. A special cause for concern is the increased use of computers to control potentially dangerous devices such as aircraft, nuclear reactors, or sensitive medical equipment. This places a strong ethical burden on the programmer to insure, as best he or she can, the reliability of the computer software.

The Department of Defense (DOD) is currently supporting research aimed at detecting and correcting programming errors. Because it spends billions of dollars annually developing software, much of it for use in situations which can be life threatening, the DOD is especially interested in having reliable programs.

As capable as computers have proven to be, we must be cautious when allowing them to replace human beings in areas where judgement is crucial. Because we are intelligent, humans can often detect that something out of the ordinary has occurred and then take actions which have not been previously anticipated. Computers will only do what they have been programmed to do, even if it is to perform a dangerous act.

We must also consider situations in which the computer can protect human life better than humans. For example, in the space program astronauts place their lives in the hands of computers which must continuously perform complicated calculations at very high speeds. No human being would be capable of doing the job as well as a computer. Computers are also routinely used to monitor seriously ill patients. Since computers are able to work 24 hours a day without becoming distracted or falling asleep, they probably perform such tasks better than most humans.

1.24 The Social and Ethical Consequences of Computers

The society in which we live has been so profoundly affected by computers that historians refer to the present time as the *information age*. This is due to the computer's ability to store and manipulate large amounts of information (data). Because of computers, we are evolving out of an industrial and into an information society, much as over a hundred years ago we evolved from an agricultural society into an industrial one. Such fundamental societal changes cause disruptions which must be planned for. For this reason it is crucial that we consider both the social and ethical consequences of our increasing dependence on computers.

Telecommunications is the sending and receiving of data over telephone lines. This makes it possible for people to work at home and communicate with the office using their computer. By allowing people to work anywhere that telephones or satellite communications are available, we have to become a more diversified society. In fact, after the Los Angeles earthquakes in 1994 a computer newspaper had the headline "A not-so-gentle push for telecommuting." Such decentralization could reduce traffic congestion, air pollution, and many of the other consequences of an urban society. Because of this, Alvin Toffler in his book *The Third Wave* called this the age of the "electronic cottage."

Robots are machines that can be programmed to perform tasks repeatedly. The advantage of using robots is their ability to work 24 hours a day. While this is obviously a major benefit to an employer, it could have a negative impact on employees. Manufacturers are increasingly able to replace factory workers with machines, thereby increasing efficiency and saving money. This trend, however, also leads to increased unemployment of those factory workers who often lack technical skills.

The argument is often used that new technologies such as robotics create jobs for the people who design, build, install, and service them. While this is true, these new jobs require well educated, highly trained people. For this reason it is important to think carefully about the educational requirements needed for employment. As we become an increasingly "high-tech" society, those properly prepared for technical jobs will be the most likely to find employment. In response to this problem many states have instituted programs to train laid-off factory workers so that they may enter technical fields.

Another concern is that the widespread dependence on information services such as the Internet will create two groups; those with access to information and those without. The *National Information Infrastructure* (NII) is a government sponsored version of the Internet created to unite the two groups. One of the goals of the NII is to provide access to the *information highway* at every school, hospital, and public library.

A Guide to Programming in C++

1.25 The Right to Privacy

With computers impacting on our lives in an ever increasing number of ways, serious ethical questions arise over their use. By ethical questions we mean asking what are the morally right and wrong ways to use computers. As human beings we want to insure that our rights as individuals are not encroached upon by the misuse of these machines.

Probably the most serious problem created by computers is invading our right to privacy. Because computers can store vast amounts of data we must decide what information is proper to store, what is improper, and who should have access to the information. Every time you use a credit card, make a phone call, withdraw money, reserve a flight, or register at school a computer records the transaction. Using these records it is possible to learn a great deal about you—where you have been, when you were there, and what you have done. Should this information be available to everyone?

Computers are also used to store information about your credit rating, which determines your ability to borrow money. If you want to buy a car and finance it at the bank, the bank first checks your credit records on a computer to determine if you have a good credit rating. If you purchase the car and then apply for automobile insurance, another computer will check to determine if you have traffic violations. How do you know if the information being used is accurate? To protect both your privacy and the accuracy of data stored about you, a number of laws have been passed.

The **Fair Credit Reporting Act of 1970** deals with data collected for use by credit, insurance, and employment agencies. The act gives individuals the right to see information maintained about them. If a person is denied credit they are allowed to see the files used to make the credit determination. If any of the information is incorrect, the person has the right to have it changed. The act also restricts who may access credit files to only those with a court order or the written permission of the individual whose credit is being checked.

The **Privacy Act of 1974** restricts the way in which personal data can be used by federal agencies. Individuals must be permitted access to information stored about them and may correct any information that is incorrect. Agencies must insure both the security and confidentiality of any sensitive information. Although this law applies only to federal agencies, many states have adopted similar laws.

The **Financial Privacy Act of 1978** requires that a government authority have a subpoena, summons, or search warrant to access an individual's financial records. When such records are released, the financial institution must notify the individual of who has had access to them.

The **Electronic Communications Privacy Act of 1986** (ECPA) makes it a crime to access electronic data without authorization. It also prohibits unauthorized release of such data.

Laws such as these help to insure that the right to privacy is not infringed by data stored in computer files. Although implementing privacy laws has proven expensive and difficult, most people would agree that they are needed.

1.26 Protecting Computer Software and Data

Because computer software can be copied electronically it is easy to duplicate. Such duplication is usually illegal unless the company that owns the rights to the software is paid for the copy. This has become an increasingly serious problem as the number of illegal software copies distributed by computer *pirates* has grown. Developing, testing, marketing, and supporting software is an expensive process. If the software developer is then denied rightful compensation, the future development of all software is jeopardized.

Software companies are increasingly vigilant in detecting and prosecuting those who illegally copy their software. In recent years, software companies have actually made "raids" on businesses and educational institutions to search their computers. An organization found guilty of using illegally copied software can be fined, and its reputation damaged. Therefore, when using software it is important to use only legally acquired copies, and to not make illegal copies for others.

Another problem that is growing as computer use increases is the willful interference with or destruction of computer data. Because computers can transfer and erase data at high speeds, it makes them especially vulnerable to acts of vandalism. Newspapers have carried numerous reports of home computer users gaining access to large computer databases. Sometimes these *hackers* change or erase data stored in the system. These acts are usually illegal and can cause very serious and expensive damage. The Electronic Communications Privacy Act of 1986 specifically makes it a federal offense to access electronic data without authorization.

One especially harmful act is the planting of a *virus* into computer software. A virus is a series of instructions buried into a program that cause the computer to destroy data when given a certain signal. For example, the instructions to destroy data might wait until a certain time or date is reached before being executed. Because the virus is duplicated each time the software is copied, it spreads to other computers, hence the name virus. This practice is illegal and can result in considerable damage. Computer viruses have become so widespread that there are now computer programs that have been developed to detect and erase viruses before they can damage data.

Contaminated disks are one way that viruses are spread from computer to computer

Most people are becoming aware that the willful destruction of computer data is no different than any other vandalization of property. Since the damage is done electronically the result is often not as obvious as destroying physical property, but the consequences are much the same. It is estimated that computer crimes cost the nation billions of dollars each year.

1.27 Computer Organizations

Many organizations have developed to help create standards and guidelines relating to issues in the computer industry. The Association for Computing Machinery (ACM) was founded in 1947 to promote international public and private standards relating to information technology and ethics. The American National Standards Institutes (ANSI) was founded in 1918 and also helps promote standards.

Chapter Summary

Humans have searched for a machine to calculate and record data for thousands of years. The earliest of these devices were mechanical, requiring gears, wheels and levers, and were often unreliable. The advent of electricity brought about machines which used vacuum tubes, and were capable of performing thousands of calculations a minute. The unreliability of the vacuum tube lead to the development of the transistor and integrated circuit. Von Neumann's concept of the central processing unit allowed computers to solve many different problems by simply typing new instructions at a keyboard. Computers became much smaller when vacuum tubes were replaced with transistors in the 1960s. A further reduction in size and cost came with the development of integrated circuits, also called chips.

Mainframes are large, expensive computers that can carry out many tasks at the same time. However, with the invention of the microprocessor, today's microcomputers rival the performance of older mainframes. All computers have the same architecture: (1) input devices (keyboard, mouse) to accept data from the user, (2) memory for storing commands and data, (3) a central processing unit for controlling the operations of the computer, and (4) output devices (monitor, printer) for the user to view the processed information. In general, a computer is a machine which accepts information, processes it according to some specific instructions in the form of software, and then returns new information as output.

Today's microcomputer makes use of a CPU on a chip, the microprocessor, which controls the actions of the computer. A computer has different types of memory that include ROM, RAM, registers, and auxiliary memory. ROM contains the most basic operating instructions for the computer and are permanent. RAM and resigters are both temporary memory. The CPU contains a special device called the Arithmetic Logic Unit (ALU) which performs any math or comparison operations. Auxiliary memory devices such as diskettes, CD-ROMs, and hard disks are used for long term storage of data and programs.

Because the electrical circuits on a chip have one of two states, OFF or ON, the binary number system is used to represent the two state: 0 for OFF and 1 for ON. In the base 2 number system, each place represents a power of two. The base 16 number system uses 16 digits with each place representing a power of 16.

The computer uses binary digits grouped into bytes to express all information. The ASCII code translates numbers and letters into a one byte binary code. The location of data stored in memory is referred to by an address.

Integers and real numbers are stored in one word in memory. Because the number of bits in a word is limited, an overflow error occurs when the number of bits that represent an integer is greater than the size of the word. A roundoff error occurs when the bits that represent the mantissa of a real number is greater than the section of the word that stores the mantissa.

A computer needs an operating system such as Windows 95 to run. An operating system is automatically booted when the computer is turned on. High-level programming languages were developed so programmers could write English-like instructions that the computer could translate. The C language was designed by Bell Laboratories in 1978 and was extended into C++ in the early 1980s. A source program is compiled into an object program.

As computers are increasingly used to make decisions in situations which can impact human life, it becomes the responsibility of programmers to do their best to insure the reliability of the software they have developed. We must continue to be cautious not to replace human beings with computers in areas where judgement is crucial.

Historians refer to the present time as the information age due to the computer's ability to store and manipulate large amounts of data. As the use of computers increases they will profoundly affect society. Therefore, it is important to analyze the social and ethical implications of computers.

A problem created by computers is their potential for invading our right to privacy. Laws have been passed to protect us from the misuse of data stored in computers.

Because computer software is easy to copy, illegal copies are often made, denying software manufacturers of rightful compensation. Another problem has been the willful destruction of computer files by erasing data or planting a virus into programs that spread when programs are copied.

The ACM and ANSI are computer organizations that help promote standards and guidelines relating to issues in the computer industry.

Vocabulary

Abacus   Ancient counting device which uses beads on a frame.

Address   Unique binary representation of the location of data in memory.

ALU   Arithmetic Logic Unit, the part of the CPU that handles math operations.

Applications software   Commercially produced programs written to perform specific tasks such as word processing.

ASCII   American Standard Code for Information Interchange, the code used for representing characters in the computer.

Auxiliary memory   Devices that store data so that it can be reused.

Binary system   Base 2 number system used by computers. Uses only two digits.

Bit   Binary Digit, a single 0 or 1 in a binary number.

Byte   A group of 8 bits.

Chips   Tiny integrated circuits etched into blocks of silicon.

CPU   Central Processing Unit, the device which electronically controls the functions of the computer.

COBOL   A high-level computer language.

Compiling   Translating a source program into machine language.

Computer   An electronic machine that accepts data, processes it according to specific instructions, and provides the results as new information.

Data   Information either entered into or produced by the computer.

Debug   To remove errors from a computer program.

Decimal system   Base 10 number system used by computers. Uses only ten digits.

Document   Also called a file.

File   Collection of data stored on a disk in a form the computer can read.

Floating point numbers   Numbers that contain decimal points.

FORTRAN   A high-level computer language.

GUI (Graphical User Interface)   An operating system that uses pictures to communicate.

Hardware   Physical devices which make up the computer and its peripherals.

Hexadecimal system   Number system used by computers. Uses sixteen digits (base 16).

Input   Data used by the computer.

K, kilobyte   Measurement of computer memory capacity. 1024 bytes.

Keyboard   Device resembling a typewriter used for inputting data into a computer.

Machine language   Computer program written in binary code, just 0s and 1s.

Mantissa   The fractional part of a real or floating point number.

MB, megabyte   Measurement of computer memory capacity. 1,048,576 bytes.

Memory   Electronic storage used by the computer.

Memory address   Binary representation of the location of data in memory.

Microprocessor   CPU on a single chip.

Monitor   Television-like device used to display computer output.

Multitasking   More than one application running at a time.

Nanosecond   Billionth of a second.

Object program   The machine language created by compiling source code.

Operating system   Software that allows the user to communicate with the computer.

Output   Data produced by a computer program.

Pascal   A high-level computer language.

Program   Series of instructions written in a special language directing the computer to perform certain tasks.

PC   Personal Computer, a small computer employing a microprocessor.

RAM   Random Access Memory. Memory that temporarily stores data and instructions.

Real numbers   Numbers that contain decimal points (also called floating point numbers).

ROM   Read Only Memory. Memory that permanently stores data and instructions, and contains the most basic operating instructions for the computer.

Roundoff error   Occurs when there are not enough bits to hold the mantissa of a number.

Software   Computer programs.

Source code   A program written in a high-level language.

Window   The area on the screen that contains an open program or file.

Words   Bits grouped in units of 8 to 64 bits.

Chapter Two
Introducing C++

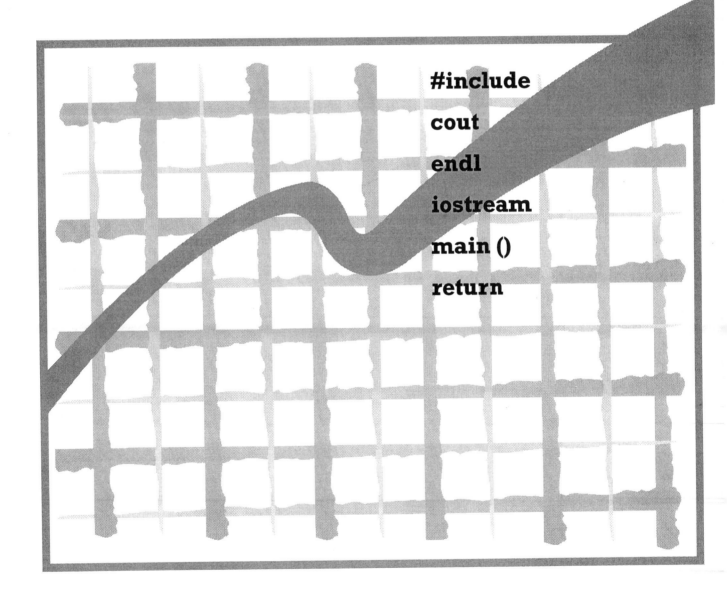

#include

cout

endl

iostream

main ()

return

2

Objectives

After completing this chapter you will be able to:

1. Understand what an object-oriented language is.

2. Read a short program containing the cout and return statements.

3. Understand a C++ program structure including comments and main().

4. Run a program and understand compiling and linking.

5. Understand syntax errors and warnings.

6. Use cout to display a string.

7. Display special characters.

8. Understand good programming style guidelines.

2

Our lives are increasingly interwoven with computers. Computers run our televisions, microwave ovens, and cars; they deliver our electronic mail; they bring us entertainment; they are revolutionizing our society. All of these applications of computing, and more, require programs. In this text you will learn how to write programs using the object-oriented language called C++.

2.1 The C++ Language

Programming languages include BASIC, Pascal, Lisp, Scheme, and FORTRAN. However, perhaps the most widely used language in the construction of commercial software is the C programming language, and more recently, the dialect of C called C++.

C was developed at Bell Laboratories in New Jersey by Brian Kernighan and Dennis Ritchie in 1978. They sought to create a simple language that would allow complex programs to be written and easily implemented on a variety of computer hardware platforms. Later, in the early 1980s, Bjarne Stroustrup and other programmers extended C to create an *object-oriented* language called C++. C++ supports object-oriented programming (OOP), a style of programming in which programs are constructed using *classes*. A class is code in a file separate from the main program. Programmers discovered that OOP in general, and C++ in particular, made it possible to handle the incredible complexity of graphical environments like Windows and the Macintosh.

2.2 About this Text

In this text you will learn the fundamentals of object-oriented programming with C++. To begin, you will learn the fundamentals of the C++ language. Next, you will learn how to use classes to create programs, and then you will learn how to write your own classes. Finally, you will write programs that use the Windows graphical user interface (GUI). In learning to program, you will use many important data structures and algorithms. All of this will give you the basics upon which you can build to become an accomplished programmer.

While you will be able to write successful programs almost immediately, you will not be able to write complex graphical programs for some time. Be patient; learning to program is a little like learning to play the piano: practice and time will lead to success.

2.3 Why learn to program?

Programming gives a sense of what computers can and cannot do, and is one of the best ways to gain a deep understanding of computer technology. Learning to program leads to a more intuitive feel for why computers and computer programs work the way they do. It also gives an appreciation for the important and difficult task of software creation.

Another benefit of learning to program is the development of problem-solving skills. Problems in real life are often complex, large, and multifaceted, as are computer programming problems. In learning to program, you will analyze a problem carefully; break it down into small, solvable parts; and put together the solutions to form a complete and correct solution to the problem. This problem-solving ability is what sets apart successful people in all walks of life.

Finally, the most obvious benefit of learning to program is that it is fun. The computer provides an immediate response to your work. When you create a solution to a complex problem, and the solution is embodied in a working program, there is a great feeling of accomplishment.

2.4 A C++ Program

All C++ programs contain *statements* that tell the computer what to do. The C++ program below contains two statements that form the *body* of the program:

```
/* Hello world program.
   A Student 8/21/97   */

#include <iostream.h>

int main()
{
   cout << "Hello, world!";   // first statement
   return(0);   // second statement
}
```

When run, the program displays:

```
Hello, world!
```

cout

In C++ input/output devices are called *streams*. cout (pronounced *see out*) is the console output stream, and the *send to operator* << (also called the insertion operator) is used to send data into the stream. In the first statement, the words following the << operator are enclosed in quotation marks to form a *string*. When executed, this statement sends the string Hello, world! to the console output device (the computer screen.)

It is important to know that all C++ symbols are case-sensitive, meaning that cout is correct but cOut, COUT, and Cout, are not. This is a common source of confusion in C++ programming.

return

The next statement is return(0) which causes the program to terminate, and the value 0 to be sent back to the computer system. The value 0 indicates to the system that the program terminated without error.

The two program statements end with a semicolon (;). Semicolons are required in C++ to indicate the end of a statement.

2.5 C++ Program Structure

Beyond the statements themselves, a C++ program must have a certain structure in order to be executed. The Hello world program begins with a comment:

```
/*Hello world program.
  A Student, 8/21/97   */
```

comments

Comments are used to explain and clarify the contents of a program for a human reader. The computer ignores them. The symbols /* and */ indicate the beginning and end of a comment, respectively. These symbols are best used with multi-line comments.

//

Comments can also be indicated by the symbols //. All characters on a line after the // symbols are considered to be a comment and are ignored. For example:

```
return(0);   // second statement
```

For style purposes, it is best to use the // symbols for a comment that follows a statement.

Following the opening comment is the line

```
#include <iostream.h>
```

library

which tells the compiler that the iostream library is needed. A *library* is a collection of program code that can be included in a program to perform a variety of tasks. The iostream library is used to perform input/output (I/O) stream tasks. For example, cout is in the iostream library. Nearly all of the programs in this text require this library, and therefore include this line.

The next line

```
int main()
```

main()

is the header of the main() function. A *function* is a set of statements that accomplish a task. A *function header* includes the return type of the function and the function name. As indicated in the main() header, main() returns an integer (int) through return(0) as explained in Section 2.3.

{ }

The body of the program is enclosed in curly braces; the { and } symbols indicate the beginning and the end of the program statements.

```
/* Opening comment. Include name and purpose of program,
   your name, date program was created, etc.              */

#include <iostream.h>

int main()
{
    statements
    return(0);
}
```

2.6 Running a C++ Program

A C++ program must be compiled and linked before it can be *executed*, or *run*, on the computer. Many compilers, such as Turbo C++ and Microsoft Visual C++, perform these steps automatically when the command for running a program is selected.

compiling

A *compiler* is a program that translates C++ code into machine language. *Machine language* is a low-level language consisting of only 1s and 0s, and is the native language of a computer. A C++ program typed by a programmer is called the *source code*; and the compiled, resulting sequence created by a compiler is called the *object code*. During compilation, the compiler checks the syntax of a program and reports errors.

linking

Before the object code can be executed, it must be *linked* to other pieces of code that interact with the computer system. The object code must also be linked to any libraries (e.g., iostream.h) used by the program. The compiled and linked program is called an *executable file* because it is ready to be run on the computer.

running

Finally, the program in linked object form is executed by the system. When a program is run, its output is displayed in a window.

2.7 Syntax Errors and Warnings

syntax error

The C++ system cannot compile a program that contains errors. Statements that violate the rules of C++ are said to contain *syntax errors*. A C++ compiler displays a message if any syntax errors are detected when the program is compiled.

After correcting a syntax error, the program must be recompiled before it will run.

warning message

In some cases, the compiler generates a *warning message* rather than an error. A warning message indicates that a statement in the program is legal, but suspicious. If a warning is generated, it is important to determine the source and fix the problem before running the program. Experienced programmers may choose to ignore certain warnings, but for beginning programmers it is important to consider warnings no different than errors.

Review 1

Enter the Hello world program, and run it.

Review 2

Write a program that displays your name. Use the Hello world program as a guide.

Review 3

Open the Hello world program. Type various errors into the program and create a chart indicating the first error message given for each error. For example:

Error	**Sample Error message**
Misspelling iostream.h	"Unable to open include file IOSTREEM.H"

2.8 Variations on cout

Previously cout was used in a statement to display a string. cout can also be used to display the result of a calculation and control the location of output. The following program calculates and displays the area of a circle with a radius of 10:

```
/*Circle Area program
   Calculates the area of a circle using the formula A=pi * r * r
   A Student, 7/13/97                                          */

#include <iostream.h>

int main()
{
   cout << "-Calculate the area of a circle-" << endl;
   cout << endl;
   cout << "Radius = " << 10 << endl;
   cout << "Area = " << (3.14*10*10) << endl;
   return(0);
}
```

When run, the program produces the output:

```
-Calculate the area of a circle-

Radius = 10
Area = 314
```

The first cout statement

```
cout << "-Calculate the area of a circle-" << endl;
```

performs two actions. The first is to display the string -Calculate the area of a circle- on the screen, and the second is to move output to the next line (i.e., it ends the line). If output is not moved to the next line, the next string sent to the screen will be displayed after the first so that both messages are on a single line. Note that while strings are enclosed in quotation marks, endl is not. If it were, it would be interpreted as a string, and displayed on the screen.

endl

To produce a blank line in the output, the statement

```
cout << endl;
```

is included. This statement does not display any characters, but it does move output to the next line.

displaying numbers

In the next statement

```
cout << "Radius = " << 10 << endl;
```

cout is given a string (Radius =), a number (10), and endl. Like endl, numeric values should not be enclosed in quotation marks. Each item requires the << operator to its left. After the last item, a semicolon indicates the end of the statement.

calculations

In the next statement

```
cout << "Area = " << (3.14*10*10) << endl;
```

a calculation is performed and the result sent to cout so that it is displayed on the screen. Note that the asterisk, *, is used to indicate multiplication. The symbols +, -, and / are used to indicate addition, subtraction, and division, respectively. The use of parentheses when performing a calculation in a cout statement is good programming style.

programming style

Review 4

Write a C++ statement that can be used in the Circle Area program to display the circumference ($2\pi r$) of the circle.

Review 5

Modify Review 2 to display your name and address separated by blank lines.

2.9 Displaying Special Characters

\

C++ provides a facility for displaying special characters in a string. Such characters are indicated by placing a backslash (\) in the string. For example, since double quotation marks are used to indicate the start and end of a string, there is no obvious way to include them within a string. Therefore, the backslash must be used as in the statement

```
cout << "You say \"Good-bye,\" and I say \"Hello\" " << endl;
```

which displays:

```
You say "Good-bye," and I say "Hello"
```

escape sequence

The double quotation marks that follow the backslashes are displayed rather than interpreted as ending the string. The backslash is often called an *escape character* and the combination of symbols an *escape sequence*. The idea is that it escapes from the normal interpretation of characters in a string.

Another special character is the *end of line* character. This is indicated by \n and can replace the use of endl. For example

```
cout << "This falls on a single line.\n";
cout << "This goes on the next line.";
```

displays:

```
This falls on a single line.
This goes on the next line.
```

Other escape sequences include:

Symbol	Effect
\n	Go to next line
\"	Double-quotation mark
\'	Single-quotation mark
\a	Alert (make a beep sound)
\\	Single backslash
\t	Tab (move eight spaces)

The following program includes most of these escape sequences:

```
/*Sailboat Picture program */

#include <iostream.h>

int main()
{
  cout << "                *\n";
  cout << "                |\\\n";
  cout << "            ___|_\\\_\n";
  cout << "~~~~~~~\_____/~~~~~~~\n";
  cout << "~~~~~~~~~~~~~~~~~~~~~~\n";
  cout << "\a\tThe \"Yankee Clipper\"";
  return(0);
}
```

When run, the program produces the output:

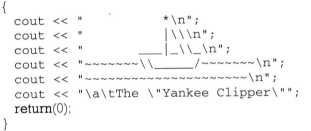

```
               *
               |\
           ___|_\_
~~~~~~~_____/~~~~~~~
~~~~~~~~~~~~~~~~~~~~~~
        The "Yankee Clipper"
```

Review 6

Write a program that displays a house. Do not use endl. When run, the program output should be similar to:

```
     /\
    /  \
   /    \
   | -- |
   |_||_|
```

Write a program that displays the following text:

```
"I think, therefore I am."
              Rene Descartes
```

2.10 Using Help

Many compilers provide online help. Online help can be very useful when learning a new language because it provides the syntax for the statements available in a language. Online help also often contains example code that can serve as a guide when learning a language for the first time.

Online help usually contains a tutorial that shows how to compile, link, and run a program.

Refer to Appendices A and B for more information about the online help available with Turbo C++ and Microsoft Visual C++.

2.11 Program Style

C++ is a *free-form* language, meaning that spaces and blank lines generally have no effect on a program's operation. Of course, comments have no effect either. Thus, the program:

```cpp
#include <iostream.h>
int main(){cout << "-Calculate the area of a circle-" << endl; cout << endl;
cout << "Radius = " << 10 << endl; cout << "Area = " << (3.14*10*10) <<
endl; return(0);}
```

will work exactly the same as the Circle Area program originally presented. The difference is that the human reader has more difficulty understanding, modifying, and debugging code that looks like this. The quality of a programmer's work depends as much upon how the code is designed as upon the output generated. Therefore, throughout the text, good programming style will be discussed.

In general, some good programming style guidelines are:

- Use one statement per line.

- Use an equal number of spaces to indent each line of the body of a program.

- Include a comment describing each program and giving the author's name and date. The description should include the purpose of the program and any key features used. Use /* and */ to enclose these comments.

- Blank lines should be used to set off sections of code.

- Place comments within the body of the code to clarify the code for a reader. However, these comments should not repeat what is obvious from the code. Generally it is best to use // for these comments.

2 Chapter Summary

Programs can be written in different languages, such as Pascal or BASIC. C++ is a popular programming language used for object-oriented programming. Object-oriented programs are programs constructed using classes. A class is code in a file separate from the main program.

There are many benefits of learning how to program. It gives you a sense of what computers can and cannot do. It also develops problem-solving skills, and helps you appreciate the task of software development. Finally, learning to program is fun.

Every C++ program has a certain structure. Comments are included to help the human reader understand the program but are ignored by the compiler. Multi-line comments are set off by the symbols /* and */. Single line comments begin with the // symbol. Any characters on a line after the // symbol are considered comments. The iostream library is included in a program to perform input/output stream tasks and should be included in nearly all programs. Every program contains a main() function which is a set of statements that accomplish a task. A statement is a line of code in the program body that tells the computer what to do. Each statement is terminated by a semicolon. One or more statements enclosed in the { and } symbols indicate the body of the program. All C++ symbols are case-sensitive.

Input/output devices are called streams. cout is the console output stream used in conjunction with the << operator to send information to the screen. cout can output strings and the results of calculations. It is good programming style to enclose any calculations in a cout statement in parentheses.

endl is used to move output onto the next line. Escape sequences are used to output special characters.

A compiler converts C++ code to machine language called object code. Object code is linked with other code to make an executable program that can be run on the computer.

A compiler cannot compile a program that contains errors. During compilation, the compiler detects syntax errors, statements that violate C++ rules. In some cases, the compiler generates a warning message which indicates that a statement is legal, but suspicious. All errors and warnings should be fixed before running the program.

C++ is a freeform language with statements separated by semicolons. Code should, however, be laid out so as to make it easy to understand by a human reader.

Body The part of a program that contains the statement(s) enclosed in the { and } symbols.

C++ Object-oriented programming language.

Comment Information placed in a program to explain and clarify the contents of a program for a human reader. Comments are enclosed by /* and */ or follow // and are ignored by the compiler.

Compiler A program that converts source code, usually written in a language like C++, into object code, a machine language version.

End-of-line A special escape sequence, \n, that when placed inside a string causes the compiler to end the line of output.

Escape character A special character, such as the backslash (\), that is used to escape from the normal interpretation of characters in a string.

Escape sequence The combination of an escape character and symbols, such as \n.

Executable File The compiled and linked version of a program ready to run on the computer.

Free form A programming language, like C++, where spaces and blank lines generally have no effect on the program's operation.

Function A set of statements that accomplish a task.

Function Header Appears as the first line of a function, and includes the return type and function name.

Library A collection of program code that can be included in a program to perform a variety of tasks.

Link To combine several pieces of compiled code into a single compiled program.

Machine language The low-level, native language of a computer that consists of only 1s and 0s.

Object A separate piece of a program.

Object code The machine language code produced by compilation.

Object-Oriented A programming language, like C++, in which programs are constructed in separate pieces.

Program A sequence of instructions that tells the computer how to accomplish a particular task.

Source code The program code written in a language like C++.

Statement A line of code in the program body that tells the computer what to do.

Stream An input/output device, such as cout.

String Characters and/or symbols enclosed in quotation marks.

Syntax error An error caused by a statement in the program that violates the rules of C++.

Warning message A message given by the compiler because a statement in the program is legal, but suspicious.

C++

#include   Used to link a library into a program.

/* */ A pair of symbols used to enclose single and multi-line comments.

// Symbols used to indicate that the rest of the current line contains only a comment.

" "   Used to enclose a string.

\ Escape character used to indicate a special character in a string.

\a Escape sequence indicating a beep sound.

\n Escape sequence indicating the end of line character.

\" Escape sequence indicating a double-quotation mark.

\t Escape sequence indicating a tab character.

\' Escape sequence indicating a single-quotation mark.

\\ Escape sequence indicating a backslash.

; Symbol used to end a statement.

{ } Symbols used to indicate the beginning and the end of a set of program statements.

cout The console output stream. Use to send program output to the screen.

<< The send to operator used to send information into a stream.

endl Inserted in an output stream (cout) to move output to the next line.

iostream   Library that performs a variety of input and output tasks.

int main() The function header in every program that indicates the main code of a C++ program.

return(0) A statement that sends the value zero back to the system indicating that the program has terminated without error.

Exercises

Exercise 1

There are five errors in the following C++ program. What are they?

```
/* Circle Area program
   Calculates the area of a circle using the formula A=pi * r * r
   A Student, 7/13/97                                          //

#include <iostream.c>

int main()
{
   cout << "-Calculate the area of a circle-" << endl
   cout >> endl;
   cout << Radius =  << 10 << endl;
   cout << "Area = " << (3.14*10*10) << endl;
   return(0);
}
```

Exercise 2

There are five errors in the following C++ program. What are they?

```
/* Circle Area program
   Calculates the area of a circle using the formula A=pi * r * r
   A Student, 7/13/97                                          */

#include <iostream.h>

{/*
   cout << "-Calculate the area of a circle-" << 'endl';
   cout << endl;
   Cout << "Radius = " << 10 << endl;
   cout << "Area = " << (3.14*10*10) << endl;
   return(0);
*/}
```

Exercise 3

Modify the Circle Area program from Section 2.8 to calculate and display the area of a circle with radius 10 with the output formatted so that the radius and area appear on the same line, clearly spaced. The program output should be similar to:

```
The area of a circle of radius 10 is 314
```

2

Exercise 4

Write a program that displays your name, class, and school address. The program output should be similar to:

```
Lauren Groon
Senior
Ivy University
Hightstown, NJ
```

Exercise 5

Write a program that calculates and displays the area and perimeter of a rectangle with length 5 and width 3.

Exercise 6

Write a program that calculates and displays the number of kilometers per liter a car gets if it travels 712.5 kilometers on a 70.3 liter tank of gas.

Exercise 7

Write a program that calculates and displays the average jump length of a long-jumper whose jumps were 3.3m, 3.5m, 4.0m, and 3.0m.

Exercise 8

Write a program that uses calculations to display the following:

```
6/5 = 1
6.0/5 = 1.2
6/5.0 = 1.2
6.0/5.0 = 1.2
```

This program illustrates how C++ handles calculations. Notice how C++ displays results with decimals only if at least one of the numbers in the calculation contains decimals.

Exercise 9

Write a program that calculates and displays the average class size of a programming course if the classes have 14, 16, 13, and 19 students. Note: In order to display a result that contains decimals, it is necessary for at least one of the numbers in the calculation to contain decimals. Thus, you might divide by 4.0 rather than 4 in your calculation.

Exercise 10

On average, the power of available computer technology increases by a factor of four every three years. Suppose that a computer can process one task per second in 1980. Write a program that displays how many tasks per second a computer can process in the next two decades. Have the calculations performed in the program. The program output should look similar to:

```
1980    1
1983    4
1986    16
1989    64
1992    256
1995    1024
1998    4096
2001    16384
```

Exercise 11

Write a program that uses cout to display a block of asterisks. The program output should be similar to:

```
* * * * * * *
*           *
*           *
* * * * * * *
```

Exercise 12

Write a program that displays a "happy face." The program output should be similar to:

```
        * * * * *
      *         *
    *   _     _   *
  *      o   o      *
  *         |        *
  *         +        *
    *     \___/    *
      *         *
        * * * * *
         "happy"
```

Exercise 13

Write a program that displays a "grouchy face." The program output should be similar to:

```
        * * * * *
       *         *
      *    \ /    *
     *    o   o    *
    *        |       *
    *        +       *
     *              *
      *    o    *
       * * * * *
        "grouchy"
```

Exercise 14

The Chemistry department has 4 computers, the Physics department has 8, the English department has 2, and the Math lab has 12. Write a program that produces the following output. Have the computer perform the calculation in the last line. Format the output using the appropriate escape sequences.

```
Chemistry      4
Physics        8
English        2
Math lab       12

Grand Total    26
```

2

A Guide to Programming in C++

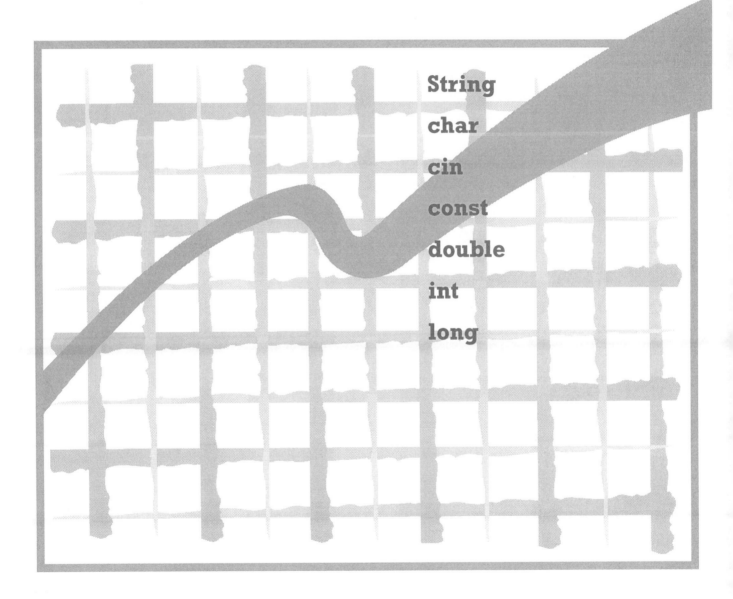

String

char

cin

const

double

int

long

Objectives

After completing this chapter you will be able to:

1. Assign values to a variable.

2. Obtain a value from the user with cin.

3. Use named constants.

4. Choose appropriate identifiers.

5. Use data types.

6. Understand promotion, integer division, type casting, modulus division, and operator precedence.

7. Use the String type.

8. Use the ignore() function.

9. Format output using width(), setf(), and precision().

10. Choose wisely how to define a variable.

3

The Circle Area program of Chapter Two showed how a calculation could be performed and its result displayed. This program was limited because it performed the calculation for a specific number, 10, written into the program. To have the program perform the calculation using a different value it would have to be modified by replacing the value 10 with the new value in three places, recompiled, and run again. To remove this limitation, variables are used to represent values within a program.

3.1 Using Variables

A *variable* is a named memory location which stores a value. To use a variable in a program it must be defined by giving its type and identifier. The *type* of the variable indicates what kind of value it will store. The name of the variable, or *identifier*, is how the value will be referred to within the program. For example, the statement

double Radius;

defines a variable named Radius which stores data of type **double**. A *double* is a numeric value possibly containing a decimal portion. Other data types will be described later in this chapter.

assignment

Once defined, a variable must be given a value. One way to do this is through *assignment*. For example, in the following assignment statement the variable Radius is assigned the value 12.3:

Radius = 12.3;

The equal sign (=) represents assignment, and the effect is to store the value 12.3 in the memory location referred to by the name Radius.

The following program demonstrates how a variable can be used:

```
/*Program to illustrate variables */

#include <iostream.h>

int main()
{
  double Radius;
  Radius = 10;
  cout << "Radius = " << Radius << endl;
  cout << endl;
  Radius = 12.3;
  cout << "Radius = " << Radius << endl;
  return(0);
}
```

When run, the program displays:

```
Radius = 10

Radius = 12.3
```

The program's assignment statements are used to change what is stored in the variable Radius so that different values are displayed by the different cout statements. There can be only one value stored in Radius at any given time. Therefore, when the value 12.3 is assigned to Radius, the value 10 is no longer available. The following illustrates this:

First, the variable is defined:

double Radius; | ? |
                    Radius

In this statement the compiler tells the computer to set aside space in memory that is identified by the variable name Radius. Until the variable is assigned a value, the value associated with Radius is unknown.

When the first assignment statement is executed, the value 10 is placed in the memory location identified by the name Radius:

Radius = 10; | 10 |
                  Radius

The first cout statement displays this value of 10. When the second assignment statement is executed, the value 10 is replaced with the value 12.3:

Radius = 12.3; | 12.3 |
                    Radius

The second cout statement displays this value of 12.3.

---

assignment statement structure   Variable assignment statements must be written so that the identifier (variable name) is on the left side of the equal sign and the value is on the right. An expression may also be used on the right side of an assignment statement. For example, in the statement

```
Area = 3.14*10*10;
```

the expression on the right is evaluated and the result stored as the value of the variable Area. Two common errors are to reverse this:

```
3.14*10*10 = Area;    // Error!
```

and to embed an assignment inside an output statement:

```
cout << Area = 3.14*10*10;    // Error!
```

Review 1

What would be the output of the following program?

```
#include <iostream.h>

int main()
{
    double Number;
    Number = 12;
    Number = 15;
    cout << (Number*Number) << endl;
    return(0);
}
```

Review 2

Modify the Circle Area program from Chapter Two so that a variable named Radius is defined and assigned the value 10, and this variable is used rather than the number 10 throughout the rest of the program.

3.2 Obtaining a Value from the User

cin

Programs can be more useful when the user is able to type a value to be assigned to a variable. cin pauses a program during execution to allow the user to type the value for a variable assignment. For example, the statement

```
cin >> Radius;
```

causes the program to wait for the user to type a value and press Enter and then assigns that value to the variable Radius. cin is the console in-put stream, part of the iostream library. The *get from operator* >> (also called the extraction operator) is used to get data from the input stream and feed it to the variable.

A cin statement makes the Circle Area program more useful:

```
/*Circle Area program */

#include <iostream.h>

int main()
{
    cout << "-Calculate the area of a circle-" << endl;
    cout << endl;

    double Radius;
    cout << "Enter radius: ";
    cin >> Radius;    // Get Radius value from user
    cout << "Radius = " << Radius << endl;
    cout << "Area = " << (3.14*Radius*Radius) << endl;
    return(0);
}
```

The program output when the user types 10 is as follows. The user input in the program output has been underlined to distinguish it from the program output:

```
-Calculate the area of a circle-

Enter radius: 10
Radius = 10
Area = 314
```

programming style

Two points should be made about the modified Circle Area program. First, the variable is declared after the heading, but just before the user is prompted for a value. It is generally considered good programming style to declare variables close to the section of code where they are first used so that the program is easier to understand. Second, the statement

```
cout << "Enter radius: ";
```

does not end with an endl to cause output to move to the next line. As a result, the user can enter the value right next to the prompt.

3.3 Using Named Constants

A *constant* is defined in a statement that begins with the keyword const followed by a type, an identifier, and then an assignment. For example, the following statement declares a constant PI with a value of 3.14:

```
const double PI = 3.14;
```

From this point forward in the execution of the program, the identifier PI represents the value 3.14. When this statement is included in the Circle Area program, the last cout statement can be modified to include the constant:

```
cout << "Area = " << (PI*Radius*Radius) << endl;
```

This formula should be easily understandable to any reader who has seen the mathematical version, $A = \pi r^2$.

Representing a value that does not change during program execution as a named constant makes the code easier for a reader to understand. Code that includes named constants is also easier to modify because the value of the constant need only be changed in one place.

A common error when defining constants is to leave out the type. When this happens, the constant is made the default type of int.

A second error is to include a program statement which tries to change the value of a constant. For example, the following statement generates a compiler error:

```
const double PI = 3.14;
PI = 22/7;   // This will generate an error
```

3.4 Choosing Identifiers

There are only a few, simple rules for C++ identifiers:

- Identifiers must start with a letter.

- Identifiers must contain only letters, digits, and the underscore character (_). However, the use of double underscores (_ _) should be avoided.

- Identifiers can be of any length.

- Identifiers are case-sensitive. For example, Radius is different than radius.

keywords

There are several identifiers that C++ reserves for use as *keywords*. A keyword has special meaning to the compiler, and therefore cannot be a user-defined variable or constant. For example, double is a keyword. In this text keywords are emphasized by formatting them in a different font, just as the word double is formatted. Refer to Appendix C for a complete list of C++ keywords.

programming style

As a matter of good programming style, one final rule is that variables and constants should be named so that they are quickly and clearly understandable to the reader. This is important for other readers of your program, for you as you try to get your program working correctly, and for you as you later modify and improve your program.

Review 3

Write a program that asks the user for the length and width of a rectangle, and then displays the value of the area of the rectangle.

Review 4

Modify the Circle Area program to use a constant for π, ask the user for the radius, and to display the area and circumference ($2\pi r$) of the circle.

Review 5

List five legal and five illegal variable names illustrating the rules for identifiers in C++. Indicate why each illegal name is incorrect.

3.5 Built-In Data Types

In addition to double, C++ supports several other built-in data types. It is important that a variable or constant be of the appropriate type for the data represented. The built-in C++ types are:

Type	Description	Range
double	real numbers, including decimals	approx. 10^{-308} to 10^{+308}, positive or negative
int	integers (no decimals)	–32,767 to +32,767
long	integers (no decimals)	–2,147,483,647 to +2,147,483,647
char	characters	all typeable or displayable characters

double

The double type is used to store positive or negative real numbers. This type is often referred to as *floating point*, meaning that it can represent values with numbers after the decimal point. When very large or very small numbers are stored and displayed, the computer will use *scientific notation*. For example

```
double j;
j = 123456789.0;
cout << j << endl;
```

displays the number 123456789 as:

```
1.23457e+08
```

which represents the number 1.23457×10^8. Note that a double value is rounded to six significant figures when displayed. The remaining digits are stored internally, and will be used in calculations.

int and long

The *int* and *long* types are used to store positive and negative integers. The only difference between int and long is the range of values that may be represented. While for many purposes, int variables are sufficient, it is often necessary to use long variables for values that may exceed 32,767 (the limit for an int). If a value with a decimal portion is assigned to an integer variable, the value is truncated (the decimal portion is not stored). For example

```
int i;
i = 12.9;
cout << i << endl;
```

displays:

```
12
```

While int and long variables may seem limited, they are the perfect choice for counting whole number quantities. Many programs throughout this text will use integer variables and constants.

char

The *char* type stores a single character. Characters include the letters of the alphabet, digits, symbols like $, %, and spaces, and in general any character that can be typed or displayed. For example:

```
char ch;
ch = 'A';
cout << ch << endl;
```

displays:

```
A
```

A char variable assignment requires using single-quotation marks. In this case, A is assigned to variable ch. If double-quotation marks are used, an error message is generated.

It is important to understand that the char value '4' is not the same as the int value 4. For example, trying to do arithmetic with char values in a statement like:

```
cout << ('4' + '5') << endl;
```

compiles without error but displays the number 105! This is because the characters are interpreted as binary numbers before being added.

3.6 Variable Definitions

Variables can be defined in single statements like Radius in the Circle Area program. Another way is to define multiple variables of the same type in a single statement. For example, the following statements define three integer variables and two character variables:

```
int x, y, z;
char ch1, ch2;
```

This style of variable definitions can lead to simpler, easier-to-read code.

A variable definition can also include assignment. For example:

```
double x = 6;
char ch1 = 'A', ch2 = 'B';
int y = 2*x;
```

The first statement defines x as a double variable and assigns it a value of 6. The next statement creates two character variables and assigns them the values A and B. The last statement defines an integer variable and assigns it the result of an expression, in this case 12.

It is sometimes tempting to think that an initial assignment establishes a relationship that is maintained throughout the program. This is not true. For example

```
int x = 12;
int y = 2*x;
x = 4;
cout << y << endl;
```

displays the value 24, not 8 (i.e., 2*4).

Review 6

Write variable definitions to represent the number of votes received by an election candidate, the percentage of votes won by the candidate, the initials of the candidate, and a constant for the year of the election. Be sure to use meaningful identifier names.

Review 7

Write a program illustrating the difference between a constant and a variable definition that includes an assignment. Your program should compile correctly if the variable is defined without the word const, and generate a compiler error if it is included.

3.7 Expressions and Operators

C++ includes a set of built-in arithmetic operators. As previously described, these include multiplication (*), addition (+), subtraction (–), and division (/). There is no standard operator for exponentiation in C++ (e.g., the ^ character on many calculators).

promotion

In general, numeric values of various types can be mixed in an expression. However, the type of the result depends upon the types used in the expression. For example, an expression involving two integers (an int or a long) results in an integer. An expression involving two doubles results in a double. Whenever an integer and a double are used, C++ *promotes* the value with the narrower range (the integer) to the type of the value with the wider range (a double) which results in a double.

integer division

Since an expression involving only integers results in an integer, division in C++ can behave somewhat surprisingly. For example

    cout << (25/4);

type casting

displays the value 6, not the expected 6.25. *Integer division* truncates the decimal portion of the quotient to result in an integer. When real division is preferred, *type casting* must be done to explicitly convert the type of one of the values into a real number. In the above example, if we cast the 25 into a double, the statement

    cout << (double(25)/4);

displays 6.25 because C++ promotes the 25 to a double and then real number division is performed. Note that casting was done by indicating the desired type and enclosing the value to convert in parentheses.

modulus division

Another built-in arithmetic operator is modulus division, %. *Modulus division* returns the remainder resulting from division. For example

    cout << (25%4);

displays the value 1 since the remainder of 25 divided by 4 is 1:

$$\begin{array}{r} 6 \;\; r1 \longleftarrow 25\%4 \\ 4\overline{)25} \\ \underline{24} \\ 1 \end{array}$$

Modulus division is often useful in examining the digits of a number, finding the number of minutes left over after hours have been accounted for, and other integer-related tasks. The modulus division operator may only be used with int or long values; an attempt to use a double value with the % operator will generate a compiler error message.

3

An expression is evaluated using a specific order of operations, or *operator precedence*. Multiplication and division (including modulus division) are performed first, followed by addition and subtraction. Two operators of the same precedence are evaluated in order from left to right.

Operator precedence can be changed by including parentheses in an expression. The operations within parentheses are evaluated first. It is also good programming style to include parentheses when there is any ambiguity or question at all so a reader will not have any doubts about what is intended.

Review 8

For each of the following expressions, indicate the value that will be calculated by the computer. If the expression is not legal, state why.

20+3	23/5
20.0+6.5	20%3
3.3–7.3	20.0%5.0
2*4	"20" + "2"
23.0/5	"3.14" * "10" * "10"

Review 9

What does the following statement display when x is 1998? When x is 1776? When x is 38?

```
cout << ((x/10)%10);
```

Explain, in general, the result of this expression.

3.8 The string Library

String type

A *string* is a sequence of characters, like a message or a name. There is no built-in string type in standard C++, but most compilers support one. Supplied with this text is the string library that is used to implement a String type. As discussed in Chapter Two, a library is included in a program so that the program can use the code in that library file. When a program is compiled, library files are expected to be in the include folder which is under the compiler's folder on the computer. The libraries supplied with this text are intended to be stored in the lvp folder under the include folder. Therefore, programs using the string library will need the statement:

```
#include <lvp\string.h>
```

If your libraries are not stored in this folder, the #include statement in your programs will need the appropriate path.

The following program demonstrates the String type and string input and output. Note the #include statement that allows String variables to be used. Also note that String **must** begin with a capital letter:

```
/* String type demo program */

#include <iostream.h>
#include <lvp\string.h>

int main()
{
   String Name;

   cout << "Enter your name: ";
   cin >> Name;
   cout << "Welcome, " << Name;
   cout << "!  Nice to meet you!" << endl;
   return(0);
}
```

String variables can be defined and used with cin and cout just like C++ built-in data types. One of the great strengths of C++ is the ability to extend the language in this way. The program output looks like:

```
Enter your name: Spike
Welcome, Spike! Nice to meet you!
```

When used with a string, cin takes input only up to the first blank. For example, if the user types a name with a space, only the first part is taken:

```
Enter your name: Mary Anne
Welcome, Mary! Nice to meet you!
```

getline()

For this reason, the string library includes the getline() function to handle full line input. If we replace the cin statement in the program above with

```
getline(cin, Name);
```

the output looks similar to:

```
Enter your name: Mary Anne
Welcome, Mary Anne! Nice to meet you!
```

The getline() syntax requires the first item in parentheses to be the name of the input stream, and the second item to be the name of the string variable which will hold the value typed.

string variable assignment

String variables can be assigned values just like other variables, as in:

```
Name = "Fedor";
```

Note that double-quotation marks are required, not single-quotation marks as with char variable assignments. It is also important to recognize that arithmetic cannot be performed with strings, even if the string contains a number. For example, given the legal definition

```
String Number = "123";
```

the following statement generates a compiler error:

```
cout << Number*2;
```

Note that the statement

```
cout << (Number+Number);
```

does compile, but produces the unexpected output:

```
123123
```

When two strings are added they are *concatenated*, or joined to form one string.

The Standard Template Library

The C++ language provides relatively simple support for strings and other types of complex data. As a result, professional programmers have created a large number of libraries that provide such support. In a movement to create standardized libraries, the Standard Template Library (STL) is under development by Hewlett-Packard.

The libraries included with this text are based on the development of the Standard Template Library and the libraries developed by the College Board. While the need for libraries may appear to be a flaw in the design of C++, it is really a tribute to the language that it is possible to easily add such libraries.

Review 10

Write a program that asks the user for a first and last name, and then displays the name as shown below (including the comma):

```
Enter your first name: Isabella
Enter your last name: Allende
Your name is Allende, Isabella
```

3.9 The ignore() Function

Unexpected results can occur in a program that reads numeric and then string input from the user. For example, when the following statements are executed

```
int x;
String Name;
cin >> x;
getline(cin, Name);
```

the getline() function will appear to be skipped, and Name will be an empty string. This happens because the cin >> x statement reads a number and leaves the end-of-line character (the Enter key pressed by the user) in the stream. The getline() statement then reads this character and assumes that it has reached the end of a line, so it stores nothing in Name and program execution proceeds to the next statement. Replacing the getline() statement with cin >> Name avoids this problem, but does not allow for multiple word entries.

A better approach to this problem is to use the ignore() function which skips over characters until a specified character is encountered. For example, the statement

```
cin.ignore(100, '\n');
```

will skip up to 100 characters stopping only after it encounters and skips the end-of-line character, which is represented as \n. The syntax of the ignore() function requires the maximum number of characters to skip and the character we want to end skipping on. For example, the code:

```
int x;
String Name;
cin >> x;
cin.ignore(100, '\n');
getline(cin, Name);
```

correctly handles both the input of a number followed by the input of a string. As a general rule, use the ignore() function prior to a getline() function.

3.10 Output Formatting

width()

A program can be made more user-friendly by carefully formatting its output. The iostream library contains functions and constants for this purpose. For example, the width() function creates a field for displaying output, as in the statements

```
cout << "12345678901234567890" << endl;
cout.width(20);
cout << "Hello" << endl;
cout.width(10);
cout << "Goodbye" << endl;
```

which display the word "Hello" on the right of a 20-character field and the word "Goodbye" on the right of a 10-character field. The numbers displayed in the first line of the output show how the words line up:

```
12345678901234567890
               Hello
     Goodbye
```

The syntax of the formatting statements use *dot notation*: cout is followed by a period then the width() function name with the field size.

The width() function is useful for lining up numbers, as in the statements

```
cout.width(10); cout << 123 << endl;
cout.width(10); cout << 12 << endl;
cout.width(10); cout << 12345 << endl;
```

which display

```
       123
        12
     12345
```

A cout.width() statement is required for each item of output.

By default, output is right aligned in a field. This is useful for columns of numbers, but names and other words are usually left aligned. To change output alignment in a field the setf() function must be used. For example, the statement

```
cout.setf(ios::left);
```

left aligns field output until the next setf(). ios::left is a constant provided by the iostream library.

As an example of setf(), consider the statements

```
cout.setf(ios::left);    // Needed only once
cout << "123456789012345678901234567890" << endl;
cout.width(20); cout << "Hello";
cout.width(10); cout << "Goodbye" << endl;
```

which display

```
123456789012345678901234567890
Hello               Goodbye
```

Each word is left aligned in a field of the specified width, padded with blanks to fill out the width on the right.

The setf() function is used with the constant ios::fixed to specify that numeric output is to be displayed with a fixed number of decimals. This is useful for formatting double output. In addition to setf(), precision() is used to specify the number of decimals, as in the statements:

```
cout.setf(ios::fixed);    // Use fixed number of decimals in output
cout.precision(3);        // Set the number of decimals to 3
```

Like setf(), precision() remains in effect until the next use of precision().

As an example of fixed output, the statements

```
cout.setf(ios::fixed);    // Needed only once
cout.precision(3);        // Needed only once
cout.width(10); cout << 123.2 << endl;
cout.width(10); cout << 12.34567 << endl;
cout.width(10); cout << 9123.0 << endl;
```

display formatted double output:

```
   123.200
    12.346
  9123.000
```

Note that values are rounded and zeroes are added to give the correct number of decimal places to each number in the list. Thus, the value 12.34567 is output as 12.346 rather than 12.345.

Review 11

Write a program that uses the width() function to display the following output:

```
LVPress
   LVPress
      LVPress
         LVPress
      LVPress
   LVPress
LVPress
```

Review 12

Write a program that displays a cast listing formatted as follows:

```
Julie Andrews       Guinevere
Richard Burton     King Arthur
Robert Goulet        Lancelot
```

Review 13

Write a program that uses the setf() and precision() functions to display the value of π (3.1415926) to various numbers of decimal places. Use a constant for π. The program output should look similar to:

```
3.1
3.14
3.142
3.1416
3.14159
3.141593
```

3.11 Choosing wisely: int vs. long vs. double; const vs. variable

It should be clear from what has been discussed that a program may be written in a variety of ways and still work correctly. In addition to the choices for program style, identifier names, and comments, the programmer may need to choose whether to define a variable as an int, a long, or a double, and as a const or not.

In choosing between an int or long and a double, the most important issue is what quantity is being represented. If the quantity can only have integer values (negative and positive whole numbers, and zero) then it should be represented as an integer (int or long). This way both the compiler and a human reader will immediately understand the possible values of the variable. To use a double in this case would be misleading. If the quantity can have values with decimals, of course, it is an easy decision: a double must be used.

It is relatively easy to choose between an int and a long. Clearly a long must be used whenever there is any chance that the variable will have to represent numbers larger than 32,767 or lower than –32,767. Although it may seem easier to simply use longs for all integer quantities, int variables require less storage space, and can perhaps improve readability by indicating that only small values will be stored.

The decision concerning the use of const is particularly interesting. A const is used to prevent errors later. If the program contains code to change the value of the const value, a compilation error will be generated. This is desirable since the intention is to create an unchangeable value. Another benefit to using a const is that a reader will immediately understand that the value is not to be changed, and this will give insight into how the identifier is being used.

If a program is easy for a reader to understand, it is easier to debug, easier to get working correctly, and easier to modify. Since most of the cost of producing software lies in debugging and modifying the code, it is crucial that it be clear and well written.

Case Study

This and all following chapters end with a *Case Study*. Each Case Study illustrates the sequence of steps and the thinking that goes into the construction of a substantial programming project. Learning to program is much more than simply learning the commands of a particular language. It is learning how to combine these commands to produce robust, clear, working code. It is learning a *process* for creating software.

The steps in the creation of software are generally given as *specification*, *design*, *coding*, and *debugging and testing*. In this first Case Study each of these steps will be explained.

specification

The first step in any programming project is defining what the program is to accomplish. This is called the *specification* of the program, or the *spec*, because it specifies what the program is to do. The specification for this Case Study is:

> Prompt the user for the names of the candidates and the number of votes for each candidate for an election. Display a table that shows the number of votes for each candidate, the percentage of votes (to two decimal places) for each candidate, and the total number of votes cast.

For the programmer, the specification is "law." If there are ambiguities in the spec, the correct response is to return to the author of the spec and ask for clarification.

The *design* of a program tells how the program will be constructed. For this Case Study, the design looks like:

> The program will first prompt the user to enter the candidate names and then store them in string variables. Next the number of votes will be entered by the user and stored in long variables. The total and the percentages will then be calculated and also stored in variables (a long and two doubles). The table is then displayed using these variables. The table will look similar to:

```
Candidate  Votes    Percent
Grassman    1276     57.27
Lee          952     42.73
    TOTAL:  2228
```

The writer of the specification only indicated that the table should be easy to read, and this presentation seems to satisfy this.

The program is written, or *coded*, based upon the design. In this Case Study, the design can be broken down into three parts. The first part obtains the input:

```
String Candidate1, Candidate2;
cout << "Enter name of first candidate: ";
cin >> Candidate1;
cout << "Enter name of second candidate: ";
cin >> Candidate2;

long Votes1, Votes2;
cout << "Enter votes for " << Candidate1 << ": ";
cin >> Votes1;
cout << "Enter votes for " << Candidate2 << ": ";
cin >> Votes2;
cout << endl;
```

The last line of this program segment places a blank line in the output between the entering of the data and the display of the table.

The second part of the program calculates the total and percentages:

```
long VotesTotal = Votes1 + Votes2;
double Percent1 = 100 * double (Votes1)/VotesTotal;
double Percent2 = 100 * double (Votes2)/VotesTotal;
```

Each of these variables is defined and given an initial value in the same statement. This programming style can be an aid to the reader because there is no need to look back to see how a variable was defined.

Note the need to typecast the long variables in the calculation of the double values for the percentages. Typecasting the first long value in the divisions (Votes1 and Votes2) is sufficient to generate real division.

The last part of the program displays the table. To make the table layout easy to change later, a named constant is used for the field width of the columns. The format of the fields must also be established:

```
const int ColWidth = 10;    // Width of columns in table
cout.setf(ios::fixed);
cout.precision(2);
```

The first line of the table displays the headings. The first column, containing the names, should be left aligned:

```
cout.setf(ios::left);
cout.width(ColWidth); cout << "Candidate";
```

The next two columns, containing the vote counts and the percentages, are right aligned:

```
cout.setf(ios::right);
cout.width(ColWidth); cout << "Votes";
cout.width(ColWidth); cout << "Percent" << endl;
```

The next row of the table displays data aligned under the column headings:

```
cout.setf(ios::left);
cout.width(ColWidth); cout << Candidate1;
cout.setf(ios::right);
cout.width(ColWidth); cout << Votes1;
cout.width(ColWidth); cout << Percent1 << endl;
```

The second and last rows of data will be coded similarly.

The complete Case Study program is shown below:

```
/*Vote Analysis program. Names and votes for two candidates are
  entered and the percentages and votes are displayed in a table     */

#include <iostream.h>
#include <lvp\string.h>

int main()
{
    cout << "--Vote Analysis Program--" << endl << endl;

    String Candidate1, Candidate2;
    cout << "Enter name of first candidate: ";
    cin >> Candidate1;
    cout << "Enter name of second candidate: ";
    cin >> Candidate2;

    long Votes1, Votes2;
    cout << "Enter votes for " << Candidate1 << ": ";
    cin >> Votes1;
    cout << "Enter votes for " << Candidate2 << ": ";
    cin >> Votes2;
    cout << endl;

    long VotesTotal = Votes1 + Votes2;
    double Percent1 = 100 * double (Votes1)/VotesTotal;
    double Percent2 = 100 * double (Votes2)/VotesTotal;
```

```
const int ColWidth = 10;    // Width of columns in table
cout.setf(ios::fixed);
cout.precision(2);

// Output column headings
cout.setf(ios::left);
cout.width(ColWidth); cout << "Candidate";
cout.setf(ios::right);
cout.width(ColWidth); cout << "Votes";
cout.width(ColWidth); cout << "Percent" << endl;

// Output election results
cout.setf(ios::left);
cout.width(ColWidth); cout << Candidate1;
cout.setf(ios::right);
cout.width(ColWidth); cout << Votes1;
cout.width(ColWidth); cout << Percent1 << endl;

cout.setf(ios::left);
cout.width(ColWidth); cout << Candidate2;
cout.setf(ios::right);
cout.width(ColWidth); cout << Votes2;
cout.width(ColWidth); cout << Percent2 << endl;

cout.width(ColWidth); cout << "TOTAL: ";
cout.width(ColWidth); cout << VotesTotal << endl;

return(0);
}
```

Running the Case Study produces output similar to:

```
--Vote Analysis Program--


Enter name of first candidate: Grassman
Enter name of second candidate: Lee
Enter votes for Grassman: 1276
Enter votes for Lee: 952

Candidate Votes    Percent
Grassman    1276     57.27
Lee          952     42.73
    TOTAL:  2228
```

debugging and testing

Debugging is the process of getting a program to work correctly. *Testing* is the process of selecting data to test different possibilities and reveal bugs.

Good test cases for this program include equal numbers of votes, and very lopsided numbers including the case where one candidate gets zero votes. In testing the program it fails when both candidates have zero votes. The statements:

```
double Percent1 = 100 * double (Votes1)/VotesTotal;
double Percent2 = 100 * double (Votes2)/VotesTotal;
```

3

generate a *run-time error* if both votes are zero because division by zero is an error. Since this is unlikely to occur, the Case Study will not be changed as the result of this test.

Review 14

Experiment with the Case Study program. What happens when the user enters zero for one of the vote values? What happens when the user enters a character instead of a number?

Review 15

Modify the Case Study program to handle three candidates.

Review 16

Modify the Case Study program to make the table look different. Change the first column of names so that it has a width of 10, while the other two columns have widths of only 6. Change the heading Percent to Pct to make this possible.

Chapter Summary

Variables are used to represent values within a program. A variable definition consists of a type and identifier. Data is stored in variables through the use of assignment statements (using =) and user input (using cin >>). A variable may also be assigned a value when it is declared.

Built-in C++ types include double, char, int, and long. A String type is accessible by including the string library supplied with this text.

Identifiers must start with a letter and contain only letters, digits, and the underscore character. Uppercase and lowercase letters are considered different, so that the variable Dog and the variable dog would be considered different variables. Keywords are identifiers reserved by C++ and cannot be used as user-defined variables or constants.

Variables may be defined anywhere in a program before they are first used. Identifiers that hold unchanging values are defined as constants in a const definition.

Arithmetic operations can be performed on numeric data types. An asterisk (*) is used to indicate multiplication, while a slash (/) is used to indicate division. The modulus division operator, %, returns the remainder of integer division. Integer division is performed when both the divisor and dividend are integers. The decimal portion of the quotient in integer division is truncated to result in an integer. To perform real division, one of the integer values can be typecast into a double by placing it in parentheses after the word double. When types are mixed in an expression, the values with the narrower range are promoted to the type of the value with the wider range before performing the calculation.

The string library function getline() is used to properly read strings that may contain spaces. The ignore() function should be used after each numeric input whenever reading numeric and string values from the user.

Output is formatted with cout functions. These include width(), setf(), and precision().

The programmer is faced with many choices in designing and writing code. In this chapter the decisions between int, long, and double types, and between const and variable definitions were explored.

Steps in creating a program include specification, design, coding, debugging, and testing. These steps are used in the Case Study program.

Vocabulary

Assignment A statement which gives a value to a variable or constant. The equal sign (=) is used for this in C++.

Coding   The process of turning a program design into code.

Concatenation   The process by which two strings are joined to form one string.

Constant An identifier given a value which cannot be changed during the execution of a program.

Debugging   The process of fixing errors in a program in order to get it to work properly.

Design   The description of how a program will satisfy its specification.

Dot Notation   The syntax required when using a function from a library, as in the statement: cin.ignore(80, '\n')

Floating Point   Another name for a double.

Identifier   The name used for a variable or constant.

Integer Division   The division performed when the / operator is used. The decimal portion of the quotient is truncated to result in an integer.

Keyword   A word that has special meaning to the compiler, and therefore cannot be a user-defined variable or constant.

Modulus Division   The operator, %, which returns the remainder of the division of two integers.

Operator Precedence   The order in which arithmetic operations are performed in an expression.

Promotion   The process by which a value with a narrower range is converted a value with a wider range.

Scientific Notation   Used by the computer to display very large or very small numbers.

Specification   A description of what a program is to accomplish.

String   A sequence of characters.

Testing   The process of running a program with various sets of data in order to reveal problems.

Type The kind of data stored in a variable or constant. For example, int, long, double, String.

Type Casting To explicitly convert the type of one value into another type.

Variable A named memory location which stores and represents a value in a program.

C++

% The modulus operator returns the remainder of the division of two integers.

>> The get from operator that gets data from the input stream and feeds it into a variable.

string.h A library that implements the String type so that string variables can be defined and string input and output be performed.

String Type limited to values containing sequences of characters. This type is available by including the string library.

char Type limited to values that are single characters.

cin The console input stream object.

const Specifies that an identifier is to represent a value that cannot be changed during the execution of a program.

double Type limited to values that are numbers possibly containing a decimal portion.

getline() String function that obtains an entire line of input from the user and places it in a single String variable.

ignore() cin function that skips over characters until a specified character is encountered.

int Type limited to values which are integer values in the range ±32,767.

setf(ios::fixed) Specifies field formatting to display fixed numbers.

setf(ios::left) Specifies field formatting to display output left aligned.

setf(ios::right) Specifies field formatting to display output right aligned.

long Type limited to values which are integer values in the range ±2,147,483,647.

precision() cout function which specifies the number of digits to display in a fixed field format.

setf() cout function which specifies a fixed field format.

width() cout function which specifies the field width for the next item of output.

Exercises

Exercise 1

The height of an object dropped from a starting height of 100 meters is given by the equation $h=100-4.9*t^2$ where t is the time in seconds. Write a program that asks the user for a time less than 20 seconds and displays the height of the object at that time using this formula. The program output should look similar to:

```
Enter the time: 2
The object is at 80.4 meters.
```

Exercise 2

Write a program to convert Fahrenheit to Celsius using the formula $C=\frac{5}{9}(F-32)$. Test the program with values 212, 32, 98.6, and –40. The program output should look similar to:

```
Enter the temperature in Fahrenheit: 212
The temperature in Celsius is 100.0 degrees.
```

Exercise 3

The cost of making a pizza at Alverto's Pizza Shop is as follows:

- A labor and rent cost of $1.20 per pizza, regardless of size.
- The cost of materials that varies by the size of the pie according to the formula $0.05*diameter*diameter.

Write a program that allows the user to enter a diameter, and then display the cost of making a pie of that size. The program output should look similar to:

```
Enter the size of the pizza: 10
The cost is $6.20
```

Exercise 4

The distance to school is 32 kilometers. Write a program that asks the user for an average speed in kilometers per hour, and then displays the time in minutes required for the trip at this speed. The program output should look similar to:

```
Enter the average speed: 88
The trip to school will take 21.8 minutes.
```

Exercise 5

Einstein's famous formula, E=MC² gives the amount of energy released by the complete conversion of matter of mass M into energy E. If M represents the mass in kilograms and C represents the speed of light in meters per second (3.0 x 10⁸ m/s), then the result is in the energy unit Joules. It takes 360000 Joules to light a 100 watt light bulb for an hour. Write a program that calculates the energy and the number of light bulbs that could be powered by a given mass of matter. The program output should look similar to:

```
Enter the mass in kg: 0.01
This mass could produce 9e+14 Joules of energy.
It could power 2.5e+09 100-watt light bulbs for an
hour.
```

Exercise 6

Write a program that allows the user to enter two integers, and then displays the results of integer (/) and modulus (%) division in either order. Program output should look similar to:

```
Enter first integer: 13
Enter second integer: 4

13 / 4 = 3
13 % 4 = 1
4 / 13 = 0
4 % 13 = 4
```

Exercise 7

Gym classes are to form volleyball teams of 7 each. Write a program that asks for the number of players, and then gives the number of teams and the number of players left over. The program output should look similar to:

```
Enter the number of players: 37
There will be 5 teams with 2 left over.
```

Exercise 8

Write a program that allows the user to enter a time in minutes and then displays the time in hours:minutes format. The program output should look similar to:

```
Enter the number of minutes: 327
This is 5:27
```

Be sure to consider times where the number of minutes left over is fewer than 10. For example, 184 minutes should display 3:04. (Hint: use the modulus operator.)

Exercise 9

Write a program that displays the coins necessary to make the change entered by the user. The change can be made up of quarters, dimes, nickels, and pennies. Assume that the amount of change is less than $1.00, and use the minimum number of coins. The program output should look similar to:

```
Enter the amount of change in cents: 68
Change:
   Quarters: 2
   Dimes: 1
   Nickels: 1
   Pennies: 3
```

Exercise 10

a) Write a program that accepts a two-digit number and displays the digits each on a single line. The program output should look similar to:

```
Enter a two-digit number: 27
The first digit is 2
The second digit is 7
```

b) Modify the program to work for a three-digit number.

c) Modify the program to report the sum of the digits of a three-digit number:

```
Enter a three-digit number: 274
The first digit is 2
The second digit is 7
The third digit is 4
The sum of the digits is 13
```

Exercise 11

Daur's Flowers ships flowers in pots around the world, and orders are placed via the Internet.

a) Write a program that asks the user for the number of flower pots to be shipped, and then displays the number of boxes required. A big box can hold four pots, and a small box only one. Have the program calculate the smallest number of boxes required. The program output should look similar to:

```
Enter the number of flower pots to ship: 25
We will ship:
   6 big box(s)
   1 small box(s)
```

b) Modify the program to allow for a very big box that can hold nine pots. The program output should look similar to:

```
Enter the number of flower pots to ship: 25
We will ship:
   2 very big box(s)
   1 big box(s)
   3 small box(s)
```

3

Exercise 12

Write a program that calculates the number of hours of your life that you have spent sleeping. Assume that you sleep 8 hours each night. To simplify the problem, assume that there are always 30 days in each month, and 365 days in each year. The program output should look similar to:

```
Enter your birthdate (using numbers for months):
  Month: 9
  Day: 27
  Year: 1984
Enter today's date (using numbers for months):
  Month: 10
  Day: 26
  Year: 2002
You have been alive for 6599 days.
You have slept 52792 hours.
```

Exercise 13

A fast food restaurant charges $1.49 for burgers, $0.89 for fries, and $0.99 for sodas.

a) Write a program that allows an employee to enter an order (the number of burgers, fries, and sodas), and then display a total, the tax (at 6%), and the final cost. The program output should look similar to:

```
Enter the number of burgers: 3
Enter the number of fries: 2
Enter the number of sodas: 5

The total before tax is: $11.20
The tax is $0.67
The grand total is $11.87
```

b) Modify the program to allow the employee to enter the amount tendered, and then display the change. Program output should look similar to:

```
...
Enter amount tendered: 20
The change is: $8.13
```

Exercise 14

Write a program to help you analyze the time taken for your C++ projects. The program should ask for the time spent designing, coding, debugging, and testing, and then display a table showing the percentage of time taken for each part.

Exercise 15

Write a program that examines the spending patterns of a user. It should ask the user for the amount spent in the last month on food, clothing, entertainment, and rent, and then display a table showing the percentage of expenditures for each category.

The results of a primary election between two candidates in three states are:

	Awbrey	Berlin
New York	314159	271860
New Jersey	89008	121032
Connecticut	213451	231034

Write a program that asks the user to enter the candidate names and election results, and then displays a summary table similar to the following:

```
Candidate          Votes      Percent
Awbrey            616618       49.71
Berlin            623926       50.29
TOTAL VOTES:     1240544
```

Chapter Four
Controlling Program Flow

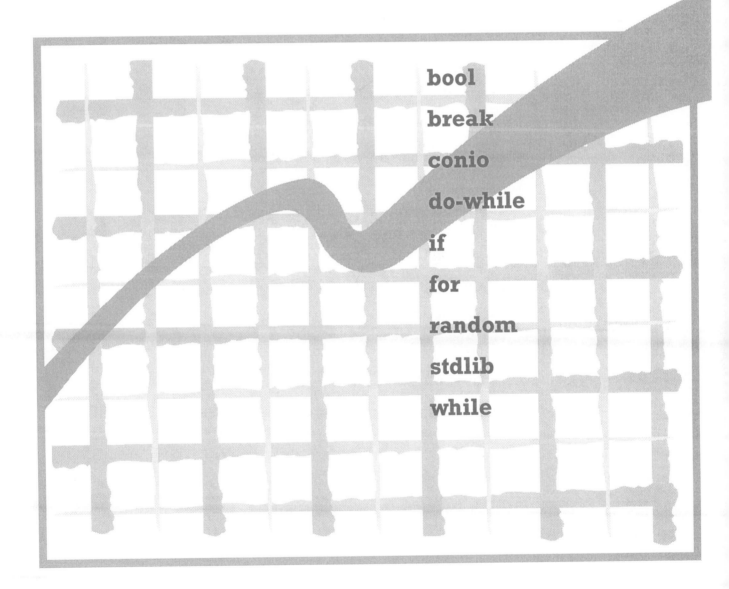

bool

break

conio

do-while

if

for

random

stdlib

while

Objectives

After completing this chapter you will be able to:

1. Allow a program to make decisions using the if statement.

2. Add an else clause to the if statement.

3. Write compound statements.

4. Use nested if statements.

5. Use an else-if ladder to decide among three or more actions.

6. Use logical operators in Boolean expressions.

7. Use do-while loops.

8. Develop an algorithm to solve a problem.

9. Use while loops.

10. Use the debugger to detect errors in logic.

11. Count or sum values.

12. Use for loops.

13. Use a Boolean variable.

14. Use the break statement to terminate the current block of code.

15. Generate random numbers.

16. Use the conio library.

4

In this chapter you will learn the C++ statements that control the flow of a program. Controlling the flow of a program allows one message to be displayed during one run of the program and a different message to be displayed during a different run. Another example of controlling program flow is when certain statements are executed a number of times.

4.1 The if Statement

The if statement allows a program to make decisions. For example, a program could make a decision based on the current temperature stored in a variable named Temp:

```
if (Temp < 5)
    cout << "Wear a coat today." << endl;
```

When this if statement is executed, the flow of the program depends upon the value of Temp. If the value of Temp is less than 5, then the cout statement is executed and the program continues on to the next statement of the program. If the value of Temp is not less than 5 (i.e., it is greater than or equal to 5), then the cout statement is not executed and the program continues on to the next statement of the program.

The if statement takes the form:

```
if (condition)
    statement;
```

Boolean expression

relational operators

The *condition* of the if statement is a Boolean expression. A *Boolean expression* is an expression that evaluates to either true or false. Boolean expressions are often formed using relational operators. In the if statement above, the less than relational operator (<) was used. There are five other *relational operators* in addition to the < operator:

Operator	Meaning
==	equal to
<	less than
<=	less than or equal to
>	greater than
>=	greater than or equal to
!=	not equal to

A Boolean expression can involve comparisons of many different types including numbers, strings, characters, and expressions formed from these, as in the following examples:

```
ch <= 'Z'
Grade == 12
FruitName == "Banana"
Radius != 0
2*pi*Radius >= Area
```

The *statement* of an if can be a single C++ statement as in the if statement on the previous page, or a compound statement as explained later.

The following program illustrates the use of a simple if statement.

```
/*Temperature program */

#include <iostream.h>

int main()
{
    double Temp;
    cout << "Enter today's temperature (Celsius): ";
    cin >> Temp;

    if (Temp < 5)
        cout << "Wear a coat today." << endl;

    cout << "Have a great day!" << endl;
    return(0);
}
```

The user's input will affect the program flow. When run, this program's output may look similar to:

```
Enter today's temperature (Celsius): -11
Wear a coat today.
Have a great day!
```

Or the program output may look similar to:

```
Enter today's temperature (Celsius): 26
Have a great day!
```

4.2 if Pitfalls

Legal C++ if statements can fail to work as expected if some simple rules are not followed. First, never make equality comparisons (== or !=) with values that may have fractional parts. For example, the code

```
if (480 == 4.8*100)
    cout << "These are equal";
```

roundoff error

does *not* output the message as expected due to computer roundoff error. In this case, when 4.8 is multiplied by 100, the result is not 480 but instead 479.999999999. Since this is not equal to 480, the if condition evaluates to false. *Roundoff error* occurs because some doubles cannot be exactly represented in binary notation by the computer. Comparisons involving inequalities (< or >) work as expected.

4

Second, it is important to compare values of only the same type. For example, comparing the character 2 to the number 3

'2' > 3

is a true Boolean expression because '2' is represented internally by the value 50.

= versus ==

There are also two common errors made with an if statement. First, the assignment operator (=) is often used when the equality relational operator (==) is intended. When this is done, an assignment rather than a comparison is made. For example, can you predict the output of the code below?

```
int x = 0;
if (x = 1)
   cout << "x is now ONE" << endl;
cout << "The value of x is now " << x << endl;
```

Because of the inadvertent use of = instead of == in the if condition, the program displays:

```
x is now ONE
The value of x is now 1
```

When an assignment is made in the condition of an if statement, the compiler generates a warning.

When an illegal assignment is made in the condition of an if statement, the compiler gives an error message. For example, the code

```
if (1= x)
   cout << "x is now ONE" << endl;
```

has a 1 on the left side of the unintended assignment statement causing the compiler to generate an error message about Lvalue. Lvalue refers to a value that can be used on the left side of an assignment statement. In this case, a 1 is on the left side rather than a variable, so the error is generated.

misplaced semicolon

Another common error is to place a semicolon after the if condition, as in the statements:

```
if (Score == 1);   // Semicolon incorrectly included!
   cout << "You got a hole in one!" << endl;
```

A semicolon indicates the if statement is complete. Therefore, when Score is equal to one the program does nothing and then goes on to the cout statement. When Score is not equal to one the program still goes on to the cout statement. The misplaced semicolon causes the message to be displayed regardless of the value of Score.

Review 1

Write a statement that could be added to the end of the Chapter Three Case Study program that will display It was a tie! if the votes entered for each candidate are the same.

Review 2 ————————————————————————————————

Modify the Circle Area program from Chapter Three to display an error message if the value entered for Radius is negative. In either case, the program may calculate and output an attempt at an answer for the area.

4.3 The if-else Statement

The if statement can include an else clause which is executed when the if condition is false. The if-else statement takes the form:

```
if (condition)
    statement;
else
    statement;
```

The *statement* in the else clause can be a single C++ statement or a compound statement as explained in the next section. For example, in the if statement

```
if (Temp < 5)
    cout << "Wear a coat today." << endl;
else
    cout << "Don't wear a coat today." << endl;
```

only the first message is displayed when the value of Temp is less than 5, and only the second message is displayed when the value of Temp is not less than 5.

programming style   The indentation used in the if statement is good programming style and has no effect on the execution of the statement. When reading the code, the indentation makes it easier to follow the logic of the statement. This is especially important as if statements become large and complex.

4.4 Compound Statements

The actions performed by an if statement can include a compound statement. A *compound statement* is more than one statement enclosed by curly braces, as in the statement:

```
if (Temp < 5) {
    cout << "Wear a coat today." << endl;
    cout << "It is cold outside!" << endl;
}
else {
    cout << "Don't wear a coat today." << endl;
    cout << "You can manage without it." << endl;
}
```

programming style   A compound statement may contain as many statements as desired. The curly braces do not slow down program execution and can be included even when there is only one statement to be executed. Always using compound statements can make the look of an if statement more consistent, and eliminate the "dangling else" problem explained later.

Review 3

The following code compiles without error but contains a bug. Find the bug and predict the output of the corrected code when Score is 1 and when Score is 2:

```
if (Score == 1)
    cout << "You got a hole in one!" << endl;
else;
    cout << "You didn't get a hole in one!" << endl;
```

Review 4

Write a statement that could be put at the end of the Chapter Three Case Study program to display the name of the winner. In the event of a tie, either name can be displayed.

Advanced

Modify the statement above to display the winner's name or It was a tie! as appropriate.

Review 5

Modify the Circle Area program to display an error message when the value entered for Radius is negative. If Radius is a positive value or zero, only the resulting area in a message should be displayed. The error message should look similar to:

```
Radius entered was -3.4
Negative radii are illegal
```

4.5 Nested if Statements

So far we have used an if-else to control program flow in one of two directions. To control program flow in one of three or more directions, a nested if can be used. A *nested if* is an if statement that contains another if statement. For example, consider the Chapter Three Case Study program. The election results can be one of three possibilities: Candidate1 as the winner, Candidate2 as the winner, or a tie. The if statement to display the appropriate message would be:

```
if (Votes1 == Votes2)
    cout << "It was a tie!" << endl;
else
    Statements to handle the non-tie case
```

This if-else statement is a simple if-else statement. To handle the non-tie case, a nested if statement is used:

```
if (Votes1 == Votes2)
    cout << "It was a tie!" << endl;
else
    if (Votes1 > Votes2)        // Nested if
        cout << Candidate1 << " is the winner!" << endl;
    else
        cout << Candidate2 << " is the winner!" << endl;
```

A logic error associated with nested if statements is known as the *dangling else* problem. For example, consider the following statement:

```
if (Temp < 13)
    if (Temp < 2)
        cout << "Cool";
else
    cout << "Hot";    // Which "if" does this belong to?
```

The indentation suggests that when the first if condition is false the message "Hot" is displayed because the else is executed. However, the else is really associated with the second if statement. This is made clear by simply changing the indentation:

```
if (Temp < 13)
    if (Temp < 2)
        cout << "Cool";
    else
        cout << "Hot";
```

In this statement, when Temp>=13 nothing is printed! To achieve the logic suggested with the first indentation, a compound statement is used:

```
if (Temp < 13) {
    if (Temp < 2)
        cout << "Cool";
}
else
    cout << "Hot";
```

4.6 The else-if Ladder

A standard format has been developed for writing if statements that are used to decide among three, four, or more actions. This format is called an else-if *ladder* because of the way the statement is written. For example, there are four options in the following else-if ladder:

```
if (Temp <= 0)
    cout << "Freezing";
else if (Temp < 13)
    cout << "Cool";
else if (Temp < 41)
    cout << "Hot";
else
    cout << "Very hot";
```

After execution of any of the cout statements, execution of the ladder is complete and program flow proceeds to the next statement after the else-if ladder.

The logic used in developing an else-if ladder is important. When if conditions are testing a range of numbers as in the example above, care must be taken to ensure that the conditions are ordered correctly. If Temp<41 were the first if condition, the message "Hot" would be displayed for every Temp value less than 41, rather than just those values from 13 to 41. Also note that the final else clause does not contain an if statement. If the program reaches this clause, it is only because all the other if conditions were false, so a default message is displayed.

4.7 Programming Style: else-if Ladder vs. Sequential ifs

Good programmers consider the clarity of their code rather than just whether it "works" or not. For example, consider the following two segments of code:

```
// else-if ladder
if (Temp <= 0)
   cout << "Freezing";
else if (Temp < 13)
   cout << "Cool";
else
   cout << "Hot";

// Sequential ifs
if (Temp <= 0)
   cout << "Freezing";
if (Temp > 0)
   if (Temp < 13)
      cout << "Cool";
if (Temp >= 13)
   cout << "Hot";
```

Although the two segments of code perform identically, the short else-if ladder is preferred for at least two reasons:

- The else-if ladder allows only one message to be displayed. In the sequential if code it is possible that zero, two, or even three messages may be displayed, depending upon the if conditions.

- The sequential if code tests basically the same conditions in several different places. This means that there is opportunity for inconsistency, and makes it harder to change the code correctly.

Review 6

In mathematics, the quantity $b^2 - 4ac$ is called the "discriminant." Write a program that asks the user for values of a, b, and c, and displays No roots if the discriminant is negative, One root if the discriminant is zero, and Two roots if the discriminant is positive. The program output may look similar to:

```
Enter the value for a: 1
Enter the value for b: 2
Enter the value for c: 1
a=1, b=2, c=1: One root
```

Review 7

Predict the output of the following code:

```
int Age = 2;
if (Age > 5)
   if (Age >= 18)
      cout << "Adult";
else cout << "Child";
```

Now use curly braces to change the logic.

Review 8

Write a program that asks the user for the number of strokes on one hole of a par 5 golf game and then displays an appropriate message according to the following table:

1	Hole in one!
2	Double-Eagle
3	Eagle
4	Birdie
5	Par
6	Bogey
7	Double-Bogey
8	Triple-Bogey
9 or over	Disaster

4.8 Logical Operators

&& and ||

A Boolean expression may also be formed using logical operators. In C++, the logical operator "and" is represented by the symbol && and the logical operator "or" is represented by the symbol ||. An expression that uses logical operators is evaluated according to the following rules:

(true) && (true) evaluates to true	(true) || (true) evaluates to true
(true) && (false) evaluates to false	(true) || (false) evaluates to true
(false) && (true) evaluates to false	(false) || (true) evaluates to true
(false) && (false) evaluates to false	(false) || (false) evaluates to false

For example, the statement

```
if ((Temp < 5) || (Wind > 24))
    cout << "Wear a coat today." << endl;
```

displays the message if the temperature is less than 5 *or* the wind is greater than 24 *or* both. As another example, the statement

```
if ((Temp < 5) && (Wind > 24))
    cout << "Wear a coat today." << endl;
```

displays the message only if *both* the temperature is less than 5 *and* the wind is greater than 24. The parentheses around each Boolean expression are optional but should be included for clarity.

A hard-to-detect error in a Boolean expression is inadvertently using the symbols & or | which have meanings in C++ that differ from that of && and ||. If the symbols & or | are used, the program may compile and may even give the correct output for many runs. However, in a later run wrong output may be given.

!

A third logical operator is "not" which is represented by the symbol !. An expression containing ! is evaluated according to the following rules:

```
!(true) evaluates to false
!(false) evaluates to true
```

For example, the statement

```
if ( !(Temp < 5) )
    cout << "DON'T wear a coat today!" << endl;
```

displays the message if it is *not* true that the temperature is less than 5. Note that the exclamation point is placed inside the parentheses that form the if condition, but outside the parentheses of the Boolean expression. It is important that the expression after the exclamation point be parenthesized so that there is not an attempt to "not" the value of Temp rather than the whole condition.

Review 9

Identify the logic errors in the following code that is intended to display a single appropriate message for any value of Height:

```
if (Height < 150)
    cout << "Short" << endl;
if ((Height > 150) && (Height < 175))
    cout << "Medium" << endl;
if (Height > 175)
    cout << "Tall" << endl;
```

Rewrite the code using an else-if ladder.

Review 10

Given the following variable definitions

```
int Age = 2, Height = 81, Weight = 13;
```

give the value, true or false, for each of the following expressions:

```
(Height > Weight) && (Weight != 10)

(Age != 2) || (Height > 60)

!(Weight == 15)

(Age*Weight > Height)

!((Age == 2) || (Age == 3))
```

Review 11

Write a program that asks the user for the length, width, and height of a package, and displays "Reject" if any dimension is greater than 10 cm, and "Accept" if all the dimensions are less than or equal to 10 cm.

4.9 Looping: The do-while Statement

Program flow can be controlled through *iteration* which means to repeat one or more statements during program execution. Iteration is often referred to as *looping*. The first of three looping statements is the do-while loop which has the form:

```
do {
   statement;
} while (condition);
```

where *statement* is one or more C++ statements that form the body of the loop. The *condition* is a Boolean expression used to determine if the loop is to be repeated. The do-while loop is executed at least once because the *condition* is not evaluated until after the first iteration of the loop. If the *condition* is true, *statement* is executed again and then the *condition* reevaluated. This looping process is repeated until the *condition* is evaluated and found to be false.

The following program demonstrates looping:

```cpp
/* Circle Area program with a do-while loop */

#include <iostream.h>

int main()
{
   char Answer;    // Whether the user wants another circle
   cout << "Circle Area Calculator" << endl;
   do {
      // Perform calculation
      const double PI = 3.14159;
      double Radius;
      cout << "Enter the radius: ";
      cin >> Radius;
      cout << "Area is " << (PI * Radius * Radius) << endl;

      // Ask if another calculation is desired
      cout << "Do another circle (Y/N)? ";
      cin >> Answer;
   } while (Answer == 'Y');
   cout << "Thanks for using the Circle Calculator" << endl;
   return(0);
}
```

The user's input will affect the program flow. When run, the program's output may look similar to:

```
Circle Area Calculator
Enter the radius: 10
Area is 314.159
Do another circle (Y/N)? Y
Enter the radius: 2
Area is 12.5664
Do another circle (Y/N)? N
Thanks for using the Circle Calculator
```

The constant PI and the variable Radius are declared within the loop body which means they are accessible by statements in the loop only. The variable Answer is accessed by the while condition outside the loop and therefore must be declared outside the loop body. Declaring Answer in the loop body will lead to an "Undefined symbol" compilation error.

Review 12 ————————————————————————————————

The Circle Area program in Section 4.9 only repeats the calculation if the user enters an upper-case Y. Modify the while condition so that the loop is executed when the user enters either Y or y.

Review 13 ————————————————————————————————

Write a simple "password" program. Have the user repeatedly enter a password until the secret word "happiness" is entered. The program output may look similar to:

```
Enter the password: money
Enter the password: success
Enter the password: happiness
You've got it!
```

Modify the program by adding an if statement that outputs a message for all incorrect tries:

```
Enter the password: money
Sorry, try again!
Enter the password: success
Sorry, try again!
Enter the password: happiness
You've got it!
```

4.10 Algorithms

Programs with more complex specifications require a method of design called an algorithm. An *algorithm* is a series of steps that tell how to solve a problem. An algorithm created using both human terms and C++ code is called *pseudocode*. For example, the pseudocode for the do-while loop in the previous section might be:

```
do
    Get Radius value from user
    Calculate the area of a circle using the Radius value
    Ask user if another calculation is desired
while (Answer == Yes)
```

Creating an algorithm forces a programmer to think through a program before actually coding it. This is helpful in two ways. First, an algorithm can be done away from the computer which usually helps a programmer focus on the overall structure of a program instead of focusing on just one statement at a time. Second, errors in logic are usually reduced.

logic error

A *logic error* is caused by statements that are syntactically correct but produce undesired or unexpected results. One logic error already discussed is the dangling else associated with nested ifs. Some logic errors associated with looping structures are discussed in Section 4.12.

Unlike syntax errors, logic errors must be found by the programmer rather than the compiler. These errors can be found only by thorough testing of the program, and by careful reading of the code. Good programming style that includes careful documentation and indentation and descriptive identifiers can be helpful when looking for logic errors.

4.11 Looping: The while Statement

The do-while loop is always executed at least once because its condition is not evaluated until after an iteration. A second looping statement is the while loop which evaluates its condition before each iteration. Therefore, the while loop body may execute *zero* or more times. The while loop has the form:

```
while (condition) {
    statement;
}
```

where *statement* is one or more C++ statements that form the body of the loop. The *condition* is a Boolean expression used to determine if the loop is to be executed. If the *condition* is true *statement* is executed and then the *condition* reevaluated. This looping process is repeated until the *condition* is evaluated and found to be false.

For example, consider the problem of asking the user for a value that falls within a certain range. If the entered value is outside the desired range, the user needs to enter a new value. This process will need to be repeated until an appropriate value is entered. However, if the user enters an appropriate value the first time then an error message need never be displayed. The pseudocode for this problem might be:

```
Ask for a positive value
While (Value < 0)
    Display an error message
    Ask for a positive value
```

This pseudocode converted into C++ looks like:

```
cout << "Enter a positive number: ";
cin >> Number;
while (Number < 0) {
    cout << "Number must be positive" << endl;
    cout << "Please re-enter: ";
    cin >> Number;
}
```

The user's input will affect the program flow. When run, the program's output may look similar to:

```
Enter a positive number: -10
Number must be positive
Please re-enter: 2
```

4.12 Infinite Loops

The condition of a loop is used to determine when it should stop executing. What happens, though, if the condition never becomes false? The result is an *infinite loop*—one which continues forever.

misplaced semicolon

A number of logic errors can lead to an infinite loop. For instance, the following loop is infinite if Number is initially negative. Can you see why?

```
while (Number < 0); {
    cout << "Please enter a positive number:";
    cin >> Number;
}
```

The semicolon after the while condition causes the statement to check the condition, *do nothing*, then check the condition again, *do nothing*, then check, and so on. This continues on indefinitely since the user is never given the chance to re-enter a value. To the user, the program appears to come to a complete halt.

A program in Windows that has gone into an infinite loop can usually be interrupted by pressing the key combination Ctrl+Alt+Sys Rq.

lack of { } around loop body

Inadvertently leaving out the curly braces that enclose the loop body will also cause an infinite loop. For example:

```
while (Number < 0)
    cout << "Please enter a positive number:";
    cin >> Number;
```

The indentation suggests that two statements make up the loop body. However, since the curly braces are missing, only the first statement is in the loop. In this case, the condition is checked and the first cout statement executed, and then the condition checked again, and so on. Since the cin statement is never executed, there is no opportunity for a positive number to be entered, and the loop goes on forever. No warning is given by the compiler for this error.

4.13 Debugging a Program

step

watch window

A compiler has tools that are useful for debugging and testing loops. The step feature is for watching and controlling program execution one statement at a time. Stepping through a program can help detect errors in logic. The watch window feature is for watching the values of variables as they change during program execution. Errors in a program can become more obvious if the values of variables are known throughout program execution. Setting up a watch window and stepping through a program can together be a very helpful way to debug a loop.

Review 14

Write a program that uses the code in Section 4.11 to verify that it correctly handles negative entries. Then modify the code to accept entries between 1 and 10, inclusive. (Hint: Change the condition.) Be sure to change the messages displayed to the user.

Review 15

Modify the Circle Area program to include a while loop so that many circle areas can be computed. Let a radius of zero indicate the end of input. The program output should look similar to:

```
Enter radius (0 to quit): 10
Area is 314
Enter radius (0 to quit): 2
Area is 12.56
Enter radius (0 to quit): 0
Have a good day!
```

Use the following pseudocode:

```
Ask for a radius
while (radius is not zero)
   Calculate and display the area
   Ask for another radius
Display good-bye message
```

Review 16

Write the pseudocode for a program that asks the user for an integer value between Low and High inclusive. The program should continue prompting the user until a value in this range is entered. Write the program using the pseudocode.

4.14 Counting and Summing

Counting or summing values is a common task performed in a program. For example, a program that allows the user to enter any number of values and then displays the average of the values does both counting and summing. For this program, the output may look similar to:

```
--Calculate Average Program--
Enter a value (0 to quit): 70
Enter a value (0 to quit): 80
Enter a value (0 to quit): 60
Enter a value (0 to quit): 84
Enter a value (0 to quit): 0
Average is 73.5
```

The pseudocode for this program could be:

```
Get a value
while (value is not zero)
   Count the value
   Sum the value
   Get another value
Display the average by dividing the sum by the count
```

A while loop can be used to get multiple values from the user. But what about counting and summing?

counting

A program that counts the number of values entered by the user is actually counting the number of loop iterations. To count loop iterations, a statement similar to the following is included in the loop body:

```
NumberOfValues=NumberOfValues+1;
```

In this assignment statement, the expression on the right is evaluated first, and then the result stored as the value of the variable on the left. Therefore, each time this statement is executed, one is added to the current value of NumberOfValues and then assigned to NumberOfValues as its new value.

initialized

Counting variables are used often in programs and are referred to as *counters*. When using counters, it is important that they first be *initialized*. A variable is initialized in an assignment statement to give the variable a starting value. In most cases, a counter should be initialized to 0.

summing

A similar assignment statement is used to sum the values entered by a user, as in the statement:

```
SumOfValues=SumOfValues+Value;
```

The expression on the right is evaluated first, and then the result stored as the value of the variable on the left. As with a counter variable, the summing variable should be initialized to zero before adding values to it.

The pseudocode converted into C++ looks like:

```cpp
/*Calculate Average program */

#include <iostream.h>

int main()
{
  int Value;    // Value entered by user
  int NumberOfValues = 0;   // Number of values entered so far
  int SumOfValues = 0;      // Sum of values entered so far
  const int Sentinel = 0;       // Indicates end of values to be entered

  cout << "--Calculate Average Program--" << endl;
  cout << "Enter a value (" << Sentinel << " to quit): ";
  cin >> Value;
  while (Value != Sentinel) {
    NumberOfValues = NumberOfValues + 1;
    SumOfValues = SumOfValues + Value;
    cout << "Enter a value (" << Sentinel << " to quit): ";
    cin >> Value;
  }
  cout << "Average is " << (double(SumOfValues)/NumberOfValues) << endl;
  return(0);
}
```

sentinel

Notice that the code uses a constant called Sentinel. This constant holds a special value to act as a *flag*, or *sentinel*, signifying the end of the loop. A program can also get the sentinel value from the user. This approach provides a clear and easy-to-change method for ending a loop.

4.15 ++ and +=

There are shortcuts for both counting and summing in C++. Placing the symbol ++ directly after a variable name indicates one should be added to the variable. For example

```
NumberOfValues++;
```

is the same as:

```
NumberOfValues=NumberOfValues+1;
```

increment operator

The ++ symbol is called the *increment operator* and its meaning was behind the decision to call this language "C++". The idea was that this object-oriented extension to the C language was "one better" than C.

For adding a value to a sum, the symbol += is used. For example

```
SumOfValues+=Value;
```

is the same as:

```
SumOfValues=SumOfValues+Value;
```

special assignment operator

The += symbol is a special form of the assignment operator (=) and indicates the value after the operator is to be added to the value of the variable on the left of the operator.

Review 17

Modify the program in Section 4.14 so that it also calculates and displays the percentage of values entered that are below 70 (Hint: Use an if statement and another counting variable.) The program output may look similar to:

```
Enter a value (0 to quit): 70
Enter a value (0 to quit): 80
Enter a value (0 to quit): 60
Enter a value (0 to quit): 84
Enter a value (0 to quit): 0
Average is 73.5
Percent below 70: 25.0%
```

Review 18

Write a program that uses a while loop and a counter to display the numbers 1 through 12 each on a line.

Review 19

Modify Review 18 so that it also calculates and displays the sum of the numbers 1 through 12.

4.16 Looping: The for Statement

4

A third looping statement is the for loop which is generally used to execute a loop body a fixed number of times. The for loop has the form:

```
for (initialization; condition; increment)
    statement;
```

The *initialization* is performed only once when the for loop is first executed. The *condition* is a Boolean expression evaluated before each iteration of the loop body (*statement*). *statement* may be a single statement or a compound statement executed only when *condition* is true. The *increment* is performed after each iteration of the loop body, and usually advances a counter. Any of these parameters may be left out, leaving the semicolons as markers.

The following for loop displays the numbers 1 through 10:

```
for (int i=1; i<=10; i++)
    cout << i << endl;
```

Note that the counter i was declared as well as initialized in the for loop. However, a variable can be declared in a block of code only once. Therefore, if i is to be used again within the same block of code, its declaration (int i;) must appear outside the for loop.

In the following example, the *initialization* parameter is left out of the for statement because Number has already been initialized:

```
// Prints a table of numbers and their squares
int Number;
cout << "Enter number to start from: ";
cin >> Number;
for ( ; Number<=10; Number++)
    cout << Number << " " << Number*Number << endl;
```

It can be confusing to determine exactly what parameters will iterate a for loop a specific number of times. A standard way of formulating the *initialization* and *condition* parameters are:

```
for (int Number=Lo; Number<=Hi; Number++)
```

The variable names will change depending upon the program. However, this format makes it clear what the starting and ending values are. The previous code can be modified to include this standard:

```
// Prints a table of numbers and their squares
const int Finish = 10;
int Start;
cout << "Enter number to start from: ";
cin >> Start;
for (int Number=Start; Number<=Finish; Number++)
    cout << Number << " " << Number*Number << endl;
```

programming style

While it is possible to modify the value of the loop control variable from within a for loop or to terminate the loop prematurely, this is generally considered poor programming style. Good programming style dictates that changes to the loop control variable will be in the *increment* only and the loop will end only when the *condition* is false.

4.17 -- and -=

4

decrement operator

A for loop is often decremented. The symbol -- is called the *decrement operator*, and is used to indicate one should be subtracted from a variable. For example

    Total--;

is the same as:

    Total=Total-1;

special assignment operator

To subtract a value from a sum, the symbol -= is used. For example

    Total-=Value;

is the same as:

    Total=Total-Value;

The -= symbol is a special form of the assignment operator (=) and indicates the value after the operator is to be subtracted from the value of the variable on the left of the operator.

Review 20

Write a for loop that displays the numbers from 2 to 20 by twos, i.e., 2, 4, 6, 8, 10, etc. (Hint: Use Number+=2 as the *increment*.)

Review 21

Write a for loop that displays the numbers from 20 to 0, i.e., 20, 19, 18, 17, etc.

Review 22

Write a for loop that computes the sum of the odd numbers from 1 to a maximum value entered by the user.

4.18 The bool Library

bool type

A *Boolean variable* can hold one of only two values, true or false. The Boolean type was just recently added to standard C++, and not all compilers support it yet. However, the bool library supplied with this text can be used in programs to implement the bool type. The bool library also contains two constants, true and false, that are useful as loop conditions, as shown in the next section.

The bool type can be implemented in a program that has the following statement:

    #include <lvp\bool.h>

The following statement declares a bool variable and assigns it a value:

    bool Continue=true;

Note that true is not enclosed in quotation marks.

4.19 The break Statement

The break statement is used to terminate the current block of code and move the flow of control to the next statement after the block. For example, a program can be simplified by coding a loop to terminate from within the loop if for example, a sentinel has been entered, or an error has been encountered. A loop written this way has the form:

```
while (true) {
   statements;
   if (ending condition)
      break;
   statements;
}
```

The Boolean constant true is used to create a while condition that is always true. Therefore, the loop iterates until the break statement is executed.

Using break, the while loop from the Calculate Average program could be rewritten as:

```
while (true) {
   cout << "Enter a value (" << Sentinel << "to quit): ";
   cin >> Value;
   if (Value==Sentinel)
      break;   // Terminate the loop
   NumberOfValues++;
   SumOfValues+=Value;
}
```

Notice the code for entry of values is not repeated as in the original code.

programming style

It is important to avoid the indiscriminate use of break statements. Do not use break to avoid thinking more deeply about a problem, but instead to simplify your code when appropriate. A good rule of thumb is that there should be no more than one break statement in a loop, and it is probably better not to use the break statement in for loops.

4.20 Generating Random Numbers

random.h

Games, simulators, screen savers, and many other types of programs require a random number generator. The random library included with this text contains the random() function which returns a random integer between 0 and one less than the value given in parentheses. For example,

```
for (int i=1; i<=10; i++)
   cout << random(100) << endl;
```

displays 10 integers in the range 0 to 99. However, when using only the random() function the same 10 "random" numbers are generated each time the program is executed! This is intentional. Often it is easier to debug a program when the behavior does not change from run to run. Once a program is debugged, the randomize() function, also in the random library, should be included to generate random numbers from run to run:

```
randomize();
for (int i=1; i<=10; i++)
   cout << random(100) << endl;
```

It is important to call randomize() only once. If it is called many times (for example, calling it from within the loop) then the program may generate the same number over and over again.

To generate a random integer between 1 and some maximum value, the following expression may be used

    1 + random(MaxRandom)

where MaxRandom represents the maximum value desired.

floating point random number

To generate a random floating point number between 0 and 1 (not including 1), the following expression can be used:

    double(random(10000))/10000

This expression generates a number between 0 and 9999, promotes it to a double, and then divides it by 10000 to get a floating point number between zero and 1. The lowest value will be 0, and the highest will be 9999/10000 or 0.9999.

4.21 The conio Library

The conio library contains many functions for controlling a program's output in its window. The conio functions include:

Function	Effect
clrscr()	Clears the entire window
clreol()	Clear the line from the current cursor position to the end of the line
getche()	Reads the key pressed by the user, and displays the character
getch()	Reads the key pressed by the user, but does not display the character
kbhit()	Returns true if a key has been pressed and false otherwise. Does not read the key pressed.
gotoxy(x,y)	Moves the cursor to the position x, y, where x indicates the column and y indicates the row from the top of the screen

clrscr() and clreol()

The program window is cleared with the clrscr() and clreol() functions. The clrscr() function can perform relatively slowly. When speed is important, only a portion of the screen should be cleared or rewritten if possible. The clreol() function is most commonly used in conjunction with the gotoxy() function to replace a message or a number on part of the screen with another message or number.

getch() and getche()

The getch() and getche() functions are used to get a single keystroke from the user. They do not require the user to press the Enter key, and are commonly used to implement simple menus, as in the statements:

```
char Choice;
cout << "A. Circle" << endl;
cout << "B. Square" << endl;
cout << "Press your choice: ";
Choice = getche();
```

The only difference between getche() and getch() is that getche() echoes the key pressed to the screen while getch() does not. In the previous statements, getche() is used in an assignment statement because it returns the value of the key pressed by the user. This value is then stored in Choice.

The getch() and getche() functions can also be used to pause a program, as in the statements:

```
cout << "Press a key to continue" << endl;
getch();    // Pause until user presses a key
```

kbhit()

The kbhit() function is often used as the condition of a loop. For example, the following loop increments a counter until a key is pressed:

```
int Number = 1;
cout << "Press any key to stop" << endl;
while (!kbhit()) {
  cout << Number << endl;
  Number++;
}
getch();    // Read in the keystroke pressed
```

The getch() statement is included to read in the keystroke so that it is not left for the next read operation later in the program.

gotoxy()

The gotoxy() function is used to move the cursor to any position in the program output window. For example, the statement

```
gotoxy(3, 6);
```

moves the cursor to the third column from the left and the sixth row from the top of the output window. The upper-left corner of the window is the first column and the first row.

The following Doodle program illustrates many of the conio functions. In the first section, the user can "draw" with asterisks by pressing the I/J/K/M keys. In the second section, the program erases the drawing by putting random asterisks and blanks in the window:

```
/*Doodle program */

#include <iostream.h>
#include <conio.h>
#include <lvp\random.h>

int main()
{
  randomize();
  cout << "Doodler!  Press I/J/K/M to move, Q to quit" << endl;
  char KeyPressed;    // Key pressed by user
  int x=40; int y=10;    // Establish initial position of cursor
  do {
    // Plot a "point"
    gotoxy(x, y);
    cout << '*';
    gotoxy(x, y);      // Move blinking cursor under current spot

    KeyPressed = getch();    // Get a key, not echoing to the screen
    if (KeyPressed == 'I' || KeyPressed == 'i')
      y--;
    else if (KeyPressed == 'M' || KeyPressed == 'm')
      y++;
```

```
                else if (KeyPressed == 'J' || KeyPressed == 'j')
                  x--;
                else if (KeyPressed == 'K' || KeyPressed == 'k')
                  x++;
                else if (KeyPressed == 'Q' || KeyPressed == 'q')
                  ;    // Do nothing
                else
                  cout << "\a";   // Beep for bad keystroke
           } while ((KeyPressed != 'Q') && (KeyPressed != 'q'));

             gotoxy(1, 1);   // Clear and display new title
             clreol();
             cout << "Random stars!  Press any key to stop." << endl;
             while (!kbhit()) {
                gotoxy(1+random(60), 2+random(20));
                cout << "* ";    // A star and a blank to draw AND erase
             }
             return (0);
           }
```

No page in a book could do this program justice! We suggest you run the program yourself to see how it behaves.

Review 23

Modify the Doodle program so that when the spacebar is pressed the drawing character is changed to a single blank rather than an asterisk and a blank. This would allow the user to "erase" by overwriting with blanks. Pressing the asterisk key should return the drawing character to an asterisk.

Review 24

Write a program that displays a counter in the middle of the window. The counter should count down from 1000 to 0, and at 0 should generate a series of beeps. Write the program so that the user can press any key during the counting to stop the counting and end the program without the beeps.

Review 25

Write a program that displays five rolls of two dice where each die is a number between 1 and 6, and shows the total. When run, program output may look similar to:

```
2  4  =  6
1  1  =  2
6  6  =  12
4  3  =  7
5  2  =  7
```

Case Study

In this Case Study a "guessing game" program will be created.

specification

Prompt the user to guess a random number generated by the computer. The program should report whether the guess is too high, too low, or correct. The user may guess as many times as desired, or may "give up" by entering a zero. At the end, the program displays the number of guesses taken.

design

Program design includes code design and data design. *Code design* is the process of determining the algorithms and program structure to be used to satisfy the specification. *Data design* is the process of deciding upon the variables and constants and their types based on the code design.

code design

A loop is needed to allow for multiple guesses. Since the number of guesses that will be taken is unknown, a while loop rather than a for (counting) loop should be used. Since there will be at least one guess entered, the do-while loop will be used. The program pseudocode looks like:

```
Generate the random number
do {
  Get a guess
  If (Guess != Sentinel to give up)
    Report if number is too high, too low, or correct
    Add one to the number of guesses
} while ((Guess != Sentinel to give up) and (Guess is not correct))
Report number of guesses
```

data design

Variables are needed for the random number (Secret), the user's guess (Guess), and a counter for the number of guesses (NumGuesses). Constants are needed for the two unchanging values: The maximum random number (MaxValue), and the sentinel to be used to give up (GiveUpValue).

coding

Translating the pseudocode to C++ gives the final code:

```cpp
/* Guessing Game program */

#include <iostream.h>
#include <lvp\random.h>

int main()
{
  // Generate secret number
  const int MaxValue = 100;
  randomize();
  int Secret = 1+random(MaxValue);

  // Have user guess secret number
  const int GiveUpValue = 0;
  int NumGuesses = 0;
  int Guess;
  cout << "--Guessing Game!--\n";
  do {
    cout << "Enter guess (" << GiveUpValue << " to give up):";
    cin >> Guess;
    if (Guess != GiveUpValue) {
      if (Guess == Secret)
        cout << "You've got it!\n";
      else if (Guess < Secret)
        cout << "Too low!  Try again!\n";
      else
        cout << "Too high!  Try again!\n";
      NumGuesses++;
    }
  } while ((Guess != GiveUpValue) && (Guess != Secret));
  if (Guess == GiveUpValue)
    cout << "You gave up after " << NumGuesses << " guesses.\n";
  else
    cout << "It took you " << NumGuesses << " guesses.\n";
  return(0);
}
```

Program output will depend on user input. When run, the Case Study output may look similar to:

```
--Guessing Game!--
Enter guess (0 to give up):50
Too high!  Try again!
Enter guess (0 to give up):25
Too low!  Try again!
Enter guess (0 to give up):37
You've got it!
It took you 3 guesses.
```

In another run, program output may look similar to:

```
--Guessing Game!--
Enter guess (0 to give up):50
Too low!  Try again!
Enter guess (0 to give up):75
Too high!  Try again!
Enter guess (0 to give up):0
You gave up after 2 guesses.
```

Logic errors are more likely in if statements and loops. Therefore, it is necessary to carefully create the pseudocode and work through each condition. For test cases, high, low, and correct guesses were made. It was also necessary to "give up" in one run in order to test that code.

Review 26

Modify the Case Study program so that it asks the user for the maximum random number to be generated (rather than using a constant).

Review 27

Modify the Case Study program so that the user has the option of playing the game repeatedly.

Review 28

Modify the Case Study program so that it prevents the user from entering numbers outside the range 0..MaxValue. If such a number is entered, the program should display an error message and then allow the user to enter that guess again.

Chapter Summary

Controlling program flow includes controlling which statements are executed and how many times statements are executed. This chapter covered the if statement and three looping statements for controlling program flow. Each of these statements evaluates a *condition* to determine program flow. The *condition* is a Boolean expression which evaluates to either true or false. A Boolean expression is formed using relational operators, and may also contain logical operators. The symbols && and || represent logical "and" and "or." The symbol ! is used in a condition to represent logical "not." When the *condition* portion of the if statement and the three looping statements is true, program flow branches to *statement* which can be a single C++ statement or a group of statements enclosed by curly braces called a compound statement.

The if statement may include an else clause that executes when *condition* is false.

Nested if statements are used to control program flow in one of three or more ways. A standard way of formatting nested ifs is called an else-if ladder. The else-if ladder is the preferred programming style where possible because it is less error-prone and because of its clarity to the reader.

The do-while loop allows statements to be repeated as often as desired. The do-while executes the statements of the loop body and then checks the while condition. If *condition* is true, the loop body is executed again and then *condition* checked again. This process is repeated until *condition* is evaluated and found to be false.

Compilers usually contain tools for debugging a program. The step feature is used for stepping through each line of code as a program executes. A watch window may be set up to watch the values of variables as a program executes.

An algorithm is a series of steps that tell how to solve a problem. When creating a program, algorithms are often written as pseudocode which is a mix of English and C++.

The while loop checks its condition before the first execution of the loop body. Therefore, this loop may not execute its loop body at all.

Flags, or sentinels, are used to signify that a loop should end. The break statement can be used inside a loop body to terminate the current block of code and move the flow of control to the next statement after the block.

A third loop, the for loop is generally used to execute a loop body a fixed number of times.

Loops are often used for counting and summing values. The expression foo++ is a shorthand for foo=foo+1 which adds one to the value of foo. The expression Sum+=foo is a shorthand for Sum=Sum+foo which adds the value of foo to the current value of Sum. Counters and summing variables must be initialized to get the expected results.

The expression foo-- is a shorthand for foo=foo-1 which subtracts one from the value of foo. The expression Sum-=foo is a shorthand for Sum=Sum-foo which subtracts the value of foo from the current value of Sum.

A Boolean variable can have one of only two values: true or false. The bool library is used to implement the bool type. The bool constants, true and false, are useful for controlling loops when used in conjunction with the break statement.

Random numbers are generated using the random() and randomize() functions in the random library. The conio library provides a number of functions for controlling a program's output in its window.

Vocabulary

Algorithm A series of steps that tell how to solve a problem.

Boolean Expression An expression that contains a relational operator and evaluates to either true or false. A Boolean expression may also contain logical operators.

Boolean Variable A variable of type bool that can store only true or false.

Code Design The process of determining the algorithm and program structure to be used to satisfy the specification.

Compound Statement A group of statements surrounded by curly braces.

Counter A variable used to count the number of loop iterations.

Data Design The process of deciding upon the variables and constants and their types based on the code design.

Dangling else A logic error that occurs in a nested if statement when an else clause is associated with the inside if instead of with the outside if as intended.

Decrement operator The symbols -- used to indicate one will be subtracted from a variable.

Flag Also called a sentinel.

Increment Operator The symbols ++ used to indicate one will be added to a variable.

Infinite Loop A loop which iterates forever because of a logic error.

Initialization An assignment statement that gives a variable a starting value. Counters are often initialized.

Iteration The repetition of the execution of one or more statements in a program.

Logical Operators Operators used in a complex if condition (&&, ||, !).

Logic Error An error caused by statements that are syntactically correct but produce an undesired or unexpected result.

Looping Also called iteration.

Lvalue An expression which can be used on the left-hand side of an assignment statement, usually a variable.

Nested if An if statement inside another if statement.

Pseudocode An algorithm created using both English terms and C++ code.

Relational Operators Operators used in an expression to make comparisons (==, <, <=, >, >=, !=).

Sentinel A value used to indicate the end of a sequence of values.

Roundoff Error Associated with floating point numbers because they cannot be exactly represented in binary notation by the computer.

! The C++ symbol for the logical "not" operator.

&& The C++ symbol for the logical "and" operator.

|| The C++ symbol for the logical "or" operator.

-- Decrement operator for subtracting one from a variable.

++ Increment operator used for adding one to a variable.

-= Special assignment operator for subtracting a value from a variable.

+= Special assignment operator used for adding a value to a variable.

bool Type limited to values of true and false.

bool.h A library that implements the bool type so that Boolean variables can be defined. Also includes constants true and false.

break Statement to terminate the current block of code and move the flow of control to the next statement after the block.

clreol() Function in the conio library for clearing the a line in the program window from the current cursor position.

clrscr() Function in the conio library for clearing the program window.

conio.h The console input/output library which includes functions for controlling a program's output in a window.

do-while Looping statement which performs its body one or more times.

else-if **Ladder** Nested ifs formatted a standard way for multiple decision branching.

getch() Function in the conio library that reads a key pressed, but does not display that key.

getche() Function in the conio library that reads a key pressed, and displays that key.

gotoxy() Function in the conio library that moves the cursor in the program window to a designated position.

if Executes a statement or a compound statement when its condition is true, and alternately executes a different statement or a compound statement when its condition is false.

kbhit() Function in the conio.h library that returns true if a key has been pressed (but not read) and false otherwise.

for Looping statement which performs its body a designated number of times.

random.h The library that includes the random() and randomize() functions.

random() Function in the random library for generating a random number.

randomize() Function in the random library for generating random numbers from run to run.

while Looping statement which performs its body zero or more times.

Exercise 1

Write a program to assist in computer repair. The user is asked if the ailing computer beeps on startup, and if the hard drive spins. If it beeps and the drive spins, have the program display "Contact tech support." If it beeps and the drive doesn't spin, have the program display "Check drive contacts." If it doesn't beep, and the hard drive doesn't spin, have the program display "Bring computer to repair center." Finally, if it doesn't beep, but the hard drive spins, have the program display "Check the speaker contacts."

Exercise 2

Geel's Overnight Delivery service accepts no package heavier than 27 kilograms, or larger than 0.1 cubic meters. Write a program that asks the input for the weight of a package and its dimensions, and displays an appropriate message if the package does not meet the requirements (e.g., too large, too heavy, or both). The program output should look similar to:

```
Enter weight of package in kilograms: 28
Enter length of package in meters: 1
Enter width of package in meters: .5
Enter height of package in meters: .5
Rejected: Too heavy and too large
```

Exercise 3

Ernesto's Eggs has different wholesale prices for their eggs, based upon the number sold:

0 up to but not including 4 dozen	$0.50 per dozen
4 up to but not including 6 dozen	$0.45 per dozen
6 up to but not including 11 dozen	$0.40 per dozen
11 or more dozen	$0.35 per dozen

Extra eggs are priced at $1/12$ the per dozen price.

a) Write a program that asks the user for the number of eggs, and then calculates the bill. The program output should look similar to:

```
Enter number of eggs: 126
Your cost is $0.40 per dozen or 0.033 per egg.
Your bill comes to $4.20
```

b) A computer is not always available, so Mr. Ernesto would like a chart showing the price for any number of eggs up to 120. Write a program that displays a chart similar to:

```
1    0.04
2    0.08
3    0.12
...
48   1.80
...
```

4

Exercise 4

Clark's Cafe pays its employees time and a half for every hour worked over 40 hours.

a) Write a program to calculate gross weekly wages (before taxes) given the hours worked and the hourly rate. The program output should look similar to:

```
Enter hours worked: 45
Enter hourly rate: 10.00

Gross wages = $ 475.00
```

b) Mr. Clark employs students who are exempt from taxes and others who are not. Modify the program so that if an employee is not exempt, 18% will be deducted from gross wages, otherwise "NO TAXES DEDUCTED" will be displayed. Two program runs are shown below:

```
Enter hours worked: 45
Enter hourly rate: 10.00
Exempt (Y/N)? Y

Gross wages = $475.00
NO TAXES DEDUCTED

Enter hours worked: 20
Enter hourly rate:  4.00
Exempt (Y/N)? N

Gross wages = $80.00
Wages after taxes = $65.60
```

Exercise 5

The Bored Auto Company has done it again. Some models of their cars may be difficult to drive because their wheels are not exactly round. Cars with model numbers 119, 179, 189 through 195, 221, and 780 have been found to have this defect. Write a program that allows customers to enter the model number of their car to find out whether or not it is defective. The program should terminate when a zero is entered as a model number. The program output should look similar to:

```
Enter your model number (0 for done): 127
Your car is OK.

Enter your model number (0 for done): 221
Your car is defective. Please have it fixed.

Enter your model number (0 for done): 0
Program complete.
```

Exercise 6

You deposit $2500.00 in a new super Certificate of Deposit (CD) at your bank. Write a program to calculate how many years it will take for your CD to be worth $5000.00 or more, if it pays 7.5% interest compounded annually.

Exercise 7

Write a program that takes a non-negative long as input and displays each of the digits on a separate line. The program output should look similar to:

```
Enter an integer: 71345
7
1
3
4
5
```

Exercise 8

Write a program that displays the sum of the digits of any non-negative integer. Two program runs are shown below:

```
Enter an integer: 145
Sum of digits is 10

Enter an integer: 8888
Sum of digits is 32
```

Exercise 9

a) Write a program that displays the sum of the cubes of the digits of any non-negative integer. Two program runs are shown below:

```
Enter an integer: 145
Sum of the cubes of the digits is 190

Enter an integer: 8888
Sum of the cubes of the digits is 2048
```

b) Modify the program to determine what integers of two, three, or four digits are equal to the sum of the cubes of their digits.

Exercise 10

An interesting problem in number theory is sometimes called the "necklace problem." This problem begins with two single-digit numbers. The next number is obtained by adding the first two numbers together and saving only the ones-digit. This process is repeated until the "necklace" closes by returning to the original two numbers. For example, if the starting numbers are 1 and 8, twelve steps are required to close the "necklace":

1 8 9 7 6 3 9 2 1 3 4 7 1 8

Write a program that asks the user for two starting numbers, and then displays the sequence and the number of steps taken. The program output should look similar to:

```
Enter first number: 1
Enter second number: 8
1 8 9 7 6 3 9 2 1 3 4 7 1 8
Your numbers required 12 steps.
```

Exercise 11

a) Write a program that asks the user for a non-negative integer and then displays a message indicating if it is prime or not. A prime number is an integer that has no factors other than one and itself. Two program runs are shown below:

```
Enter an integer: 51
Not prime

Enter an integer: 53
Prime
```

b) Modify the program to display the number of primes found between two numbers entered by the user.

```
Enter starting number: 50
Enter ending number: 59
Number of primes in range: 2
```

Exercise 12

Write a program that displays the prime factors of an integer entered by the user. If a number is a prime factor more than once, it should be printed more than once. The program output should look similar to:

```
Enter a number: 140
Prime factors: 2,2,5,7
```

Use the following algorithm:

> Initialize a counter at 2
> So long as the counter is less than or equal to the number
>   if the counter divides the number evenly
>   display the counter
>   divide the number by the counter to get a new number
>   else add one to the counter

Exercise 13

Write a program that asks the user for two non-negative integers and then prints the greatest common divisor (GCD) of the two numbers. The GCD is the largest integer that divides into both numbers evenly. Two program runs are shown below:

```
Enter an integer: 12
Enter an integer: 18
The GCD is 6

Enter an integer: 102
Enter an integer: 68
The GCD is 34
```

Exercise 14

Amy's Garden Emporium uses mailing labels for shipping boxes. Write a program to display a mailing label for each box to be shipped. The program output should look similar to:

```
How many boxes? 2
    AMY'S GARDEN EMPORIUM
    SUNTAN, IOWA 12345
    BOX NUMBER 1 OF 2

    AMY'S GARDEN EMPORIUM
    SUNTAN, IOWA 12345
    BOX NUMBER 2 OF 2
```

Exercise 15

Write a program that displays the sum of all of the integers between two input numbers, inclusive. The program output should look similar to:

```
Enter starting number: 25
Enter ending number: 47

The sum of integers from 25 to 47 is 828
```

Exercise 16

a) Write a program that reads in letter grades for a class of 20 students and displays the number of students who passed (D or better) and the number who failed (E or F). The program output should look similar to:

```
Enter a grade: C
Enter a grade: A
...

16 students passed
4 students failed
```

b) Modify the program to work for a class of any size. Use Z as the value of the sentinel, making sure not to count the Z as a grade. Program output should display the percentage of students passing and failing using formatted output:

```
Enter a grade: C
Enter a grade: E
Enter a grade: A
...

Enter a grade: Z

12 students passed: 80.00%
3 students failed: 20.00%
```

Exercise 17

Write a program that asks the user for starting and ending values and then display a formatted table of squares and cubes. Write the program so that it is easy to change the column widths. The program output should look similar to:

```
Enter starting value: 5
Enter ending value: 12

X    X SQUARED    X CUBED
5           25        125
6           36        216
           ...
12         144       1728
```

Exercise 18

a) Write a program that calculates the average and total for a known number of test grades. The program should first read in the number of grades and then the grades. The program output should look similar to:

```
How many grades? 12

Enter a grade: 95
...

Enter a grade: 69

The total is 1020
The average is 85.00
```

b) Modify the program to include error checking so that it will give an error message and not accept test grades outside the range 0 – 100. The program output should look similar to:

```
How many grades? 3

Enter a grade: 82
Enter a grade: -12
-12 is not an acceptable grade
Enter a grade: 75
Enter a grade: 93

The total is 250
The average is 83.33
```

c) Modify the program to accept any number of grades terminated with a sentinel, –1. The program output should look similar to:

```
Enter a grade: 82
Enter a grade: 75
Enter a grade: -1

The total is 157
The average is 78.5
```

Exercise 19

The factorial of a positive number is the product of all positive integers less than or equal to the number. For example, 5 factorial (written 5!) is equal to 5*4*3*2*1, or 120.

a) Write a program that reads a positive integer and displays its factorial. The program output should look similar to:

```
Enter an integer: 5

5! = 120
```

b) 0! is defined as 1, but all negative factorials are considered to be undefined. Modify the factorial program to ask the user for an integer until a positive integer or 0 is entered. The program output should look similar to:

```
Enter an integer: -5

-5! is undefined.

Enter an integer: 0

0! = 1
```

4

Exercise 25

Write a program that plays a guessing game where the computer tries to guess a number picked by the user. The program asks the user to think of a secret number and then asks the user a sequence of guesses. After each guess, the user must report whether it is too high or too low or correct. The program should count the guesses. (Hint: Maintain HighestPossible and LowestPossible variables, and always guess midway between the two. This is called a binary search.) The program output should look similar to:

```
Think of a number between 1 and 100 and then press Enter.
Is the number 50 (Correct, Low, High)? h
Is the number 25 (Correct, Low, High)? h
Is the number 13 (Correct, Low, High)? l
Is the number 19 (Correct, Low, High)? c
```

Exercise 26

Write a program that acts as a simple "slot machine." The user starts with 100 tokens and with each "pull" of the handle loses 1 token. The computer "spins" three wheels each consisting of the numbers 1, 2, and 3. If all three numbers are 1, the user gets 4 tokens; if all three are 2, the user gets 8 tokens; if all are 3, the user gets 12 tokens. Program output should look similar to:

```
You have 100 tokens. Pull? Y
[1] [3] [2]
You lost.
You have 99 tokens. Pull? Y
[2] [2] [2]
You won 8 tokens!
You have 106 tokens. Pull? N
Thanks for playing!
```

Exercise 27

Modify the Doodle program in Section 4.21 so that when the C key is pressed the drawing character is changed to the next key pressed. Thus, if the user pressed C and then $, the program will use $ characters instead of * characters when drawing.

Exercise 28

Modify the Doodle program in Section 4.21 so that it uses the numeric keypad keys to move and includes diagonal moves.

Exercise 29

Write a program that uses gotoxy() to display an "x" formed from asterisks on the screen. Let the user specify the size of the "x" as an odd number between 1 and 15. The program output should look similar to:

```
What size x would you like (an odd number)? 5
*     *
 *   *
   *
 *   *
*     *
```

Exercise 30

In the "random walk" problem, a person is placed at the center of a 7 meter long bridge. Each step, the person moves 1 meter either forward or backward at random.

a) Write a program to determine how many steps the person will walk before taking a step off the bridge. Have the program average 50 trials, and report the average and greatest number of steps. (Hint: Use random(2), with 0 meaning to go forward and 1 meaning to go backward.)

b) Modify the program to display the position of the person at each stage of a run:

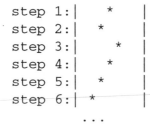

```
step 1:|    *    |
step 2:|   *     |
step 3:|      *  |
step 4:|    *    |
step 5:|   *     |
step 6:|  *      |
        . . .
```

Exercise 31

A simple form of animation is done by drawing characters, then erasing them by redrawing them with blanks, and then drawing them in a new location. The pseudocode might be:

```
Set location to starting spot
Draw black character at location
While not done do
    Draw white character at location
    Change location
    Draw black character at (new) location
```

The line "Change location" may mean adding one to the location, or changing the location according to a command key pressed.

a) Write a program that animates an asterisk moving across the screen from left to right.

b) Modify the program so that the user can specify the direction with L meaning left to right and T meaning top to bottom.

c) Modify the program so that the "character" is formed of several characters, e.g.,

```
o  o
   ,
\_/
```

Exercise 32

Modify the Case Study so that it prevents the user from entering a foolish guess (i.e., one lower than a number previously reported to be too low, or higher than a number previously reported to be too high). (Hint: Maintain HighestPossible and LowestPossible variables, updating one of them after each guess.)

The exercise section of this and all succeeding chapters will end with one or more advanced exercises. These exercises provide the specification; your task is to produce design, coding, debugging, and testing steps just as those used in the Case Study problem.

Advanced Exercise 33

Write a program to simulate a simplified version of the game "21." A deck of cards numbered 1 to 10 is used and any number can be repeated. The computer starts by asking you (the user) how many cards you want. It then deals you the cards, which are randomly picked, and deals itself three randomly picked cards. If both scores are over 21, or if both are equal but under 21, the game is declared a draw. Otherwise, the winner is the one with the highest score equal to or less than 21. If one score is over 21, but the other is 21 or less, the player with 21 or less is declared the winner. Write your program so that the game can be played as often as desired with the winner of each game winning one point. At the end of the games display the total winnings for you and the computer and the number of draws. The program output should look similar to:

```
How many cards do you want? 3
You: 8 5 1
Computer: 8 3 3
I have 14 and you have 14 so we draw.
Would you like to play again? (Y/N)? Y

How many cards do you want? 2
You: 7 2
Computer: 8 7 4
I have 19 and you have 9 so I win
Would you like to play again? (Y/N)? Y

How many cards do you want? 3
You: 8 7 4
Computer: 2 1 7
I have 10 and you have 19 so you win
Would you like to play again (Y/N)? N

Computer wins = 1
Your wins = 1
Draws = 1
```

4

A Guide to Programming in C++

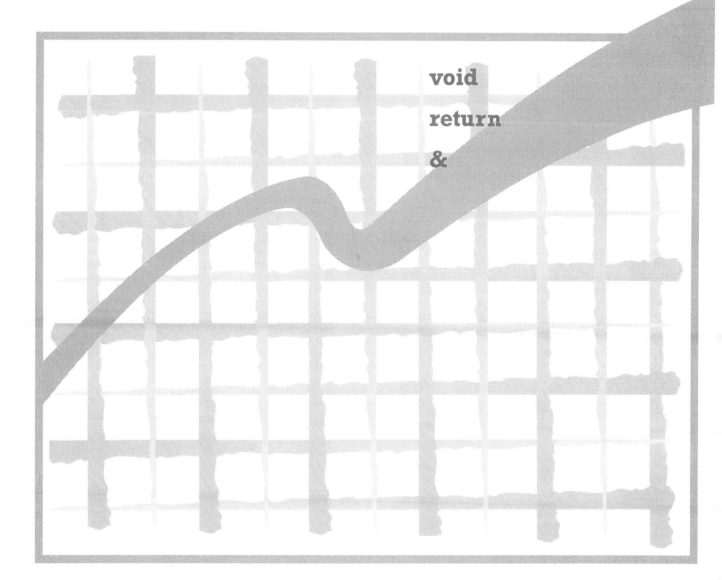

void

return

&

Objectives

After completing this chapter you will be able to:

1. Write user-defined functions.

2. Use parameters to pass values to a function.

3. Write overloaded functions.

4. Use default parameters.

5. Use the return statement to return a value from a function.

6. Use reference parameters in a function.

7. Develop methodologies for building functions.

8. Use preconditions and postconditions to document functions.

9. Build a library containing code to perform related tasks.

10. Use top-down design in constructing large programs.

11. Understand function prototypes.

5

As the complexity of your programs increases, you may wonder how large programs containing hundreds of thousands of lines of code are ever written. Software applications such as these are often written by a team of from tens to hundreds of programmers. But how can so many individuals work together effectively? A complex programming task is broken down into small, independent parts that can work together in a clearly defined way. In C++, these small, independent parts are called functions. Understanding and using functions is central to becoming a C++ programmer.

5.1 The Function

A C++ *function* performs a single, well-defined task. For example, Chapters Three and Four introduced functions getline(), gotoxy(), and random().

A program's algorithm can be used to identify several well-defined tasks. In many cases, these well-defined tasks can be accomplished using functions from libraries that are included in the program. Other tasks require *user-defined functions*. For example, the following user-defined function converts the number of days entered by the user to the corresponding number of hours:

```
void DaysToHours()
/* Converts days to hours */
{
  int Days, Hours;

  cout << "Enter the number of days: ";
  cin >> Days;

  Hours = Days*24;
  cout << "The number of hours in " << Days << " days is: " << Hours;
}
```

void

A user-defined function has the same format as a main() function. The function above does not return a value, therefore it begins with the keyword void instead of int and does not contain a return statement. A comment describing the function is included as good programming style.

A *function definition* is the actual code of a function. To execute a function it is *called* by main() or another function using its name and parentheses. In this way, user-defined functions extend the C++ language. The program below includes the DaysToHours() function and a similar function HoursToDays():

```
/* Time Conversion program.
   Illustrates user-defined functions. */

#include <iostream.h>

//---------------------------------------------------------------------------
void DaysToHours()
/* Converts days to hours */
{
   int Days, Hours;

   cout << "Enter the number of days: ";
   cin >> Days;

   Hours = Days*24;
   cout << "The number of hours in " << Days << " days is: " << Hours;
}
//---------------------------------------------------------------------------
void HoursToDays()
/* Converts hours to days */
{
   int Hours, Days;

   cout << "Enter the number of hours: ";
   cin >> Hours;

   Days = Hours/24;
   cout << "The number of days in " << Hours << " hours is: " << Days;
}
//---------------------------------------------------------------------------
int main()
{
   char Choice;
   cout << "1  Days to Hours" << endl;
   cout << "2  Hours to Days" << endl;
   cout << "Enter your choice: ";
   cin >> Choice;
   if (Choice == '1')
      DaysToHours();    // function call
   else
      HoursToDays();    // function call

   return(0);
}
```

When run, the program output may look similar to:

```
1 Days to Hours
2 Hours to Days
Enter your choice: 1
Enter the number of days: 3
The number of hours in 3 days is: 72
```

A function definition must appear before the function can be called. For this reason, the order of function definitions must be considered if one function calls another. This is also why the main() function appears last in the program. To summarize, the structure of a program becomes:

```
#include <libraries>
function definitions
main() function
```

Review 1

Modify the Time Conversion program to include an Introduction() function that gives instructions to the user on the use of the program. Have the main() function call Introduction() before asking for the user's choice.

Review 2

Modify the Time Conversion program to include a third function HoursToMinutes().

5.2 Function Parameters

A function can be given values through *parameters*, also called *arguments*. For example, the built-in function gotoxy() requires two parameters:

```
gotoxy(3,5);
```

In this case, 3 and 5 are the function parameters. These parameters are used to position the cursor in the third row of the fifth column in the program output window.

A function uses parameters when they have been specified in the function definition. For example, a user-defined function DrawBar() displays a bar of asterisks across the screen. The length of the bar is determined with a parameter:

```
void DrawBar(int Length)
/*Displays a bar of asterisks of length Length.
   Length assumed >= 0                              */
{
   const char Mark = '*';
   for (int i=0; i<Length; i++)
      cout << Mark;
   cout << endl;
}
```

The function heading includes the type and name of the parameter, in this case, Length. Length can then be used in the function like a variable. The initial value of Length is determined by the argument given in the function call. For example, the statements

```
DrawBar(30);
int i = 5;
DrawBar(i);
```

produce the output:

```
* * * * * * * * * * * * * * * * * * * * * * * * * * * * * *
* * * * *
```

In the function heading, int Length is the *formal parameter*, also called the *formal argument*. It defines the type of the value required in the function call. The value 30 in the function call is the *actual parameter*, also called the *actual argument*. It is the value being passed to the function in a call. Note that the actual parameter can also be the value stored in a variable.

multiple parameters

When specifying more than one parameter in a function definition, the parameters are separated by a comma. For example, a modified DrawBar() requires both the character to display as well as a length:

```
void DrawBar(int Length, char Mark)
/*Displays a bar of length Length using the character Mark.
  Length assumed >= 0                                      */
{
  for (int i=0; i<Length; i++)
    cout << Mark;
  cout << endl;
}
```

Using this modified function, a call to DrawBar() could look like

DrawBar(10,'$');

which produces the output:

$$$$$$$$$$

parameter order

The order of the parameters is significant. In a function, the first actual parameter corresponds to the first formal parameter, and the second actual parameter to the second formal parameter, as illustrated below:

DrawBar(10, '$')

void DrawBar(int Length,char Mark)

programming style

As many parameters as desired can be placed in a function header. However, well-designed functions usually have only a few parameters.

Review 3

Write a main() function that uses four calls to DrawBar() to create a triangle:

```
*
* *
* * *
* * * *
```

Review 4

Write a function SpanishNum() that displays the spanish equivalent of its int parameter that is in the range 1 to 5:

1	uno
2	dos
3	tres
4	cuatro
5	cinco

Write a program where main() uses a for loop to display a table similar to the one above.

A Guide to Programming in C++

5.3 Function Overloading

The name and arguments in a function call are used to determine the function to be executed. Therefore, function names do not need to be unique as long as the functions with the same name have different arguments. Defining more than one function by the same name is called *function overloading*. For example, both versions of DrawBar() may be used in the same program since their arguments are different:

```
/*Overloaded DrawBar() program.
   Illustrates overloaded DrawBar functions */

#include <iostream.h>

//-----------------------------------------------------------------------
void DrawBar(int Length)
/*Displays a bar of asterisks of length Length.
   Length assumed >= 0                                    */
{
   const char Mark = '*';
   for (int i=0; i<Length; i++)
     cout << Mark;
   cout << endl;
}
//-----------------------------------------------------------------------
void DrawBar(int Length, char Mark)
/*Displays a bar of length Length using the character Mark.
   Length assumed >= 0                                    */
{
   for (int i=0; i<Length; i++)
     cout << Mark;
   cout << endl;
}
//-----------------------------------------------------------------------
int main()
{
   DrawBar(40);
   DrawBar(10,'$');
   DrawBar(40);

   return(0);
}
```

When run, the program displays:

```
* * * * * * * * * * * * * * * * * * * * * * * * * * * * * * * * * * * * * * * * *
$$$$$$$$$$
* * * * * * * * * * * * * * * * * * * * * * * * * * * * * * * * * * * * * * * * *
```

The DrawBar(40) calls invoke the first function, while the DrawBar(10,'$') call invokes the second. The compiler makes this decision based upon the *types*, *order*, and *number* of the actual arguments in a call.

5.4 Default Parameters

A function definition can include a *default parameter* which is used when that parameter is not specified in the function call. For example, the following program includes a DrawBar() function with a default parameter:

```
/* Default Parameter DrawBar() program.
   Illustrates DrawBar function with default parameter */

#include <iostream.h>

//-----------------------------------------------------------------------------
void DrawBar(int Length, char Mark = '*')
/* Displays a bar of length Length using the character Mark.
   Length assumed >= 0                                                     */
{
   for (int i=0; i<Length; i++)
     cout << Mark;
   cout << endl;
}
//-----------------------------------------------------------------------------
int main()
{
   DrawBar(40);
   DrawBar(10,'$');
   DrawBar(40);

   return(0);
}
```

When run, the program displays:

```
* * * * * * * * * * * * * * * * * * * * * * * * * * * * * * * * * * * * * * * *
$$$$$$$$$$
* * * * * * * * * * * * * * * * * * * * * * * * * * * * * * * * * * * * * * * *
```

In the function header, Mark is declared with a default value. If only a single argument is given in the call, then the default value (an asterisk) is used. If both arguments are given in the call, the default value is overridden. Note how the function definition with the default parameter can take the place of *both* the previous DrawBar() functions.

When using default parameters:

- All nondefault parameters must come first, followed by any parameters that have defaults.

- There is often ambiguity introduced when using default parameters and overloading on the same function. It is generally best to use one or the other, but not both for any given function.

Review 5

Write a function GiveHint() that has two int arguments, Secret and Guess, and displays one of
the following messages as appropriate:

```
Too high! Try again!
Too low! Try again!
You've got it!
```

Review 6

Write a function DrawBox() that has an int and a char argument, and displays a square using the
char argument. DrawBox() should make calls to DrawBar() to perform its work. For example, the
call DrawBox(4,'%') should display:

```
%%%%
%%%%
%%%%
%%%%
```

Review 7

Write a function DrawBox() that is based on the function in Review 6. This DrawBox() should
include three parameters, two of which are int arguments giving the height and width of a rectangle to be drawn. The function header should be:

```
void DrawBox(int Height, int Width, char Mark)
/*Draws a rectangle of size Height and Width using the character Mark.
    Height, Width assumed >= 0                                        */
```

Write a program where main() makes calls to this DrawBox() and the one in Review 6 to illustrate how overloading allows these two functions to coexist.

Review 8

Write a function DrawBox() that is based on the function in Review 7. This DrawBox() should
include two int arguments giving the height and width of a rectangle to be drawn and a third
default parameter for Mark. To test this DrawBox(), write a program where main() makes a call
that uses the default parameter and a call that doesn't.

5.5 The return Statement

A user-defined function can return a value. For example, the CubeOf()
function returns the cube of its parameter:

```
double CubeOf(double x)
/*Returns the cube of x */
{
    double Result = x*x*x;
    return(Result);
}
```

The function definition begins with double indicating the type of value it
will return to the calling function. The value returned by the function is
in a return statement. A *return statement* can return a single value only.

Functions can return any type of value, including built-in types (int, double, char) and those implemented in a library (String, bool). The void type is used to indicate that a function does not return any value at all, as was the case with the previous user-defined functions in this chapter. Functions defined using void do not include a return statement.

Calculations can be performed within the return statement. For example, CubeOf() could be rewritten as:

```
double CubeOf(double x)
/*Returns the cube of x */

{
   return(x*x*x);
}
```

Functions that return a value can be used in calculations, assignments, or streams. For example, the statement

```
for (Row=1; Row<=4; Row++)
   cout << Row << "   " << CubeOf(Row) << endl;
```

displays:

```
1    1
2    8
3    27
4    64
```

programming style

In the statement above, the value returned by CubeOf() is passed to cout to be displayed, and these values form the second column above. Note that the actual parameter is the variable Row, while the formal parameter is x. Throughout a program, descriptive variable names should be used without regard to matching parameter names in function definitions.

Understanding the return statement permits better understanding of the main() function used in every C++ program:

```
int main()
{
   // statements
   return(0);
}
```

The int in the main() header indicates that this function returns an integer. As discussed in Chapter Two, the value returned by main() is used to indicate if the function terminated without error. A 0 indicates no error.

Review 9

Write a function PowerOf() that calculates and returns the value of x^n. (Hint: A for loop can be used to calculate the power.) Use the function header:

```
double PowerOf(double x, int n)
/*Returns x to the nth power.
   n assumed >= 0           */
```

Review 10

Write a program that uses PowerOf() in Review 9 to display a table of the first ten powers of 2. The program output should look similar to:

```
2 to the 1 is 2
2 to the 2 is 4
2 to the 3 is 8
2 to the 4 is 16
. . .
2 to the 10 is 1024
```

5.6 Reradalarameters

value parameters

The function parameters discussed so far are *call-by-value parameters*, or *value parameters*, because they are used to only pass values in to a function. The variables representing actual parameters are unaltered by a function with value parameters, as demonstrated by the following program:

```
/*Value Parameters program */

#include <iostream.h>

//----------------------------------------------------------------
void Swap(int x, int y)
/*Exchanges the values of x and y */
{
   int Temp;
   Temp = x;
   x = y;
   y = Temp;
}
//----------------------------------------------------------------
int main()
{
   int a = 3, b = 5;
   cout << "Before Swap(): a=" << a << " and b=" << b << endl;
   Swap(a, b);
   cout << "After Swap(): a=" << a << " and b=" << b;
   return (0);
}
```

produces the undesired output:

```
Before Swap(): a=3 and b=5
After Swap(): a=3 and b=5
```

reference parameters

Reference parameters, or *call-by-reference parameters*, pass values both in to and out of a function. The variables representing actual parameters are automatically and immediately altered by a function with reference parameters, as demonstrated in the following program:

```
/*Reference Parameters program */

#include <iostream.h>

//----------------------------------------------------------------
void Swap(int &x, int &y)
/*Exchanges the values of x and y */
{
   int Temp;
   Temp = x;
   x = y;
   y = Temp;
}
//----------------------------------------------------------------
int main()
{
   int a = 3, b = 5;
   cout << "Before Swap(): a=" << a << " and b=" << b << endl;
   Swap(a, b);
   cout << "After Swap(): a=" << a << " and b=" << b;
   return (0);
}
```

produces the output:

```
Before Swap(): a=3 and b=5
After Swap(): a=5 and b=3
```

&

Note that x and y are preceded by an ampersand (&) in the Swap() header to indicate that they are reference parameters. When reference parameters are used, the values of the actual parameters are passed to the formal parameters, and then may be altered by the function and passed back to the actual parameters, as illustrated below:

Swap(a, b)

void Swap(int &x,int &y)

Reference parameters are used when a function needs to return more than one value. As demonstrated by the Swap() function, two values were passed in to a function (a and b) and two values were passed out (new a and b). As another example, a function BreakUp() converts a total number of seconds to hours, minutes, and seconds that are returned in three parameters:

```
void BreakUp(int TotalSeconds, int &Hours, int &Minutes, int &Seconds)
/*Returns the Hours, Minutes, and Seconds in TotalSeconds.
   TotalSeconds assumed >= 0                                       */
{
   Hours = TotalSeconds/3600;
   int Left = TotalSeconds%3600;
   Minutes = Left/60;
   Seconds = Left%60;
}
```

The first parameter, TotalSeconds, is a value parameter (no ampersand) that sends information in to the function. Hours, Minutes, and Seconds are preceded by an ampersand to indicate that they are reference parameters to be modified by the function. For example, the code

A Guide to Programming in C++

```
int h, m, s, TotalSecs = 5000;
BreakUp(TotalSecs, h, m, s);
cout << "Hours: " << h << endl;
cout << "Minutes: " << m << endl;
cout << "Seconds: " << s << endl;
```

displays:

```
Hours:   1
Minutes: 23
Seconds: 20
```

Unlike Swap(), the three reference parameters were not given initial values because the purpose of the BreakUp() is to pass out three values.

It is important that the actual parameter corresponding to a reference parameter be a variable. If a constant is used instead, the compiler generates a warning, and any changes made within the function cannot be reflected in the calling function because there is no variable in the call to be changed.

Review 11

Write a function DaysToHrsMins() that takes an int as its first parameter and returns the corresponding Hours and Mins as its second and third parameters. The function should not communicate directly with the user, but should only use the parameters to pass information in and out. Write a program that uses DaysToHrsMins() to display a table similar to:

```
1 day(s)  is 24 hours  or 1440 minutes
2 day(s)  is 48 hours  or 2880 minutes
. . .
10 days(s) is 240 hours or 14400 minutes
```

Review 12

Write a function FindLoHi() that takes two int values and returns the lesser of the two as its third parameter and the greater of the two as its fourth parameter. Use the function header:

    void FindLoHi(int x, int y, int &Lo, int &Hi)

Overload this function by writing another function that does the same task using double as the type for all its arguments. Write a program that illustrates the use of these functions.

Review 13

Write a function SetLoHi() that reorders the values of its two int parameters into low-high order. If x is less than y when the function is called, it should do nothing. Use the function header:

    void SetLoHi(int &x, int &y)

5.7 Methodology for Building Functions

The same method used to construct good programs should be applied to the construction of good functions. This method, as discussed in Chapter Three, is specification, design, coding, and debugging and testing.

specification

The first step in creating a function is determining what the function is to accomplish. This is called its specification.

design

A function is designed according to its specification. The design includes determining what information the function needs from the caller, and what information the function should return. The following table can be used as a guide:

If the function must return...	then...
no information	use a void function
one item of information	use a return statement
more than one item of information	use reference parameters

If reference parameters are to be used in a function, consider whether it is possible and logical for a parameter to provide both input and output from the function.

A function should be designed with the following in mind:

- A function should perform a single, well-defined task.

- The function's name and parameter names should be descriptive of the task being performed by the function so that it is understandable to someone reading only the function and not the rest of the program.

- A function should be short; a long function implies that the code should be further decomposed into other functions as described below.

Another part of designing a function is determining whether a function should be written as two or more different functions. For example, rather than a single function:

```
void BreakUp(int TotalSeconds, int &Hours, int &Minutes, int &Seconds)
/*Returns the Hours, Minutes, and Seconds in TotalSeconds.
   TotalSeconds assumed >= 0                                    */
```

It might be preferable to have three functions, each returning just one piece of information:

```
int SecondsFrom(int TotalSeconds)
/*Returns the number of seconds left when converting
   TotalSeconds to H/M/S form. TotalSeconds assumed >= 0 */

int MinutesFrom(int TotalSeconds)
/*Returns the number of minutes when converting
   TotalSeconds to H/M/S form. TotalSeconds assumed >= 0 */

int HoursFrom(int TotalSeconds)
/*Returns the number of hours when converting
   TotalSeconds to H/M/S form. TotalSeconds assumed >= 0 */
```

These functions offer the advantage of calculating only the desired quantity rather than all three quantities. The disadvantage is that there are more names to remember and some redundant calculations performed within the functions. There is no best choice—the programmer has to consider the options for the particular application being written.

coding

The third step in creating a function is coding. This includes carefully commenting a function as discussed in the next section. Code can also be made clearer by separating functions with a delimiter. For example:

```
//--------------------------------------------------------------------
```

debugging and testing

The last step in creating a function is debugging and testing. The best method for debugging is to write just enough code to test each function in isolation during the development process. A common error is to write an entire program containing many functions and only test when the program is completely coded. This makes it much harder to find the source of bugs, and greatly increases the chance that bugs will go undetected through the testing process.

5.8 Documenting Functions

A function's documentation should be based in part on the specification and include a description, followed by a precondition and a postcondition. For example:

```
void DrawBar(int Length)
/*Writes a bar across the screen using asterisks
   Pre: Length >= 0
   Post: Bar drawn of length Length, cursor moved to next line */
```

The initial requirements of a function are called the *preconditions*. Up to this point, we have been referring to these comments as "assumptions." If the preconditions are met when a function is called, a correctly written function will satisfy a *postcondition*. A function may not have a precondition, as in a function that can act on any data values. However, a function with no postcondition implies that it accomplishes nothing!

Good guidelines for writing preconditions and postconditions are:

- The precondition is a statement that must be true at the beginning of a function for the function to work properly.

- The postcondition is a statement that must be true at the end of the execution of a function if the function has worked properly.

- Preconditions and postconditions should not state facts that the compiler has already verified or refer to variables or other information outside the function.

- The postcondition should not tell how the function accomplished its task.

As another example, PowerOf() would be documented like:

```
double PowerOf(double x, int n)
/* Returns x to the nth power.
   Pre: n >= 0
   Post: x to the nth power returned */
```

Note that the precondition does not state that n is an integer since the compiler checks for this.

The goal in function documentation is to create a function header which fully describes the actions of the function. When reading a program segment that includes a function call, the programmer should only need to read the header of the function called to understand what is happening. As our programs become more and more complex, this will become increasingly important.

In addition, the use of preconditions and postconditions are an effective tool in debugging. Often it is possible to place code at the beginning of a function to verify that the precondition has been met. Code can also often be placed at the end of the function to verify that the postcondition has been met. If a function's precondition is not satisfied, the problem must be in the calling function. If the precondition is satisfied but the postcondition is not, then the problem must lie within the function.

Review 14

Write a function DisplayWithDecimals() that displays a double value with a given number of decimals. Use the header:

```
void DisplayWithDecimals(double Num, int NumDecimals)
/* Displays Num to NumDecimals places
   Post: Num displayed to NumDecimals places */
```

Review 15

Write a function FindDigits() that has a parameter for a three-digit number and three other parameters for returning the three individual digits of the three-digit number.

Review 16

Complete the functions SecondsFrom(), MinutesFrom(), and HoursFrom() by writing the code for the bodies of the functions. Write a program that uses each of these functions. (The main() can be similar to the code in Section 5.7.)

A Guide to Programming in C++

5.9 Building a Library

Professional programmers seldom write a program using only code written entirely from scratch. They start by analyzing the problem to be solved, and then identify previously written and debugged code that can be used to form part of the solution. The recent history of programming languages has shown an effort to make this process more reliable, powerful, and convenient. C++ has a large number of facilities for combining existing code with new. For example, the line

```
#include <iostream.h>
```

combines the code from the iostream library with the current program.

A library usually contains code to perform related tasks. For example, the iostream library contains code related to the input/output stream. In this section a "utility" library will be written that might be useful in a variety of programs. The utility library will contain the user-defined functions Pause() and GetInt() described below.

Pause()

A common need is to pause program execution until the user presses a key. This can be accomplished with the following two lines of code:

```
cout << "Press a key to continue" << endl;
getch();   // Wait for user to hit a key
```

The getch() function is defined in the conio library. Therefore, the conio library will need to be included in the utility library.

GetInt()

A program commonly prompts the user for an integer in a specific range. A function that returns an integer in the desired range from the user while providing appropriate error messages would have the following header:

```
int GetInt(int Lo, int Hi)
/*Obtains and returns an integer from the user in the range Lo..Hi.
   Pre: Lo < Hi
   Post: An integer between Lo and Hi inclusive returned              */
```

The body of this function uses a loop to check the user entry, and displays an error message if the entry is out of range. Once the user enters a correct value, the loop terminates and the value is returned:

```
int Entry;
cin >> Entry;
while ((Entry < Lo) || (Entry > Hi)) {
   cout << "Value must be between " << Lo << " and " << Hi << endl;
   cout << "Please re-enter: ";
   cin >> Entry;
}
return(Entry);
```

To create the utility library the desired functions are coded in a file by themselves, along with the necessary include statements:

```
/*Utility Library
    void Pause()
    int GetInt(int Lo, int Hi)                    */

#include <iostream.h>
#include <conio.h>

//---------------------------------------------------------------------------
void Pause()
/*Displays a message and waits for the user to hit a key
    Post: Key pressed                                      */
{
    cout << "Press a key to continue" << endl;
    getch();  // Pause for user to hit a key
}
//---------------------------------------------------------------------------
int GetInt(int Lo, int Hi)
/*Obtains and returns an integer from the user in the range Lo..Hi.
    Pre: Lo < Hi
    Post: An integer between Lo and Hi inclusive returned          */
{
    int Entry;
    cin >> Entry;
    while ((Entry < Lo) || (Entry > Hi)) {
        cout << "Value must be between " << Lo << " and " << Hi << endl;
        cout << "Please re-enter: ";
        cin >> Entry;
    }
    return(Entry);
}
```

This file may be saved with any name. However, by convention, it should be saved with a .h extension. Since this is a utility library, the file is saved as utility.h in the same folder with our other C++ program files. The utility library can be included in a program with the statement:

```
#include "utility.h"
```

Note that, rather than angle brackets, < and >, double-quotation marks are used. When a library is included with angle brackets, the compiler looks for the file in the include directory. When double-quotation marks are used, it looks in the current directory.

The following program illustrates the utility library:

```
/*English to Spanish Translator program */

#include <iostream.h>
#include "utility.h"

int main()
{
  cout << "Welcome to the translator program!" << endl;
  int Choice;
  do {
    cout << "Choose to see the Spanish translation" << endl;
    cout << " 0  End program" << endl;
    cout << " 1  Hello" << endl;
    cout << " 2  Good-bye" << endl;
    cout << " 3  Tomorrow" << endl;
    cout << "Enter your choice: ";
    Choice = GetInt(0, 3);

    if (Choice == 1)
      cout << "Buenos dias" << endl;
    else if (Choice == 2)
      cout << "Adios" << endl;
    else if (Choice == 3)
      cout << "Manana" << endl;
    else
      cout << "Gracias!" << endl;
    Pause();
  } while (Choice != 0);
  cout << "Thanks for using the translator!" << endl;
  return(0);
}
```

When run, the program output may look similar to:

```
Welcome to the translator program!
Choose to see the Spanish translation
  0 End program
  1 Hello
  2 Good-bye
  3 Tomorrow
Enter your choice: 3
Manana
Press a key to continue
Choose to see the Spanish translation
  0 End program
  1 Hello
  2 Good-bye
  3 Tomorrow
Enter your choice: 6
Value must be between 0 and 3
Please re-enter: 0
Gracias!
Press a key to continue
Thanks for using the translator!
```

The program uses Pause() and GetInt() almost as if they were built into C++. The utility library has, in a sense, extended the language. Note that the program includes the iostream library. The utility library also included iostream. Libraries are constructed so that duplication is detected and the library is linked in only once—there is no cost in terms of efficiency. This feature will be discussed later in the text.

Review 17

Add to the utility library a function Signature() that displays a declaration of authorship:

```
This program was written by Liam Carr.
```

Review 18

The random() function in random.h is sometimes inconvenient to use since it only generates values between 0 and one less than its integer argument. Add to the utility library a function RandomInRange() that takes integer parameters Lo and Hi and returns a random number in the range Lo..Hi. Write a program that illustrates its use.

5.10 Top-Down Design

There are many approaches to the construction of large computer programs. One common method is *top-down design*, also called *step-wise refinement*. In the top-down approach, the programmer first conceives of the major tasks to be accomplished (the "top") and writes the main() function with the major tasks as function calls. Each major task is refined into smaller subtasks. These subtasks may, in turn, be further refined. The entire process continues until the resulting subtasks are single, specific tasks that are easily translated into C++ code.

Top-down design has many advantages. It helps the programmer (and whoever else may need to read the program) to keep things organized. It allows difficult, lower-level coding to be done after the major ideas have been clearly specified. It makes it possible to get a program running quickly, and then to progressively add features. Finally, it allows the program to be broken up into specific tasks that can be worked on and tested separately from the whole, and possibly even by different programmers. Top-down design is demonstrated in the Case Study.

5.11 Prototype-Style Program Organization

Some programmers prefer a different layout for their C++ programs, one that may emphasize top-down design. In this layout, the sequence is as follows:

```
#include <libraries>
function prototypes
main() function
function definitions
```

A *function prototype* is a statement that consists of a function header terminated by a semicolon. For example, the Time Conversion program given at the beginning of the chapter could be written as:

```
/*Time Conversion program with prototypes */

#include <iostream.h>

//-----------------------------------------------------------------------
void DaysToHours();
/* Converts days to hours */
void HoursToDays();
/* Converts hours to days */

//-----------------------------------------------------------------------
int main()
{
   char Choice;
   cout << "1  Days to Hours" << endl;
   cout << "2  Hours to Days" << endl;
   cout << "Enter your choice: ";
   cin >> Choice;
   if (Choice == '1')
     DaysToHours();
   else
     HoursToDays();

   return(0);
}
//-----------------------------------------------------------------------
void DaysToHours()
/* Converts days to hours */
{
   int Days, Hours;

   cout << "Enter the number of days: ";
   cin >> Days;

   Hours = Days*24;
   cout << "The number of hours in " << Days << " days is: " << Hours;
}
//-----------------------------------------------------------------------
void HoursToDays()
/* Converts hours to days */
{
   int Hours, Days;

   cout << "Enter the number of hours: ";
   cin >> Hours;

   Days = Hours/24;
   cout << "The number of days in " << Hours << " hours is: " << Days;
}
```

This program will perform identically to the version at the beginning of this chapter. The advantage is that main() (the "top" in top-down design) is near the top of the program, making it easy to see what functions it calls. The disadvantage is that the prototypes make the program longer and must be updated each time a function changes, introducing the possibility of inconsistency.

In this Case Study a "game of 21" program will be created. Note that this game is the Advanced Exercise at the end of Chapter Four.

specification

The program asks the user how many cards are wanted. It then "deals" cards to the user which are random numbers from 1 to 10. The program then "deals" itself three cards. If both scores are over 21, or if both are equal but less than or equal to 21, the game is declared a draw. Otherwise, the winner is the one with the highest score equal to or less than 21. If one score is over 21, but the other is 21 or less, the player with 21 or less is declared the winner. The program allows the game to be played as often as desired. At the end of the games the program displays the total wins, losses, and draws. A sample run illustrates the game:

```
How many cards do you want? 3
You: 8 5 1 = 14
Computer: 8 3 3 = 14
A draw!
Would you like to play again? (Y/N)? Y

How many cards do you want? 2
You: 7 2 = 9
Computer: 8 7 4 = 19
Computer wins!
Would you like to play again? (Y/N)? Y

How many cards do you want? 3
You: 8 7 4 = 19
Computer: 2 1 7 = 10
You win!
Would you like to play again (Y/N)? N

Your wins = 1
Computer wins = 1
Draws = 1
```

design—level 1

The method for constructing this program will be top-down design. Through this approach, the main() function is written first. The major tasks to be accomplished are to play a game, maintain the wins, losses, and draws, determine if another game is to be played, and report the wins, losses, and draws. The pseudocode for main() is:

```
Initialize counters
do
    Play a game
    Update counters as needed
    Ask the user for another game
while (the user wants to play again)
Display the final results
```

To complete the design for main(), the pseudocode is used to determine the data design. Counters are needed for the wins, losses, and draws. A variable is needed to hold the result of a game. Another variable is needed to hold the result of prompting the user to play another game.

At the first level of a top-down design, there are no details for accomplishing the major tasks. These details are addressed in the next level of refinement.

coding—level 1

The top-down design approach to programming dictates that main() be translated into code before continuing on to the next level of refinement. This will help resolve any ambiguities in the logic, and clearly identify the tasks remaining to be accomplished. The main() code is based on its pseudocode and data design:

```
int main()
{
  int Wins = 0, Losses = 0, Draws = 0;
  char Answer;
  do {
    int Result;  // 0=draw  1=user win  2=computer win
    Result = PlayGame();
    UpdateCount(Result, Wins, Losses, Draws);
    Answer = AskRepeat();
  } while ((Answer != 'N') && (Answer != 'n'));
  Report(Wins, Losses, Draws);
  return(0);
}
```

The main() function cannot be compiled because the functions that handle the major tasks of playing the game, maintaining the counters, and reporting are not yet written. However, we can make a compilable level 1 version of the program by adding *stub functions* which are functions with carefully written headers and empty bodies:

```
/* Game of 21 program */

#include <iostream.h>

//----------------------------------------------------------------------------
int PlayGame()
/*Plays one game of 21 and returns an indication of the winner
   Post: One game has been played, and a code returned indicating
   the winner: 0=Draw  1=user Won  2=Computer Won            */
{
}
//----------------------------------------------------------------------------
void UpdateCount(int Result, int &Wins, int &Losses, int &Draws)
/*Increments one of the counters as determined by Result
   Pre: Result is either 0, 1, or 2
   Post: Either Wins, Losses, or Draws has been incremented based
   upon whether Result is 1, 2, or 0 respectively              */
{
}
//----------------------------------------------------------------------------
char AskRepeat()
/*Asks the user if another game is desired and returns response
   Post: User has been asked and has responded with Y, y, N, or n.
   The response is returned.                                   */
{
}
```

```
//-----------------------------------------------------------------
void Report(int Wins, int Losses, int Draws)
/* Reports the current results
    Pre: Wins, Losses, Draws represent the current results
    Post: The current results have been displayed            */
{
}
//-----------------------------------------------------------------
int main()
{
  int Wins = 0, Losses = 0, Draws = 0;
  char Answer;
  do {
    int Result;  // 0=draw  1=user win  2=computer win
    Result = PlayGame();
    UpdateCount(Result, Wins, Losses, Draws);
    Answer = AskRepeat();
  } while ((Answer != 'N') && (Answer != 'n'));
  Report(Wins, Losses, Draws);
  return(0);
}
```

This code will compile without error to produce a level 1 version of the program that can be refined. However, the stub functions generate a warnings indicating that parameters and variables are not used and values are not returned.

At this point, the Case Study may be illustrated as:

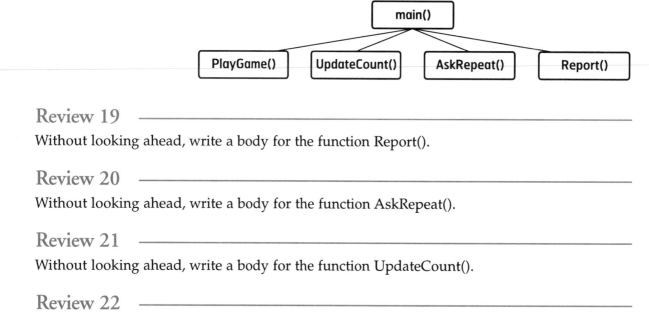

Review 19 ———————————————————————————————

Without looking ahead, write a body for the function Report().

Review 20 ———————————————————————————————

Without looking ahead, write a body for the function AskRepeat().

Review 21 ———————————————————————————————

Without looking ahead, write a body for the function UpdateCount().

Review 22 ———————————————————————————————

Write a function Introduction() that gives the rules, etc. for the game of 21.

design—level 2

In the next level of design, the functions called by main() are refined. The UpdateCount(), AskRepeat(), and Report() functions are straightforward in their design. The PlayGame() function is more complex. Using the top-down design approach, PlayGame() and the functions it calls will be designed and coded at this level.

PlayGame()
design—level 1

The pseudocode for PlayGame() is:

> Play user hand
> Play computer hand
> Determine winner
> Report result of the game

The data design for PlayGame() is a variable to hold the score of the human hand, a variable to hold the score of the computer hand, and a variable to hold the winner.

PlayGame()
coding—level 1

The PlayGame() code is based on its pseudocode and data design:

```
int PlayGame()
/*Plays one game of 21 and returns an indication of the winner
   Post: One game has been played, and a code returned indicating
   the winner: 0=Draw  1=user Won  2=Computer Won              */
{
   int UserSum = DealUser();
   int ComputerSum = DealComputer();
   int Winner = FindWinner(UserSum, ComputerSum);
   ReportResult(Winner);
   return(Winner);
}
```

PlayGame()
design—level 2

In the next level of the PlayGame() design, the functions called by PlayGame() are refined.

The DealUser() pseudocode is:

> Ask the user the number of cards
> For (CardCount=0, CardCount<NumCards, CardCount++)
>   Get a card
>   Add the card to the score
> Return the score

The DealComputer() pseudocode is:

> For (CardCount=0, CardCount<3, CardCount++)
>   Get a card
>   Add the card to the score
> Return the score

The FindWinner() pseudocode is:

> An else-if ladder comparing UserSum and Computer Sum
> Return a 0 for a draw, a 1 for a User win, and a 2 for a
>   computer win

PlayGame()
coding—level 2

The DealUser(), DealComputer(), and FindWinner() functions will be coded in the next level of coding for the program.

The complete design can be represented as:

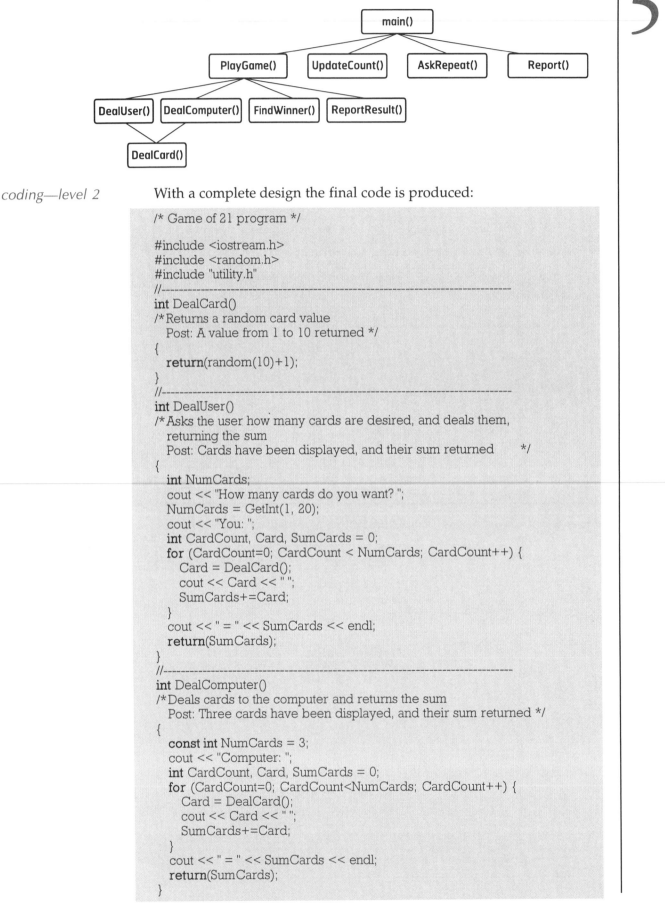

coding—level 2

With a complete design the final code is produced:

```
/* Game of 21 program */

#include <iostream.h>
#include <random.h>
#include "utility.h"
//------------------------------------------------------------------------
int DealCard()
/*Returns a random card value
   Post: A value from 1 to 10 returned */
{
   return(random(10)+1);
}
//------------------------------------------------------------------------
int DealUser()
/*Asks the user how many cards are desired, and deals them,
   returning the sum
   Post: Cards have been displayed, and their sum returned      */
{
   int NumCards;
   cout << "How many cards do you want? ";
   NumCards = GetInt(1, 20);
   cout << "You: ";
   int CardCount, Card, SumCards = 0;
   for (CardCount=0; CardCount < NumCards; CardCount++) {
      Card = DealCard();
      cout << Card << " ";
      SumCards+=Card;
   }
   cout << " = " << SumCards << endl;
   return(SumCards);
}
//------------------------------------------------------------------------
int DealComputer()
/*Deals cards to the computer and returns the sum
   Post: Three cards have been displayed, and their sum returned */
{
   const int NumCards = 3;
   cout << "Computer: ";
   int CardCount, Card, SumCards = 0;
   for (CardCount=0; CardCount<NumCards; CardCount++) {
      Card = DealCard();
      cout << Card << " ";
      SumCards+=Card;
   }
   cout << " = " << SumCards << endl;
   return(SumCards);
}
```

A Guide to Programming in C++

```
//----------------------------------------------------------------------
int FindWinner(int UserSum, int ComputerSum)
/*Determines winner and returns code indicating winner.
  Post: Winner determined according to rules in the specification and
  code returned indicating the winner: 0=Draw  1=User Won
  2=Computer Won                                                      */
{
  const int Limit = 21;
  if ((UserSum==ComputerSum) || ((UserSum>Limit)
     && (ComputerSum>Limit)))
    return(0);
  else if ((ComputerSum>Limit) || ((UserSum>ComputerSum)
     && (UserSum<=Limit)))
    return(1);
  else
    return(2);
}
//----------------------------------------------------------------------
void ReportResult(int Result)
/*Reports the result of the game
  Pre: Result is either 0, 1, or 2
  Post: Result has been displayed. */
{
  if (Result == 0)
    cout << "A draw! \n";
  else if (Result == 1)
    cout << "You win! \n";
  else
    cout << "Computer wins! \n";
}
//----------------------------------------------------------------------
int PlayGame()
/*Plays one game of 21 and returns an indication of the winner
  Post: One game has been played, and a code returned indicating
  the winner: 0=Draw  1=User Won  2=Computer Won                     */
{
  int UserSum = DealUser();
  int ComputerSum = DealComputer();
  int Winner = FindWinner(UserSum, ComputerSum);
  ReportResult(Winner);
  return(Winner);
}
//----------------------------------------------------------------------
void UpdateCount(int Result, int &Wins, int &Losses, int &Draws)
/*Increments one of the counters as determined by Result
  Pre: Result is either 0, 1, or 2
  Post: Either Wins, Losses, or Draws has been incremented based
  upon whether Result is 1, 2, or 0 respectively                     */
{
  if (Result==0)
    Draws++;
  else if (Result==1)
    Wins++;
  else
    Losses++;
}
```

```
//------------------------------------------------------------------
char AskRepeat()
/* Asks the user if another game is desired and returns response
   Pre: none
   Post: User has been asked and has responded with Y, y, N, or n.
   The response is returned.                                      */
{
  char Answer;
  cout << "Would you like to play again? (Y/N)? ";
  cin >> Answer;
  while ((Answer != 'Y') && (Answer != 'y') && (Answer != 'N')
    && (Answer != 'n')) {
    cout << "Answer Y or N please: ";
    cin >> Answer;
  }
  return(Answer);
}
//------------------------------------------------------------------
void Report(int Wins, int Losses, int Draws)
/* Reports the current results
   Pre: Wins, Losses, Draws represent the current results
   Post: The current results have been displayed           */
{
  cout << "Your wins = " << Wins << endl;
  cout << "Computer wins = " << Losses << endl;
  cout << "Draws = " << Draws << endl;
}
//------------------------------------------------------------------
int main()
{
  randomize();
  int Wins = 0, Losses = 0, Draws = 0;
  char Answer;
  do {
    int Result;  // 0=draw  1=user win  2=computer win
    Result = PlayGame();
    UpdateCount(Result, Wins, Losses, Draws);
    Answer = AskRepeat();
  } while ((Answer != 'N') && (Answer != 'n'));
  Report(Wins, Losses, Draws);
  return(0);
}
```

Note that the utility library was included so that GetInt() could be used to obtain the number of cards desired by the user.

debugging and testing

In developing such a large program, it is necessary to test subparts of the program in isolation. For example, to test the logic used in writing FindWinner(), main() was replaced with the following code:

```
while (true) {
  cout << "Enter User total: " << endl;
  cin >> UserSum;
  cout << "Enter Computer total: " << endl;
  cin >> ComputerSum;
  cout << "Result: " << FindWinner(UserSum, ComputerSum) << endl;
}
```

This allowed any combination of sums to be entered to make sure that the program consistently gave the correct results. The test data included:

User	Computer	Expected Result
21	21	0
15	15	0
23	25	0
23	23	0
15	10	1
21	18	1
10	24	1
10	15	2
18	21	2
24	10	2

It is best to try to include in the test data each possible way the program could execute, and also include edge cases. An *edge case* occurs when the data is right on the edge between two behaviors. In this case, the value 21 lies on the edge between a successful score and a score that is too high to win. In order to verify that <= was used when < is needed, the edge cases must be tested carefully.

It can be difficult to read through a lengthy program such as this one. The best way to learn about a large program is to attempt to revise it, as in the Reviews below. When doing them, take careful note of what portions of the code need to be changed, and what portions do not. Note how the program organization makes it easier to make modifications.

Review 23

The cards "dealt" are unrealistic in that it is just as likely to draw a 1 as a 10 where in actuality 10s, Jacks, Queens, and Kings all count as ten-point cards. Modify the Case Study so that cards are drawn from 1 to 13, with cards 1 to 10 counting as their value, and cards 11 through 13 counting as ten points.

Review 24

Modify the Case Study so that the user is initially dealt two cards, and then is asked one-by-one for any additional cards. For example:

```
You:  3 7
Another?  Y
6
Another?  N
Total: 16
```

Review 25

Modify the Case Study so that the computer, rather than always taking three cards, takes cards one-by-one until the total reaches 16 or higher.

A function performs a single, well-defined task. User-defined functions can be written to extend the C++ language. A function is executed by calling it from main() or another function. The function call includes the function name and parentheses with any required parameters. A function can return a single value through the return statement.

A function definition is the actual code of the function, and includes a header. The header begins with a keyword indicating what type of value the function returns. void indicates a function returns nothing. The header also contains a descriptive function name and any parameters required by the function.

A function's parameters, also called arguments, can be value parameters, default parameters, or reference parameters. Value parameters can only pass values into a function. The variables representing value parameters are not changed by a function. Default parameters use a value assigned to a parameter in the function header when that parameter is not specified in a function call. Reference parameters pass values into and out of a function. Reference parameters are indicated with a preceding & in the function header. The variables representing reference parameters can be changed by a function.

Function overloading is defining more than one function by the same name. Function overloading is allowed because the compiler evaluates the types, order, and number of parameters in a function call as well as the function name.

The same method used to construct good programs should be used to construct functions. This method is specification, design, coding, and debugging and testing.

The initial requirements of a function are called the preconditions. A correctly written function will satisfy a postcondition. A function's documentation should include a header with the precondition and postcondition as well as a description of the function's purpose.

A library can be created by writing functions and saving them in a file traditionally named with a .h extension. This file can then be included in any program. User-defined libraries are enclosed with quotation marks in an include statement.

One common method used in the construction of a large program is top-down design, also called step-wise refinement. In the top-down approach main() is constructed first and then the major tasks are refined. Refinement of tasks is done in levels with each level being coded and tested before continuing to the next level.

One method of coding that emphasizes top-down design is using function prototypes. A function prototype is a statement that consists of the function header terminated by a semicolon. Function prototypes are included at the beginning of a program and allow main() to be defined before the bodies of the other functions.

5 | Vocabulary

Actual Argument See Actual Parameter.

Actual Parameter The variable or value being passed to a function through a function call.

Argument See parameter.

Call Including a function name and its parameters to execute the function. For example, DrawBar(2).

Call-By-Reference Parameter See Reference Parameter.

Call-By-Value Parameter See Value Parameter.

Default Parameter A formal parameter with a default value that is used if the actual parameter is not specified in a function call.

Edge Case A case in which program data is on the edge between two behaviors.

Formal Argument See Formal Parameter.

Formal Parameter The parameter type and name in the function header.

Function C++ code written in a specific format to perform a single, well-defined task.

Function Definition The actual code of the function.

Function Overloading Defining more than one function by the same name.

Function Prototype A statement at the top of a program consisting of the function header terminated by a semicolon.

Parameter Values included in a function call that are passed to the function.

Precondition A statement that must be true at the beginning of a function for the function to work properly.

Postcondition A statement that must be true at the end of the execution of a function if the function has worked properly.

Reference Parameter A parameter that can receive as well as pass a value to a function.

Top-Down Design A method for constructing a large program where the main() is written first and then the subtasks refined.

Step-Wise Refinement See Top-Down Design.

Stub Function A function header with no body that is used to create a compilable level 1 of a program.

User-Defined Function A function written by the user.

Value Parameter A parameter that passes only its value to a function.

void   Used at the beginning of a function definition to indicate that a function returns nothing.

return   Statement used to return a value from a function to the calling function.

&   Used to indicate a reference parameter.

5 Exercises

Exercise 1

Write a program that calls functions Roof(), Base(), and Walk() to display:

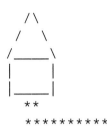

Exercise 2

a) Write a function Triangle() that takes a parameter and displays a right triangle with that many lines. Use the DrawBar() function as a basis. For example, the function call Triangle(4) displays:

```
*
* *
* * *
* * * *
```

b) Write a program using Triangle() to draw triangles of sizes 1, 3, 5, and 7, each separated by a blank line.

Exercise 3

Write a function IsoTriangle() that takes a size parameter and displays an isosceles triangle with that many lines. Use the DrawBar() function as a basis. (Hint: Use another function Spaces() to display the leading spaces before the start of the asterisks on each line.) For example, the function call IsoTriangle(4) displays:

```
   *
  * * *
 * * * * *
* * * * * * *
```

Exercise 4

Write a function DisplayWithCommas() that displays any long up to 10 digits using commas. For example, 1234567 should be displayed as 1,234,567. Be sure your function correctly handles negative numbers as well.

Exercise 5

a) Write a function DisplayFormatted() with the following header:

```
void DisplayFormatted (int n, int Width)
/*Displays the value of n left-aligned in a field of size Width.
    Post: Value displayed left-aligned in a field of size Width    */
```

Write a program illustrating its use.

b) Overload the DisplayFormatted() function to work for double values. In this case, include a width parameter and also a decimals parameter giving the number of decimals to display.

c) Write a program illustrating both DisplayFormatted() functions.

d) Add these functions to the utility library.

Exercise 6

A prime number is an integer that has no factors other than one and itself. For example, 2, 3, 5, and 7 are prime while 9, 10, and 15 are not.

a) Write a function IsPrime() that accepts a long greater than 1 as a parameter and returns a bool. The function should return true if and only if the integer is prime. (Hint: An integer can be tested for primeness by repeatedly dividing it by integers smaller than itself but larger than 1, and checking whether the remainder is zero. Use the modulus operator, %.)

b) Write a program that uses IsPrime() to display all the prime numbers between 2 and 100.

Exercise 7

Write a function GetChar(), modeled on GetInt(), that obtains a character from the user that falls within the two character arguments given. Use the header:

```
char GetChar(char Lo, char Hi)
```

For example, the following code will return A, B, C, D, E, or F and assign it to Grade:

```
Grade = GetChar('A', 'F');
```

5

Exercise 8

a) Write a function BreakUp() that takes an integer in the range 0–999 as a parameter and returns each of the digits in three integer reference parameters.

b) Write a function Build() that takes three integer parameters and returns a value which consists of the number represented by the three digits.

c) Write a program illustrating BreakUp() and Build() using the specification: Every number from 0 to 999 is first broken up and then rebuilt and the result compared to the original value. An error message should be displayed if the original and rebuilt numbers do not match.

Exercise 9

Programs such as racing programs must manipulate times in minutes and seconds.

a) Write two utility functions, ReadTime() and DisplayTime(), that handle reading and writing of times. Test the functions with the code:

```
{
    int Min, Sec;
    cout << "Enter a time: ";
    ReadTime(Min, Sec);
    cout << "Your time was: ";
    DisplayTime(Min, Sec);
}
```

The program output may look similar to:

```
Enter a time:
   Enter minutes: 65
   Enter seconds: 32
Your time was 1:05:32
```

Note that the time was displayed in hours, minutes and seconds and that a zero was inserted when needed to display the proper number of minutes.

b) Write a function AddTime() that takes two times in four parameters and returns their sum as a third pair of reference parameters. Test the function using the code:

```
{
    int Min1, Sec1, Min2, Sec2, MinTot, SecTot;
    cout << "Enter first time: ";
    ReadTime(Min1, Sec1);
    cout << "Enter second time: ";
    ReadTime(Min2, Sec2);
    cout << "Your total time was: ";
    AddTime(Min1, Sec1, Min2, Sec2, MinTot, SecTot);
    DisplayTime(MinTot, SecTot);
}
```

When run, the program output may look similar to:

```
Enter a time:
   Enter minutes:  12
   Enter seconds:  32
Enter another time:
   Enter minutes: 21
   Enter seconds: 43
Your total time was:  0:34:15
```

Exercise 10

It is useful to have a program to manipulate fractions.

a) Write a function Reduce() that takes the integer numerator and denominator of a fraction and reduces the fraction, changing the numerator and denominator as necessary. A fraction may be reduced by finding the largest common factor and dividing both the numerator and denominator by this factor. The function can be tested using the code:

```cpp
{
   int Num, Denom;
   cout << "Enter the numerator: ";
   cin >> Num;
   cout << "Enter the denominator: ";
   cin >> Denom;
   Reduce(Num, Denom);
   cout << "The reduced fraction is "<< Num << "/" << Denom << endl;
}
```

When run, the program output may look similar to:

```
Enter the numerator: 12
Enter the denominator: 16
The reduced fraction is 3/4
```

b) Write a program that adds two fractions, reporting the result in reduced form. Use functions ReadFraction(), DisplayFraction(), and AddFraction(). ReadFraction() and AddFraction() should return their fractions in reduced form using Reduce().

Exercise 11

Using a top-down design approach, write a program that displays one month of a calendar using the specification: The user enters the number of days in the month and the day of the week on which the month starts (1=Monday, etc.). The output for a 30 day month that starts on a Wednesday should be:

A Guide to Programming in C++

```
        Sun      Mon      Tue      Wed      Thu      Fri      Sat
* * * * * * * ∗ * * * * * * * * * * * * * * * * * * * * * * * * * * * * * * * * * * * * * * * * * * * * *
   *        *        *        *        1*       2*       3*       4*
   *        *        *        *        *        *        *        *
   *        *        *        *        *        *        *        *
* * * * * * * * * * * * * * * * * * * * * * * * * * * * * * * * * * * * * * * * * * * * * * * * * *
   *        5*       6*       7*       8*       9*      10*      11*
   *        *        *        *        *        *        *        *
   *        *        *        *        *        *        *        *
* * * * * * * * * * * * * * * * * * * * * * * * * * * * * * * * * * * * * * * * * * * * * * * * * *
   *       12*      13*      14*      15*      16*      17*      18*
   *        *        *        *        *        *        *        *
   *        *        *        *        *        *        *        *
* * * * * * * * * * * * * * * * * * * * * * * * * * * * * * * * * * * * * * * * * * * * * * * * * *
   *       19*      20*      21*      22*      23*      24*      25*
   *        *        *        *        *        *        *        *
   *        *        *        *        *        *        *        *
* * * * * * * * * * * * * * * * * * * * * * * * * * * * * * * * * * * * * * * * * * * * * * * * * *
   *       26*      27*      28*      29*      30*      *        *
   *        *        *        *        *        *        *        *
   *        *        *        *        *        *        *        *
* * * * * * * * * * * * * * * * * * * * * * * * * * * * * * * * * * * * * * * * * * * * * * * * * *
```

a) Write a compilable level 1 version of the program. Be sure to document and write headers for the level 2 functions.

b) Complete the program and debug and test it.

Note: You should judge your program by how little redundant code it contains and how easy it is to modify column widths and heights.

Exercise 12

The game of Nim is played as follows: The game starts with a random number of stones between 15 and 30. Two players alternate turns and on each turn may take either 1, 2, or 3 stones from the pile. The player forced to take the last stone loses.

a) Write a program that allows the user to play Nim against the computer. The specification: The computer generates the random number of stones, and the user is allowed to go first. On each user turn, the program displays the current number of stones and asks for the number to be removed. On each computer turn, the program displays the number of stones and the number taken (a random number from 1 to 3.) When the last stone is drawn, the program displays the winner. Code should be included to prevent the user or the computer from trying to take an illegal amount of stones. In particular, neither should be allowed to take three stones when there are only 1 or 2 left. The program output should be similar to that shown on the next page:

```
There are 16 stones. How many would you like? 3
There are 13 stones. The computer takes 3.
There are 10 stones. How many would you like? 4
Value must be between 1 and 3
How many would you like? 3
There are 7 stones. The computer takes 2.
There are 5 stones. How many would you like? 3
There are 2 stones. The computer takes 1.
There is 1 stone. How many would you like? 3
Value must be between 1 and 1
How many would you like? 1
The computer wins!
```

b) Write a compilable level 1 version of the program. Be sure to comment and write headers for the level 2 functions.

c) Complete the program and debug and test it.

d) *Advanced*: Try to make the computer play "smart" rather than random. See if you can come up with a strategy that will allow the computer to win as often as the user.

Exercise 13

The game of Mastermind is played as follows: One player (the code maker) chooses a secret arrangement of colored pegs and the other player (the code breaker) tries to guess it. The code breaker puts forth an arrangement of colored pegs, and the code maker reports two numbers:

1. The number of pegs that are the correct color and in the correct position

2. The number of pegs that are the correct color regardless of whether they are in the correct position.

a) Write a program that plays the part of the code maker in this game. The code will consist of an arrangement of 3 "pegs" each with a "color" from 1 to 5. The program output may look similar to:

```
Guess 1:
    First peg: 3
    Second peg: 4
    Third peg: 2
You have 1 correct peg(s) and 2 correct color(s)
Guess 2:
    First peg: 3
    Second peg: 4
    Third peg: 5
You have 1 correct peg(s) and 3 correct color(s)
Guess 3:
    First peg: 3
    Second peg: 5
    Third peg: 4
You have 3 correct peg(s) and 3 correct color(s)
You have broken the code in 3 guesses.
```

A Guide to Programming in C++

Note: For simplicity, do not allow either the guess or the code to contain duplicates. You should write a function that checks for duplicate pegs and use it to prevent duplicates.

b) Write a compilable level 1 version of the program. Be sure to comment and write headers for the level 2 functions.

c) Write the next level functions, and so on until the program is complete.

d) Debug and test the program.

Exercise 14 ⟳

a) Write a program that uses functions to solve the random walk problem from Chapter Four Exercise 30. Include a function that displays the bridge and the person.

b) Modify the Random Walk program to display a table of bridge length vs. average time taken to step off of it. Use 50 trials for each bridge length, and try odd lengths from 5 to 21 meters long. The program output may look similar to:

Length	Average Time
5	5.6
7	7.2
9	8.0
. . .	. . .
21	37.5

In generating this table, do not display the picture of the bridge.

c) *Advanced*: See if you can determine what the relationship is between the length of the bridge and the time taken to fall off it.

Exercise 15

Write a program that plays a dice game with the user. The specification: The user begins with a score of 1000. The user is asked how many points to risk and then the computer rolls two dice. If an even total is rolled, the user loses the points at stake. If an odd total is rolled, the user receives double the points at stake. The program output may look similar to:

```
You have 1000 points.
Points to risk: 100
Roll is 3 and 5
You lose.
Play again? Y

You have 900
Points to risk: 200
Roll is 1 and 2
You win.
Play again? N

Final score: 1300
```

Exercise 16

Write a program which plays the game of Hi-Lo with the user. The specification: The user begins with a score of 1000. The user is asked the number of points to risk and to choose High or Low. The computer then chooses a random number between 1 and 13. If the number is between 1 and 6 inclusive, it is considered "Low." If it is between 8 and 13 inclusive, it is considered "High." The number 7 is considered neither High nor Low, and the user loses the points at risk. If the user guesses correctly, the user receives double the points. If the user guesses incorrectly, the user loses the points at risk. The program output may look similar to:

```
You have 1000 points.
How many points to risk: 100
Predict (1=High, 0=Low): 1
Number is 3
You lose.
Play again? Y

You have 900 points.
How many points to risk: 200
Predict (1=High, 0=Low): 1
Number is 11
You win.
Play again? N

Final amount: 1300
```

Exercise 17 ☙

Chapter Four Exercise 31 described a simple form of animation. This sort of work can be simplified by using a function that draws the figure at a specific location. Modify the program using a function with the following header:

```
void SmileyFace(int x, int y, bool Black)
/*Draws a simple smiley face with upper-left corner at position x, y on the screen.
  If Black is true, the face is drawn with black characters. If Black is false, the face is
  drawn with blanks, effectively erasing the face.
  Pre: x and y are valid screen coordinates
  Post: Face is drawn with either black characters or blanks                      */
```

Exercise 18

Write a program that runs a random horse race. The specification: There are three horses. During each round, a random number from 1 to 100 is generated for each horse. The horse advances one square if the random number is greater than 50. Show the track this way:

```
1|--------H------|
2|-------H-------|
3|---------H-----|
```

Write a function ShowHorse() that takes a horse number (1 to 3) and a position on the track, and shows the current position of the horse. Have the program run until one of the horses reaches the finish line.

Advanced
Exercise 19

Computers have been widely used to test students on their ability to solve arithmetic problems. Write a program that will test a student on addition, subtraction, or multiplication using random integers between 1 and 100. The student begins by choosing the type of problem and is then asked 10 problems with 3 chances to answer each correctly. If after 3 chances the answer is still incorrect, the correct answer is displayed. A score is calculated by awarding 10 points for a correct answer on the first try, 5 points on the second try, 2 points on the third try, and 0 points if all three attempts are wrong. The program output may look similar to:

```
Enter the number for the problem type desired.
   1. Addition
   2. Subtraction
   3. Multiplication

Enter choice: 1

25 + 73 = 79
WRONG Try again.
25 + 73 = 98
CORRECT

12 + 94 = 106
CORRECT

15 + 6 = 19
WRONG Try again.
15 + 6 = 18
WRONG Try again.
15 + 6 = 20
You have missed 3 times. The answer is 21.

36 + 49 = 85
CORRECT

    . . .
17 + 65 = 82
CORRECT

Your score = 70
```

5

A Guide to Programming in C++

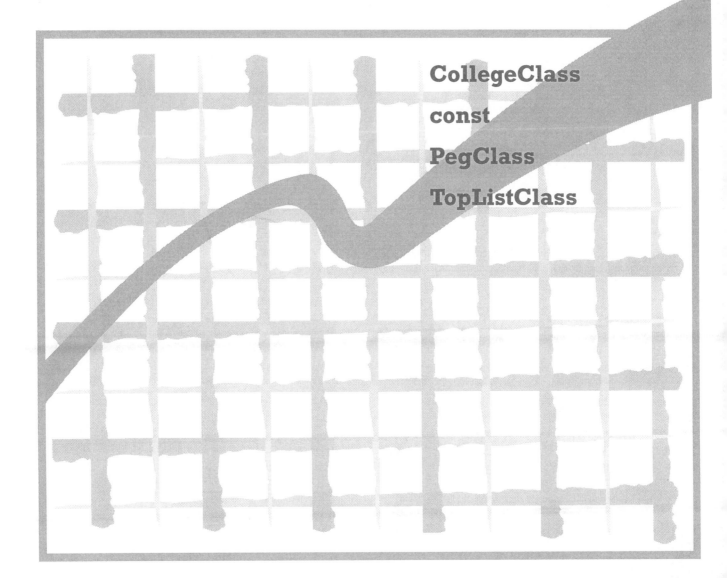

CollegeClass

const

PegClass

TopListClass

Objectives

After completing this chapter you will be able to:

1. Understand classes and objects including the concepts instantiation and member function.

2. Use classes in programs.

3. Use String class member functions.

4. Use the ios class.

5. Understand constructors.

6. Pass an object as a parameter.

7. Use the PegClass class.

8. Write a program to solve the towers of Hanoi puzzle.

9. Use the TopListClass class.

6

Akey skill in object-oriented programming is learning how to use classes that have been written by someone else. In this chapter you will learn how to use classes and objects in the construction of programs. The String class, two utility classes, and the cout and cin objects will be used. In Chapter Ten you will learn how to create classes.

6.1 Classes and Objects

The types int, long, and double are examples of simple, or built-in types. For example, the statement

double Radius;

defines a variable of type double with the identifier Radius.

Just as user-defined functions extend the C++ language so do user-defined types. A user-defined type is called a *class*. A class is used to create an *object*. Objects are declared with the name of the class followed by an identifier. For example, the statement

CircleClass B;

instantiation

declares an object of class CircleClass with the identifier B. Declaring an object is often called *instantiation*. In this case, B is an *instance* of CircleClass. Several instances of CircleClass can be created at once:

CircleClass LeftCircle, MiddleCircle, RightCircle;

A variable has just one value associated with it. However, an object has all the properties of its class associated with it. Properties of a class include member functions.

member function

A *member function* is a function belonging to a class. It is also sometimes called a *method* of the class. A member function is called by giving the object's identifier, a period, and then the function name and any needed arguments. For example, CircleClass has member functions SetRadius() and Area() that can be used in statements similar to

```
double Radius;
cout << "Enter radius:";
cin >> Radius;
B.SetRadius(Radius);
cout << "Area is " << B.Area() << endl;
```

which display:

```
Enter radius: 10
Area is 314.159
```

As discussed in Chapter Three, there are many libraries written by professional programmers. These libraries often contain classes. The properties of the classes are usually described in printed documentation that comes with the library files. Compiler software comes with a book that describes their libraries and classes. Professional programmers are also very careful to document their code so that a user can open the .h library file and understand its features by reading the comments. In Chapter Ten you will learn how to write classes and properly document them.

A class stored in a library can be used in a program once its library name appears in an #include statement at the beginning of the program. Three classes have been included with this text for demonstration purposes: PegClass in the pegclass library, TopListClass in the toplist library, and CollegeClass in the college library. Their documentation is included in this chapter. The string class from the string library and the ios class from the iostream library are also discussed in this Chapter.

programming style

Classes can be given a descriptive name that ends with the word Class as good programming style. This naming procedure makes it easy to know when an identifier is associated with a class.

CircleClass, like PegClass and TopListClass, was written for demonstration purposes. CircleClass has member functions SetRadius(), Area(), and Circumference(). The following program demonstrates classes:

```
/* Classes Demonstration Program */

#include <iostream.h>
#include <lvp\circle.h>

int main()
{
  cout << "-Calculate the area of a circle-" << endl;
  cout << endl;

  CircleClass B;
  double Radius;
  cout << "Enter radius: ";
  cin >> Radius;
  B.SetRadius(Radius);
  cout << "Area = " << B.Area() << endl;
  cout << "Circumference = " << B.Circumference() << endl;

  return(0);
}
```

When run, the program displays:

```
-Calculate the area of a circle-

Enter radius: 10
Area = 314.159
Circumference = 62.8318
```

6

6.3 The String Class

It may surprise you to know that you have already made extensive use of classes and objects without being aware of it. The string library implements the string type with a class. For example, the statement

```
String FirstName, LastName;
```

creates two instances of the String class. The author of the string class has written the class so that its objects can be displayed on the screen, assigned values that are read from the user, used in assignment statements, and passed as arguments to functions.

length()

The string class has a member function length() that returns the length of the string stored by a string object. For example, the statements

```
String FirstName = "Samuel";
cout << FirstName.length() << endl;
```

display 6 since there are six characters stored by FirstName.

substr()

Another string member function is substr() that returns part of the string stored by a string object. The part returned is specified with one argument that gives the starting position and another argument that gives the number of characters to return. Positions in a string object are counted from the left, starting with zero:

```
Characters:   S    a    m    u    e    l
Position:     0    1    2    3    4    5
```

The following code demonstrates substr():

```
String FirstName, Nickname, Leftovers;
FirstName = "Samuel";
Nickname = FirstName.substr(0, 3);
Leftovers = FirstName.substr(3, 3);
cout << Nickname << " + " << Leftovers << " = " << FirstName << endl;
```

When run, the code displays:

```
Sam + uel = Samuel
```

FirstName.substr(0, 3) returns the substring of FirstName consisting of characters in positions 0, 1, and 2. FirstName.substr(3, 3) returns the substring of FirstName consisting of characters in positions 3, 4, and 5. The precondition of substr() is that a substring be a valid part of the string object.

find()

A third string member function is find() that takes a string argument and returns the position of the first occurrence of this string in an object. For example, the statements

```
String FirstName = "Samuel";
cout << FirstName.find("mu") << endl;
```

display

2

indicating that the string "mu" was found starting in position 2 of FirstName. If the string is not found, then find() returns a special constant value, npos. For example, the statements

```
String FirstName = "Samuel";
if (FirstName.find("pi")==npos)
    cout << "Not found." << endl;
```

display

```
Not found.
```

The find() function is overloaded so that it can also be called with a character argument. For example, the statements

```
String FirstName = "Samuel";
cout << FirstName.find('e') << endl;
```

display 4 because the letter e is in position 4 of FirstName.

c_str()

atoi() atof()

A member function c_str() returns a C-style (not C++) string. This function is sometimes needed when using strings with functions from other libraries. For example, a useful function in the stdlib library is atoi(). This function converts a string to an int. Similarly, the atof() function in stdlib converts a string to a double. Both of these functions require a C-string parameter. atoi() is used in the code below:

```
String s;
cout << "Enter an integer: ";
cin >> s;
cout << s << " doubled is " << (2*atoi(s.c_str()));
```

which displays

```
Enter an integer: 23
23 doubled is 46
```

operator member function

+

A class can include *operator member functions* that redefine, or overload, the built-in C++ operators. The String class contains many of these functions. For example, the addition operator (+) is overloaded to return a string consisting of concatenated String objects, as in the statements

```
String Part1 = "wood", Part2 = "chuck", Whole;
Whole = Part1 + Part2;
cout << Whole << endl;
```

which display:

```
woodchuck
```

+=

Similarly, the special assignment operator, +=, concatenates one string onto the end of another. For example, the statements

```
String FirstName = "Samuel", LastName = "Clemens", Whole = "";
Whole+=FirstName;
Whole+=" ";
Whole+=LastName;
cout << Whole << endl;
```

display:

```
Samuel Clemens
```

6

Review 1 ───────────────────────────────

Write a function WriteFirstLast() that takes a String argument containing a name in last-comma-first format (e.g., "Twain, Mark") and displays it in first-last format (e.g., "Mark Twain"). Use the find() function to identify the position of the comma, and the substr() function to display the parts. Assume there is a space after the comma.

Review 2 ───────────────────────────────

Write a function ConvertToFirstLast() that *returns* (not *displays*) a first-last formatted string corresponding to a last-comma-first string sent as an argument. See Review 1 for the definition of first-last and last-comma-first formats.

6.4 The ios Class

the cin and cout objects

The iostream library provides a class called ios that is the basis for C++ input and output operations. In addition, iostream.h predeclares several objects, including cout and cin, making these objects available without being explicitly declared.

You have already used many of the ios member functions, including width(), precision(), setf(), and ignore(). In addition, iostream.h defines the send to operator << for output and the get from operator >> for input, as in the statement

```
cout << "Hello, world!";
```

which will output the string "Hello, world!" to the console (the cout object.)

constant data members

There are also *constant data members* defined in the ios class. To use these constants, they must begin with a prefix ios:: to indicate the source of the constant. For example, ios::fixed is a constant used as an argument to the setf() member function. Others include ios::left and ios::right.

6.5 Constructors

A class automatically executes a *constructor member function* whenever an object of that class is instantiated. Constructors make sure that objects of the class are properly initialized.

A constructor member function can be given values through parameters. An argument to the constructor may give an initial value to the object, or specify its size, or some other aspect of the object. This allows variations on the object instantiated. For example, a String object may be instantiated with the declaration

```
String FirstName("Samuel");
```

which creates an object FirstName with the value Samuel.

Constructors, like any function, can be overloaded. Commonly, classes have a number of different constructors. In the statement above, a string class object was created by passing an argument to the constructor. This was possible because the class contains a constructor with no arguments and a constructor with a string argument.

6.6 Object Parameters

const parameter

Objects can be passed as function parameters just as variables can. When an object is passed as a value parameter, a copy of the argument is automatically made, and the copy used within the function. Since objects are often large, local copies that consume memory space and time may be undesirable. The solution would seem to be to pass objects as reference parameters since these do not produce local copies. However, objects as reference parameters may allow the function to inadvertently change the object. The solution is to pass objects as *const parameters*.

To demonstrate const parameters, imagine a function CountVowels() that takes a string object as an argument and returns the number of vowels in the string:

```
int CountVowels(const String &Word);
/*Returns the number of vowels in String Word
   Post: The total number of vowels (a, A, e, E, i, I, o, O, u, U) in
   Word returned                                                     */
```

As with any const value, the compiler will prevent the value of Word from being changed within the function. Any attempt to change the value should generate a compiler error. However, because this is a recent feature of C++, some compilers generate a warning rather than an error.

6.7 The PegClass Class

The PegClass library contains the PegClass class which is useful in game programs and other simulations. This section includes the PegClass documentation and a program demonstrating PegClass.

PegClass (pegclass.h)

Peg with three rings

Constructor
```
PegClass(int Height);
/*Creates a PegClass object and draws the peg on the screen.
   Requires parameter h that correspond to the height of the peg.
   Post: A peg of height h created                                 */
```

Functions
```
void AddRing(int Size);
/*Adds a ring of the given size to the peg, and updates screen
   Pre: 1 <= Size <= 7
   Post: Peg with ring of size Size displayed on screen            */

int RemoveRing();
/*Removes a ring from the peg, returns its size, and updates screen
   Pre: Peg is not empty
   Post: Peg displayed on screen with top ring removed             */

int TopRing();
/*Returns size of top ring
   Pre: Peg is not empty
   Post: Size of top ring on peg returned */

int RingsOnPeg();
/*Returns number of rings on peg
   Post: Number of rings on peg returned */
```

```
void ShowAll();
/*Shows all declared and configured pegs
   Post: All declared and configured pegs are displayed */
```

The following program demonstrates the PegClass class:

```
/*PegClass Class Demonstration program  */

#include <lvp\pegclass.h>
#include "utility.h"

int main()
{
  PegClass P(7), Q(7);

  P.AddRing(3); Q.AddRing(2);
  P.AddRing(4); Q.AddRing(3);
  P.AddRing(5); Q.AddRing(4);
  P.ShowAll(); Pause();

  P.RemoveRing();
  P.RemoveRing(); Q.RemoveRing();
  P.ShowAll();

  return(0);
}
```

To instantiate P and Q, parameters must be included to display the pegs. At the first call to Pause(), three rings have been added to the pegs and the following displayed. Note how only one call to ShowAll() displays all the PegClass objects:

```
          |              |
          |              |
          |              |
          |              |
     XXXXX | XXXXX   XXXX | XXXX
     XXXX | XXXX     XXX | XXX
      XXX | XXX       XX | XX
    --------------------------------
          Press a key to continue
```

The first ring, of size 3, ends up on the bottom.

At the second call to ShowAll(), two rings have been removed:

```
          |              |
          |              |
          |              |
          |              |
          |          XXX | XXX
      XXX | XXX       XX | XX
    --------------------------------
```

Review 3

Assume the following code is in the main() function of a program that includes the pegclass library. Sketch the status of the pegs at the end of the program and indicate the output generated by the last statement:

```
PegClass P(7), Q(5);

for (int i=1; i<=5; i++) {
   P.AddRing(i);
   Q.AddRing(3);
}
P.RemoveRing();
cout << P.TopRing() << " " << Q.TopRing() << endl;
```

Review 4

What effect would the following statement have as the last statement in the program above?

```
P.AddRing(Q.RemoveRing());
```

Review 5

Write a function TotalRings() that takes three pegs as arguments and returns the total number of rings on the three pegs. Write a program that uses PegClass to create three pegs of height 8 and tests the TotalRings() function by placing a number of rings on the various pegs and then calling the function. Note that pegs cannot be passed as value parameters or assigned.

6.8 The Towers of Hanoi Puzzle

An ancient puzzle involving three pegs is called the Towers of Hanoi. The initial set up has two empty pegs and one peg containing a number of rings from largest (on the bottom) to smallest (on the top), similar to:

```
       |             |             |
    X | X            |             |
   XX | XX           |             |
  XXX | XXX          |             |
  ----------------------------------------
```

The puzzle is to move the rings from the left peg to the middle peg according to the following rules:

- Each move takes a ring from the top of one peg, and moves it to another peg.

- At no time may a larger ring be placed on a smaller ring.

The three-ring puzzle can be solved with seven moves. You may wish to experiment with a physical model (coins work well) to see this.

The following program uses PegClass to demonstrate the solution to the three-ring puzzle. A function MoveRing() was written to move a ring from one peg to another:

```
/*Towers of Hanoi program.
    Demonstrates the solution to a three-ring puzzle */

#include <lvp\pegclass.h>
#include "utility.h"

//-------------------------------------------------------------------------
void MoveRing(PegClass &FromPeg, PegClass &ToPeg)
/*Moves a ring from the FromPeg to the ToPeg
    Pre: FromPeg is not empty
    Post: ring has been moved                           */
{
    int Size = FromPeg.RemoveRing();
    ToPeg.AddRing(Size);
}
//-------------------------------------------------------------------------
int main()
{
    PegClass Left(7), Middle(7), Right(7);

    const int NumRings = 3;

    // Fill Left ring with NumRings, starting with biggest
    for (int Ring=NumRings; Ring>=1; Ring--)
        Left.AddRing(Ring);

    MoveRing(Left, Middle); Pause(); Left.ShowAll();
    MoveRing(Left, Right); Pause(); Left.ShowAll();
    MoveRing(Middle, Right); Pause(); Left.ShowAll();
    MoveRing(Left, Middle); Pause(); Left.ShowAll();
    MoveRing(Right, Left); Pause(); Left.ShowAll();
    MoveRing(Right, Middle); Pause(); Left.ShowAll();
    MoveRing(Left, Middle); Pause(); Left.ShowAll();

    return(0);
}
```

The MoveRing() function changes the status of each peg (by moving a ring off or on). Therefore, the pegs are passed as reference parameters.

Since the code demonstrates the moves, a static diagram would poorly illustrate the output. If possible, run the program and view the output.

Review 6

Write a function FillPeg() that takes a peg P and an integer N as arguments. It should add N rings to the peg, from size N down to 1. Show how this could be used in the program above.

Reviews 7 through 9 develop a version of the Towers of Hanoi program that allows the user to solve the puzzle.

Review 7

Write a function GetUserMove() that asks the user for a source peg and a destination peg (L, M, or R) and returns the input as two reference parameters.

Review 8

Write a function MakeUserMove() that takes two characters representing the user move and the three pegs as arguments and moves the ring as desired by the user.

Modify main() in the Towers of Hanoi program to use the functions in Reviews 7 and 8 to allow the user to play until Middle.RingsOnPeg() == NumRings.

6.9 The TopListClass Class

Virtually every game program has a feature in which the top scores of previous players are recorded. Of course, this would not be very interesting if the list were restarted every time the program were run! Instead, the list is stored in permanent form on disk. The TopListClass class was created to perform just this task. This section includes the TopListClass documentation and a program demonstrating TopListClass.

TopListClass (toplist.h)

Constructor

TopListClass(**const** String &Filename, **int** MaxItems=10);
/*Opens a file on disk, creating it first if necessary. If the file is created it is filled with MaxItems items each with score 0 and name Empty. The constructor requires a String parameter that corresponds to the name of the file on disk. MaxItems is 10 by a default parameter. A second parameter can be passed to the constructor to change the number of items stored.
   Post: A file on disk is opened.   */

Functions

void AddItem(**long** Score, String Name);
/*Adds a score and name to the list if Score ranks in the list, otherwise does nothing.
   Post: A score and name have been inserted if score is greater than any one of the current scores   */

String GetName(**int** Rank);
/*Determines the Name in Rank position in the list. Rank of 1 is the highest score.
   Pre: Rank is in range 1 to maximum number of items in list.
   Post: Name in Rank position returned   */

long GetScore(**int** Rank);
/*Determines the Score in Rank position in the list. Rank of 1 is the highest score.
   Pre: Rank is in range 1 to maximum number of items in list.
   Post: Score in Rank position returned   */

void Clear();
/*Clears TopListClass object back to empty items.
   Post: List contains only scores of 0 and names of Empty */

int GetListSize();
/*Determines the number of items that can be stored in the list
   Post: The number of items that can be stored in the list returned */

void Display (ostream os);
/* Displays list to output stream
   Post: Names and scores displayed */

The following program demonstrates the TopListClass class:

```
/* TopListClass Class Demonstration program */

#include <iostream.h>
#include <lvp\string.h>
#include <lvp\toplist.h>
#include <lvp\bool.h>

int main()
{
  TopListClass DemoList("samplist.dat");
  DemoList.Display(cout);    // Display current scores to console

  String Name;
  const String Sentinel = "END";
  long Score;
  while (true) {
    cout << "Enter your name (" << Sentinel << " to end): ";
    getline(cin, Name);
    if (Name == Sentinel)
      break;
    cout << "Enter your score: ";
    cin >> Score;
    cin.ignore(80, '\n');
    DemoList.AddItem(Score, Name);
    DemoList.Display(cout);
  }
  return(0);
}
```

When run, program output may look similar to:

```
Empty  0
Empty  0
Empty  0
Empty  0
Empty  0
Empty  0
Empty  0
Empty  0
Empty  0
Empty  0
Enter your name (END to end): Tristan
Enter your score: 1200
Tristan 1200
Empty  0
Empty  0
Empty  0
Empty  0
Empty  0
Empty  0
Empty  0
Empty  0
Empty  0
Enter your name (END to end): Marie
Enter your score: 825
Tristan 1200
Marie 825
Empty  0
Empty  0
Empty  0
```

```
Empty 0
Empty 0
Empty 0
Empty 0
Empty 0
Enter your name (END to end): Vickie
Enter your score: 910
Tristan 1200
Vickie 910
Marie 825
Empty 0
Empty 0
Empty 0
Empty 0
Empty 0
Empty 0
Empty 0
Enter your name (END to end): END
```

The program stores the list on disk using the file name given. This way the list is maintained from one run to the next. Note how a class can make file manipulation transparent: code to open the disk file, load information from the file, and store it, is executed almost invisibly.

The DemoList is displayed by simply inserting it into the cout stream. This generates legible, but poorly formatted output. A better approach would be to use the GetName() and GetScore() member functions to obtain the information and then display it formatted. This task is presented as Review 10.

Review 10

Write a function PrintFormatted() that takes TopListClass P as its argument and displays a neatly formatted table from rank 1 to the highest rank stored. Use GetName(), GetScore(), and GetListSize() member functions, and cout.width() in the function.

Review 11

Write a function with the following header:

```
bool NewPersonalBest(String Name, long Score, const TopListClass &TL)
/*Returns true if and only if Score is higher than any other score in
   TL associated with Name, and Name appears in TL somewhere.
   Post: true returned if Name's score is higher than a previous score by Name */
```

The idea is that the player has previously made the list, but now has a new score that is higher than any previous score achieved.

Review 12

Modify the TopListClass demonstration program to use a list of only five items. Write a main() that tries to insert more than five items to verify that TopListClass objects restrict the list to the top five scores.

6

Review 13

Run the TopListClass demonstration program and then open the data file produced (e.g., samplist.dat) to see how the list is stored. What would the file look like if the only items inserted were a score of 3141 for Euclid and a score or 2718 for Euler? Does it matter in which order the scores were inserted?

Case Study

In this Case Study, data from a college database will be displayed.

specification

Use the information in a database of colleges to produce a list of the five colleges with the highest enrollments and display the average enrollment of all the colleges in the database. The CollegeClass class, implemented in the college library, provides access to a database of over 400 colleges. The CollegeClass documentation follows:

CollegeClass (college.h)

Constructor
CollegeClass();
/*Opens a database file on disk making the first item the current item.
   Post: First item of database is current item   */

Functions
bool GetNext();
/*Move to next item in database (next college); returns false if fails
   Post: Next item in database is current item or false returned   */

bool CurrentIsValid();
/*Returns true if current item is valid (i.e. not past end of database)
   Post: true returned if current item is valid   */

void Reset();
/*Moves back to the start of the database
   Post: First item of database is current item */

// These functions obtain information from the current item
String GetName();
String GetTown();
String GetState();
String GetPubOrPri(); // Public or Private
long GetEnrollment();
long GetTuition();
long GetRoomAndBoard();

Operators
<<   Inserts the data from the current item into the output
      stream

design

The specification requires a list of the top five colleges by enrollment. This is a natural task for a TopListClass object. To output a formatted list a user-defined function WriteTopColleges() is required.

The specification also requires the average enrollment of all the colleges in the database. The algorithm for this is count the colleges, sum their enrollments, and then divide the total enrollments by the total number of colleges.

Using the CollegeClass class, the TopListClass class, and the algorithm for the average enrollments, the Case Study pseudocode becomes:

```
while CurrentIsValid()
    Add college to count of colleges
    Add enrollment of college to sum of enrollments
    Insert college in toplist
    GetNext()
Display average enrollment
Display list of top 5 colleges by enrollment
```

coding

With so much left to the classes, the coding is relatively simple:

```cpp
/*Top Colleges by Enrollment program.
   Displays the average enrollment of all colleges, and a list of the five
   colleges with the largest enrollments according to the database
   accessed by college.h.                                            */

#include <iostream.h>
#include <lvp\college.h>
#include <lvp\toplist.h>

//-----------------------------------------------------------------------------
void WriteTopColleges(const TopListClass &CollegeList)
/*Displays the CollegeList in a tabular format
   Post: A formatted list is displayed          */
{
    for (int i=1; i<=CollegeList.GetListSize(); i++) {
        cout.setf(ios::left);
        cout.width(40);
        cout << CollegeList.GetName(i);
        cout.setf(ios::right);
        cout << CollegeList.GetScore(i) << endl;
    }
}
//-----------------------------------------------------------------------------
int main()
{
    CollegeClass College;

    const int ListSize = 5;
    TopListClass EnrollmentList("enroll.dat", ListSize);

    EnrollmentList.Clear();
    int Count = 0;
    long Sum = 0;
    while (College.CurrentIsValid()) {
        Count++;
        Sum += College.GetEnrollment();
        EnrollmentList.AddItem(College.GetEnrollment(),College.GetName());
        College.GetNext();
    }
    cout << "Average enrollment over " << Count << " colleges: "
        << double(Sum)/Count << endl;

    WriteTopColleges(EnrollmentList);
    return (0);
}
```

When run, the program displays:

```
Average enrollment over 452 colleges: 10454
Ohio State University                  38958
Indiana University - Bloomington       35551
Texas A&M University                   33479
Arizona State University               31906
Pennsylvania State University Park      31732
```

It is impressive to see how just forty lines of code (including documentation) can, with the judicious use of classes, solve a complex task.

Review 14

Modify the Case Study so that the average enrollment and top five schools by enrollment are displayed for just the state specified by the user.

Review 15

Modify the Case Study so that it displays a list of the top five colleges by tuition cost *and* another list of the top five by enrollment. Use the WriteTopColleges() function for both lists.

Review 16

Predict what would happen if the statement EnrollmentList.Clear() were removed from the main function and the program executed several times. Then test your prediction by actually removing the line and running the program.

Chapter Summary

Classes are user-defined types that extend the C++ programming language. A class is used to create an object. When an object is created it is said to be instantiated. Objects can be used like other variables. When an object is used as a parameter, it is usually best to pass it as a const parameters which is a reference parameter that is not allowed to change.

Classes contain member functions that define the properties of an object of that class. Operator member functions overload the built-in C++ operators. A constructor member function is automatically called when an object is instantiated. Constructors can have parameters that specify the aspects of an object, and a constructor can be overloaded. Classes can also contain member constants.

The String class contains a length() member function that returns the number of characters in the calling string object. The substr() function, also in the string class, returns a part of the string object. The find() function returns the position of a character or string in the calling string object. The c_str() function returns a C-style string, and is useful when using functions atoi() and atog() from stdlib which require C-style parameters. The String class also overloads the + and += operators.

The ios class is in the iostream library. cin and cout are predeclared objects. The ios class also defines the << and >> operators, and contains several constants.

The PegClass class has a constructor that requires parameters. When a class has a constructor that requires parameters, the parameters must be given to instantiate the object. The PegClass class is useful for solving the Towers of Hanoi puzzle.

The TopListClass class is useful for storing data in a file. A game program often uses this approach for storing top scores. This class was also useful for maintaining a list of items that met certain requirements, as in the Case Study which printed the top five colleges by enrollment.

Vocabulary

Class A user-defined type.

Constant Data Member A constant belonging to a class.

Constructor A member function that is automatically called when an object is instantiated.

Instance An identifier associated with a class.

Instantiate Declare an object.

Member Function A function that belongs to a class.

Method Sometimes used to refer to a member function.

Operator Member Function A member function that overloads a C++ built-in operator.

Object An instance of a class.

C++

+ Overloaded operator in the string class that concatenates strings.

+= Overloaded operator in the string class that concatenates strings.

atof() A stdlib library function that returns a double from a C-style string.

atoi() A stdlib library function that returns an int from a C-style string.

c_str() A String member function that returns a C-style string.

CollegeClass A class in the college library that is used to view the information in a college database.

const Keyword used to define an object as a parameter that cannot be changed.

find() A String member function that returns the position of a character or string in the calling String object.

ios A class in the iostream library that is used for input/output.

length() A String member function that returns the number of characters of the calling String object.

PegClass A class in the pegclass library that is used for creating and displaying "pegs."

6

substr() A String member function that returns a substring of the calling String object.

TopListClass A class in the toplist library that is used to create a file of data items.

Exercises

Exercise 1

A "Scrolling" message display shows a message with characters entering from the right. For example, if the message is "Vote YES!", the display first shows

```
                Vote YES!
```
then
```
                ote YES! V
```
then
```
                te YES! Vo
```
and so on.

a) Write a function RotateOne() that takes a string parameter and returns it with one character moved from the left to the right as illustrated above. (Hint: Be sure the message includes a space at the end so the words do not run together in the scroll.)

b) Write a program that displays 10 sequences of a message.

c) Write a program that asks the user for a message and then uses gotoxy() to display it as a scrolling message at the top of the screen. You may need to include a "delay loop" to slow down the scrolling process. A simple one is:

```
for (long i=1; i<=2000000; i++);
```

This loop does nothing for 2,000,000 iterations which causes a brief pause in the program.

Exercise 2

Write a function Reverse() that returns a string containing the reverse of its string parameter, e.g. "Testing" returns "gnitseT".

Exercise 3

a) When an integer expression with a value between 65 and 90 is cast into a char the result is an uppercase letter. For example, cout << char(65); displays an A. Write a function RanWord() that returns a word formed of random letters, of the length given as a parameter. Use the function header:

```
String RanWord(int NumLetters)
/* Returns a word of length NumLetters formed of random letters
   Pre: NumLetters >= 1
   Post: Random word of length NumLetters returned          */
```

b) Write a program to display 5 six-letter "words."

c) Modify RanWord() so that it always returns words with at least one vowel. Have the function do this by repeatedly generating words until a word with a vowel (A, E, I, O, U) is generated.

Exercise 4

Write a function IsPalin() that returns true if and only if its string parameter is a palindrome. A palindrome is any word that is spelled the same backwards and forwards, for example DAD.

Exercise 5

Reading of numeric values from the user is error-prone. If the user mis-types by entering a letter the program may behave unpredictably. Use the atoi() and atof() functions to create more robust functions GetInt() and GetDouble() which read a string, and convert it to the numeric value to be returned. Test these functions, and then add them to the Utility library.

Exercise 6

It is often necessary to ask a user for a character input, and then to check it against a list of valid entries. This is cumbersome when a condition contains many choices, as in the code:

```
char Choice;
cout << "Enter your choice (A, B, or C): ";
cin >> Choice;
while ((Choice != 'A') && (Choice != 'B') && (Choice != 'C')) {
   cout << "Choose from among A, B, and C" << endl;
   cin >> Choice;
}
```

Write a function GetChoice() using the following header:

```
char GetChoice(const String &LegalChoices)
/*Forces the user to enter a character in LegalChoices and returns it
   Post: Character in LegalChoices returned                            */
```

GetChoice() should display error messages until the user enters a valid character, and allow the code above to be rewritten as:

```
cout << "Enter your choice (A, B, or C): ";
char Choice = GetChoice("ABC");
```

Exercise 7

In many applications it is necessary to take a string containing a command and divide it into pieces for further processing. Usually those pieces are separated by blanks. For example, the string "Pick up 2 sticks" would be divided into 4 pieces: "Pick," "up," "2," and "sticks."

a) Write a function ExtractFirstWord() using the following header:

```
void ExtractFirstWord(String &Sentence, String &Word)
/*Removes the first word from Sentence and returns it in Word.
   Pre: Words in Sentence are separated by blanks
   Post: First word of Sentence returned with blanks before and after word discarded.
   Sentence returned with first word and spaces before and after the word removed.
   Sentence and Word returned as empty strings if Sentence contained no words. */
```

b) Test ExtractFirstWord() in a program with the following main():

```
int main()
{
  String S, W;
  getline(cin, S);
  while (S != "") {
    ExtractFirstWord(S,W);
    cout << W << endl;
  }
  return(0);
}
```

Exercise 8

Modify the Towers of Hanoi program developed in Reviews 7 through 9 so that:

- It counts and reports the number of moves taken by the user.
- It allows the user to "give up" by entering a peg of Q.
- It provides an option to specify the number of rings at the start (3 or 4).

Exercise 9

Modify the Towers of Hanoi program developed in Reviews 7 through 9 so that it counts the number of moves taken by the user and maintains a top scorer list. Note that since TopListClass ranks the highest score as best, and in this case the lowest score is to be considered the best, some creative programming is required. Store the number of moves by subtracting from 1000 first. That is, a score of 12 moves is stored as 988 (1000–12). When printing the list of top scores, reconvert the scores by subtracting from 1000 (1000–988).

Exercise 10

One variation of the game of Nim, described in Chapter Five Exercise 12, is played with four pegs. Initially, the pegs contain 1, 2, 3, and 4 rings (all rings are the same size). On each turn, a player may take 1, 2, or 3 rings from a single peg. The player who takes the last ring loses.

Write a program that uses the pegclass library to allow two players to play Nim. Be sure the program allows only legal moves. A typical screen may look similar to:

```
        |             |             |             |
        |             |             |             | XXX | XXX
        |             |             | XXX | XXX      XXX | XXX
        |             | XXX | XXX      XXX | XXX      XXX | XXX
  XXX | XXX      XXX | XXX      XXX | XXX      XXX | XXX
  ------------------------------------------------------------

    Player 1:
      Choose a peg: 3
      Choose the number to take: 2
```

Exercise 11

Modify a game program from a previous Exercise to include a top scores list.

6

Exercise 12

Use the TopListClass class in a program that tracks results of a gymnastics competition. Names of up to 20 competitors and their numerical scores are entered, and at the end of the competition, a full list of all competitors and their scores is displayed. Finally the names of the Gold, Silver, and Bronze winners are displayed. Note: Gymnastics scores are usually given to one decimal place (1.0 to 10.0), but a TopListClass object only stores integer values. Multiply the scores by 10 before storing them, and divide by ten before displaying them.

Exercise 13 ♻

Modify Exercise 12 to include several different events: Balance Beam, Floor Exercises, and Uneven Bars. Provide the user with a menu of options:

```
A.  Enter Balance Beam result
B.  Enter Floor Exercises result
C.  Enter Uneven Bars result
D.  Display all current standings
E.  Display all medal winners
F.  Quit
```

Exercise 14

Modify the Case Study so that the average and top enrollment lists are generated for public schools, private schools, and both. Have the program also provide a count of the number in each category.

Exercise 15

Modify the Case Study so that it gives the average and top five colleges based upon the total cost combining tuition and room and board.

Exercise 16

Write a program that displays the names of the lowest tuition and highest tuition colleges in the college database. Refer to the CollegeClass class used in the Case Study. You do not need to use TopListClass for this program.

Exercise 17

Write a program that uses the CollegeClass class from the Case Study to allow the user to search for information on a given college. Have the program require the user to enter just the first few letters of the college name, and then display the information on all colleges that match these letters. (Note that the names of some colleges are stored in the form: "Foobar, University of")

Exercise 18

a) The college database used in the Case Study stores many college names in the form: "Foobar, University of." Write a function that converts names in this form to "University of Foobar." The function should return college names that do not originally contain commas as unchanged.

b) Modify the Case Study to include the function from part (a).

Advanced
Exercise 19

Use the CollegeClass class from the Case Study to write a Find-a-College program that asks the user a number of questions, and then displays the names of all colleges that match the responses. For example:

```
A. Public
B. Private
C. Either
Enter choice: B

A. Large (above 2000)
B. Small (below 2000)
C. Either
Enter choice: C

Enter maximum tuition:   12000

Colleges fitting your criteria are:
     American University of Puerto Rico
     Baldwin-Wallace College
     ...
```

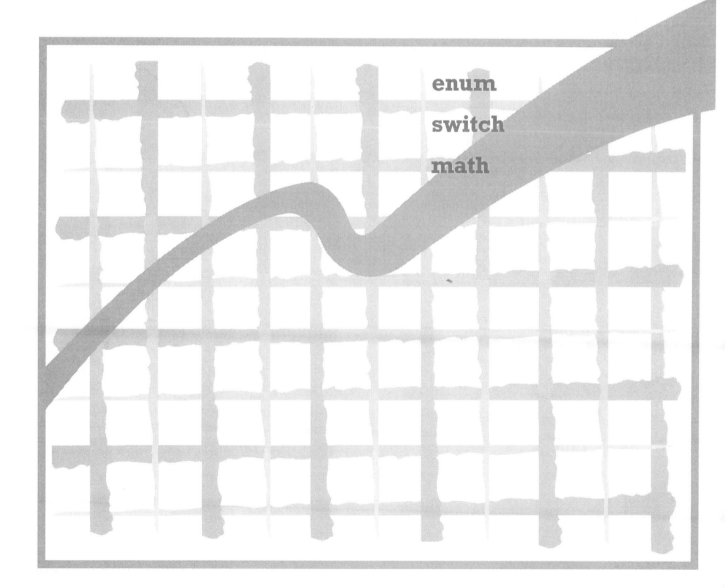

enum

switch

math

Objectives

After completing this chapter you will be able to:

1. Use the mathematical (trigonometric, logarithmic, exponential) functions contained in the math library.

2. Avoid problems created by roundoff error.

3. Round a double value to the nearest integer.

4. Write recursive functions.

5. Use the ASCII code.

6. Use enumerated types.

7. Control program flow with the switch statement.

7

The earliest uses for electronic computers were largely mathematical. One of the very first programming languages was called FORTRAN which means FORmula TRANslator. C++, like all modern languages, provides special facilities for performing mathematical tasks.

7.1 The math Library

math.h

The math library includes many useful mathematical functions. The prototypes for exponentiation and square root functions are:

```
double pow(double x, double y);
/*Returns x to the power of y
   Pre: x and y are not both zero
   if x is negative, y must be a whole number
   Post: x to the y returned                    */
```

```
double sqrt(double x);
/*Returns the square root of x
   Pre: x >= 0
   Post: square root of x returned */
```

```
int abs(int x);
/*Returns the absolute value of x
   Post: absolute value of x returned */
```

```
double fabs(double x);
/*Returns the absolute value of x
   Post: absolute value of x returned */
```

The pow() and sqrt() functions can also be called with integer arguments. When this is done, int values are promoted to double if needed. The abs() and fabs() functions should be used with int and double arguments respectively. The abs() function was not overloaded to handle both types because the math library is carried over from traditional C programming where overloading is not possible.

Note carefully the preconditions. If they are violated in a call to one of these functions, the program will terminate with an error message.

The math library also includes trigonometric functions:

```
double tan(double x);
/* Post: The tangent of x returned */

double sin(double x);
/* Post: The sine of x returned */

double cos(double x);
/* Post: The cosine of x returned */
```

The arguments to these functions are assumed to be in radians. A value in degrees may be converted to radians using the formula:

```
ValueInRadians = (PI/180)*ValueInDegrees;
```

To demonstrate the trigonometric functions, the following program displays a table of sine and cosine values for angles from 0 to 90 degrees, stepping by 5 degrees:

```
/* Sine and Cosine program.
   Displays a table of sine and cosine values for various angles
   from 0 to 90 degrees                                           */

#include <math.h>
#include <iostream.h>

int main()
{
  const double PI = 3.14;
  const int Width = 6;
  const int Precision = 3;
  cout.setf(ios::fixed);
  cout.precision(Precision);
  const int MaxAngle = 90;
  const int AngleStep = 5;
  cout << " Angle sin() cos()" << endl;
  for (int Angle=0; Angle<=MaxAngle; Angle+=AngleStep) {
    cout.width(Width);
    double RadAngle = (PI/180)*Angle;
    cout << Angle;
    cout.width(Width);
    cout << sin(RadAngle);
    cout.width(Width);
    cout << cos(RadAngle);
    cout << endl;
  }
  return (0);
}
```

When run, the program output looks like:

```
Angle  sin()  cos()
    0  0.000  1.000
    5  0.087  0.996
   10  0.174  0.985
   15  0.259  0.966
   20  0.342  0.940
   25  0.423  0.906
   30  0.500  0.866
   35  0.574  0.819
   40  0.643  0.766
   45  0.707  0.707
. . .
```

Mathematical work often requires finding the angle that corresponds with a trigonometric value. This is called the *inverse* trigonometric function, also supplied in the math library:

```
double atan(double x);
/*Post: The arctangent of x in radians returned
   -PI/2 < atan() < +PI/2                              */

double asin(double x);
/*Pre: -1 <= x <= 1
   Post: The arcsine of x in radians returned
   -PI/2 < asin() < +PI/2                              */

double acos(double x);
/*Pre: -1 <= x < = 1
   Post: The arccosine of x in radians returned
   0 < acos() < +PI                                    */
```

7.3 Logarithmic and Exponential Functions

The math library also provides functions that calculate base 10 and base e (natural) logarithms:

```
double log(double x);
/*Returns the natural logarithm of x
   Pre: x > 0
   Post: natural log of x returned     */

double log10(double x);
/*Returns the base 10 logarithm of x
   Pre: x > 0
   Post: base 10 log of x returned       */
```

The exp() function raises e to a given power:

```
double exp(double x);
/*Returns e to the power of x
   Post: e to the x returned     */
```

Integer values may be used as arguments to any of these functions.

7.4 Other math.h Functions

The simplest way to learn more about the math library is to use online help. Help contains information about all the functions supplied with a library.

Review 1

Write a program to display powers of 2 in a table like the following:

```
2^1      2
2^2      4
2^3      8
. . .
2^10   1024
```

Review 2

Write a function PerfectSquare() that takes an integer argument and returns true if and only if it is a perfect square. You can determine this by finding the square root, rounding it, then squaring the result, and checking to see if it is equal to the original number. Write a program that calls PerfectSquare() for integers 1 through 20 and displays the result.

Review 3

Modify the Sine and Cosine program so that it displays a fourth column that displays the sum of the squares of the sine and cosine values.

7.5 Precision of double Values

roundoff error

As discussed in Chapter Four, noninteger values are necessarily rounded slightly by the computer which can result in *roundoff error*. For example, the value 1.0/3.0 is represented as 0.333333333... in decimal. However, to be represented in binary, the system used internally by the computer, a repeating decimal must be rounded off, preventing an exact representation. This is important to remember when programming with nonintegers (e.g., doubles).

For example, consider the following statement:

```
if (4.80*100 == 480)
    cout << "equal";
else
    cout << "not equal";
```

It appears that equal should be displayed since 4.80 times 100 is 480. However, this code displays not equal. The number 4.80 cannot be exactly represented in binary. Therefore, when 4.80 is multiplied by 100 this rounding error becomes large enough so that it is slightly different from 480. The following code demonstrates this:

```
cout << (4.80*100 – 480) << endl;
```

Rather than zero, the output is:

-1.77636e–14

Though a very small number (–0.0000000000000177636) it is enough so that 4.80*100 is not *exactly* 480.

A simple rule should be followed when comparing noninteger values: Never use == or != in comparisons. The result will often be unexpected. If two double values must be compared for equality, use a *tolerance*, an acceptable difference. For example, instead of:

if (x == y)...

write:

if (fabs(x–y) < 0.00001)...

This way if the difference between x and y is very small (smaller than the tolerance, 0.00001), then the condition will be true.

tolerance

7.6 Rounding double Values

It is often necessary to round a double value to the nearest integer. The decimal portion of a value is used to determine how the value should be rounded. The fractional part of a value can be obtained by casting the double into an int, and then subtracting the int from the original double (assume x is a double):

FractionalPart = x – int(x);

The Round() function returns a rounded double value (an integer):

```
int Round(double x)
/*Returns x rounded to the nearest integer
   Pre: x >= 0
   Post: rounded x returned                    */
{
   double FractionalPart = x – int(x);
   if (FractionalPart < 0.5)
      return (int(x));
   else
      return (int(x) + 1);
}
```

Review 4 ————————————————————————————————————

Modify the Round() function in Section 7.6 so that is works correctly for negative numbers. For example, Round(–1.6) should return –2, and Round(–1.4) should return –1, and so on.

Review 5 ————————————————————————————————————

Overload the Round() function in Section 7.6 by writing a new version with the following header:

```
double Round(double x, int NumDecimals)
/*Returns x rounded to the NumDecimals decimal places
   Post:  x to NumDecimals decimal places returned      */
```

Predict the behavior of the following code:

```
double S = 0;
do {
   S += 0.1;
   cout << "Value is " << S << endl;
} while (S != 1);
```

7.7 Recursion

A function can include calls to itself. This process is called *recursion* and the calls are referred to as *recursive calls*. Recursion is a programming technique that can be used whenever a problem can be solved by solving one or more smaller versions of the same problem and combining the results. The recursive calls solve the smaller problems.

One problem which has a recursive solution is raising a number to a power. For example, 2^4 can be thought of as:

$2^4 = 2 * 2^3$ which can be thought of as
$2^3 = 2 * 2^2$ which can be thought of as
$2^2 = 2 * 2^1$ which can be thought of as
$2^1 = 2 * 2^0$ which can be thought of as
1

In each case, the power problem is reduced to a smaller power problem. A more general solution is:

$$x^n = x * x^{n-1}$$

A function IntPower() that raises a number to an integer power to return an integer (as opposed to pow() which returns a double) could be written with the header:

long IntPower(double x, int n)

Using the general solution above, the body of IntPower() becomes:

return (x * IntPower(x, n–1));

infinite recursion   A call to find 2^8 returns 2 times 2^7, which returns 2 times 2^6, and so on. However, this statement has no place to stop! This is called *infinite recursion* and clearly is not desirable.

To provide a solution, recursion requires a case that has no recursive solution. In this problem, when n is zero the answer is simply 1. IntPower() then becomes:

```
long IntPower(long x, int n)
/* returns x to the power of n
   Pre: x and n are not both zero
   Post: x to the n returned         */
{
   if (n == 0)
      return(1);
   else
      return(x * IntPower(x, n–1));
}
```

Review 7

Rewrite IntPower() without using recursion and compare this solution to the recursive solution.

Review 8

IntPower() only works for positive values of n. Modify IntPower() to work with negative values of n using the solution:

$$x^n = \frac{1}{x^{-n}}$$

Review 9

Write a recursive function Factorial() that returns the factorial (a long) of its int argument. The factorial of a positive integer is the product of it and all the positive integers less than it. For example, the factorial of 5 is 5*4*3*2*1 or 120. The symbol for factorial is the exclamation point, therefore 5! = 120. Computing this factorial can also be thought of as 5! = 5*4! or more generally, N! = N*(N-1)! By definition, 0! is equal to 1.

7.8 More on Recursion

Consider the following function:

```
void Example(int N)
{
    cout << "Entering function, N = " << N << endl;
    if (N > 1)
        Example(N-1);
    cout << "Leaving function, N = " << N << endl;
}
```

When the call Example(1) is made the if condition is false. This is the nonrecursive case which produces the output:

```
Entering function, N = 1
Leaving function, N = 1
```

Now consider what happens when the call Example(2) is made. First, the cout statement displays

```
Entering function, N = 2
```

and then the if statement is executed. The condition N>1 is true, therefore a recursive call, Example(N-1), is made. Since N-1=1, the nonrecursive call Example(1) produces

```
Entering function, N = 1
Leaving function, N = 1
```

and then the statement after the if is executed, producing:

```
Leaving function, N = 2
```

The total effect of the call Example(2) is to produce four lines of output:

```
Entering function, N = 2
Entering function, N = 1
Leaving function, N = 1
Leaving function, N = 2
```

To review, the call Example(2) starts the N=2 function, then performs the N=1 function (via the recursive call), and then finishes the N=2 function. With this in mind, the call Example(3) can be predicted to produce:

```
Entering function, N = 3
Entering function, N = 2
Entering function, N = 1
Leaving function, N = 1
Leaving function, N = 2
Leaving function, N = 3
```

The diagram below shows a recursive call tree for the call Example(3). Keep in mind that each call maintains its own, private value for N:

Review 10

Using a recursive call tree diagram, illustrate the effect of the call IntPower(2, 3).

Review 11

Predict the output of the call Review(9):

```cpp
void Review(int N)
{
   cout << "Entering function, N = " << N << endl;
   if (N > 0)
      Review(N/2);
   cout << "Leaving function, N = " << N << endl;
}
```

7.9 The Towers of Hanoi

In Chapter Six, the Towers of Hanoi program solved the puzzle for three rings. This program can be modified to use a recursive function.

To develop a recursive solution to a problem, there must be a way to solve the problem by solving smaller versions of the same problem. In the case of the Towers of Hanoi three rings can be moved from the left peg to the middle peg with the following steps:

1. Move two rings from the left peg to the right peg.
2. Move the remaining ring from the left peg to the middle peg.
3. Move the two rings from the right peg to the middle peg.

The first and third steps are smaller versions of the three-ring problem. Instead of moving three rings, steps one and three only require two rings to be moved.

Next, a recursive solution requires a case which has no recursive solution. For the Towers of Hanoi problem moving zero rings requires nothing at all.

The pseudocode for the recursive Hanoi function is:

> if the number of rings is greater than zero
>> move the top n–1 rings from the source peg to the spare peg
>> move the bottom ring from the source peg to the destination peg
>> move the n–1 rings from the spare peg to the destination peg

Rather than referring to left, right, and middle pegs, the pseudocode refers to the source peg (from which the rings are to be moved), the destination peg (to which all the rings are to be moved) and the spare peg (available for temporary use during the transfer). During recursive calls, the pegs may change roles. For example, a source peg in one call may be a spare peg in another.

The actual code is surprisingly concise. There are more lines of documentation than there are statements:

```
void Hanoi(int NumRings, PegClass &SourcePeg, PegClass &DestPeg,
           PegClass &SparePeg)
/*Moves NumRings rings from SourcePeg to DestPeg using SparePeg for
  temporary storage.                                               */
{
  if (NumRings > 0) {
    // Move N–1 rings to the SparePeg for storage
    Hanoi(NumRings–1, SourcePeg, SparePeg, DestPeg);

    // Move the single big ring over
    MoveRing(SourcePeg, DestPeg);

    // Move the N–1 ring back from SparePeg to destination
    Hanoi(NumRings–1, SparePeg, DestPeg, SourcePeg);
  }
}
```

The call Hanoi(3, L, M, R) where L means left peg, M means middle peg, and R means right peg, could be represented with the recursive call tree:

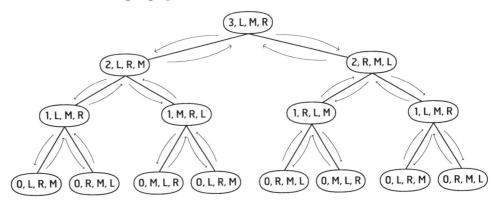

With the Hanoi function, the modified Towers of Hanoi program:

```
/*Recursive Towers of Hanoi program */

#include <lvp\pegclass.h>
#include "utility.h"
#include <conio.h>
#include <iostream.h>

//---------------------------------------------------------------
void MoveRing(PegClass &FromPeg, PegClass &ToPeg)
/*Moves a ring from the FromPeg to the ToPeg
  Pre: FromPeg is not empty
  Post: ring has been moved                        */
{
  int Size = FromPeg.RemoveRing();
  ToPeg.AddRing(Size);
}
//---------------------------------------------------------------
void Hanoi(int NumRings, PegClass &SourcePeg, PegClass &DestPeg,
           PegClass &SparePeg)
/*Moves NumRings rings from SourcePeg to DestPeg using SparePeg for
  temporary storage.                                             */
{
  if (NumRings > 0) {
    // Move N-1 rings to the Aux peg for storage
    Hanoi(NumRings-1, SourcePeg, SparePeg, DestPeg);

    // Move the single big ring over
    MoveRing(SourcePeg, DestPeg); getch(); SourcePeg.ShowAll();

    // Move the N-1 ring back from Aux peg to destination
    Hanoi(NumRings-1, SparePeg, DestPeg, SourcePeg);
  }
}
//---------------------------------------------------------------
int main()
{
  PegClass Left(7), Middle(7), Right(7);

  const int NumRings = 3;

  // Fill Left peg with NumRings, starting with biggest
  int RingCount;
  for (RingCount = NumRings; RingCount >= 1; RingCount--)
    Left.AddRing(RingCount);

  Pause();
  Hanoi(NumRings, Left, Middle, Right);
  return(0);
}
```

The Hanoi() function was modified to include a call to getch() after each move so that the action does not take place too quickly. This program illustrates the solution to the three-ring problem. However, by changing the value of NumRings, it will correctly show the solution to larger (or smaller) sized problems. A note of caution: the Towers of Hanoi problem requires over 1000 moves for the ten-ring problem!

Recursion is a difficult concept and deep understanding takes time. Later we will present more examples and explanation, and your mastery of this technique will increase.

Review 12

Modify the Towers of Hanoi program so that the user is asked how many rings are desired. Build the pegs so that they hold just one more than the number of rings (e.g., if the user asks for three rings, build the pegs with height four.)

Review 13

Write a function HanoiMoves() that returns the number of moves required to solve the Towers of Hanoi problem with the number of rings given as an argument. Hint: To solve a five-ring Tower, you must solve two four-ring Towers and also move the base ring. The sum of all these moves is the total for the five-ring problem.

7.10 Character Data Storage

ASCII code

A computer stores characters through a standard conversion table called the American Standard Code for Information Interchange, or *ASCII code*. The ASCII code specifies a character equivalent for every decimal value below 127. Values above 127 may be assigned by the individual computer manufacturer, and generally may not be transferable to other systems. The characters corresponding to these assignments are called *extended characters*.

In C++, casting integer values into characters results in a character corresponding to the ASCII code. For example, the ASCII code for A is 65. Therefore, the statement

```
cout << char(65);
```

displays A. Conversely, casting a character into an integer results in the ASCII integer code corresponding to that character, as in the statement

```
cout << int('A');
```

which displays 65.

The following page contains the ASCII table for displayable characters. It is often useful to create a character constant to represent an ASCII value in a program. For example:

```
const char POUND = char(163);
```

A named constant makes code easier to read, as in

```
Amount = 200;
cout << "Total cost is " << Amount << POUND;
```

which displays:

```
Total cost is 200£
```

bell	7	B	66	f	102	–	150	½	189	á	225
tab	9	C	67	g	103	—	151	¾	190	â	226
space	32	D	68	h	104	~	152	¿	191	ã	227
!	33	E	69	i	105	™	153	À	192	ä	228
"	34	F	70	j	106		154	Á	193	å	229
#	35	G	71	k	107	›	155	Â	194	æ	230
$	36	H	72	l	108	œ	156	Ã	195	ç	231
%	37	I	73	m	109		159	Ä	196	è	232
&	38	J	74	n	110	¡	161	Å	197	é	233
'	39	K	75	o	111	¢	162	Æ	198	ê	234
(	40	L	76	p	112	£	163	Ç	199	ë	235
)	41	M	77	q	113	¤	164	È	200	ì	236
*	42	N	78	r	114	¥	165	É	201	í	237
+	43	O	79	s	115	¦	166	Ê	202	î	238
,	44	P	80	t	116	§	167	Ë	203	ï	239
-	45	Q	81	u	117	¨	168	Ì	204	ð	240
.	46	R	82	v	118	©	169	Í	205	ñ	241
/	47	S	83	w	119	ª	170	Î	206	ò	242
0	48	T	84	x	120	«	171	Ï	207	ó	243
1	49	U	85	y	121	¬	172	Ð	208	ô	244
2	50	V	86	z	122	-	173	Ñ	209	õ	245
3	51	W	87	{	123	®	174	Ò	210	ö	246
4	52	X	88	|	124	–	175	Ó	211	÷	247
5	53	Y	89	}	125	•	176	Ô	212	ø	248
6	54	Z	90	~	126	±	177	Õ	213	ù	249
7	55	[	91	ƒ	131	²	178	Ö	214	ú	250
8	56	\	92	„	132	³	179	×	215	û	251
9	57	]	93	…	133	´	180	Ø	216	ü	252
:	58	^	94	‡	135	µ	181	Ù	217	ý	253
;	59	_	95	‰	137	¶	182	Ú	218	þ	254
<	60	`	96	‹	139	·	183	Û	219	ÿ	255
=	61	a	97	'	145	¸	184	Ü	220		
>	62	b	98	'	146	¹	185	Ý	221		
?	63	c	99	"	147	º	186	Þ	222		
@	64	d	100	"	148	»	187	ß	223		
A	65	e	101	•	149	¼	188	à	224		

7.12 Enumerated Types

A user-defined type can be created through enumeration. An *enumerated type* is a named set of constants. For example

enum DayType {Monday, Tuesday, Wednesday, Thursday, Friday, Saturday, Sunday};

creates a type called DayType that has five possible values. By default, each identifier in an **enum** list corresponds to the integer value representing the position in the list. In this case, Monday is equal to 0, Tuesday is equal to 1, Wednesday is equal to 2, and so on. An enumerated type must be defined before any functions that use it. Therefore, enumerated types are usually placed at the beginning of a program before any function definitions. The following statements show how an enumerated type might be used:

```
enum DayType {Monday, Tuesday, Wednesday, Thursday, Friday, Saturday,
Sunday};

DayType Today = Wednesday;    // enum type in an assignment statement
if (Today == Monday)
   cout << "Go to work." << endl;
else if (Today == Saturday)
   cout << "Go to the beach!" << endl;

for (Today = Monday; Today <= Sunday; Today++)    // enum type counter
   ...

DisplaySchedule(Monday);    // enum type in a function call
```

Because an enumerated type is simply a set of constants, the statements

```
DayType Today = Wednesday;
cout << Today;
```

display

2

rather than the string `Wednesday` as might be desired. To improve the usage of enumerated types, functions to read and write them should be written. For example, the PrintDay() function displays the string corresponding to the constant's value:

```
void PrintDay(DayType Day)
/*Displays a string corresponding to Day
   Post: string corresponding to Day displayed */
{
   if (Day == Monday)
      cout << "Monday";
   else if (Day == Tuesday)
      cout << "Tuesday";
   else if (Day == Wednesday)
      ...
```

The identifiers in an enumerated type may be assigned a value if the default values are not to be used. For example:

enum SummerType {June=6, July=7, August=8}

7.13 The switch Statement

The switch statement controls program flow and takes the form:

```
switch (integer expression) {
   case integer constant: statement; break;
   case integer constant: statement; break;
   ...
}
```

where *integer expression* is an integer, constant of type int, variable storing an integer, or an expression that results in an integer. The *integer expression* is called the *selector* of the switch statement. Based upon its value, the *statement* of the matching case *integer constant* is executed. *statement* is a legal C++ statement or compound statement. Once a correctly matching case *integer constant* value is found, all of the remaining code in the switch statement is executed until a break is encountered.

The switch statement is especially useful for handling enumerated types. For example, the PrintDay() function could be rewritten using a switch statement:

```
void PrintDay(DayType Day)
/*Displays a string corresponding to Day
   Post: string corresponding to Day displayed */
{
   switch (Day) {
     case Monday: cout << "Monday"; break;
     case Tuesday: cout << "Tuesday"; break;
     case Wednesday: cout << "Wednesday"; break;
     case Thursday: cout << "Thursday"; break;
     case Friday: cout << "Friday"; break;
     case Saturday: cout << "Saturday"; break;
     case Sunday: cout << "Sunday"; break;
   }
}
```

Because the switch statement executes all the code after a matching case, it allows simplicity when multiple values are to execute the same statements. For example, when Day is equal to Tuesday, the statement

```
switch (Day) {
   case Monday:
   case Tuesday:
   case Wednesday:
   case Thursday:
   case Friday: cout << "Weekday"; break;
   case Saturday:
   case Sunday: cout << "Weekend"; break;
}
```

displays

```
Weekday
```

If any of the first five case integer constants match the selector, then Weekday is displayed. If either of the last two match, then Weekend is displayed.

default case

A switch statement can also have a default case. The default executes if none of the case is a match. This is accomplished with the keyword default. For example:

```
switch (Day) {
   case Monday:
   case Tuesday:
   case Wednesday:
   case Thursday:
   case Friday: cout << "Weekday"; break;
   case Saturday:
   case Sunday: cout << "Weekend"; break;
   default: cout << "Invalid day value"; break;
}
```

programming style

As with any C++ statement, alignment in the switch statement is irrelevant to the compiler. Often it is preferable to put code indented underneath the corresponding case, as in:

```
switch (Day) {
   case Monday:
      cout << "Monday";
      break;
   case Tuesday:
      cout << "Tuesday";
      break;
   case Wednesday:
      cout << "Wednesday";
      break;
   ...
```

The style used should make the code as clear as possible, given the number and length of the statements within the switch.

Review 14

Write a function LowerCase() that returns the lowercase equivalent of its char argument. If the argument is not an uppercase letter, it should just return the value of the argument unchanged.

Review 15

Write a declaration of an enum type MonthType that holds the months of the year. Write a function NextMonth() that returns the month following the month given as its argument.

Review 16

Write a switch statement that displays the season (Winter, Spring, Summer, Fall) corresponding to the value of Month of type MonthType declared in Review 15.

Case Study

In this Case Study, a program will be written to perform numerical integration for several mathematical functions.

Among the most useful and important discoveries in mathematics is the collection of techniques for finding the area under a curve, also called *integration*. A curve can be specified in a mathematical function that gives the height (y-value) of the curve for every legal x value.

A technique for finding the area under a curve is called *numerical integration*. Numerical integration approximates an area by summing the areas of a large number of trapezoids under the curve. A trapezoid is a four-sided figure with two sides parallel. For example, the area under the curve specified by the function $f(x)=1/x$ is overlaid with a trapezoid:

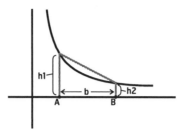

Notice how the trapezoid roughly approximates the area under the curve between the limits A and B. The area of the trapezoid can be found using the formula Area $= 0.5*(h1+h2)*b$ where $h1$ and $h2$ are the y-values of the curve for x values A and B, and b is the width (base) of the trapezoid.

A more precise approximation can be obtained by using multiple trapezoids. For example, the sum of the areas of six trapezoids give a better approximation of the area under the curve:

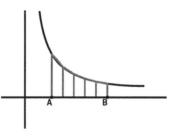

specification

Write a program that calculates the area under a curve using numerical integration. Have the program display some introductory information to the user, and then display a menu with an option to quit and a list of mathematical functions to choose from. The functions should include x^2, x^2+1, sqrt(x), sin(x), and log(x). For the selected function, allow the user to enter the endpoints of the area to be found and the number of trapezoids to be used in the approximation. The program should then display the approximate area, and then display the menu again to allow the user to continue experimenting with numerical integration.

design—level 1

The main() function is designed first. The pseudocode for the major tasks is:

```
Give the description
while (true)
    Get the user's mathematical function choice (or quit)
    if the choice is to quit
        break
    Find the approximation desired
```

To complete the design for main(), the pseudocode is used to determine the data design. A variable is not needed for loop control since the boolean constant true will be used to control the while loop. However, a variable is needed to hold the users menu choice.

At this point, the Case Study may be illustrated as:

```
                    ┌──────────┐
                    │  main()  │
                    └──────────┘
          ┌──────────────┼──────────────┐
┌──────────────────┐ ┌──────────────────┐ ┌──────────────┐
│ GiveDescription()│ │ ChooseFunction() │ │  FindArea()  │
└──────────────────┘ └──────────────────┘ └──────────────┘
```

coding—level 1

main() is coded before continuing to the next level of refinement:

```cpp
/*Area Under a Curve program.
   Approximates the area under curve by summing the area of a number
   of trapezoids that represent the area under the curve. The user specifies
   the function, the endlimits, and the number of trapezoids.                 */

#include <iostream.h>
#include <lvp\bool.h>

//--------------------------------------------------------------------------
void GiveDescription()
/*Provides a description of the program
   Post: A description of the program displayed */
{
}
//--------------------------------------------------------------------------
int ChooseFunction()
/*Allows user to choose a function from a menu.
   Post: The function number chosen by the user returned
   or 0 to quit returned                                   */
{
   return(0);   // For debugging purposes
}
//--------------------------------------------------------------------------
void FindArea(int FunctionNum)
/*Prompts user for endlimits and the number of trapezoids to use,
   and then calculates and displays the area under the curve
   FunctionNum using these values
   Post: area of selected function returned                  */
{
}
//--------------------------------------------------------------------------
int main()
{
   GiveDescription();
   while (true) {
      int FunctionNum = ChooseFunction();
      if (FunctionNum == 0)
         break;
      FindArea(FunctionNum);
   }
   return(0);
}
```

A return(0) was included in ChooseFunction() to make the program a compilable level 1 program.

design—level 2

In the next level of design, the functions called by main() are refined.

GiveDescription() displays introductory information using cout.

ChooseFunction() displays a menu of functions and an option to quit using cout. User input is handled with GetInt() from the utility library. As our first-level design indicates, ChooseFunction() returns the menu selection as an integer.

FindArea() obtains the limit information from the user and the number of trapezoids desired, and then calculates and displays the area. The area calculation is a major task that requires a separate function Approximate().

Approximate() calculates the area of a function for the specified limits using a specified number of trapezoids. The parameters needed by Approximate() are FunctionNum, LowLimit, HighLimit, and NumTraps. Approximate() returns a double for the area.

Level 2 design may be represented as:

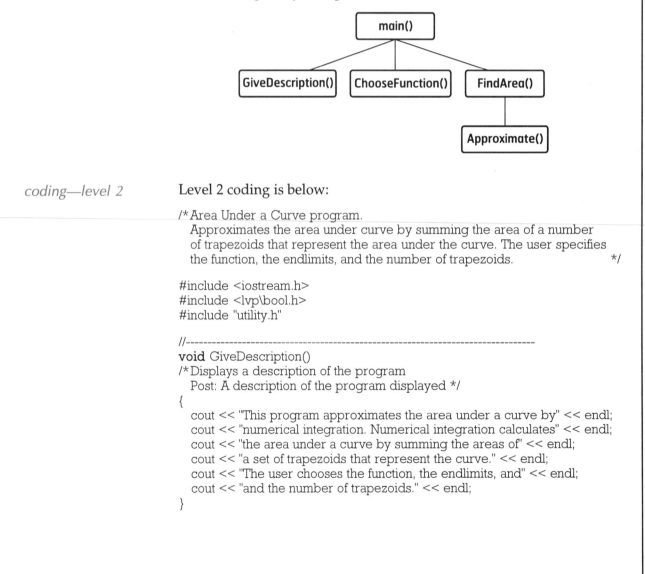

coding—level 2

Level 2 coding is below:

```
/* Area Under a Curve program.
   Approximates the area under curve by summing the area of a number
   of trapezoids that represent the area under the curve. The user specifies
   the function, the endlimits, and the number of trapezoids.              */

#include <iostream.h>
#include <lvp\bool.h>
#include "utility.h"

//-------------------------------------------------------------------------------
void GiveDescription()
/* Displays a description of the program
   Post: A description of the program displayed */
{
    cout << "This program approximates the area under a curve by" << endl;
    cout << "numerical integration. Numerical integration calculates" << endl;
    cout << "the area under a curve by summing the areas of" << endl;
    cout << "a set of trapezoids that represent the curve." << endl;
    cout << "The user chooses the function, the endlimits, and" << endl;
    cout << "and the number of trapezoids." << endl;
}
```

```
//-----------------------------------------------------------------
int ChooseFunction()
/*Allows user to choose a function from a menu.
  Post: The function number chosen by the user returned
  or 0 to quit returned                                         */
{
  cout << "Function list" << endl;
  cout << "  0. QUIT" << endl;
  cout << "  1. x^2" << endl;
  cout << "  2. x^2 + 1" << endl;
  cout << "  3. sqrt(x)" << endl;
  cout << "  4. sin(x)" << endl;
  cout << "  5. log(x)" << endl;
  cout << "Enter your choice: ";
  int Choice = GetInt(0, 5);
  return (Choice);
}
//-----------------------------------------------------------------
double Approximate(int FunctionNum, double LowLimit,
                   double HighLimit, int NumTraps)
/*Approximates the area under a curve using trapezoids
  Pre: FunctionNum is a defined function
  LowLimit..HighLimit values are defined for the function
  NumTraps >= 1
  Post: The area under the function between LowLimit and
  HighLimit returned                                            */
{
  return(0);  // For debugging purposes
}
//-----------------------------------------------------------------
void FindArea(int FunctionNum)
/*Prompts user for endlimits and the number of trapezoids to use,
  and then calculates and displays the area under the curve
  FunctionNum using these values
  Post: area of selected function returned                      */
{
  double LowLimit, HighLimit, Area;
  int NumTraps;
  cout << "Enter the low limit: ";
  cin >> LowLimit;
  cout << "Enter the high limit: ";
  cin >> HighLimit;
  cout << "Enter the number of trapezoids: ";
  cin >> NumTraps;
  Area = Approximate(FunctionNum, LowLimit, HighLimit, NumTraps);
  cout << "The area is approximately " << Area << endl;
}
//-----------------------------------------------------------------
int main()
{
  GiveDescription();
  while (true) {
    int FunctionNum = ChooseFunction();
    if (FunctionNum == 0)
      break;
    FindArea(FunctionNum);
  }
  return(0);
}
```

At this level, the program will run and generate some output. Therefore, program flow can be tested and debugged. A sample run is shown below:

```
This program approximates the area under a curve by
numerical integration. Numerical integration calcu-
lates
the area under a curve by summing the areas of
a set of trapezoids that represent the curve.
The user chooses the function, the endlimits, and
the number of trapezoids.
Function list
   0. QUIT
   1. x^2
   2. x^2 + 1
   3. sqrt(x)
   4. sin(x)
   5. log(x)
Enter your choice: 1
Enter the low limit: 1
Enter the high limit: 10
Enter the number of trapezoids: 100
The area is approximately 0
Function list
   0. QUIT
   1. x^2
   2. x^2 + 1
   3. sqrt(x)
   4. sin(x)
   5. log(x)
Enter your choice: 0
```

This run shows that the flow of control appears to work correctly. However, the screen display is hard to read because it runs together. At the next level of coding, Pause() from the utility library and clrscr() from the conio library will be used to improve the readability.

At the next level of design, the Approximate() function must be refined. The Approximate() pseudocode is based on numerical integration theory:

> Determine the base length for each trapezoid
> For each trapezoid
>   Calculate its area
>   Add its area to the summation of trapezoid areas
> Return the summation of the trapezoid areas

When calculating trapezoid area, the values of h1 and h2 are required. This task is substantial enough to require another function, f(), which returns a y-value based on parameters FunctionNum and x. f() uses a switch statement to select the correct mathematical function.

The final design can be represented as:

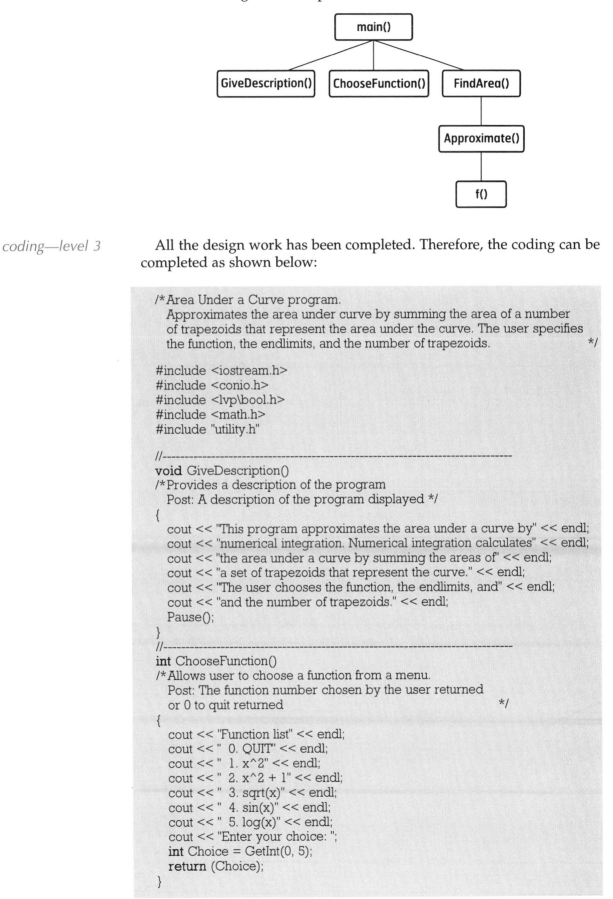

coding—level 3

All the design work has been completed. Therefore, the coding can be completed as shown below:

```
/*Area Under a Curve program.
   Approximates the area under curve by summing the area of a number
   of trapezoids that represent the area under the curve. The user specifies
   the function, the endlimits, and the number of trapezoids.            */

#include <iostream.h>
#include <conio.h>
#include <lvp\bool.h>
#include <math.h>
#include "utility.h"

//-------------------------------------------------------------------------
void GiveDescription()
/*Provides a description of the program
   Post: A description of the program displayed */
{
   cout << "This program approximates the area under a curve by" << endl;
   cout << "numerical integration. Numerical integration calculates" << endl;
   cout << "the area under a curve by summing the areas of" << endl;
   cout << "a set of trapezoids that represent the curve." << endl;
   cout << "The user chooses the function, the endlimits, and" << endl;
   cout << "and the number of trapezoids." << endl;
   Pause();
}
//-------------------------------------------------------------------------
int ChooseFunction()
/*Allows user to choose a function from a menu.
   Post: The function number chosen by the user returned
   or 0 to quit returned                                              */
{
   cout << "Function list" << endl;
   cout << " 0. QUIT" << endl;
   cout << " 1. x^2" << endl;
   cout << " 2. x^2 + 1" << endl;
   cout << " 3. sqrt(x)" << endl;
   cout << " 4. sin(x)" << endl;
   cout << " 5. log(x)" << endl;
   cout << "Enter your choice: ";
   int Choice = GetInt(0, 5);
   return (Choice);
}
```

```
//--------------------------------------------------------------------
double f(int FunctionNum, double x)
/* Returns the value of the function at x
   Pre: FunctionNum represents a valid function
   f(x) is defined for the function
   Post: The value of the function at x is returned or
   0 if FunctionNum is not valid.                                  */
{
  switch (FunctionNum) {
    case 1: return(x*x);
    case 2: return(x*x + 1);
    case 3: return(sqrt(x));
    case 4: return(sin(x));
    case 5: return(log(x));
    default: return(0);
  }
}
//--------------------------------------------------------------------
double Approximate(int FunctionNum, double LowLimit,
                    double HighLimit, int NumTraps)
/* Approximates the area under a curve using trapezoids
   Pre: FunctionNum is a defined function
   LowLimit..HighLimit values are defined for the function
   NumTraps >= 1
   Post: The area under the function between LowLimit and
   HighLimit returned                                            */
{
  double TrapWidth = (HighLimit – LowLimit)/NumTraps;
  double x = LowLimit;
  double Area = 0;
  for (int TrapCount = 1; TrapCount <= NumTraps; TrapCount++) {
    Area += 0.5*(f(FunctionNum, x)+f(FunctionNum, x+TrapWidth))
            *TrapWidth;
    x += TrapWidth;
  }
  return(Area);
}
//--------------------------------------------------------------------
void FindArea(int FunctionNum)
/* Prompts user for endlimits and the number of trapezoids to use,
   and then calculates and displays the area under the curve
   FunctionNum using these values
   Post: area of selected function returned                        */
{
  double LowLimit, HighLimit, Area;
  int NumTraps;
  cout << "Enter the low limit: ";
  cin >> LowLimit;
  cout << "Enter the high limit: ";
  cin >> HighLimit;
  cout << "Enter the number of trapezoids: ";
  cin >> NumTraps;
  Area = Approximate(FunctionNum, LowLimit, HighLimit, NumTraps);
  cout << "The area is approximately " << Area << endl;
  Pause();
}
```

```
//-----------------------------------------------------------------
int main()
{
   GiveDescription();
   while (true) {
      clrscr();
      int FunctionNum = ChooseFunction();
      if (FunctionNum == 0)
         break;
      FindArea(FunctionNum);
   }
   return(0);
}
```

Because of the use of clrscr() it is hard to show a full run of this program on paper. However, a portion is shown below:

```
Function list
   0. QUIT
   1. x^2
   2. x^2 + 1
   3. sqrt(x)
   4. sin(x)
   5. log(x)
Enter your choice: 4
Enter the low limit: 0
Enter the high limit: 3.14
Enter the number of trapezoids: 20
The area is approximately 1.99589
Press a key to continue
```

Review 17

Suppose that, in violation of the precondition, Approximate() is called with a negative value for NumTraps. What would be the result? Modify the Case Study so that the user must enter a positive value for the number of trapezoids.

Review 18

Modify the Case Study to include three more mathematical functions: x^3, exp(x), and fabs(x).

Review 19

The Case Study used trapezoids in approximating the area under a curve. Another method of approximating the area under a curve uses rectangles rather than trapezoids. The height of each rectangle is taken to be the height of the curve at the midpoint of the rectangle. Modify the Case Study to implement this method. Compare the results obtained from each method.

Chapter Summary

This chapter introduced many of the functions available in the math library. These functions included pow(), sqrt(), abs(), and fabs(). Trigonometric functions are also available in math.h These include tan(), sin(), and cos() and the inverse trigonometric functions atan(), asin(), and acos(). Logarithmic and exponentiation functions include log(), log10(), and exp(). Online help can be used to learn more about the math library.

The precision of double values is limited due to roundoff error. An equality should not be used to compare doubles. If an equality comparison must be made, it should be done with a tolerance included for an acceptable difference.

Type casting can be used in a function that rounds a double.

Recursion is a programming technique that can be used whenever a problem can be solved by solving one or more smaller versions of the same problem. Infinite recursion occurs if a stopping condition has not been included in a recursive function. The Towers of Hanoi can be solved using a recursive function.

A computer stores characters through a standard conversion called the ASCII code. In C++, casting integer values into characters results in the ASCII character corresponding to the integer.

An enumerated type is a named set of constants that can make a program easier to read and modify. Enumerated types are created using the keyword enum. When using enumerated types functions should be written to handle reading and writing them.

The switch statement controls program flow and is especially useful for handling enumerated types.

Vocabulary

ASCII American Standard Code for Information Interchange. Specifies a character equivalent for every decimal value below 127.

Extended Characters Character equivalents for decimal values above 127.

Infinite Recursion A recursive function call in which no stopping point has been designated.

Integration Technique for finding the area under a curve. See Numerical Integration.

Numerical Integration A technique in which the area under a curve is determined by representing the area as a number trapezoids and then summing the areas of the trapezoids.

Recursion A programming technique that can be used whenever a problem can be solved by solving one or more smaller versions of the same problem. A process by which a function calls itself.

Recursive Call A function call in which the calling function is the same as the function being called.

Roundoff Error An error in representation of a double because the computer cannot exactly represent values with decimal portions.

C++

abs() A function in the math library that returns the absolute value of an integer x.

acos() A function in the math library that returns the arcosine of x in radians.

asin() A function in the math library that returns the arcsine of x in radians.

atan() A function in the math library that returns the arctangent of x in radians.

cos() A function in the math library that returns the cosine of x, an angle in radians.

enum Keyword used to define an enumerated type.

exp() A function in the math library that raises *e* to the power of x.

fabs() A function in the math library that returns the absolute value of a double x.

log() A function in the math library that returns the natural logarithm of x.

log10() A function in the math library that returns the base 10 logarithm of x.

pow() A function in the math library that returns x to the power of y.

sin() A function in the math library that returns the sine of x, an angle in radians.

sqrt() A function in the math library that returns the square root of x.

switch Statement used to control program flow.

tan() A function in the math library that returns the tangent of x, an angle in radians.

Exercises

Exercise 1

Write a program that displays a table of powers as follows:

```
x     x^2     x^3     x^4     x^5
1      1       1       1       1
2      4       8      16      32
3      9      27      81     243
4     16      64     256    1024
5     25     125     625    3125
6     36     216    1296    7776
```

Exercise 2

Write a boolean function IsFactor() that takes two integers parameters and returns true if and only if the first is a factor of the second. A factor of a number is an integer value which divides evenly into the number. For example, 3 is a factor of 9 but 4 is not.

Exercise 3

Write a program that displays all perfect integers up to 100. A perfect integer is a number which is equal to the sum of all its factors except itself. For example, 6 is a perfect number because $1 + 2 + 3 = 6$. Write a boolean function IsPerfect() to use in the program.

Exercise 4

Write a program that compares the square of the square root of a number with the number itself, for all whole numbers from 1 to 100. If they are not equal, have the program display the original number and the difference between the two values. What could cause this?

Exercise 5

Write a program that gives the solution to any quadratic equation. Have the program accept values for a, b, and c ($ax^2 + bx + c = 0$) and then display the roots, if any. Recall the quadratic formula:

$$\frac{-b \pm \sqrt{b^2 - 4ac}}{2a}$$

7

Exercise 6   *trigonometry required*

a) Write a function SinD() that returns the sine of its argument, an angle given in degrees.

b) Write a function CosD() that returns the cosine of its argument, an angle given in degrees.

c) Write a program that calls SinD() and CosD() to produce a table of sine and cosine values for all angles from 0 to 360 degrees in 10 degree increments.

Exercise 7   *trigonometry required*

a) Write a function Quadrant() that takes the X and Y coordinates of a point as parameters and returns either 1, 2, 3, or 4 depending upon the Cartesian quadrant the point lies in.

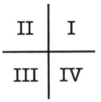

b) Write a function RectToPolar() that takes the X and Y coordinates of a point and returns (using reference parameters) the radius R and angle θ of the point in polar coordinates. The formulae are:

$$R = sqrt(X^2 + Y^2) \qquad θ = atan(Y/X)$$

In finding θ, be sure to consider the quadrant of the angle and the value of X.

c) Write a function PolarToRect() that takes the radius and angle θ of a point in polar coordinates and returns the X, Y Cartesian coordinates of the point. The formulae are:

$$X = R * cos(θ) \qquad Y = R * sin(θ)$$

In finding X and Y, be sure to consider the quadrant of the angle to determine the signs of X and Y.

d) Write a program that contains the functions from (a) through (c) above and gives the user an opportunity to test each one via a menu.

Exercise 8

A Pythagorean triple is a set of three integers that fits the equation $A^2 + B^2 = C^2$. Use PerfectSquare() from Review 2 in a program that displays all Pythagorean triples with values of A and B less than 100. (Hint: You will need to generate all possible combinations of A and B and display just those that work.)

Exercise 9

The following formula can be used to calculate powers:

$$X^Y = \exp(Y * \log(X))$$

Write a function MyPow() and compare the output to that produced by pow() from the math library for a variety of values.

Exercise 10

Can the body of the Round() function in Section 7.6 be replaced with the single line below?

```
return(int(x+0.5));
```

Compare the results of this version with those of the one in the text, and explain.

Exercise 11

A faster recursive IntPower() function can be constructed by using the equations:

$$X^N = (X^{N/2})^2 \text{ for even values of N}$$

$$X^N = X * (X^{N/2})^2 \text{ for odd values of N}$$

If one is careful to calculate the value of $X^{N/2}$ only once and then square it, this is much more efficient than the algorithm used in the chapter. Use this algorithm to construct a new IntPower() function.

Exercise 12

Consider the following recursive function:

```
void Exer(int N)
{
   cout << "Starting " << N << endl;
   if (N > 0) {
      Exer(N/3);
      cout << "Middle " << N << endl;
   }
}
```

What output is generated when it is called with Exer(13)? with Exer(3)? With Exer(0)?

Exercise 13

Consider the following recursive function:

```
void Exer(int N)
{
   cout << N << endl;
   if (N > 0) {
      if (N % 2 == 1)
         Exer(N/3);
      else
         Exer(N/2);
   }
}
```

What output is generated when it is called with Exer(13)? with Exer(14)? With Exer(15)?

Exercise 14

Consider the following recursive function:

```
void Exer(int N)
{
   if (N > 0) {
      Exer(N/10);
      cout << (N % 10);
   }
}
```

What output is generated when it is called with Exer(13)? with Exer(124)? With Exer(21785)? State, in general, what this function does.

Exercise 15

Describe the output of the following function when the user enters the characters T, E, S, T, . ?

```
void WhatzItDo()
{
   char ch = getche();
   if (ch != '.') {
      WhatzItDo();
      cout << ch;
   }
   else
      cout << endl;
}
```

State, in general, what this function does.

Exercise 16

Write a recursive function SumUp() that returns the sum of all positive integers less than or equal to its argument. Use the idea that the sum of all numbers from 1 to N is equal to the N plus the sum of all numbers from 1 to N-1.

Exercise 17

Write a recursive function NumDigits() that returns the number of digits in its integer parameter. Numbers –9 through 9 have one digit; numbers –99 to –10 and 10 to 99 have two digits, and so on. (Hint: the number of digits of a number N is one more than the number of digits in N/10.)

Exercise 18

Newton's method is taught in calculus classes as a way of finding roots of functions. One application is in finding cube roots. To do this, take an initial guess (say 1.00) and generate a new guess at the root using the formula:

$$NewGuess = OldGuess - (pow(OldGuess, 3)-N)/(3*pow(OldGuess, 2))$$

where N is the number whose root is to be determined. The NewGuess becomes the old guess in the next round. For example, if N=29 and the initial guess is 1.00, the next guess is:

$$NewGuess = 1.0 - (1.0*1.0*1.0 - 29)/(3*1.0*1.0)$$

$$= 10.3333$$

which is then put in the equation to get the next guess:

$$NewGuess = 10.3333 - (10.3333*10.3333*10.3333 - 29)/(3*10.3333*10.3333)$$

$$= 6.97941959$$

Write a function to find cube roots using this process. Repeat the process until two consecutive guesses are equal within 0.000001.

Exercise 19

You are a spy who will use the computer to produce a secret code. A simple code can be produced by replacing each letter in a message with another letter several letters later in the alphabet. For example, 'A' could be replaced with 'D', 'B' with 'E', and so on, replacing 'X' with 'A', 'Y' with 'B', and finally 'Z' with 'C'. Write a function Code() that takes a character and an integer as arguments and returns the coded character using the system described. For example,

```
cout << Code('A', 3) ;
```

should display:

```
D
```

You may assume that the integer value is between 1 and 25 inclusive, and that the character is an uppercase letter.

7

Exercise 20

The Approximate() function in the Case Study returns an approximation of the area under a curve. A better approximation can be calculated by increasing the number of trapezoids used. This process can be repeated using an even greater number of trapezoids, and so on. Write a function PerfectArea() that uses Approximate() to produce a "perfect" approximation. The idea is to call Approximate() repeatedly with greater and greater numbers of trapezoids until two consecutive calls return similar numbers. By similar, we mean within 0.00001 of each other. Start with eight trapezoids, and each time the function is called, double the number of trapezoids. Modify the Case Study to include PerfectArea(). Allow the user to test this function by allowing a response of zero when asked for the number of trapezoids to use.

Advanced
Exercise 21

A *root* of a mathematical function is the x-value that makes the function equal to zero. With some functions, it is easy to find the root or roots. For example, the root of 2x + 6 is the value –3 because the function is zero when x is –3. For other functions, the root may be harder to find. Visually, the root is where the curve crosses the x-axis, as shown below:

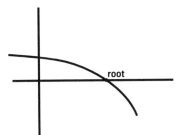

The method of finding roots by *bisection* is as follows. Begin with two x-values, low and high, that have corresponding y-values that are of different signs. That is, one value produces a y-value that is above the x-axis, and the other produces a y-value that is below the x-axis. This means that the curve must cross the x-axis somewhere between the two points.

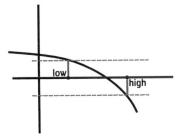

Calculate the midpoint of the two x-values, and determine whether its y-value is above or below the x-axis. Choose to make this midpoint the new high or new low so that the high and low continue to be on different sides of the x-axis. In our example, the midpoint has a y-value above the x-axis, so it becomes a new low.

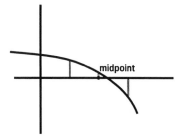

Continue this process until the low and high x-values are within 0.000001 of each other.

Modify the Case Study to display the roots of an equation using bisection. Have the program ask the user whether roots or areas are desired. If roots are chosen, low and high values must be obtained from the user. The program must verify that the low and high values are on opposite sides of the x-axis. Use the same set of functions as in the current Case Study.

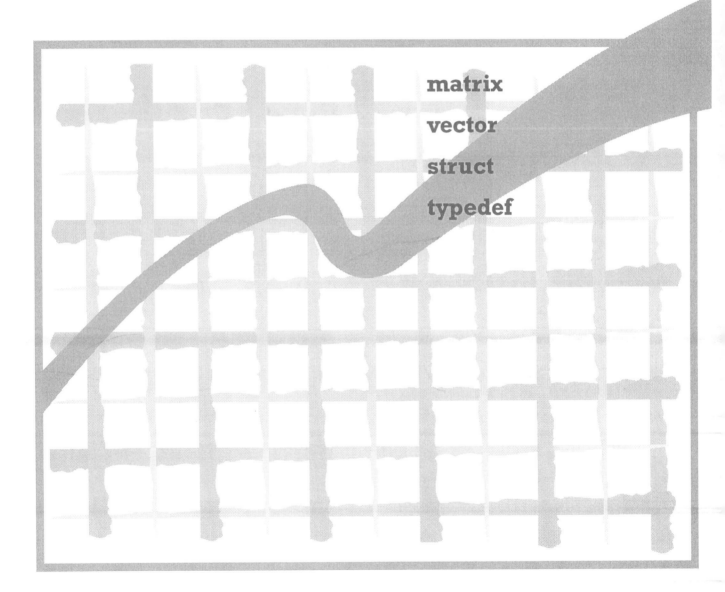

matrix

vector

struct

typedef

Objectives

After completing this chapter you will be able to:

1. Use arrays to store values.

2. Implement arrays using the vector class.

3. Understand range errors.

4. Search an array for a specific value.

5. Use dynamic arrays.

6. Use a typedef statement to associate an identifier with a type.

7. Manipulate a String object as an array of chars.

8. Employ arrays with meaningful indexes.

9. Use two-dimensional arrays to represent a matrix.

10. Use the struct statement to create a user-defined type.

11. Understand three-dimensional arrays.

8

$\mathbf{I}$n this chapter you will learn about array and matrix data types for storing many values of the same type. The struct statement will be used to create user-defined types that can store many values of different types. The typedef statement will be used to simplify code.

8.1 The Array Type

An *array*, sometimes called a *vector*, is a data type that can store many values. For example, a variable of type String can store only one string, but a String array can store many strings:

string Name | Tristan |

string NameArray | Tristan | Chris | Jodi | Connie | Don | Debi |

A value in an array is accessed by giving its *index* number in the array. In C++, the index number is given in square brackets, and counting starts from zero. For example, the statement

```
cout << NameArray[1];
```

displays

```
Chris
```

because Chris is the second value in array NameArray. The second item has an index number of 1 since counting begins at zero.

C++ has a built-in array type that is widely regarded as difficult to use and prone to error. Therefore, in this text the vector library will be used to implement arrays, as described in the next section.

8.2 The vector Library

array type

template

The vector library supplied with this text contains the vector class to implement an array type. The vector class is a class template that allows creation of arrays of any type. A *template* is a body of code in which one or more types are initially left unspecified. These types are specified when the template is actually used. For example, the following statement instantiates a vector object:

```
vector<String> NameArray(6);
```

More simply, this statement declares an array NameArray that can contain six strings, indexed from 0 to 5. The portion <String> specifies the type to be used by the template. The type is specified in angle brackets directly after the class name.

Following is the vector class documentation:

vector (vector.h)

Constructors
```
vector();
/*Creates an array of capacity 0
   Post: An array of a capacity of 0 items created.
   Array will need to be resized                        */

vector(int size);
/*Creates an array of capacity size
   Post: An array of a capacity of  size items created. */

vector(int size, const ItemType &FillValue);
/*Creates an array of capacity size with each element
   containing FillValue
   Post: An array of a capacity of size items with each element
   containing FillValue created.                         */
```

Functions
```
int length();
/*Determines the size of the array
   Post: Size of array returned      */

void resize(int NewSize);
/*Resizes an array
   Pre: NewSize >= 0
   Post: Array resized to NewSize */
```

Operators
```
[ ]    Returns the item at the index number in [ ]
 =     Assigns one array to another.
```

The following program demonstrates the vector class:

```
/* vector class demonstration program */

#include <iostream.h>
#include <lvp\string.h>
#include <lvp\vector.h>

int main()
{
  const int NumItems = 3;
  vector<String> NameArray(NumItems);
  int Index;

  // Load array
  for (Index=0; Index<NumItems; Index++) {
    cout << "Enter a name: ";
    cin >> NameArray[Index];
  }
```

```
// Display array
for (Index=0; Index<NumItems; Index++)
   cout << NameArray[Index] << endl;
return(0);
}
```

A constant value, NumItems, is used for the number of items stored in the array. This clarifies the code and makes it easier to change the number of values if needed. The for loops access elements 0 through 4 (NumItems–1) of the array, since array indexing starts at zero.

When run, program output may look similar to:

```
Enter a name: Angelou
Enter a name: Austin
Enter a name: Dickinson
Angelou
Austin
Dickinson
```

8.3 Range Errors

In an array declared with 10 elements, only references to indices 0 through 9 are permissible. If code refers to any index outside this range, program execution is stopped with a run-time error. For example, the following code will generate a run-time error because it references index 12 when only indices 0 through 9 are permitted:

```
#include <iostream.h>
#include <lvp\vector.h>

int main()
{
   vector<char> Foo(10);
   cout << "Starting" << endl;
   Foo[12] = 'x';      // Error here!
   cout << "Ending" << endl;
   return(0);
}
```

Review 1 ───────────────────────────────────────

Write declarations for an array storing 12 int values, an array storing 100 double values, and an array storing 80 char values.

Review 2 ───────────────────────────────────────

What is the output of the following program segment?

```
vector<int> Num(3);
Num[0] = 23;
Num[1] = 61;
Num[2] = 98;
cout << Num[0] << '|' << Num[1] << endl;
cout << Num[0] + Num[1] << '|' << Num[0+1] << endl;
Num[1] = Num[2];
Num[2] = Num[0];
Num[0] = Num[1];
cout << Num[0] << '|' << Num[1] << '|' << Num[2] << endl;
```

Review 3

Modify the vector class demonstration program to include an array VoteArray that stores five long values. Have the program ask the user for the number of votes associated with each name, and then display a table. The program output should be similar to:

```
Enter name: Pooh
Enter votes: 123
Enter name: Piglet
Enter votes: 32
. . .
Results:
Pooh        123
Piglet       32
. . .
```

8.4 The vector Member Functions

To better understand the vector member functions, examples involving each of the functions are given below.

resize()

The resize() member function is used to modify the size of an array during program execution. For example, the statement

```
NameArray.resize(10);    //Array now holds 10 names, indexed from 0 to 9
```

allows NameArray to hold 10 values. If an array is resized to be smaller, values after the new maximum index are discarded. If an array is resized to be larger, the original items are maintained, and space for additional items is made available.

length()

Since the size of an array may vary during a program run, it is sometimes necessary to determine the current array size. The length() member function is used to do this, as in the statement:

```
cout << "The array now holds " << NameArray.length() << endl;
```

length() is also used in loops that process an array, as in the statement:

```
for (int Index=0; Index<NameArray.length(); Index++)
    cout << NameArray[Index] << endl;
```

Note that the loop executes until one less than the length since array indexing starts at zero.

assignment

The assignment operator member function allows one array to be assigned to another. The sizes of the arrays need not be the same before the assignment. After the assignment, they both hold the same number of values and the same values. For example, the statements

```
vector<double> BigArray(100), SmallArray(10);

// Code here to put values in SmallArray
BigArray = SmallArray;
cout << BigArray.length() << endl; // Displays 10
```

display

```
10
```

8.5 vector Parameters

Like other C++ object parameters, it is usually best to pass arrays as reference parameters. If a function should not modify the array, the array should be passed as a const parameter.

The syntax of a template class object parameter requires the object type be given in angle brackets. The following program asks the user for values and then displays the average of the values using two functions with vector parameters:

```
/*Average of Array Elements program */

#include <iostream.h>
#include <lvp\vector.h>


//-------------------------------------------------------------------
double SumOfItems(const vector<double> &NumArray)
/*Returns the sum of all values in NumArray
   Post: Sum of values in NumArray returned          */
{
  double Sum = 0;
  for (int Index=0; Index<NumArray.length(); Index++)
    Sum += NumArray[Index];
  return(Sum);
}
//-------------------------------------------------------------------
void LoadArray(vector<double> &NumArray)
/*Loads all elements of NumArray with values entered by user
   Post: NumArray contains values entered by user          */
{
  for (int Index = 0; Index<NumArray.length(); Index++) {
    cout << "Enter number " << Index << ": ";
    cin >> NumArray[Index];
  }
}
//-------------------------------------------------------------------
int main()
{
  const int NumItems = 5;
  vector<double> DataArray(NumItems);

  LoadArray(DataArray);
  cout << "Average is " << (SumOfItems(DataArray)/DataArray.length());
  return(0);
}
```

SumOfItems() and LoadArray() both use reference parameters. However, SumOfItems() does not need to change the array, so its reference parameter is a const.

When run, program output may look similar to:

```
Enter number 0: 78.6
Enter number 1: 87.5
Enter number 2: 105.7
Enter number 3: 55.6
Enter number 4: 67.8
Average is 79.04
```

Review 4

Modify Review 3 so that it uses two functions: LoadData() and DisplayResults().

Review 5

Most users prefer to count from one on up rather than from zero. Modify the program in Section 8.5 to display prompts similar to the following:

```
Enter number 1: 78.6
Enter number 2: 87.5
Enter number 3: 105.7
Enter number 4: 55.6
Enter number 5: 67.8
Average is 79.04
```

8.6 vector Constructors

The vector class template contains three constructors. The constructor used so far requires one parameter specifying the array size. A second constructor allows an additional parameter specifying a value to be stored in each array element. For example, the statements

```
vector<double> ValueArray(10, 0);
vector<String> NameArray(30, "Empty");
```

create an array ValueArray with 10 elements each containing a value of 0, and an array NameArray with 30 elements each containing a string Empty.

default constructor   A third constructor, called the *default constructor*, takes no parameters and creates an array with zero elements. This constructor is useful when the size of an array is unknown at the start of a program. For example, the statement

```
vector<double> DataArray;
```

creates an array of zero double elements. An array with zero elements must be resized in order to be used. The resize() member function can be used to change the array size.

Review 6

Modify the Average of Array Elements program to allow the user to specify the number of items to be entered. Have the program declare an array to a size of zero, and then resize it once the number of values desired is obtained from the user. The program output should look similar to:

```
How many numbers to enter? 7
Enter number 0: 78.6
Enter number 1: 87.5
Enter number 2: 105.7
Enter number 3: 55.6
Enter number 4: 67.8
Enter number 5: 15.7
Enter number 6: 59.0
Average is 67.1286
```

8.7 Searching an Array

linear search

There are many ways to search an array for a specific value. The simplest searching algorithm is called *linear search* and works by proceeding from one element to the next through the array until the desired value is found or the entire array has been searched. The function FindItemIndex() below uses this algorithm:

```
int FindItemIndex(const vector<String> Array, const String Goal)
/*Returns the index of the first occurrence of Goal in Array,
    or -1 if Goal not in Array.
    Post: The index of the first occurrence of Goal in Array returned,
    or -1 returned if Goal not in Array                              */
{
  for (int i=0; i<Array.length(); i++)
    if (Array[i] == Goal)
      return(i);
  return(-1);
}
```

If the Goal is found, its index is returned and the function terminates. If the loop completes without finding Goal, the value -1 is returned.

8.8 Dynamic Arrays

A *dynamic array* varies in size throughout program execution. For example, when the maximum size of an array is unknown at run time, a dynamic array must be used. The vector class template allows for dynamic arrays through assignment and resize(). A program that uses a dynamic array creates an array of zero elements and then uses functions similar to the following to add to and delete from the array:

```
void AddToArray(vector<String> &Array, const String &ValToAdd)
/*Increases size of Array by 1 and adds ValToAdd to Array
   as the last element
   Post: Array length increased by 1 and ValToAdd is last element of array */
{
  Array.resize(Array.length()+1);
  Array[Array.length()-1] = ValToAdd;
}
//-----------------------------------------------------------------------------
void RemoveFromArray(vector<String> &Array, const String &ValToDelete)
/*Deletes ValToDelete from Array and decreases size of Array by 1
   Pre: Array is of size >= 1. ValToDelete is present in Array.
   Post: Array length has decreased by 1 and ValToDelete is removed */
{
  int Index=FindItemIndex(Array, ValToDelete);
  for(; Index<Array.length()-1; Index++)
    Array[Index]=Array[Index+1];
  Array.resize(Array.length()-1);
}
```

Note that RemoveFromArray() uses FindItemIndex() from Section 8.7 to determine the index of the element to delete.

Review 7

Write a program that uses a dynamic array to add and delete names to an array. Have the program allow the user to find names. Initially, the array should contain no names. When run, program output should look similar to:

```
Choose action (Add/Delete/Find/Quit):A
Enter name to add: Zaphod
Choose action (Add/Delete/Find/Quit):A
Enter name to add: Trillian
Choose action (Add/Delete/Find/Quit):F
Enter name to find: Adams
Not found.
Choose action (Add/Delete/Find/Quit):F
Enter name to find: Trillian
Found in location 1
Choose action (Add/Delete/Find/Quit):D
Enter name to delete: Zaphod
Choose action (Add/Delete/Find/Quit):F
Enter name to find: Trillian
Found in location 0
Choose action (Add/Delete/Find/Quit):Q
```

8.9 Using typedef

A typedef statement allows an identifier to be associated with a type. typedefs may make code easier to understand for the reader and less prone to error. The typedef statement takes the form

typedef *type identifier;*

where *type* is a built-in C++ type or a user-defined type, and *identifier* is a legal C++ identifier. For example, the statement

typedef String ItemType;

establishes that the name ItemType represents the type String. With this statement, the AddToArray() function header in Section 8.8 can be written:

void AddToArray(vector<ItemType> &Array, const ItemType &ValToAdd)

typedef can also be used to define names for more complex types. For example, the statements:

typedef String ItemType;
typedef vector<ItemType> ArrayType;

define the name ArrayType to represent a vector of String values. With these definitions, an array can be declared like:

ArrayType MyList;

and the AddToArray() header can be written more simply as:

void AddToArray(ArrayType &Array, const ItemType &ValToAdd)

typedef declarations must come before any functions that use the defined type. Therefore, they are usually placed at the beginning of a program before any function definitions. For example:

```
/*typedef program */

#include <iostream.h>
#include <lvp\string.h>
#include <lvp\vector.h>

typedef String ItemType;

//-------------------------------------------------------------------------
// Definitions of functions, i.e. AddToArray()
//-------------------------------------------------------------------------

int main()
{
  // Variable definitions, possibly using ItemType
  // Statements
  return(0);
}
```

Review 8

Modify Review 7 to use typedef statements for both ItemType and ArrayType. Demonstrate the fact that changing a single statement will convert the program from manipulating an array of strings to an array of integers.

8.10 Strings as Arrays

A String object can be manipulated as an array of chars. For example, the statements

```
String FirstName = "Tristan";
cout << FirstName[2];
```

display

```
i
```

As an array of chars, a String can be displayed in reverse with a simple for statement

```
for (int Letter=FirstName.length()-1; Letter>=0; Letter--)
  cout << FirstName[Letter];
```

that in this case displays:

```
natsirT
```

Uppercase()

Many useful functions can be written based on the array properties of a String. For example, a function to allow string comparisons that are not case sensitive. With this function, the strings "apple," "APPLE," and "Apple" would be recognized as the same. The following program uses this function:

```
/* Compare Strings program */

#include <iostream.h>
#include <lvp\string.h>

//-----------------------------------------------------------------------------
String Uppercase(String S)
/* Returns a copy of S with all lowercase characters converted to
   uppercase characters
   Post: String in all uppercase letters returned                    */
{
  for (int Letter=0; Letter<S.length(); Letter++)
    if ((S[Letter]>='a') && (S[Letter]<='z'))
      S[Letter]=S[Letter]-'a'+'A';
  return(S);
}
//-----------------------------------------------------------------------------
int main()
{
  String String1, String2;
  cout << "Enter a string: ";
  cin >> String1;
  cout << "Enter another string: ";
  cin >> String2;
  if (Uppercase(String1)==Uppercase(String2))
    cout << "Strings are equal." << endl;
  else
    cout << "Strings are not equal." << endl;
  return(0);
}
```

When run, program output may look similar to:

```
Enter a string: Apple
Enter another string: apple
Strings are equal.
```

The vector library is not included in this program because the String class automatically creates a String object as an array of chars. In Uppercase(), S is a value parameter so that a local copy is made. This local copy is then manipulated, and returned by the function.

Review 9

Write a function Reverse() that returns the reverse of its single String argument. For example, if the argument is "able," it should return "elba."

Review 10

Write a function Palindrome() that returns true if its string argument is the same backwards and forwards, regardless of case. For example, Palindrome() should return true for "Dad" and "Mom," and false for "kids." Palindrome() may make calls to Reverse() and Uppercase().

8 | 8.11 Arrays with Meaningful Indexes

An array's structure can be thought of as a set of storage boxes where each box stores only certain information. This scenario uses the indexes as labels for that array's data. Many algorithms make use of this aspect of an array's structure to simplify storage, as demonstrated in the following program.

To analyze a sequence of rolls of a pair of dice, the number of times for each outcome could be stored in an int array at the index number corresponding to the outcome. For example, if the array is called Count, then the number of 2s rolled will be stored in Count[2], the number of 3s in Count[3], and so on. The program below simulates 1000 dice rolls and then displays the counts of each possible outcome:

```
/* Dice Rolls program */

#include <iostream.h>
#include <lvp\vector.h>
#include <lvp\random.h>

typedef vector<int> CountType;

//-----------------------------------------------------------------------
void DisplayCounts(const CountType &Count)
/*Displays the contents of Count[2] through Count[12] in two columns
   Post: Contents of Count displayed                                    */
{
  cout << "Roll" << " " << "Count" << endl;
  for (int Roll=2; Roll<=12; Roll++) {
    cout << Roll << "    " << Count[Roll] << endl;
  }
}
//-----------------------------------------------------------------------
void CountTrials(CountType &Count, int NumTrials)
/*Simulates NumTrials rolls of two dice and stores the counts of each
   outcome in Count
   Post: NumTrials dice rolls simulated. Count of outcomes of NumTrial
   simulated rolls stored in Count                                      */
{
  for (int Trial=1; Trial<=NumTrials; Trial++) {
    int Roll = (random(6) + 1) + (random(6) + 1);
    Count[Roll]++;
  }
}
//-----------------------------------------------------------------------
int main()
{
  randomize();
  CountType Count(13, 0);  // Array with indexes 0 through 12,
                           // each element initialized to 0
  const int NumTrials = 1000;
  CountTrials(Count, NumTrials);
  DisplayCounts(Count);
  return(0);
}
```

In CountTrials(), the statement

```
Roll = (random(6) + 1) + (random(6) + 1);
```

generates a random roll of two dice, and then the outcome of the trial is used to update a counter in the statement:

```
Count[Roll]++;
```

In this statement, one is added to the location in Count corresponding to the roll outcome. If a three was rolled, Count[3] is incremented. There is no need to search for the location where the 3s are counted since the index is used as a label.

A typedef statement was used to create a name, CountType, to represent the array. The elements of the Count array were initialized to zero using the vector constructor.

When run, program output may look similar to:

Roll	Count
2	21
3	71
4	90
5	114
6	151
7	151
8	145
9	94
10	74
11	56
12	33

offsetting indexes   In the Dice Rolls program, the outcomes ranged from 2 through 12 making it possible to store counters at array indexes directly corresponding to the outcomes. However, this approach for a range of years 1900 through 2000 would require an array of 2001 elements with only the last 100 elements in use. For ranges such as these, the solution is to store counters at offset array indexes. For example, for an outcome of 1900, a counter at index 0 would be updated. For an outcome of 1901, a counter at index 1 would be updated, and so on.

A standard way of formulating the array size to handle an offset is:

```
vector<int> Count(High–Low+1);
```

where High is the highest value in the range and Low is the lowest value in the range. The following statement updates a counter stored at an offset index:

```
Count[Value–Low]++;
```

A program that counts the frequency of uppercase characters in a string could use an array to store the counts. To further simplify storage of the counters, the indexes could be used to determine which counter corresponds to which letter. For example, the letter A in ASCII is 65, B is 66, and so on. Therefore, the counters could be stored at offset array indexes corresponding to the ASCII equivalent of uppercase letters. The Uppercase Characters program implements this algorithm:

```
/* Uppercase Characters program */

#include <iostream.h>
#include <lvp\vector.h>
#include <lvp\string.h>

int main()
{
  const char Low = 'A';
  const char High = 'Z';
  vector<int> Count(High–Low+1, 0);

  String S;
  cout << "Enter a string:" << endl;
  getline(cin, S);

  // Count frequency of uppercase characters
  for (int index=0; index<S.length(); index++) {
    char Letter = S[index];
    if ((Letter >= Low) && (Letter <=High))
      Count[Letter–Low]++;
  }

  // Display counts
  for (char Letter=Low; Letter<=High; Letter++)
    cout << Letter << " " << Count[Letter–Low] << endl;

  return(0);
}
```

In the declaration of Count, C++ automatically typecast the characters to ints to determine the size of the array. Automatic typecasting came into effect again when the elements of Count were accessed (Count[Letter–Low]). Here is part of a sample run:

```
Enter a string:
THE QUICK BROWN FOX JUMPS OVER THE LAZY DOG.
A  1
B  1
C  1
D  1
E  3
F  1
G  1
H  2
I  1
J  1
K  1
L  1

. . .
```

Review 11

Modify the Dice Rolls program so that it allows the user to specify the number of trials to make, and displays the results as percentages. The program output should look similar to:

```
Enter number or trials to perform: 2000
Roll  Percent
   2     2.1%
   3     4.5%
   4    10.2%
...
```

Review 12

Modify the Dice Rolls program so that it counts rolls of three dice rather than two and displays the counts of each roll. The program output should look similar to:

```
Roll  Count
   3     20
   4     43
   5    110
...
```

Review 13

Write a complete set of definitions to create an array that would store the number of times the word "Internet" appeared in the New York Times during each of the years 1960 through 1996.

8.12 The matrix Library

two-dimensional array

Two-dimensional arrays are used to represent a *matrix*, or two-dimensional grid of information. For example, a checkerboard, a tic-tac-toe board, a system of streets and avenues, and the seats in a theater can be represented in a two-dimensional grid.

matrix type

The matrix library supplied with this text contains the matrix class to implement a two-dimensional array type called matrix.

Like the vector class, matrix is a class template that allows creation of two-dimensional arrays of any type. For example, the following statement instantiates a matrix object:

matrix<char> Board(3, 3);

More simply, this statement declares a two-dimensional array Board that can contain nine chars. The first argument is the number of rows, and the second is the number of columns. The following illustrates a matrix with a character stored in each element:

```
     0   1   2
  0 | X | O | O |
  1 | X | X | X |
  2 | O | X | O |
```

To access a matrix element, both its column and row numbers must be given in square brackets. For example, the statement

    cout << Board[0][1]

displays the element in the first row and the second column:

    O

Following is the matrix class documentation:

matrix (matrix.h)

Constructors
matrix();
/*Creates a matrix of capacity 0
   Post: A matrix of a capacity of 0 items created.
   Matrix will need to be resized   */

matrix(int rows, int cols);
/*Creates a matrix of rows rows by cols columns
   Post: A matrix of a capacity of rows rows by cols
   columns items created.   */

matrix(int rows, int cols, const ItemType &FillValue);
/*Creates a matrix of capacity rows rows by cols columns
   with each element containing FillValue
   Post: An array of a capacity of rows rows by cols columns
   with each element containing FillValue created.   */

Functions
int numrows();
/*Determines the number of rows in the matrix
   Post: Number of rows in matrix returned   */

int numcols();
/*Determines the number of columns in the matrix
   Post: Number of columns in matrix returned   */

void resize(int NewRows, int NewCols);
/*Resizes a matrix
   Pre: NewRows, NewCols >= 0
   Post: Array resized to NewRows by NewCols */

Operators
[ ]   Returns one row of a matrix whose type is vector
=   Assigns one matrix to another.

A tic-tac-toe program will be used to demonstrate matrices. Consider the tic-tac-toe board. It has three columns and three rows:

Each cell of the board can hold an X, an O, or be empty. A space character can represent an empty cell. Therefore, the board can be represented as a matrix of characters.

The Tic-Tac-Toe program allows two players to play a game of tic-tac-toe using the computer to keep track of the board:

```cpp
/* Tic-Tac-Toe program */

#include <iostream.h>
#include <lvp\matrix.h>
#include <lvp\bool.h>

typedef matrix<char> TTTBoard;

//-------------------------------------------------------------------------------
void DisplayBoard(const TTTBoard &Board)
/*Displays board
   Post: Board displayed */
{
  for (int Row=0; Row<Board.numrows(); Row++) {
    // Display a row
    for (int Col=0; Col<Board.numcols(); Col ++)
      cout << "[" << Board[Row][Col]<< "]" ;
    cout << endl;
  }
}
//-------------------------------------------------------------------------------
void GetMove(int &Row, int &Col, const TTTBoard &Board)
/* Obtains a valid move (Row, Col) from user
   Post: Row and Col of matrix returned as valid move */
{
  while (true) {
    cout << "Enter row of move (0, 1, 2): ";
    cin >> Row;
    cout << "Enter column of move (0, 1, 2): ";
    cin >> Col;
    if ((Row >= 0) && (Row < Board.numrows()) &&
       (Col >= 0) && (Col < Board.numcols()) && (Board[Row][Col] == ' '))
       break;
    cout << "Invalid move, please re-enter!" << endl;
  }
}
//-------------------------------------------------------------------------------
char Winner(const TTTBoard &Board)
/*Returns X or O indicating the winner. If no winner, a blank is returned.
   If there are multiple winning sets, returns the first one encountered
   Post: X, O, or a blank returned                                          */
{
  int Row, Col;
  // Try all rows
  for(Row = 0; Row < Board.numrows(); Row++)
    if (Board[Row][0]==Board[Row][1] &&  Board[Row][1]==Board[Row][2]
       && Board[Row][0] != ' ')
       return(Board[Row][0]);
  // Try all columns
  for(Col = 0; Col < Board.numcols(); Col++)
    if (Board[0][Col]==Board[1][Col] &&  Board[1][Col]==Board[2][Col]
       && Board[0][Col] != ' ')
       return(Board[0][Col]);
  // Try one diagonal
  if (Board[0][0]==Board[1][1] &&  Board[1][1]==Board[2][2]
     && Board[0][0] != ' ')
     return(Board[0][0]);
```

```
        // Try the other diagonal
        if (Board[0][2]==Board[1][1] && Board[1][1]==Board[2][0]
            && Board[0][2] != ' ')
            return(Board[0][2]);
        // Return blank, if all others fail
        return(' ');
}
//----------------------------------------------------------------------
int main()
{
    TTTBoard Board(3, 3, ' ');
    char CurrPlayer;
    int Row, Col, NumMoves = 0;

    CurrPlayer = 'X';
    do {
        DisplayBoard(Board);
        GetMove(Row, Col, Board);
        Board[Row][Col] = CurrPlayer;
        NumMoves++;
        if (CurrPlayer == 'X')
            CurrPlayer = 'O';
        else
            CurrPlayer = 'X';
    } while ((Winner(Board) == ' ') && (NumMoves != 9));
    DisplayBoard(Board);
    cout << "Winner is " << Winner(Board) << endl;
    return(0);
}
```

matrix parameters   DisplayBoard() has a matrix parameter. As with array objects, matrix objects that are not to be changed should be passed as a const reference parameter. Nested for loops are used in DisplayBoard() to process all the elements in the matrix.

When run, program output may look similar to:

```
[ ][ ][ ]
[ ][ ][ ]
[ ][ ][ ]

Enter row to move (0,1,2): 1
Enter column to move (0,1,2): 1
[ ][ ][ ]
[ ][X][ ]
[ ][ ][ ]

Enter row to move (0,1,2): 0
Enter column to move (0,1,2): 0
[O][ ][ ]
[ ][X][ ]
[ ][ ][ ]

Enter row to move (0,1,2): 1
Enter column to move (0,1,2): 0
[O][ ][ ]
[X][X][ ]
[ ][ ][ ]
```

```
. . .
Enter row to move (0,1,2): 2
Enter column to move (0,1,2): 2
[O][ ][X]
[X][X][O]
[ ][ ][O]

Enter row to move (0,1,2): 2
Enter column to move (0,1,2): 0
[O][ ][X]
[X][X][O]
[X][ ][O]

Winner is X
```

Review 14

Modify the Tic-Tac-Toe program so that the user enters rows and columns in the range 1 to 3 instead of 0 to 2, and so that the display shows the row and column numbers. The program output should look similar to:

```
    1   2   3
1 [X][O][ ]
2 [ ][X][O]
3 [ ][X][O]
```

Review 15

Modify the Tic-Tac-Toe program so that the user may play against the computer, with the computer picking a random but legal move on its turn. Write a function GetComputerMove() to use in the program.

8.13 The struct Type

A struct is a user-defined type that is a simpler form of a class. A struct type is often created so that related data can be stored in one structure. Unlike an array which can store many values of the same type, a struct can store many values of different types. For example, rather than storing the data about a student in separate variables, struct can be used to create a type that allows all the data to be stored under one identifier, as in the statements:

```
struct StudentType {
    String Last;
    String First;
    char Initial;
    int Class;
};
```

Note the semicolon that must be included to end the type definition. A struct type must be defined before any functions that use it. Therefore, struct types are usually placed at the beginning of a program before any function definitions.

The StudentType struct has four *data members*. The data members are accessed using the same dot notation used with classes. For example, the statements

```
StudentType Student;
cout << "Enter class: ";
cin >> Student.Class;
```

declare a struct Student of type StudentType, and ask the user for the value to assign to the Class data member of Student.

struct parameters

A struct variable can be passed as a parameter, just as any other variable. For example, the function below has a struct reference parameter:

```
void GetStudentData(StudentType &Student)
/*Obtains values for all data members of Student from user
   Post: Values entered for data members of Student        */
{
  cout << "Enter last name: ";
  cin >> Student.Last;
  cout << "Enter first name: ";
  cin >> Student.First;
  cout << "Enter middle initial: ";
  cin >> Student.Initial;
  cout << "Enter class: ";
  cin >> Student.Class;
}
```

This function obtains values from the user and places them in the Student data members.

Review 16

Write a function DisplayStudentData() that displays the values of its StudentType argument. Write a program that uses GetStudentData() and DisplayStudentData() to generate output similar to:

```
Enter last name: Yamaguchi
Enter first name: Kristi
Enter middle initial: A
Enter class: 2004
Kristi A. Yamaguchi     2004
```

Review 17

Write a definition for a struct named CollegeType that holds information about a college. Include data members for name, state, and enrollment.

8.14 Complex structs

A struct may contain any types. For example, StudentType could be expanded to include a class object (array) and an enum:

```
typedef vector<int> IntArray;
enum GenderType {male, female};
struct StuType {
    String Last;
    String First;
    char Initial;
    int Class;
    GenderType Gender;
    IntArray Grades;
};
```

The Grades data member is declared as an IntArray. However, no constructor parameters are given because variables and objects cannot be initialized in a struct definition. Like classes, structs can have member functions that are constructors. To initialize variables and instantiate objects, a struct constructor must be written, as described in the next section.

8.15 struct Constructors

A struct *constructor* is a member function that is automatically called when a struct variable is declared. The struct constructor prototype is part of the struct, and the constructor must have the same name as the struct. For example, StudentType could be expanded to include a constructor:

```
struct StudentType {
    StudentType();  // Constructor member function
    String Last;
    String First;
    char Initial;
    int Class;
    GenderType Gender;
    IntArray Grades;
};
```

A struct constructor should be defined after the struct definition, and has the following form:

```
struct name::constructor name(parameters)
    :initializer list
{
    statements
}
```

initializer list

struct *name* and *constructor name* should be the same as the identifier used for the struct. The *parameters* of the constructor are optional. The colons are part of the constructor syntax. A special feature of a constructor is an *initializer list* that is used to instantiate objects or make assignments to data members of the struct. The colon preceding *initializer list* may be omitted if there is no initialization of data members.

StudentType()

The StudentType constructor takes the form:

```
StudentType::StudentType()
  : Grades(10,-1)
/*Grades initialized to 10 items with each element storing –1 */
{
}
```

The body of this constructor is empty. This is common for constructors because much of the work can be done in the initializer list.

In addition to calling data member constructors, a struct constructor can initialize variables. For example, the StudentType constructor could be written:

```
StudentType::StudentType()
  : Grades(10,–1), Gender(female), Class(0)
/*Grades initialized to 10 items with each element storing –1;
  Gender and Class initialized to default values.              */
{
}
```

programming style

It is good programming style to use a constructor initializer list, rather than making simple assignments to these data members in the body of the constructor. The following constructor is an example of poor programming style:

```
StudentType::StudentType()    // Poor programming style!
  : Grades(10,-1)
/*Example of poor programming style */
{
Gender = female;
Class = 0;
}
```

8.16 const Data Members

struct data members can include constants. Like any struct data member, const data members are declared in the struct definition and then given a value in the initializer list of the struct constructor.

The StudentType struct could be expanded to include a const for the maximum number of grades in the Grades array:

```
struct StudentType  {
    StudentType();   // Constructor member function
    String Last;
    String First;
    char Initial;
    int Class;
    GenderType Gender;
    const int MaxGrades;
    IntArray Grades;
};
```

The StudentType constructor would then take the form:

```
StudentType::StudentType()
   : MaxGrades(10), Grades(MaxGrades, –1)
/* Grades initialized to 10 items with each element storing –1;
   Gender and Class initialized to default values.          */
{
}
```

After giving a const a value, it may be used in other initializations. In this case, MaxGrades is used in the Grades initialization.

The order in which data members appear in a struct is the order in which they are initialized. Therefore, it is important that a struct declare data members in the order in which they are needed. For example, the StudentType struct declared MaxGrades before Grades because the initialization of Grades depends on the definition of MaxGrades:

```
struct StudentType {
   StudentType();   // Constructor member function
   …
   const int MaxGrades;   // Must come before Grades
   IntArray Grades;   // Requires MaxGrades
};
```

Review 18

Write a struct PegBoard with a constructor that initializes three pegs of size 7.

Review 19

Write a function TotalRings() that takes a PegBoard argument from Review 18 and returns the total number of rings on the three pegs. Write a program to test the function.

8.17 Arrays of structs

An array can store elements of any type including a user-defined type, or a struct. For example, 500 students would best be represented as an array of StudentType variables:

```
vector<StudentType> School(500);
```

Each element of School has data members that can be given values through assignment, as in the following statements:

```
School[7].Last = "Morrison";
School[7].First = "Toni";
```

To demonstrate an array of structs, the following Student Records program maintains student information. For this program, a dynamic array is used because the actual number of students may vary due to new admissions. To efficiently handle additions to the array, the array will initially be size 10, then resized to 20 when the first 10 elements are taken, then resized to 30 when the first 20 elements are taken, and so on. Increasing the array by 10 elements at a time is much more efficient than resizing the array every time a new student is added. However, in order to use this algorithm for resizing the array, a variable must be used to store the number of array elements taken. The array is then resized only if the addition of a student record means that the number of array elements taken will be greater than the current array size.

For example, an array currently of size 20 with 17 student records can be illustrated as:

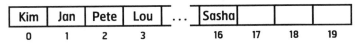

Adding students Ollie, Kurt, and Lily does not require the array to be resized, as illustrated below:

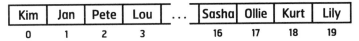

Adding a fourth student, Vito, requires resizing the array. Since 10 elements are added at a time, there is now room for nine more students, as illustrated below:

To better implement this algorithm, a struct SchoolType is used in the program:

```
struct StudentType {
   String Last;
   String First;
   int Class;
};
struct SchoolType {
   SchoolType();    // Constructor
   const int SizeChange;    // Amount to increase array by
   int NumStudents;    // Current number of students
   vector<StudentType> Students;    // Student records
};
```

A constructor for SchoolType initializes NumStudents and SizeChange:

```
SchoolType::SchoolType()
   : SizeChange(10), NumStudents(0), Students(10)
/*Start with space for 10 students, increase by SizeChange when needed */
{
}
```

The complete program code is shown below:

```
/* Student Records program */

#include <iostream.h>
#include <lvp\bool.h>
#include <lvp\vector.h>
#include <lvp\string.h>
#include <conio.h>

struct StudentType {
  String Last;
  String First;
  int Class;
};
//------------------------------------------------------------------------
void GetStudentData(StudentType &Student)
/* Obtains values for all data members of Student from user
   Post: Values entered for data members of Student         */
{
  cout << "Enter last name: ";
  cin >> Student.Last;
  cout << "Enter first name: ";
  cin >> Student.First;
  cout << "Enter class: ";
  cin >> Student.Class;
}
//------------------------------------------------------------------------
void DisplayStudentData(const StudentType &Student)
/* Displays the data in Student, one element per line
   Post: Data in Student displayed                         */
{
  cout << Student.First << " " << Student.Last << " "
    << Student.Class << endl;
}
//------------------------------------------------------------------------
struct SchoolType {
  SchoolType();   // Constructor
  const int SizeChange;   // Amount to increase array by
  int NumStudents;   // Current number of students
  vector<StudentType> Students;   // Student records
};
//------------------------------------------------------------------------
SchoolType::SchoolType()
  : SizeChange(10), Students(10), NumStudents(0)
/* Start with space for 10 students, increase by SizeChange when needed */
{
}
//------------------------------------------------------------------------
void DisplaySchool(const SchoolType &School)
/* Displays a list of all students in School, one per line
   Post: Elements of School displayed                      */
{
  for (int i=0; i<School.NumStudents; i++)
    DisplayStudentData(School.Students[i]);
}
```

```
//------------------------------------------------------------------------
void AddStudent(SchoolType &School, const StudentType &NewStudent)
/*Adds NewStudent to School, increasing size of School.Students if needed
   Post: NewStudent added to School                                      */
{
   if (School.NumStudents == School.Students.length())
      School.Students.resize(School.NumStudents+School.SizeChange);
   School.Students[School.NumStudents] = NewStudent;
   School.NumStudents++;

}
//------------------------------------------------------------------------
int main()
{
   StudentType Student;
   SchoolType School;

   bool Quit=false;
   do {
      cout << "Press choice Add, Display, Quit: ";
      char Choice = getche();
      cout << endl;
      switch (Choice) {
        case 'A':
        case 'a': GetStudentData(Student);
                  AddStudent(School, Student);
                  break;
        case 'D':
        case 'd': DisplaySchool(School);
                  break;
        case 'q':
        case 'Q': Quit=true; break;
      }
   } while(!Quit);
   return(0);
}
```

The organization of this program is important. First, the StudentType struct is defined followed by all its support functions (GetStudentData(), DisplayStudentData()). Next, the SchoolType struct is defined followed by its support functions (constructor SchoolType() and DisplaySchool()). The SchoolType declarations must come after the StudentType declarations because SchoolType requires StudentType. Finally, main() is written. This "building block" approach will become increasingly important.

When run, the program output may look similar to:

```
Press choice Add, Display, Quit: A
Enter last name: Howell
Enter first name: Louis
Enter class: 1997
Press choice Add, Display, Quit: a
Enter last name: Wu
Enter first name: Shiu
Enter class: 1996
Press choice Add, Display, Quit: A
Enter last name: Kubak
Enter first name: Michael
Enter class: 1999
Press choice Add, Display, Quit: D
```

```
Louis Howell 1997
Shiu Wu 1996
Michael Kubak 1999
Press choice Add, Display, Quit: Q
```

Review 20

Modify the Student Records program to allow the user to search for a record matching an entered last name and first name. To do this, write a function that returns the student record, if any, that matches the name. The program output should look similar to:

```
. . .
Enter choice Add, Display, Search, Quit: S
Enter last name: Kubak
Enter first name: Michael
Michael Kubak 1999
Enter choice Add, Display, Search, Quit: S
Enter last name: Cenker
Enter first name: Brian
Brian Cenker not found!
. . .
```

8.18 Three-Dimensional Arrays

In some cases, it is possible to represent information using a multi–dimensional array. However, the use of multidimensional arrays is rare because a more structured organization is usually preferred. For example, to store sales information on 10 employees for five products over the course of 12 months, a three-dimensional structure Sales could be used where Sales[3][0][11] would represent the sales of the fourth employee for the first product in the twelfth month. A three-dimensional array is created by nesting structures. In this case, a matrix with each element an array:

```
typedef vector<double> MonthArray;
typedef matrix<MonthArray> SalesType;
```

With these definitions, the declaration of the three-dimensional array would be:

```
SalesType Sales(10, 5, MonthArray(12, 0.0));
```

Sales is a three-dimensional array of 10 by 5 by 12 elements, all initialized to 0.0. The third argument to the Sales constructor is itself a constructor that creates array MonthArray of size 12 filled with 0.0 values. Each element of the matrix contains a MonthArray array. Data is accessed using three indices. For example, the statement

```
Sales[3][0][11]+=234.95;
```

adds 234.95 to the value stored in the twelfth element of the array stored in the fourth column and the first row of the matrix.

Rather than represent the sales with a three-dimensional array, a more common approach is for some part of the nesting to be handled by a struct. Using the above example, EmployeeType could be defined as follows:

```
struct EmployeeType {
    EmployeeType(); // Constructor
    String Last;
    String First;
    matrix<double> Sales;
};
EmployeeType::EmployeeType()
    : Sales(5, 12, 0.0)  // 5 products, 12 months
{
}
typedef vector<EmployeeType> SalesType;
```

While it still has the characteristics of a three-dimensional array, the nesting is more subtle, and code is easier to understand:

```
SalesType Employee(10);  // Make room for 10 employees
...
Employee[3].Sales[0][11]+=234.95;
```

programming style

When designing a data structure, carefully consider whether the information to be stored falls naturally into a multidimensional structure, or whether a more structured organization is possible and preferable.

Case Study

In this Case Study, a vote analysis program will be written.

specification

Write a program to provide vote analysis for an election, as might be needed by a television station covering the election. There are three candidates and five precincts. The program should be menu-driven to allow the names of the candidates to be entered, the precinct data to be entered as it arrives, and a grid of the data to be displayed. When run, the programs output should be similar to:

```
Enter name for candidate 1: Carter
Enter name for candidate 2: Ford
Enter name for candidate 3: McCarthy

Enter precinct, Display results, Quit: e
What precinct? 3
Enter votes for this precinct for Carter: 342
Enter votes for this precinct for Ford: 300
Enter votes for this precinct for McCarthy: 65

Enter precinct, Display results, Quit: d
Candidate   1       2       3       4       5  Total
Carter      0       0     342       0       0    342
Ford        0       0     300       0       0    300
McCarthy    0       0      65       0       0     65

Enter precinct, Display results, Quit: e
What precinct? 1
Enter votes for this precinct for Carter: 427
Enter votes for this precinct for Ford: 432
Enter votes for this precinct for McCarthy: 48
```

```
Enter precinct, Display results, Quit: d
              1        2       3       4       5  Total
    Carter    427      0     342       0       0    769
    Ford      432      0     300       0       0    732
    McCarthy  48       0      65       0       0    113

Enter precinct, Display results, Quit: Q
```

design—level 1 The main() function is designed first. The pseudocode for the major tasks is:

```
Get candidates names
do
  Display menu of choices (Enter precinct, Display results, Quit)
  switch
    E or e: Load precinct with votes
    D or d: Display candidates and votes for each precinct
    Q or q: quit is true
while (!Quit)
```

Next, the main() pseudocode is used to determine the data design. A char variable Choice is needed to hold the user's menu choice. A bool variable Quit is needed to end the do loop. An array can be used to store the candidates names:

```
vector<String> Candidates;
```

A matrix can be used to store the votes for each precinct for each candidate:

```
matrix<int> Votes;
```

The matrix should have three rows (const **int** NumCandidates) and five columns (const **int** NumPrecincts). The array and matrix data is related information that would best be represented by a struct:

```
struct ResultsType {
   ResultsType();   // Constructor
   const int NumCandidates;
   const int NumPrecincts;
   vector<String> Candidates;
   matrix<int> Votes;
};
//----------------------------------------------------------------------
ResultsType::ResultsType()
   : NumCandidates(3), NumPrecincts(5),
     Votes(NumCandidates, NumPrecincts, 0), Candidates(NumCandidates)
{
}
```

The constructor initializes the Votes matrix to all zeroes. These zeroes will be replaced by votes entered by the user. Candidates was not initialized since the names will be entered by the user at the start of the program.

ResultsType could be pictured as:

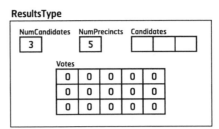

coding—level 1

At this point, rather than coding main() as designed, a main() that tests the ResultsType struct will be coded. To test ResultsType, the LoadNames() function, which gets candidate names from the user, must be coded:

```
void LoadNames(ResultsType &R)
/*Prompts user to enter all candidate names, and stores them in R
  Post: Candidate names are stored in R                          */
{
  for (int CNum=0; CNum<R.NumCandidates; CNum++) {
    cout << "Enter name for candidate " << (CNum+1) << ": ";
    cin >> R.Candidates[CNum];
  }
}
```

const NumCandidates is used to control the for loop. A variable, CNum is used as the loop control and the array index. However, CNum+1 is displayed in the program output as defined by the specification because, while the array is indexed from 0 to 2, the numbers 1 to 3 are more understandable to the user.

Although not needed in the final program, a function DisplayNames() is written to test LoadNames() and the ResultsType struct:

```
void DisplayNames(const ResultsType &R)
/*Function to test loading and retrieval of names
  Post: Contents of R displayed                   */
{
  for (int CNum=0; CNum< R.NumCandidates; CNum++)
    cout << (CNum+1) << ": " << R.Candidates[CNum] << endl;
}
```

Finally, a main() to test LoadNames() and the ResultsType struct:

```
int main()
{
  ResultsType Results;
  LoadNames(Results);
  DisplayNames(Results);
  return(0);
}
```

A program with the declaration of ResultsType, the function definitions, and the main() above displays output similar to the following:

```
Enter name for candidate 1: Carter
Enter name for candidate 2: Ford
Enter name for candidate 3: McCarthy
1: Carter
2: Ford
3: McCarthy
```

In the next level of design, the real main() and the functions it calls are refined. The refined main() pseudocode is:

```
ResultsType Results
bool Quit=false
LoadNames(Results)
do
   Display menu of choices (Enter precinct, Display results, Quit)
   switch
      E or e: LoadAPrecinct(Results)
      D or d: DisplayAll(Results)
      Q or q: quit is true
while (!Quit)
```

A boolean variable controls the loop. The "quit" commands, Q and q, need only be specified in the switch statement.

LoadNames() was created in level 1 of coding.

The LoadAPrecinct() pseudocode is:

```
Ask user for precinct number
for each candidate
   Ask user for votes received
```

The data design of LoadAPrecinct() includes variables UserPct and PctNum to account for the user entering a precinct number that is one greater than its matrix position. For example, data for precinct number 1 (UserPct) is stored in the 0th column (PctNum) of the matrix.

The DisplayAll() pseudocode is:

```
for each precinct
   display precinct number as a title
for each candidate
   Display candidate name
   Display votes for each precinct
   Display total votes for all precincts
```

The task of the second for loop is complex enough that another function DisplayCandidateRow() should be written. DisplayCandidateRow() will require parameters for the Results and the current candidate number. The DisplayCandidateRow() pseudocode is:

```
Display candidate name corresponding to candidate number
for each precinct
   Display votes corresponding to candidate number
Display total votes for that candidate
```

With a complete design the final code is produced:

```
/*Election Summary program.
   Allows entry and display of election results for a multiprecinct election
   as precinct data is entered                                              */

#include <iostream.h>
#include <lvp\vector.h>
#include <lvp\matrix.h>
#include <lvp\string.h>
#include <lvp\bool.h>

struct ResultsType {
   ResultsType();    // Constructor
   const int NumCandidates;
   const int NumPrecincts;
   vector<String> Candidates;
   matrix<int> Votes;
};
//-----------------------------------------------------------------------
ResultsType::ResultsType()
   : NumCandidates(3), NumPrecincts(5),
     Votes(NumCandidates, NumPrecincts, 0), Candidates(NumCandidates)
{
}
//-----------------------------------------------------------------------
void LoadNames(ResultsType &R)
/*Prompts user to enter all candidate names, and stores them in Results
   Post: Candidate names are stored in Results                           */
{
   for (int CNum=0; CNum<R.NumCandidates; CNum++) {
      cout << "Enter name for candidate " << (CNum+1) << ": ";
      cin >> R.Candidates[CNum];
   }
}
//-----------------------------------------------------------------------
void LoadAPrecinct(ResultsType &R)
/*Prompts user to choose a precinct, and then prompts for and
   stores votes for each candidate for that precinct
   Post: Votes entered for a precinct                                    */
{
   int UserPct;
   cout << "What precinct? " ;
   cin >> UserPct;
   int PctNum = UserPct – 1;
   for (int CNum=0; CNum<R.NumCandidates; CNum++) {
   cout << "Enter votes for this precinct for " << R.Candidates[CNum] << ": ";
      cin >> R.Votes[CNum][PctNum];
   }
}
```

```
//--------------------------------------------------------------------------------
void DisplayCandidateRow(const ResultsType &R, int CNum,
                              const int CField, const int VField)
/*Displays data for one candidate in the format: Name  p1  p2  p3 ... Total
   Pre: 0 <= CNum < R.NumCandidates
   Post: Data for candidate CNum displayed                                */
{
   cout.setf(ios::left);
   cout.width(CField); cout << R.Candidates[CNum];
   cout.setf(ios::right);
   int Total = 0;
   for (int PNum=0; PNum<R.NumPrecincts; PNum++) {
      cout.width(VField); cout << R.Votes[CNum][PNum];
      Total = Total + R.Votes[CNum][PNum];
   }
   cout.width(VField); cout << Total << endl;
}
//--------------------------------------------------------------------------------
void DisplayAll(const ResultsType &R)
/*Displays all data entered as well as totals for each candidate
   Post: Candidate names, votes, and total votes displayed        */
{
   const int CandidateField = 10;
   const int VotesField = 6;

   // Display headings
   cout.setf(ios::left);
   cout.width(CandidateField); cout << "Candidate";
   cout.setf(ios::right);
   for (int PNum=0; PNum<R.NumPrecincts; PNum++) {
      cout.width(VotesField); cout << (PNum+1);
   }
   cout.setf(ios::right);
   cout.width(VotesField); cout << "Total" << endl;

   // Display rows
   for (int CNum=0; CNum<R.NumCandidates; CNum++)
      DisplayCandidateRow(R, CNum, CandidateField, VotesField);
}
//--------------------------------------------------------------------------------
int main()
{
   ResultsType Results;
   bool Quit=false;
   LoadNames(Results);
   do {
      cout << endl;
      char Choice;
      cout << "Enter precinct, Display results, Quit: ";
      cin >> Choice;
      switch (Choice){
         case 'E':
         case 'e': LoadAPrecinct(Results); break;
         case 'D':
         case 'd': DisplayAll(Results); break;
         case 'Q':
         case 'q': Quit = true; break;
      }
   } while (!Quit);
   return (0);
}
```

A Guide to Programming in C++

DisplayCandidateRow() has parameters for field widths. This requires field widths changes be made in only one function, which may avoid bugs later.

debugging and testing

Some testing and debugging was done at level 1 coding. However, additional runs with different sets of test data need to be done at this point.

Review 21

Modify DisplayCandidateRow() in the Case Study so that percentages are displayed for each candidate, similar to:

```
Candidate    1     2     3     4     5   Total     %
Carter     427     0   342     0     0     769   48%
Ford       432     0   300     0     0     732   45%
McCarthy    48     0    65     0     0     113    7%
```

Review 22

Modify the Case Study so that it prevents a precinct from being entered twice with a message similar to:

```
What precinct? 3
That precinct has already been entered.
Choose another: 2
```

(Hint: One approach is to use an array of bools with false indicating that a precinct has not been entered, and true indicating that it has. This array should be added to the ResultsType struct, and it should be initialized to all false in the constructor.)

Review 23

The Case Study is not "user proof." There are a variety of ways in which the user may crash the program, or enter nonsensical values. Create a list of all of the potential problems, and then indicate how they might be solved.

Chapter Summary

An array, sometimes called a vector, is used to store many values of the same type. Elements of an array are accessed using an index number enclosed in square brackets (Array[0]). An attempt to access an array element outside the declared array size causes a range error.

The vector class is used to implement arrays. The vector class includes member functions that allow for dynamic arrays which vary in size throughout program execution.

An algorithm for finding an element in an array is linear search, which proceeds from one element to the next until the desired value is found.

The typedef statement allows an identifier to be associated with a type, and it can make code easier to read and less error-prone.

A string can be manipulated as an array of chars. This allows many useful functions to be written.

Many algorithms can be developed using an array's indexes as labels to simplify data storage. Array indexes usually do not directly correspond to the data to be stored, and an algorithm must include offsetting index numbers.

A two-dimensional arrays is called a matrix. Matrices are implemented using the matrix library. Elements of a matrix are accessed using row and column numbers enclosed in square brackets following the matric name. Game[0][4] refers to the element in the first row (0) and fifth column (4).

The vector and matrix classes are class templates that allow creation of objects of any type. To indicate the type of value that will be stored in the array or matrix, angle brackets enclose the type after the class name when the object is instantiated (vector<int> GradeArray).

A struct is a user-defined type that is a simpler form of a class. A struct can contain member functions and data members. A struct often contains a constructor member function to initialize variables, instantiate objects, and assign values to constants. Most of the work done by a struct constructor is in the initializer list.

Three-dimensional arrays are created using a matrix of arrays. However, multidimensional arrays are rarely used because a more structured organization is usually preferred.

Vocabulary

Array A data type that can store many values of the same type where each element is accessed with an index number.

Data Members Variables of a struct which are accessed using dot notation.

Default Constructor A constructor that takes no parameters.

Dynamic Array An array that varies in size throughout program execution. The vector class enables dynamic arrays to be used in a program.

Index The number by which the element in an array is accessed.

Initializer List A part of a struct constructor that is used to invoke struct object constructors and make assignments to struct data members.

Linear Search A searching algorithm that works by proceeding from one element to the next in an array until the desired value is found.

Matrix A two-dimensional array.

struct A user-defined type that is a simpler form of a class.

struct Constructor A struct member function that is automatically called when a struct variable is declared.

Template A body of code in which one or more types are left initially unspecified.

Two-Dimensional Array A matrix implemented with the matrix class.

Vector See Array.

< >   Used to enclose the type for a class template declaration.

matrix.h   The library that implements the matrix type.

matrix   A two-dimensional array type. This type is available by including the matrix library.

vector.h   The library that implements the vector type.

vector   An array type. This type is available by including the vector library.

struct   Keyword used to create a user-defined type that can include data members and member functions.

typedef   Keyword used to associate an identifier with a type.

Exercises

Exercise 1

Write a program that generates 25 random numbers between 0 and 99, and then displays all the odd numbers in one list and the even numbers in another. The program output should look similar to:

```
ODD: 13 21 97 ...
EVEN: 22 4 84 ...
```

Exercise 2

Write a program that picks 500 random numbers between 0 and 9, and then displays the number of occurrences of each number. The program output should look similar to:

```
NUMBER    OCCURRENCES
  0            45
  1            32
  2            67
 ...          ...
  9            81
```

Exercise 3

Write a program to ask the user for 15 integers, and then display them in reverse order.

Exercise 4

A program that analyzes a set of numbers can be very useful. Write a program that allows the user to enter numbers in the range 1 through 50, terminated by a sentinel, and then perform the following functions on the numbers:

- Determine the average number
- Determine the maximum number
- Determine the range (maximum–minimum)
- Determine the mode (the number that occurs most often)
- Display a bar graph called a histogram showing the numbers in each five unit range (i.e., 1–5, 6–10, 11–15, etc.). The histogram may look similar to:

```
 1-5:   ***
 6-10:  *****
11-15:  ******
16-20:  ****
21-25:  ******
26-30:  ********
31-35:  ****
36-40:  ******
41-45:  ******
46-50:  **
```

Exercise 5

Write a function StrUpperCase() that returns the uppercase equivalent of its String argument. (Hint: A lowercase letter can be converted to uppercase by subtracting the quantity ('a'–'A'))

Exercise 6

When reading an integer from the keyboard, a single incorrect character typed (e.g. a letter rather than a digit) causes the program to crash with a run-time error. This could be prevented by storing the user's input in a string variable and then converting the string to an integer. If an error is detected, the value can be re-entered.

Write a function StrToInt() that takes a String argument and returns its numerical value. The function should also have a bool reference parameter indicating whether or not an error was detected. (Hint: A single digit character, NumChar, can be converted to an integer by using NumChar–'0') Use the header:

```
int StrToInt(const String &S, bool &Error)
/*If S contains only digits which represent an int value, then this value is
    returned and Error is false. Otherwise, error is true.
    Post: S converted to an integer returned and Error false. If S cannot be
    converted,  0 returned and Error true.                                    */
```

Exercise 7 ☼

One variation of the game of Nim, described in Chapter 5 Exercise 12, is played with four piles of stones. Initially, the piles contain 1, 2, 3, and 4 stones. On each turn, a player may take 1, 2, or 3 stones from a single pile. The player who takes the last stone loses.

a) Write a program that allows two players to play Nim. Be sure to allow only legal moves. The program should be written so that it can easily be modified for more or less than four piles. The program output should look similar to:

```
Name for player #1: Petra
Name for player #2: Elaine
Board: 1   2   3   4
Petra
   Which pile? 3
   How many? 2

Board: 1   2   1   4
Elaine
   Which pile? 4
   How many? 3

Board: 1   2   1   1
Petra
. . .
```

b) Modify the program to use an array of PegClass objects to represent the piles as stacks of rings, similar to:

```
     |              |              |              |
     |              |              |          XXX | XXX
     |              |          XXX | XXX      XXX | XXX
     |          XXX | XXX      XXX | XXX      XXX | XXX
 XXX | XXX      XXX | XXX      XXX | XXX      XXX | XXX
----------------------------------------------------------
```

Exercise 8

In the game of Hangman one player determines a word that another player tries to guess one letter at a time.

a) Write a hangman program that allows one person to enter a word to be guessed, and then clears the screen. Another person can then guess the word by entering letters. The program output should look similar to:

```
Enter word to be guessed: BANANA (screen clears)
Word is ------
Your letter ($ to guess the word)? S
Sorry, there are no S's
Your letter ($ to guess the word)? N
Word is --N-N-
Your letter ($ to guess the word)? B
Word is B-N-N-
Your letter ($ to guess the word)? $
Your guess? BANANA
CORRECT! You took 3 tries.
```

b) Modify the hangman program to keep track of the letters that have been guessed, and give an error message if the user enters the same guess twice. The program output should look similar to:

```
. . .
Word is -N-N-
. . .
Your letter ($ to guess the word)? S
Sorry, you guessed S already. Try again.
. . .
```

c) *Advanced.* In traditional hangman, one piece of a stick figure is drawn for each wrong guess. Modify the hangman program to use gotoxy() to illustrate the traditional "hangman" near the top of the window. When six wrong guesses have been made, the hangman part of the program output should look similar to:

```
 ------
 |
 o
/|\
/ \
```

8

Exercise 9 ✑

Modify the Mastermind program from Chapter 5 Exercise 13 to use arrays with the following features:

- Permit the number of pegs (from 1 to 10) to be specified at the start of the program.
- Permit the number of colors (from 1 to 9) to be specified at the start of the program.
- Permit both the guess and the secret code to contain duplicates. This will require extra care when counting the number of pegs of the correct color. For example, if the secret code is 1, 2, 3, 4, 5 and the guess is 2, 1, 1, 2, 2 then the program should only report two correct colors (a single 1 and a single 2).

Exercise 10

An array is said to be sorted if its elements are in either increasing or decreasing order. The selection sort algorithm works by repeatedly taking the lowest item from an array and adding it to a new array, so that all the elements in the new array are sorted from low to high.

a) Write a function FindLowest() that returns the index of the lowest value in the array. Use the following typedef and function header:

```
typedef vector<int> ArrayType;

int FindLowest(const ArrayType &A)
/*Returns the index of the lowest value in the array
    Post: Index of lowest value in array returned     */
```

b) Write a function Sort() that repeatedly finds the lowest value in an array A, removes it, and adds it to an array T. When all values of A have been moved, T is copied to A with an assignment statement. Use the following header and functions FindLowest() from part (a) and AddToArray() and RemoveFromArray() from the text:

```
void Sort(ArrayType &A)
/*Sorts elements of A from low to high
    Post: Elements of A are in order from lowest to highest. */
```

Exercise 11

Use the following steps to write a program to store grades for a class. There are 20 students in the class and each student has five grades during the term.

a) Write a type declaration that will store these grades and student names.

b) Write a function LoadGrades() that asks the user for the five grades for each student and stores them in the array declared in (a).

c) Write a function DisplayGrades() that displays a table of the data in the array:

```
                         TEST
   STUDENT        1    2    3    4    5
   Brewer         85   77   89   97   88
   Reynolds       66   75   66   77   85
   Warren         89   88   94   90   93
                 . . .
```

d) Write a function StuAvg() that displays a list of student averages similar to:

```
   STUDENT        AVERAGE
   Brewer           87.2
   Reynolds         73.8
     . . .
```

e) Write a function TestAvg() that displays the averages on each test:

```
   TEST        AVERAGE
    1            77.4
    2            67.9
    3            90.1
    4            86.2
    5            83.1
```

f) Write a menu-driven program that allows the user to select from the four functions above.

Exercise 12

The Penny Pitch game is popular in amusement parks. Pennies are tossed onto a board that has certain areas marked with different prizes. For example:

PUZZLE			POSTER		DOLL
	POSTER			DOLL	BALL
	PUZZLE	GAME			
PUZZLE	BALL			POSTER	GAME
DOLL	GAME				BALL

The prizes available on this board are puzzle, game, ball, poster, and doll. At the end of the game, if all of the squares that say BALL in them are covered by a penny, the player gets a ball. This is also true for the other prizes. The board is made up of 25 squares (5 x 5). Each prize appears on 3 randomly chosen squares so that 15 squares contain prizes.

Write a penny pitch game program that simulates ten pennies being randomly pitched onto the board. At the end of the game display a list of the prizes won or NONE.

8

Exercise 13

The game Life was devised by a mathematician as a model of a very simple world. The Life world is a two-dimensional plane of cells. Each cell may be empty or contain a single creature. Each day, creatures are born or die in each cell according to the number of neighboring creatures on the previous day. A neighbor is a cell that adjoins the cell either horizontally, vertically, or diagonally. The rules in pseudocode style are:

- If the cell is alive on the previous day
    Then if the number of neighbors was 2 or 3
        the cell remains alive
        otherwise the cell dies (of either loneliness or overcrowding)
- If the cell is not alive on the previous day
    Then if the number of neighbors was exactly 3
        the cell becomes alive
        otherwise it remains dead.

For example, the world displayed as:

```
OOOOOOOOOO
OOOOOOOOOO
OOOXXXOOOO
OOOOOOOOOO
OOOOOOOOOO
OOOOOOOOOO
```

where X's indicate live cells, becomes

```
OOOOOOOOOO
OOOOXOOOOO
OOOOXOOOOO
OOOOXOOOOO
OOOOOOOOOO
OOOOOOOOOO
```

Write a program to play Life on a 20 x 20 grid. To initialize the grid, have the program ask the user for the coordinates of live cells on the first day. Generate each day's world so long as the user wishes to continue, or until there are no more live cells.

Exercise 14

A shoe store manager wishes to maintain an inventory of shoes on hand. There are 22 styles of shoes, each of which come in four colors (black, brown, tan, and suede) and 8 sizes (6 through 13). Write a menu-driven program that uses a three-dimensional array to store data, and displays output similar to:

```
Add shoe, Remove shoe, Find Shoe, Quit: A
Enter style: 3
Enter color (Black/Brown/Tan/Suede): Tan
Enter size: 6
Shoe added.
...
Add shoe, Remove shoe, Find Shoe, Quit: F
Enter style: 14
Enter color (Black/Brown/Tan/Suede): Brown
Enter size: 8
There are 3 shoes of this type.
Add shoe, Remove shoe, Find Shoe, Quit: F
...
```

Exercise 15

Modify the Case Study so that it begins by asking the user for the number of candidates and the number of precincts rather than using constants 3 and 5.

Advanced
Exercise 16

In order to better organize its business, the Lawrenceville Lawn Service wants to computerize its customer list. The information for each customer (name, address, size of lawn, and day of the week that they wish their lawn to be mowed) should be stored in parallel arrays. Write a program that allows the user to perform the following functions:

- Add a new customer
- Remove a customer
- Display a table of jobs for a given day. The table should be similar to the one shown in the sample run below, showing the name, address, and total charge including 6% sales tax. LLS charges 2 cents per square yard for cutting.

When run, the program output should look similar to:

```
Enter Display, Add, dElete, Quit: a
ADD
Enter name to be added: Tiger Woods
Enter address: 65 Lakeshore Drive
Enter lawn size: 1262
Enter day to be cut: Saturday
```

```
Enter Display, Add, dElete, Quit: a
ADD
Enter name to be added: Julia Winitsky
Enter address: 16 Manor Dr
Enter lawn size: 2500
Enter day to be cut: Tuesday
Enter Display, Add, dElete, Quit: e
DELETE
Enter name for deletion: Tiger Woods
** Deleted **
Enter Display, Add, dElete, Quit: e
DELETE
Enter name for deletion: Josephine Bouchard
** Error Name not on list **
Enter Display, Add, dElete, Quit: X
** Please enter D, A, E, or Q **
Enter Display, Add, dElete, Quit: d
DISPLAY
Enter day to display: Tuesday

LAWRENCEVILLE LAWN SERVICE
Schedule for: Tuesday

NAME                ADDRESS             COST
Julia Winitsky  16 Manor Dr.           $50.00

Enter Display, Add, dElete, Quit: q
QUIT
** Program complete **
```

Advanced Exercise 17

The game of Mankala is played on a board like that illustrated below:

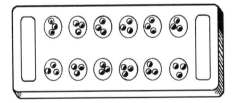

Players sit on opposite sides with the large bin to a player's right designated her home bin. On a turn, a player selects one of the six pits nearest her, removes the stones, and "sows" them counterclockwise around the board, placing one stone in each pit including her home bin (but excluding her opponent's home bin). If the last stone lands in her home bin, she gets another turn. If the last stone lands in an empty pit on her side of the board, she takes all stones on the corresponding pit of the opponent's side and places them in her home bin. When a player cannot play, the game is over and all stones remaining in the opponent's pits go to the opponent's home bin. The winner is the player with the most stones in his home bin at the end of the game.

For example, if the bottom player plays first and chooses the fourth pit to play from, the board looks like:

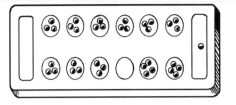

Since the last stone landed in her bin, she plays again. She may choose the first pit this time in order to capture her opponent's stones:

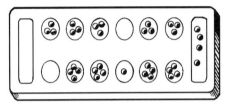

Her turn is now over, and her opponent now has a turn.

Write a Mankala program. Use simple characters to illustrate the board, and letters to identify the pits, similar to that shown below:

```
        3   3   3   3   3   3
    0                           0
        3   3   3   3   3   3
        A   B   C   D   E   F
```

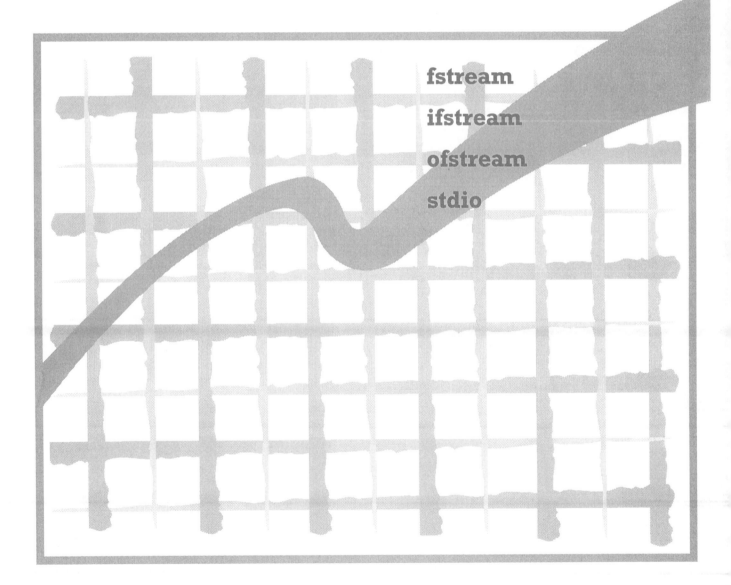

fstream

ifstream

ofstream

stdio

Objectives

After completing this chapter you will be able to:

1. Understand how a stream processes characters.

2. Use the fstream library.

3. Read numeric and character data from a file.

4. Use the ofstream class.

5. Pass and return stream objects as parameters.

6. Use sequential and random access files.

9

In this chapter you will learn how to read, write, and manipulate files on disk. Files are used by programs to store user data, configuration information, and the results of calculations. Files can also be used as input to a program. Programs of any complexity usually require access to files stored on disk.

9.1 Streams

A *stream* processes characters, and in C++, streams are implemented with classes. The ios class, discussed in Chapter Six, is the basis of all stream classes. The ios objects, cin (console input stream) and cout (console output stream), are the standard console stream objects. For example, the statement

```
cout << "This is output";
```

displays

```
This is output
```

because the string was processed by the console output stream which sends characters to the screen. To process the data in a file, a file stream is used, as discussed in the next section.

9.2 The ifstream Class

fstream.h

The fstream library contains the ifstream class which is used to create an input file stream. For example, the following statement instantiates an ifstream object:

```
ifstream InFile("ask-not.txt", ios::nocreate);
```

ios::nocreate

More simply, this statement creates an input file stream InFile that can be used to read the data in the file ask-not.txt stored on disk. The constant ios::nocreate prevents the file from being created if it does not exist, which is preferred when opening a file for input.

inheritance

The ifstream class is derived from the ios class, its base class. A *derived class* has all the properties of its *base class*. This means that an ifstream object has all the properties of an ios object. For example, an ifstream object can use all the member functions in the ios class. This property of object-oriented programming in which a class can be derived from another class is called *inheritance*.

Following is the ifstream documentation. The most useful functions are described, including some found in the ifstream base class, the ios class:

ifstream (fstream.h)

Constructors

ifstream();
/*Creates an input file stream
    Post: Input file stream created that is not attached to a file */

ifstream(**const** C-string FileName, **int** Mode);
/*Creates an input file stream and opens FileName.
    Mode should be ios::nocreate
    Pre: File with FileName exists
    Post: Input file open   */

Functions

void open(**const** C-string FileName, **int** Mode);
/*Opens FileName
    Mode should be ios::nocreate
    Post: Input file open   */

void close();
/*Closes file associated with calling ifstream object
    Post: FileName closed   */

int fail();
/*Determine if last operation on the stream failed
    Post: true (1) returned if last operation failed,
    false (0) returned if last operation succeeded   */

int eof();
/*Determines if calling ifstream object is at the end of file
    Post: 1 returned if ifstream object is at end of file,
    0 returned if ifstream object is not at end of file.   */

istream & get(**char** character);
/*Assigns the next character in calling ifstream object to character
    Post: character assigned the next character in ifstream object   */

istream & ignore(**int** NumChars = 1, **int** Delimiter = EOF);
/*Extracts up to NumChars from the ifstream until Delimiter is read
    Post: Characters extracted from ifstream until Delimiter
    read or NumChars characters read   */

istream & seekg(**long** StreamPos);
/*Moves read pointer to position StreamPos
    Post: Current read position at StreamPos   */

long tellg();
/*Returns the current position of read pointer
    Post: Current position of read pointer returned */

Operators
>>   Extracts one data item from the stream into a variable.

Many of the ifstream member functions are discussed later in this chapter. The Read File program demonstrates the basic ifstream functions:

```
/* Read File program */

#include <iostream.h>
#include <fstream.h>
#include <lvp\string.h>

int main()
{
  ifstream InFile("ask-not.txt", ios::nocreate);
  if (InFile.fail()) {
    cout << "File could not be opened";
    return(0);
  }
  else {
    String S;
    while (getline(InFile, S))
      cout << ">" << S << endl;
    cout << "Done" << endl;
    return(0);
  }
}
```

testing an attempt to open a file

The first line of main() instantiates an ifstream object InFile that is the file stream associated with disk file ask-not.txt. When an ifstream object is instantiated, the associated file is opened. If an attempt to open the file fails, C++ does not generate a runtime error. Therefore, it is up to the programmer to include code to test for this condition, as is done in the condition of the if statement. The fail() member function returns a value that evaluates to true if the last operation on the stream failed, and false if it succeeded.

fail()

getline()

getline(), as used with cin, processes the file through the file stream one line at a time. Each line is then sent to the console output stream for displaying. For this program, a ">" symbol was also sent to cout to clarify the output. When run, the program displays:

```
>Ask not, what your country can do for you;
>Ask what you can do for your country!
>John F. Kennedy, Inaugural Speech, 1961
Done
```

testing for end of file

The getline() function is used as the condition of the while loop because it returns a value that evaluates to false when an input operation is false. For example, when the end of the file is reached, getline() returns false. In general, all functions and operators that process a file stream return a value that evaluates to true when an operation is successful and false when an operation fails.

Text files, sometimes called ASCII files, contain only ASCII characters. There are no special formatting codes or extended ASCII characters in a text file. Most importantly, a text file is in a file format that can be read by any program. For example, an Excel spreadsheet file is saved in a format that can be read only by Excel. This is indicated by the extension .xls that is part of the filename. A text file usually has the extension .txt and contains plain text that can be read by any file. ASCII files may also use the extension .dat to indicate they contain characters that should be interpreted as numbers. For example, a file grades.dat may contain the characters 98 77 60 100.

A text file can be created in Turbo C++ or Microsoft Visual C++ by creating a new file, typing the desired data, and then saving the file with a .txt extension. By default, Turbo C++ and Microsoft Visual C++ do not add any special formatting codes to a file.

A word processor may also be used to create a text file. However, it is important that the file be saved in the text or ASCII file format. This is usually a special option available in the Save As dialog box of the word processor.

Review 1

Modify the Read File program to display a summary of the file contents. The program output should look similar to:

```
lines: 3
characters: 118
```

Review 2

Modify the Read File program to count the number of times the word "you" occurs in the file. The word "you" embedded in the word "your" should count as an occurrence. The program output should look similar to:

```
"you" occurs 4 times
```

9.3 Reading Numeric Data

A file on disk is a set of characters. However, a program accessing the file can read the characters as integers, reals, strings, or characters. For example, the Read File program read ask-not.txt as a file of strings. The Read Scores program below manipulates scores.dat as a list of numbers. The file scores.dat contains:

```
77 66 88 78 98
```

```
/* Read Scores program */

#include <iostream.h>
#include <fstream.h>
```

```
int main()
{
  ifstream InFile("scores.dat", ios::nocreate);
  if (InFile.fail()) {
    cout << "File could not be opened";
    return(0);
  }
  else {
    int Num;
    int Sum = 0;
    while (InFile >> Num) {
      cout << ">" << Num << endl;
      Sum += Num;
    }
    cout << Sum << endl;
    return(0);
  }
}
```

When run, the program displays:

```
>77
>66
>88
>78
>98
407
```

In this program, each number is read, sent to cout, and then added to Sum to create a running total. The ">" symbol was also sent to cout to indicate which values were read from the file.

>>
whitespace

The >> operator automatically skips whitespace, and is usually used to process a file containing numeric data. *Whitespace* is spaces, tabs, and newline (end of line) characters. For example, the Read Scores program would produce the same output if scores.dat looked like

```
77      66
88    78
98
```

because the extra spaces and new lines would be ignored.

read error

Like getline() used in the Read File program, the >> operator is used within the condition of the while loop because it returns a value that evaluates to false when an input operation is false. For example, when the end of the file is reached, >> returns false. When reading data as numeric values, false is also returned when there is an attempt to read non-numeric data. For example, if scores.dat looked like:

```
77 66 eighty-eight 78 98
```

the Read Scores program would produce the output:

```
>77
>66
143
```

Review 3

Modify the Read Scores program to display the number of integers and the following statistics on the values in the data file. The program output should look similar to:

```
Average: 81.4
Number of values: 5
Maximum: 98
Minimum: 66
```

Review 4

Create a text file that contains the following:

```
Objectville
23094
10239
-1
Bjarne City
4562
328
125
-1
```

In the file above, each group of lines represents a city. The first line holds the name of the city. The remaining lines hold the number of voters in each district of the city. A value of –1 indicates the end of the list of districts. Write a program that displays a summary of this file. The program output should look similar to:

```
Objectville: 33333
Bjarne City: 5015
```

9.4 Reading Character Data

get()

The get() member function is used to read data from a file character-by-character. For example, the Read Characters program below reads and displays every character in a file quick.txt:

```
/*Read Characters program */

#include <iostream.h>
#include <fstream.h>
#include <lvp\string.h>

int main()
{
  ifstream InFile("quick.txt", ios::nocreate);
  if (InFile.fail()) {
    cout << "File could not be opened";
    return(0);
  }
  else {
    char Character;
    while (InFile.get(Character))
      cout << ">" << Character << endl;
    cout << "Done" << endl;
    return(0);
  }
}
```

The file quick.txt contains:

```
Hi and
Bye!
```

When the Read Characters program is run, the following is displayed:

```
>H
>i
>
>a
>n
>d
>


>B
>y
>e
>!
>


Done
```

The blank line after the word and is the end-of-line character that was read from the file. This character can be recognized by comparing it to the newline character, \n. For example, the while loop can be written as:

```
while (InFile.get(Character))
  if (Character == '\n')
    cout << ">end-of-line" << endl;
  else
    cout << ">" << Character << endl;
```

When run, the program now displays:

```
>H
>i
>
>a
>n
>d
>end-of-line
>B
>y
>e
>!
>end-of-line
Done
```

Tab characters (\t) can be detected in the same way.

Review 5

Modify the Read Characters program to display a summary of the number of characters in quick.txt. Do not count end-of-line characters.

9.5 The eof() and ignore() Member Functions

The eof() member function is used to detect the end-of-file. eof() returns a value that evaluates to true if the input stream is at the end-of-file, and false otherwise. For example, the following loop:

```
while (true) {
    // Read an item of data
    if (InFile.eof())
        break;
    // Process the data
}
```

reads an item from the InFile stream. If the end-of-file has been reached, the loop is exited, otherwise the loop continues. However, unexpected data (a letter when numbers are being read) or a missing file do not return true for eof() and may lead to an infinite loop. It is good programming style to use the return value of a read operation as the loop condition to determine file status. For example, InFile >> Num used in the Read Scores program is preferred over eof().

programming style

The ignore() function is used to read and then discard characters from the input file stream. For example, the statement

```
MyFile.ignore(20);    // extracts 20 characters
```

reads and discards 20 characters from the MyFile stream. By default the ignore delimiter is end-of-file. If there are fewer than 20 characters left in the file, all the remaining characters are discarded until end-of-file is read.

A delimiter may also be specified in ignore(), as in the statement

```
MyFile.ignore(80,'\n');    // extracts up to 80 chars until '\n' is reached
```

which extracts characters until 80 characters have been extracted or an end-of-line character is extracted. This form of ignore() is often used to "skip" the rest of a line of input from a file.

9.6 The ofstream Class

The fstream library contains the ofstream class which is used to create an output file stream. For example, the following statement instantiates an ofstream object:

```
ofstream OutFile("my-data.txt");
```

More simply, this statement creates an output file stream OutFile that can be used to write data to the file my-data.txt on disk.

Like the ifstream class, the ofstream class is derived from the ios class. Following is documentation of some of the most useful ofstream functions:

ofstream (fstream.h)

Constructors

ofstream();
/*Creates an output file stream
   Post: Output file stream created that is not attached to a file */

ofstream(**const** C-string FileName);
/*Creates an output file stream and opens FileName,
   creating a file with FileName if necessary.
   Post: Output file open   */

Functions

void open(**const** C-string FileName);
/*Opens FileName
   Post: Output file open */

void close();
/*Closes file associated with calling ofstream object
   Post: FileName closed   */

int fail();
/*Determine if last operation on the stream failed
   Post: false (0) returned if last operation failed,
   true (1) returned if last operation succeeded   */

ostream & seekp(**long** StreamPos);
/*Moves write pointer to position StreamPos
   Post: Current write position at StreamPos   */

long tellp();
/*Returns the current position of write pointer
   Post: Current position of write pointer returned */

int width(**int** FieldWidth);
/*Sets field width used when data written to a file
   Post: Field width set for writing data to a file   */

long setf(ios::fixed);
/*Uses floating point notation when writing data to a file
   Post: Data formatted as floating point for writing to a file */

int precision(**int** NumDecimals);
/*Sets number of decimals to use in floating point notation
   Post: Data formatted as floating point to NumDecimals
   decimal places for writing to a file   */

Operators

<<   Inserts one data item into the file stream.

Many of the ofstream member functions are discussed later in this chapter. The Write File program demonstrates the basic ofstream functions:

```
/* Write File program */

#include <iostream.h>
#include <fstream.h>
#include <lvp\string.h>

int main()
{
    ofstream OutFile("my-data.txt");
    if (OutFile.fail()) {
        cout << "File could not be opened";
        return(0);
    }
    else {
        OutFile << "The first line of the file." << endl;
        OutFile << (12 + 34) << endl;
        OutFile << "PI=";
        OutFile.setf(ios::fixed);
        OutFile.precision(2);
        double PI=3.1415926;
        OutFile.width(10); OutFile << PI << endl;
        OutFile << "The last line of the file.";
        return(0);
    }
}
```

The first line of main() instantiates an ofstream object OutFile that is the file stream associated with disk file my-data.txt. When an ofstream object is instantiated, the associated file is opened. If the file does not exist, the ofstream object creates one. If an attempt to open or create the file fails, C++ does not generate a runtime error. Therefore, it is up to the programmer to include code to test for this condition, as done in the condition of the if statement. The fail() member function returns a value that evaluates to false if the last operation on the stream failed, and true if it succeeded.

fail()

<<

The << operator is used to send data to the OutFile stream for writing to a file. Formatted data is written to a file using the width(), setf(), and precision() member functions. When run, the program displays no output unless there is a problem creating or opening my-data.txt.

After running the program, opening my-data.txt displays:

```
The first line of the file.
46
PI=      3.14
The last line of the file.
```

A Guide to Programming in C++

9.7 The open() and close() Member Functions

Both the ifstream and ofstream classes contain open() and close() member functions. The open() member function can be used when an ifstream or ofstream constructor is called with no parameters. For example, the statements

```
ifstream MyFile;
MyFile.open("my-data.txt", ios::nocreate);
```

instantiate an ifstream MyFile and then associate the file my-data.txt with the MyFile stream.

Files are closed automatically by the ifstream and ofstream classes. However, by explicitly closing a file within a program, a different file can be associated with a stream, as in the statements:

```
ifstream MyFile;
MyFile.open("my-data.txt", ios::nocreate);
// process file
MyFile.close();
MyFile.open("progdata.txt", ios::nocreate)
// process file
```

9.8 User-Specified File Names

Programs often ask the user to enter the file name to be opened. This is accomplished by having the user enter a string, and then using the string as the file name in a call to open(). However, the open() member function expects a C-style (not C++) string as an argument. The String class includes a member function, c_str(), for this purpose. c_str() returns a C-style string corresponding to the calling string object, as in the statements:

c_str()

```
String FileName;
ifstream InFile;
cout << "Enter the name of the file to process: ";
getline(cin, FileName);
InFile.open(FileName.c_str());
```

9.9 Stream Object Parameters

Like any object, streams can be passed as arguments to functions. Stream objects are required to be passed as reference arguments because it does not make sense for "local copies" of a stream object to be made.

Stream objects can also be passed as const parameters. However, this is rarely done since nearly every member function and operation on a stream modifies the stream.

The File Statistics program on the next page includes a function with a stream parameter:

```
/*File Statistics program.
  Counts number of characters and lines in one or more text files specified
  by the user. End-of-line characters are not counted as characters.        */

#include <iostream.h>
#include <fstream.h>
#include <lvp\string.h>
#include <lvp\bool.h>

//------------------------------------------------------------------------------
void DisplayStats(ifstream &InFile)
/*Displays the number of characters and lines in InFile.
  End-of-line characters are not counted as characters.
  Pre: InFile open.
  Post: File statistics displayed.                              */
{
  String S;
  long TotalChars = 0;
  long TotalLines = 0;
  while (getline(InFile, S)) {
    TotalChars+=S.length();
    TotalLines++;
  }
  cout << "Total characters: " << TotalChars << endl;
  cout << "Total lines: " << TotalLines << endl;
}
//------------------------------------------------------------------------------
int main()
{
  ifstream InFile;
  String FileName;

  while (true) {
    cout << "Enter name of file (Enter to quit): ";
    getline(cin, FileName);
    if (FileName.length() == 0)
      break;
    InFile.open(FileName.c_str(), ios::nocreate);
    if (InFile.fail())
      cout << "File cannot be opened" << endl;
    else {
      DisplayStats(InFile);
      InFile.close();
    }
  }
  return(0);
}
```

When run, the program may display output similar to:

```
Enter name of file (Enter to quit): ask-what.txt
File cannot be opened
Enter name of file (Enter to quit): ask-not.txt
Total characters: 118
Total lines: 3
Enter name of file (Enter to quit): filestat.cpp
Total characters: 1244
Total lines: 47
Enter name of file (Enter to quit):
```

Review 6

Modify the File Statistics program so that its output is written to a file, stats.dat, rather than to the screen. Do this by including an argument for the output stream in DisplayStats(). Run the program and then verify that it worked by opening stats.dat.

Review 7

Write a function FileExists() that returns a bool value that is true if and only if its argument is an existing filename. Use the prototype:

bool FileExists(**const** String & FileName);

9.10 The remove() and rename() Functions

stdio.h

The remove() and rename() functions in the stdio library can be used to manipulate files. The remove() function deletes a file from disk. For example, the statement

```
remove("my-file.txt");
```

deletes my-file.txt from disk. The remove() function requires a C-style string as an argument. If a String type variable is used as an argument, it must call c_str(). For example:

```
String FileToDelete;
cout << "Enter name of file to delete: ";
getline(cin, FileToDelete);
remove(FileToDelete.c_str());
```

The rename() function takes the name of a file as its first argument and the new name of the file as a second argument. For example, the statement

```
rename("foo.txt", "bar.txt");
```

renames the file foo.txt as bar.txt. The rename() function also requires C-style string arguments.

Both the remove() and rename() functions return integer values indicating the result of the operation. A returned value of 0 indicates success; a returned value of –1 indicates an error occurred. The return values may be used as follows:

```
String FileToDelete;
cout << "Enter name of file to delete: ";
getline(cin, FileToDelete);
if (remove(FileToDelete.c_str())!=0)
    cout << "Remove operation failed" << endl;
else
    cout << FileToDelete << " has been removed" << endl;
```

A file must be closed before it can be removed or renamed.

9.11 Returning Stream Objects References

A function may return a reference, just as it may return values of other types. This is important when working with streams because a function may only return a reference to a stream. For example, in the ifstream documentation, the getline prototype is:

```
istream & getline(ifstream FileName, String &S);
/* Assigns the next string in FileName to S
   Post: String from FileName assigned to S */
```

istream class

Note the ampersand used to indicate that this function returns a reference to a stream. The istream class (input stream) is in the iostream library, and is inherited by the ifstream class.

To demonstrate a function that returns a reference, the following getline() function reads a long value and then ignores the rest of the line:

```
istream & getline(istream &InFile, long &N)
/* Assigns the next value in InFile to N
   Post: Value from InFile stream assigned to N */
{
  InFile >> N;
  InFile.ignore(80,'\n');
  return(InFile);
}
```

This getline() assumes that there are no more than 80 characters after the long value in the stream. The syntax in the return statement does not vary when a reference is returned.

Review 8

Write two variations of getline() that obtain a particular value type from a line in a file and ignores the rest of the characters on the line. One function should obtain an int from a line in a file. The other should obtain a char value from a line in a file.

Review 9

Write a variation of getline() that obtains a bool value from a line in a file and ignores the rest of the characters. It should return true if and only if the first characters on the line are TRUE or true, and false otherwise.

9.12 Random Access Files

sequential access files

The programs so far have accessed files sequentially. In *sequential access files*, each item in the file is accessed one after the other in the order stored. Files can also be accessed in an arbitrary order, usually determined by an algorithm implemented in a program. Files accessed this way are called *random access files*. For example, consider the file stock.dat:

widgets 115 gadgets 203 thingamajigs 31 knickknacks 9

If sequential file access is used to determine the stock of thingamajigs, five items would need to be read before the desired item is found. A more efficient program could use random file access to implement an algorithm

A Guide to Programming in C++

to read every other item until the desired item is found, which means only three items would need to be read.

file pointers

Random access to a file is possible because the file stream maintains a pair of position indicators or *pointers*. The *get pointer* tells where the next reading operation will start. The *put pointer* tells where the next writing operation will occur. For example, a stream may look like:

A write operation to this stream would take place at the put pointer. For example, writing the character R overwrites the character N, and the put pointer moves to the next character, B:

Similarly, a read operation to this stream reads the character T and moves the get pointer to the next character, H.

seekp() seekg()

A program that uses random access files must manipulate the get and put pointers. To move the pointers, the seekg() and seekp() functions are used. These function prototypes appear in the ifstream and ofstream documentation.

The positions of the pointers are indicated in bytes (characters) with the first character in the file considered to be at position 0. For example, if file composer.txt contains BEETHOVENBACH, and MyFile is the file stream, then the statements:

```
char ch;
MyFile.seekg(4);      // Move the get pointer to character 4 ("H")
MyFile >> ch;         // Read character at get pointer
MyFile.seekp(0);      // Move the put pointer to character 0 ("B")
MyFile << ch;         // Write ch ("H") at put pointer (overwriting "B")
```

will modify the file to contain HEETHOVENBACH.

The get and put pointers are moved to the beginning of the file stream with the statements:

```
MyFile.seekg(0);
MyFile.seekp(0);
```

ios::end

To move a pointer to the end of the file stream, the constant ios::end can be used. For example, the statement

```
MyFile.seekp(0, ios::end);
```

moves the put pointer 0 characters past the end of the file.

appending data to a file

To append data to a file, the put pointer must first be moved to the end of the file before writing the data to the file. For example, the statements

```
MyFile.seekp(0, ios::end);
MyFile << "MOZART" << endl;
```

add the characters MOZART to the end of the file.

The fstream library contains the fstream class which is used to create a file stream that can be read from and written to. For example, the following statement instantiates an fstream object for both input and output:

```
fstream MyFile("composer.txt", ios::in | ios::out);
```

More simply, this statement creates a file stream MyFile that can be used to read or write data to the file composer.txt on disk.

fstream()

The fstream constructor requires two parameters. The first parameter indicates the filename, the second indicates how the stream should be used. The ios constant in indicates the stream will be read from. The ios constant out indicates the stream will be written to. In this case, the | symbol was used in the parameters to tell the compiler that both in and out are to be used.

The fstream class is derived from the ios class. The fstream class includes all the functions and operators found in the ifstream and ofstream classes, and therefore its documentation will not be included here.

The Read and Write File program demonstrates the fstream class:

```
/*Read and Write File program. */

#include <iostream.h>
#include <fstream.h>

int main()
{
  fstream MyFile("composer.txt", ios::in | ios::out);
  if (MyFile.fail()) {
    cout << "File could not be opened";
    return(0);
  }
  else {
    char Character;
    MyFile.seekg(4);          // Advance to character 4
    MyFile >> Character;      // Read character at get pointer
    MyFile.seekp(0);          // Move the put pointer to character 0
    MyFile << Character;      // Write the character at put pointer
    MyFile.close();
    return(0);
  }
}
```

When run, the program displays no output unless there is a problem opening composer.txt.

Before running the program, composer.txt contains:

BEETHOVENBACH

After running the program, composer.txt contains:

HEETHOVENBACH

9.14 The tellg() and tellp() Functions

The current positions of the get and put pointers can be determined with the tellp() and tellg() functions. The tellp() function returns the position of the put pointer, and tellg() returns the position of the get pointer. For example, the following statements display the number of characters in the file associated with MyFile:

```
MyFile.seekg(0, ios::end);
cout << MyFile.tellg() << endl;
```

\n

The end-of-line character (\n) is stored as two characters in a file. This is important to note when manipulating data with file pointers.

Review 10

Write a program that encodes a file by replacing each letter in the file with a coded version, leaving non-letters unchanged. Use the function CodeChar() to encode each letter:

```
char CodeChar(const char Plain)
/*Encodes Plain
    Pre: Plain is a letter, uppercase or lowercase
    Post: Coded version of Plain returned        */
{
  switch(Plain) {
    case 'Z': return ('A');
    case 'z': return ('a');
    default: return(char(Plain+1));
  }
}
```

Review 11

Write a function that appends one file to another, with the file names given as String arguments. For example, if the two files are foo.txt and bar.txt, then the program should copy the contents of bar.txt onto the end of foo.txt. Assume that the files can be processed as lines of text using String and getline().

Case Study

In this Case Study, an inventory management program will be written.

The programs in this chapter are simplistic in that they only use character-level access. More commonly, a program manipulates larger units of data, for example structures containing information about a student in a school or a book in a bookstore. In more sophisticated C++ programming, this is accomplished by carefully formatting the data into a memory buffer, which is beyond the scope of this text. However, we can accomplish the same thing at only a small cost in efficiency by using random access files.

specification

Write an inventory management program for a bookstore. The program should be menu-driven to allow a title to be recorded (the author and copies in stock), a list of all the titles to be displayed, a selected title examined, and to update the stock for a title. Each book has a unique identification number. When run, the program output should be similar to:

```
Add title, Check/Change, List, Quit: L
0. The Shipping News    E. Annie Proulx      12
1. A Good Scent         Robert Butler         6
2. A Thousand Acres     Jane Smiley           8
Add title, Check/Change, List, Quit: A
Enter title: Rabbit at Rest
Enter author: John Updike
Enter number of copies: 3
Add title, Check/Change, List, Quit: C
Enter number of book to change: 2
2. A Thousand Acres     Jane Smiley           8
Add one to copies, Subtract one, Cancel: A
Add title, Check/Change, List, Quit: L
0. The Shipping News    E. Annie Proulx      12
1. A Good Scent         Robert Butler         6
2. A Thousand Acres     Jane Smiley           9
3. Rabbit at Rest       John Updike           3
Add title, Check/Change, List, Quit: Q
```

design—level 1

The main() function is designed first. The pseudocode for the major tasks is:

```
do
    Display menu of choices (Add title, Check/Change, List, Quit)
    switch
        A or a: AddBook
        C or c: ChangeBook
        L or l: ListBooks
        Q or q: Quit is true
while (!Quit)
```

Next, the main() pseudocode is used to determine the data design. A char variable Choice is needed to hold the user's menu choice. A bool variable Quit is needed to end the do loop. To store the book data permanently, a file on disk will be used. Since the file will be both read from and written to, an fstream object BookFile is needed.

The best data structure for storing the related information about a single book, or record, is a struct:

```
struct BookType {
    long CopiesInStock;
    String Title;
    String Author;
};
```

An algorithm for storing and locating the book records must now be developed. To store records, each data member in the struct could be written to the file separated by end-of-line characters (endl). To efficiently locate the records in the random access file, each record should take up the same amount of space. With each record having the same length the file is essentially divided into units. This makes it possible to know where to move the get and put pointers to access a specific record. In this case, the unit length could be computed as 80 characters for the book title, 50 characters for the author, 3 characters for the number of copies, and 2 characters for each end-of-line so in this case 6 characters for each record, for a total unit size of 139 characters. As a measure of safety, 150 characters will be allowed per record. The random access file could be thought of as:

Using this algorithm, the following statement moves the put pointer to the beginning of the second record:

F.seekp(1*150);

In general, the statement

F.seekp(RecNum*150);

could be used to move the put pointer. A RecNum of 0 will move the pointer to the 0th character in the file; a RecNum of 1 will move the pointer to the 150th character in the file, and so on.

This algorithm requires a constant to store the maximum record size:

const long MaxRecSize = 150;

coding—level 1

At this point, rather than coding main() as designed, a main() that tests writing and reading book records will be coded. For writing and reading records, a function NumRecords is needed for determining the number of records in the file:

```
long NumRecords(fstream &F)
/*Determines number of records in F based on record size of MaxRecSize
   Pre: F is open
   Post: Number of records in F returned                                    */
{
   F.seekp(0, ios::end);
   if (F.tellp()==0)
      return(0);
   else
      return(1+F.tellp()/MaxRecSize);
}
```

This function moves a pointer to the last character in the file and determines the location of the pointer. If the pointer is at 0, then the file contains no records. If the pointer is at some value greater than 0, the location of the pointer is divided by MaxRecSize. Since the last record will likely not use all 150 characters available for it, the number of characters in the file will not be a multiple of 150. Therefore, the integer division truncates any decimals and then 1 added to the quotient to compute the number of records. For example, if there are three records in the file, and the last record has 107 characters, tellp() returns 407. The expression 407/150 results in 2.71333, which is truncated to 2. Adding 1 results in 3.

To write a record to the file, the WriteBook() function must be coded:

```
bool WriteBook(fstream &F, const long RecNum, const BookType &Book)
/* Writes Book to F at position RecNum
   Pre: F is open for reading
   Post: Book written to F at RecNum record.
   false returned if read fails, true returned otherwise */
{
  if ((RecNum <= NumRecords(F)) && (F.seekp(RecNum*MaxRecSize))) {
    F.seekp(RecNum*MaxRecSize);
    F << Book.CopiesInStock << endl
    << Book.Title << endl
    << Book.Author << endl;
    return(true);
  }
  else
    return(false);
}
```

The order of the if condition is important. Checking for a valid RecNum must be done before checking the success of seekp(). If a seek is performed with a bad value, the results are unpredictable. A RecNum equal to the number of records occurs when a new record is to be appended.

To read a record in the file, the ReadBook() function must be coded:

```
bool ReadBook(fstream &F, const long RecNum, BookType &Book)
/* Reads record RecNum into Book
   Pre: F is open for reading
   Post: Book contains record RecNum.
   false returned if the read fails, otherwise true returned */
{
  if ((RecNum < NumRecords(F)) && (F.seekg(RecNum*MaxRecSize))) {
    getline(F, Book.CopiesInStock);
    getline(F, Book.Title);
    getline(F, Book.Author);
    return(true);
  }
  else
    return(false);
}
```

ReadBook uses the getline() for long values created in Section 9.11, as well as the getline() for strings.

All three functions require the constant, MaxRecSize. Defining this constant inside each function may lead to inconsistency and bugs. Defining the constant in main() and then passing it as a parameter is cumbersome. A third approach is to define the constant before the definitions of the functions, which makes the constant accessible from any function. Defin-

global declaration

ing a constant this way is called a *global declaration*. Global constants should be used only when absolutely necessary because they can make a program harder to understand. A more elegant solution is presented in the next chapter.

A Guide to Programming in C++

The following program tests reading and writing book records:

```
/*Bookstore test program */

#include <iostream.h>
#include <fstream.h>
#include <lvp\string.h>
#include <lvp\bool.h>

const long MaxRecSize = 150;  // Global constant
struct BookType {
  long CopiesInStock;
  String Title;
  String Author;
};
//-----------------------------------------------------------------------
istream & getline(istream &InFile, long &N)
/*Assigns the next value in InFile to N
   Post: Value from InFile stream assigned to N */
{
  InFile >> N;
  InFile.ignore(100,'\n');
  return(InFile);
}
//-----------------------------------------------------------------------
long NumRecords(fstream &F)
/*Determines number of records in F based on record size of MaxRecSize
   Pre: F is open
   Post: Number of records in F returned                              */
{
  F.seekp(0, ios::end);
  if (F.tellp()==0)
    return(0);
  else
    return(1+F.tellp()/MaxRecSize);
}
//-----------------------------------------------------------------------
bool ReadBook(fstream &F, const long RecNum, BookType &Book)
/*Reads record RecNum into Book
   Pre: F is open for reading
   Post: Book contains record RecNum.
   false returned if the read fails, otherwise true returned */
{
  if ((RecNum < NumRecords(F)) && (F.seekg(RecNum*MaxRecSize))) {
    getline(F, Book.CopiesInStock);
    getline(F, Book.Title);
    getline(F, Book.Author);
    return(true);
  }
  else
    return(false);
}
```

```
//-------------------------------------------------------------------------------
bool WriteBook(fstream &F, const long RecNum, const BookType &Book)
/* Writes Book to F at position RecNum
     Pre: F is open for reading
     Post: Book written to F at RecNum record.
     false returned if read fails, true returned otherwise */
{
  if ((RecNum <= NumRecords(F)) && (F.seekp(RecNum*MaxRecSize))) {
    F.seekp(RecNum*MaxRecSize);
    F << Book.CopiesInStock << endl
      << Book.Title << endl
      << Book.Author << endl;
    return(true);
  }
  else
    return(false);
}
//-------------------------------------------------------------------------------
int main()
{
  fstream BookFile("BookTest.txt", ios::in | ios::out);
  cout << NumRecords(BookFile) << endl;
  BookType Book1, Book2;
  Book1.Title = "First Book!";
  Book1.Author = "Author Name";
  Book1.CopiesInStock = 12;
  WriteBook(BookFile, 0, Book1);
  ReadBook(BookFile, 0, Book2);
  cout << Book2.Title << "/"
    << Book2.Author << "/"
    << Book2.CopiesInStock << endl;
  cout << NumRecords(BookFile) << endl;
  return(0);
}
```

When run, the program displays:

```
0
First Book!/Author Name/12
1
```

This simple test shows that the functions appear to work. However, more complex test programs are usually desired to thoroughly test functions.

Review 12

Write a function ListBooks() that displays a list of all books in the file used in the Case Study. Use the header:

```
void ListBooks(fstream &F)
/* Displays a list of the books in F
     Pre: F is open for reading
     Post: List of books displayed    */
```

Review 13

Modify WriteBook() in the Case Study so that it first checks the total length of the fields to verify that they do not exceed MaxRecSize.

design—level 2

In the next level of design, the real main() and the functions it calls are refined. The refined main() pseudocode is:

```
fstream BookFile("bookdata.txt", ios::in | ios::out)
char Choice
bool Quit = false
do
   Display menu of choices (Add title, Check/Change, List, Quit)
   switch
      A or a: AddBook(BookFile)
      C or c: ChangeBook(BookFile)
      L or l: ListBooks(BookFile)
      Q or q: Quit=true
while (!Quit)
```

The AddBook() pseudocode is:

```
Get book title, author, and stock from user
WriteBook(BookFile, NumRecords(BookFile), Book)
```

The ChangeBook() pseudocode is:

```
Get book number from user
Show book selected by user
Display menu of choices (Add one to copies, Subtract one,
   Cancel)
switch
   A or a: add one to copies in stock
   S or s: subtract one from copies in stock
   C or c: make no changes
```

The ListBooks() pseudocode is:

```
for each book in the file
   ReadBook(BookFile, RecNum, Book)
   show book
```

The ChangeBook() and ListBooks() functions include a step that shows a book's data. The show book step should also be a function.

Using the final design, the graphical representation of the program is:

The diagram shows that there is a set functions handling BookType operations (WriteBook(), ShowBook(), ReadBook(), NumRecords()), and two utility functions (the two getline() functions) to access the file.

coding—level 2   The final code is:

```
/* Bookstore Inventory program. */

#include <iostream.h>
#include <fstream.h>
#include <conio.h>   // for getche()
#include <lvp\string.h>
#include <lvp\bool.h>

const long MaxRecSize = 150;  // Global constant
struct BookType {
  long CopiesInStock;
  String Title;
  String Author;
};
//------------------------------------------------------------------------
istream & getline(istream &InFile, long &N)
/* Assigns the next value in InFile to N
   Post: Value from InFile stream assigned to N */
{
  InFile >> N;
  InFile.ignore(100,'\n');
  return(InFile);
}
//------------------------------------------------------------------------
long NumRecords(fstream &F)
/* Determines number of records in F based on record size of MaxRecSize
   Pre: F is open
   Post: Number of records in F returned                              */
{
  F.seekp(0, ios::end);
  if (F.tellp()==0)
    return(0);
  else
    return(1+F.tellp()/MaxRecSize);
}
//------------------------------------------------------------------------
bool ReadBook(fstream &F, const long RecNum, BookType &Book)
/* Reads record RecNum into Book
   Pre: F is open for reading
   Post: Book contains record RecNum.
   false returned if the read fails, otherwise true returned */
{
  if ((RecNum < NumRecords(F)) && (F.seekg(RecNum*MaxRecSize))) {
    getline(F, Book.CopiesInStock);
    getline(F, Book.Title);
    getline(F, Book.Author);
    return(true);
  }
  else
    return(false);
}
```

```
//--------------------------------------------------------------------------------
bool WriteBook(fstream &F, const long RecNum, const BookType &Book)
/*Writes Book to F at position RecNum
  Pre: F is open for reading
  Post: Book written to F at RecNum record.
  false returned if read fails, true returned otherwise */
{
  if ((RecNum <= NumRecords(F)) && (F.seekp(RecNum*MaxRecSize))) {
    F.seekp(RecNum*MaxRecSize);
    F << Book.CopiesInStock << endl
      << Book.Title << endl
      << Book.Author << endl;
    return(true);
  }
  else
    return(false);
}
//--------------------------------------------------------------------------------
void ShowBook(const long N, const BookType &Book)
/*Displays a book's data in a formatted line
  Post: N, Book displayed on a formatted line */
{
  cout.width(2); cout << N << ". ";
  cout.setf(ios::left);
  cout.width(20); cout << Book.Title << " ";
  cout.width(20); cout << Book.Author << " ";
  cout.setf(ios::right);
  cout.width(5); cout << Book.CopiesInStock << endl;
}
//--------------------------------------------------------------------------------
void ChangeBook(fstream &BookFile)
/*Displays a book and allows user to change its stock.
  Pre: BookFile is open for read/write
  Post: Book selected by user has been displayed and
  stock may have been changed.                        */
{
  long BookNum;
  BookType Book;
  while (true) {
    cout << "Enter number of book to change: ";
    getline(cin, BookNum);
    if (ReadBook(BookFile, BookNum, Book))
      break;
    cout << "Bad book number" << endl;
  }
  ShowBook(BookNum, Book);
  char Choice;
  cout << "Add one to copies, Subtract one, Cancel: ";
  Choice = getche(); cout << endl;
  switch (Choice) {
    case 'A':
    case 'a': Book.CopiesInStock++;
              WriteBook(BookFile, BookNum, Book);
              break;
    case 'S':
    case 's': Book.CopiesInStock--;
              WriteBook(BookFile, BookNum, Book);
              break;
    case 'C':
    case 'c': cout << "Change canceled" << endl;
              break;
  }
}
```

```
//-----------------------------------------------------------------------
void AddBook(fstream &BookFile)
/* Adds a book record to BookFile
    Pre: BookFile is open for read/write
    Post: Book data entered by user appended to BookFile. */
{
    BookType Book;
    cout << "Enter title: ";
    getline(cin,Book.Title);
    cout << "Enter author: ";
    getline(cin,Book.Author);
    cout << "Enter number of copies: ";
    getline(cin,Book.CopiesInStock);
    WriteBook(BookFile, NumRecords(BookFile), Book);
}
//-----------------------------------------------------------------------
void ListBooks(fstream &BookFile)
/* Displays a formatted table of book data.
    Pre: BookFile is open for reading
    Post: List of books displayed              */
{
    long i;
    for (i=0; i < NumRecords(BookFile); i++) {
        BookType Book;
        ReadBook(BookFile, i, Book);
        ShowBook(i, Book);
    }
}
//-----------------------------------------------------------------------
int main()
{
    fstream BookFile("BookData.txt", ios::in | ios::out);
    bool Quit = false;
    char Choice;
    do {
        cout << "Add title, Check/Change, List, Quit: ";
        Choice = getche();
        cout << endl;
        switch (Choice) {
            case 'A':
            case 'a': AddBook(BookFile); break;
            case 'C':
            case 'c': ChangeBook(BookFile); break;
            case 'L':
            case 'l': ListBooks(BookFile); break;
            case 'q':
            case 'Q': Quit = true; break;
            default: cout << "Bad command" << endl;
        }
    } while (!Quit);
    return(0);
}
```

When run, the program output is similar to that shown in the specification.

Review 14

Modify the Case Study to use the struct BookType with two additional data members, Publisher and PubYear. Be sure to modify all the code to use the two additional data members.

A Guide to Programming in C++

Review 15

Modify the Case Study to display titles that contain a word entered by the user. The program output should look similar to:

```
...
Enter a word from the title: good
Matches:
    1. A Good Scent                 Robert Butler
    2. Good Grief, Charlie Brown!   Charles Schultz
Choose by number: 2
...
```

Review 16

Modify the Case Study to include a purge command that removes all the records from the file with zero CopiesInStock. To do this, copy all the nonzero records to a new file, and then use remove() and rename() to make this new file the one used by the program.

Chapter Summary

A stream processes characters, and in C++, streams are implemented with classes. The fstream library contains the ifstream class, ofstream class, and the fstream class. The fstream classes are derived from the ios class and therefore inherits all the properties of the ios class. The ifstream class is used to instantiate an input (read) file stream. The ofstream class is used to instantiate an output (write) file stream. The fstream class is used to instantiate a file stream for input or output. In general, all functions and operators that process a file stream return a value that evaluates to true when an operation is successful and false when an operation fails.

A file on disk is a set of characters. To process a file, it must have a file stream associated with it. Characters can be read from the file stream as numbers, strings, or characters. The >> operator automatically skips whitespace and is usually used to process a file containing numbers. The get() member function is usually used to process a file containing characters. The getline() function is usually used to process a file containing strings. The ignore() function is used to read and then discard characters from the file stream. The eof() function is used to detect the end-of-file.

The << operator is used to write data to the output stream. The width(), setf(), and precision() member functions can be used to write formatted data to a file.

The open() and close() member functions can be used to change the file associated with a file stream. This is useful when opening a file specified by the user. The c_str() function is a member function of the string class and is used to convert a string entered by the user to a C-style string which is required by the open() function.

Stream object parameters must be passed as reference arguments. A function may return a reference to a stream object.

The remove() and rename() functions in the stdio library are used to rename or delete a file.

The items in a sequential access file are accessed one item at a time in the order that they are stored. The items in a random access file are accessed in any order, usually determined by an algorithm implemented in a program. Random file access is possible because the file stream maintains the get and put pointers for reading and writing to a file. The pointers are moved with the seekg() and seekp() functions, respectively. The tellg() and tellp() functions are used to determine the positions of the get and put pointers, respectively.

Vocabulary

Base Class A class that is used as the basis of an inherited class.

Derived Class A class that has all the properties of its base class.

Get Pointer The file stream pointer that tells where the next read operation will start.

Global Declaration Defining a constant before function definitions to make it accessible from any function.

Inheritance The property of object-oriented programming in which a class can be derived from another class.

Put Pointer The file stream pointer that tells where the next write operation will occur.

Random Access File A file with items that are accessed in an arbitrary order, usually determined by an algorithm implemented in a program.

Sequential Access File A file with items that are accessed one after the other in the order stored.

Stream Processes characters.

Whitespace Spaces, tabs, and newlines in a file.

C++

& Used to indicate that a reference is being returned by a function.

>> Operator used to read data from a file stream.

c_str() A String member function that converts a string to a C-style string.

fstream A class in the fstream library that is used to create an output or input file stream.

ifstream A class in the fstream library that is used to create an input file stream.

ios::end The ios constant that moves the file pointer to the end of a file.

ofstream A class in the fstream library that is used to create an output file stream.

stdio.h The standard input/output library that contains the rename() and remove() functions for renaming and deleting a file.

9 | Exercises

Exercise 1

Write a program that displays the number of words and the average word length in the text file source.txt. Consider a word to be any sequence of letters terminated by nonletters. For example, forty-nine is two words.

Exercise 2

Write a program that replaces all occurrences of a word or phrase in a file with a specified word or phrase. The program output should be similar to:

```
Enter name of file: myfile.txt
Enter word to search for: gotta
Enter word to replace it with: got to
```

Exercise 3

Write a program that copies a file named source.cpp containing C++ code to another file named src.cpp with all comments eliminated. Be sure to consider both /* */ and // formatted comments.

Exercise 4   *Pascal required*

Write a program that provides some Pascal to C++ translation. The program should replace Pascal keywords and symbols with their C++ equivalents. Store the list of translations in a file so that it can be easily extended. The following table provides some of the translations:

Pascal	C++	Pascal	C++
begin	{	end	}
{	/*	}	*/
(*	/*	*)	*/
:=	=	=	==
<>	!=	not	!
if	if (	then	)
else	; else	repeat	do {
while	while (	until	} while (
do	)		

Exercise 5

a) Write a program that lists all the unique words in a file, and how many times they occurred. Ignore capitalization. The program output should be similar to:

```
Enter name of file: myfile.txt
WORD                NUMBER
the                     57
boy                      8
and                     12
...
```

b) Modify the program to list the words in alphabetical order. Do this by using either the sorting algorithm presented in Chapter Eight Exercise 10, or by keeping the words in order as they are read.

Exercise 6

Test results for a multiple choice test can be stored in a text file as follows:

Line 1: The correct answers, one character per answer
Line 2: Name of the first student (length <= 30 chars)
Line 3: Answers for the student in line 2
The remaining lines: student names and answers on separate lines

For example:

```
BADED
Smithgall
BADDD
DeSalvo
CAEED
Darji
BADED
```

Write a program that processes the test results file for any number of students. The program output should be similar to:

```
Smithgall    80%
DeSalvo      60%
Darji        100%
```

Exercise 7

Write a program that processes the data file described in Exercise 6 to produce a statistical analysis showing the responses given to each question, and the percent of students who gave the correct answer. To easily understand the output, the correct answers should be marked with an asterisk. For example:

	A	B	C	D	E	%
1	0	2*	1	0	0	67
2	3*	0	0	0	0	100
3	0	0	0	2*	1	67
4	0	0	0	1	2*	67
5	0	0	0	3*	0	100

Exercise 8

A Mad-Lib story is a story where nouns and verbs in a paragraph are randomly replaced with other nouns and verbs, usually with humorous results. Write a program that displays a Mad-Lib story. The program should use three files:

- story.txt which contains a story with # signs as noun placeholders, and % signs as verb placeholders. For example:

  Bugsy Kludge is a # with our company.
  His job is to % all of the #s.

- verbs.txt which contains verbs, one per line. For example:

  run
  display
  eat

- nouns.txt which contains nouns, one per line. For example:

  banana
  soprano
  elephant
  vegetable

The program output may be similar to:

  Bugsy Kludge is a vegetable with our company.
  His job is to display all of the elephants.

Exercise 9

The idea of merging two or more files is an important one in programming. One approach is to merge the ordered data of two files into a third file, keeping the data in order.

Write a program that merges the integers ordered from low to high in two files into a third file, keeping the order from low to high. First, create two files containing about 15 to 20 integer values, each file in order from low to high. Have the files hold different numbers of integers. For example:

  File 1: 12 23 34 45 56 67 69 123 133
  File 2: 4 5 10 20 35 44 100 130 150 160 180

The program should not use an array to temporarily store the numbers, but should merge the two files by taking one element at a time from each. Do not use the seekp() or seekg() functions in the program. After running the program, the third file should look similar to:

  4 5 10 12 20 23 34 35 44 45 56 67 69 100 123 130 133 150 160 180

Exercise 10

The algorithm used in the program in Exercise 9 is sometimes used as part of a sorting algorithm with data that is too large to be stored in memory at once. For example, to sort a large file large.dat that is twice as large as will fit in memory, half can be read into an array, the array sorted and then written to a file numbers1.dat. Next, the second half of large.dat can be read into the array, sorted, and then written to numbers2.dat. Finally, the two files can be merged in order back into large.dat. All of this can be done without using the seek functions. Implement this algorithm in a program. Test the program with a file that contains 30 integers sorted from low to high.

Exercise 11

The early success of the World Wide Web is largely due to the simplicity of HTML (HyperText Markup Language), the code used to represent pages. HTML provides a way to describe Web pages that can be interpreted by any computer, any screen width, etc. A Web page might be stored in a file like this:

Do not go gentle into that good night,
 Old age should burn and rave at close of day;
 Rage, rage against the dying of the light. <P> Though wise men at their end know dark is right,
 Because their words had forked no lightning they
 Do not go gentle into that good night.<P> <HR>

Tags are enclosed in angle brackets, < >. The command <BR> means to start a new line. The command <P> means to start a new paragraph (a blank line). The command <HR> means to draw a horizontal rule. When these commands are interpreted, the following is displayed:

```
Do not go gentle into that good night,
Old age should burn and rave at close of day;
Rage, rage against the dying of the light.

Though wise men at their end know dark is right,
Because their words had forked no lightning they
Do not go gentle into that good night.

------------------------------------------------
```

a) Write a program that properly displays a file containing these HTML format codes.

b) Modify the program so that the user may specify the display line width. For example, a width of 30 should display the HTML document as:

```
Do not go gentle into that
good night,
Old age should burn and rave
at close of day;
Rage, rage against the dying
of the light.
...
```

9

Exercise 12

The manager of the campus radio station needs a program to keep track of the CDs in the station's library. Write a program that stores each CD title, artist, status, and location in a file. The status may be OK, damaged, or lost. The location should be the shelf number (an integer). The station librarian should be able to perform the following functions on the file:

- Add CDs
- Find and change the information stored for a CD by specifying the title
- Display the information for all of the lost CDs
- Display the information for all of the CDs on a given shelf
- Display the information for all of the CDs by a given artist

Exercise 13 ☼

Modify the HangMan program from Chapter Eight Exercise 8 to use words stored in a file. Have the program choose words from the file at random. One algorithm for doing this is to generate a random number and then use the word that correlates to that number. For example, if the number generated is 7, the 7th word in the file is used.

Exercise 14

All database programs perform basically the same tasks, whether the database stores student, CD, book, or soccer game records. This realization led to general database programs like dBase and Access.

Write a small-scale general database program. Have the program get the filename from the user. If it is found on the disk, it will be opened. If not, it will be set up as a new file. The user specifies the names of the fields, the field types (number or text), and their field lengths (if text). The program writes the setup information to the 0th record of the file, along with the maximum record size. The user then has the option of adding or listing records.

The program output should be similar to:

```
Enter name of file to use: soccer.dat
File not found. Set up a new file (Y/N)? Y
Enter a field (blank to quit): Opponent
Text or Numeric: T
Enter length: 25
Enter a field (blank to quit): OppScore
Text or Numeric: N
Enter a field (blank to quit): OurScore
Text or Numeric: N
Enter a field (blank to quit):
Setup, Add, List, Quit: A
Enter Opponent: South Fork High
Enter OppScore: 2
Enter OurScore: 3
Setup, Add, List, Quit: L
Opponent            OppScore    OurScore
South Fork High     2           3
Setup, Add, List, Quit: Q
```

Exercise 15

Owners of Web servers like to monitor access to their servers so they can determine if their servers are getting used, if customers are visiting, etc. All servers create a log file of requests. A typical log file may look like this:

```
38.249.60.78 - - [22/Mar/1996:08:07:13 -0500] "GET / HTTP/1.0" 200 1260
38.249.60.78 - - [22/Mar/1996:08:07:14 -0500] "GET /new.gif HTTP/1.0" 200 285
38.249.60.78 - - [22/Mar/1996:08:07:16 -0500] "GET /seal.gif HTTP/1.0" 200 9529
202.32.234.125 - - [22/Mar/1996:09:42:43 -0500] "GET /new.gif HTTP/1.0" 200 285
202.32.234.125 - - [22/Mar/1996:09:42:46 -0500] "GET / HTTP/1.0" 200 1260
202.32.234.125 - - [22/Mar/1996:09:42:57 -0500] "GET /seal.gif HTTP/1.0" 200 9529
159.164.29.128 - - [22/Mar/1996:09:51:14 -0500] "GET / HTTP/1.0" 200 1260
159.164.29.128 - - [22/Mar/1996:09:51:14 -0500] "GET /new.gif HTTP/1.0" 200 285
159.164.29.128 - - [22/Mar/1996:09:51:16 -0500] "GET /seal.gif HTTP/1.0" 200 9529
159.164.29.128 - - [22/Mar/1996:09:51:48 -0500] "GET /coll3.htm HTTP/1.0" 200 8665
159.164.29.128 - - [22/Mar/1996:09:51:51 -0500] "GET /grads.gif HTTP/1.0" 200 3705
159.164.29.128 - - [22/Mar/1996:09:53:02 -0500] "GET /gallry.htm HTTP/1.0" 200 279
```

The first group of numbers is the Internet address of the computer accessing the server. This is followed by the date and time, some other data, the GET command, and the page requested (e.g., "/new.gif" or "/coll3.htm") and finally some other information. If the GET command shows just a slash character, /, it indicates a request for the home page of the site.

Write a program that processes a log file in the format shown above to produce a breakdown of "hits" in output similar to:

```
home page   3
new.gif     3
seal.gif    3
coll3.htm   1
grads.gif   1
gallry.htm  1
```

Exercise 16

Modify the Case Study to include a backup command that makes a copy of the data file to a new file using a name entered by the user.

Advanced
Exercise 17

Write a data-driven Survey Administrator program that conducts a survey and stores the data in a file. The program should give the user the option to tabulate data, as well as add data. The program output with the survey questions to ask should look similar to:

```
Enter data, Display stats, or Quit: E
Do you know programming languages other than C++? Y
What computer do you own (Pc, Mac, Other, None)? N
Have you ever used a word processor (Y/N)? N

Enter data, Display stats, or Quit: E
Do you know programming languages other than C++? N
What computer do you own (Pc, Mac, Other, None)? M
Have you ever used a word processor (Y/N)? Y

Enter data, Display stats, or Quit: D
Do you know programming languages other than C++?
   Yes   17
   No    23
What computer do you own (Pc, Mac, Other, None)?
   P   13
   M    5
   O    3
   N   10
Have you ever used a word processor (Y/N)?
   N   15
   Y   25
```

In the sample run above, the statistics displayed are for more than the two entries because previous respondents to the survey are stored in a file.

The program should be *data-driven*. This means that the behavior of the program is substantially modified simply by changing the contents of one or more data files. In this case, the data driving the program is the survey questions contained in a text file:

> Do you know programming languages other than C++?
> What computer do you own (Pc, Mac, Other, None)?
> Have you ever used a word processor (Y/N)?

The program is to read this text file, and then provide the menu options. The results should be stored so that users can enter more data at any time.

9

A Guide to Programming in C++

Chapter Ten
Building Classes

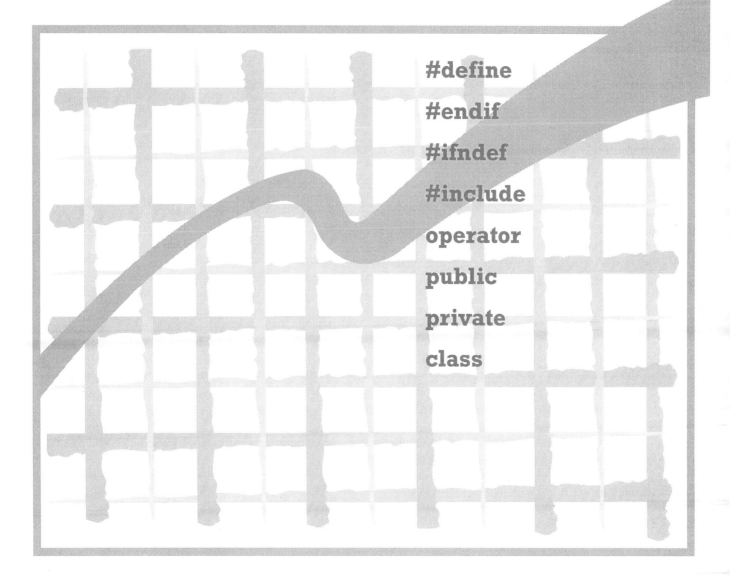

#define

#endif

#ifndef

#include

operator

public

private

class

Objectives

After completing this chapter you will be able to:

1. Create classes and include them as part of a library.

2. Build utility classes.

3. Use compiler directives.

4. Understand the concepts of object-oriented programming and design.

0

The central concept of C++ programming is the class. In this chapter you will learn how to create classes.

10.1 The C++ Class

As defined in Chapter Six, a class is a user-defined type that can include data members and member functions. Up to this point, the documentation of pre-existing classes has been presented for programs using these classes. Classes used so far include string, PegClass, TopListClass, CollegeClass, ofstream, ifstream, fstream, vector<>, and matrix<>.

A class may contain a constructor member function that is automatically called when an object is instantiated to properly initialize the object. For example, when a PegClass object is instantiated the height of the peg must be included as a parameter for the PegClass constructor. A class may contain other member functions that act on an object. For example, PegClass contains AddRing(), RemoveRing(), and RingsOnPeg().

encapsulation

data hiding

Classes, like the ones used so far, are often coded as part of a library that can then be included in a program. The property of object-oriented programming in which code is self-contained in a separate unit is called *encapsulation*. With proper documentation, libraries can be used without regard to how the classes they contain work. This property of object-oriented programming is called *data hiding*.

10.2 The AccountClass Class

A program that maintains bank account information would keep track of each account name, opening date, and current balance, and would be able to provide a complete list of transactions. At a bank, it is important that every transaction for each account be recorded for security and information reasons. In this section, a class for maintaining bank account information will be implemented.

The same method used to construct good programs and functions should be used to construct classes. This method is specification, design, coding, and debugging and testing.

The specification of a class defines how an object may be accessed by a programmer, and is called the *public* section of a class. The AccountClass public member functions are:

```
// Constructor
AccountClass(String AcctName, String AcctOpenDate);
/* Opens AcctName account on AcctOpenDate.
   Post: AcctName balance is zero, and transaction recorded */

void Deposit(double Amt, String Date);
/* Adds deposit to Acct and records transaction
   Post: Amt added to account, and transaction recorded */

bool Withdrawal(double Amt, String Date);
/* Subtracts withdrawal from account and records transaction
   Post: if Amt<=Balance, Amt deleted from account, transaction recorded,
   and true returned. Otherwise, false returned, attempt recorded,
   and balance unchanged.                                           */

double GetBalance() const;
/* Determines current balance
   Post: Current balance returned */

void WriteTransactions(ostream & OutFile) const;
/* Writes transactions to OutFile
   Post: All information about the account written to OutFile,
   including a list of all transactions.                       */
```

The public member functions of a class specify the only way that objects of the class can be accessed. In other words, the data associated with an object can be changed only through public member functions. In this case, these member functions guarantee that all transactions are recorded because both Deposit() and Withdrawal() record the transaction. The constructor requires the account name and opening date as arguments, and also records the opening transaction. Part of the power of classes is the ability to restrict access to data so that the integrity and consistency of the data can be maintained.

The AccountClass member functions do not have preconditions because the only prerequisite for their proper operation is that an AccountClass object has been instantiated, which is guaranteed by the constructor.

The functions GetBalance() and WriteTransactions() do not change their calling object in any way. To strictly reinforce this, the keyword const appears in the member function header. A const member function cannot change any object data.

The WriteTransactions() function has an ostream (output stream) object as its parameter. This allows the function to be passed the console output stream (cout) for transactions to be written to the screen, or a file output stream (ofstream object) for transactions to be written to a file.

In designing the class, there are also *private* functions and data members that are not accessible to code outside of the class, but are needed by the public part of the class.

The variables associated with a class are called data members, and are usually private. The AccountClass class needs data members that store the account name (String Name), opening date (String Date), and current balance (double Balance). Arrays are the best data structure to store the date (vector<String> TransDates), type (vector<String> TransKinds), and amount (vector<double> TransAmts) of transactions.

class declaration

The *class declaration* includes the public member function and private data member declarations, and has the form:

```
class classname {
  public:
    // public members listed here
  private:
    // private members listed here
};
```

The AccountClass class declaration is:

```
class AccountClass {
public:
    // Constructor
    AccountClass(String AcctName, String AcctOpenDate);
    /* Opens AcctName account on AcctOpenDate.
       Post: AcctName balance is zero, and transaction recorded */

    void Deposit(double Amt, String Date);
    /* Adds deposit to Acct and records transaction
       Post: Amt added to account, and transaction recorded */

    bool Withdrawal(double Amt, String Date);
    /* Subtracts withdrawal from account and records transaction
       Post: if Amt<=Balance, Amt deleted from account,
       transaction recorded, and true returned. Otherwise, false returned,
       attempt recorded, and balance unchanged.                       */

    double GetBalance() const;
    /* Determines current balance
       Post: Current balance returned */

    void WriteTransactions(ostream & OutFile) const;
    /* Writes transactions to OutFile
       Post: All information about the account written to OutFile,
       including a list of all transactions.                       */

private:
    String Name;
    String OpenDate;
    double Balance;
    vector<String> TransDates, TransKinds;
    vector<double> TransAmts;
};
```

Note that the declaration ends with a semicolon. Coding the member functions and testing the class still remain.

Review 1

Write a program with main() instantiating an AccountClass object and exercising each of the member functions. Write down the expected output of the program.

A struct is a simpler form of a class. Using the struct syntax described in Chapter Eight, write a constructor for AccountClass according to its specification.

10.3 Defining Member Functions

Member functions require the class name as well as the function name separated by two colons (::) in the following form:

return type class name::member function name(parameters)
```
{
   statements
}
```

For example, the AccountClass GetBalance() member function is written:

```
double AccountClass::GetBalance() const
/* Determines current balance
   Post: Current balance returned */
{
   return (Balance);
}
```

The AccountClass Deposit() member function may be defined similarly:

```
void AccountClass::Deposit(double Amt, String Date)
/* Adds deposit to Acct and records transaction
   Post: Amt added to account, and transaction recorded */
{
   Balance += Amt;
   TransDates.resize(TransDates.length() + 1);
   TransDates[TransDates.length()–1] = Date;

   TransKinds.resize(TransKinds.length() + 1);
   TransKinds[TransKinds.length()–1] = "Deposit";

   TransAmts.resize(TransAmts.length() + 1);
   TransAmts[TransAmts.length()–1] = Amt;
}
```

The remaining AccountClass member functions are implemented similarly.

constructor

A class constructor member function has the same form as a struct constructor described in Chapter Eight. Constructors cannot have a return type, and therefore never include a return statement. A constructor is used to initialize data members. As with a struct constructor, it is good programming style to perform initializations in the initializer list. For example, the AccountClass class constructor is defined as:

```
AccountClass::AccountClass(String AcctName, String AcctOpenDate)
   : Name(AcctName), OpenDate(AcctOpenDate), Balance(0),
   TransDates(0), TransKinds(0), TransAmts(0)
/* Opens AcctName account on AcctOpenDate.
   Post: AcctName balance is zero, and transaction recorded */
{
}
```

10.4 The account Library

header file

interface file

implementation file

coding

A library is coded in two files. The first, called the *header file* is saved with a .h extension and contains the class declarations and any required #include statements. The header file is also called the *interface file* since it describes the interface between the library and a program that uses it. The second file, called the *implementation file* is saved with a .cpp extension and contains class member function definitions.

To create an account library that contains the AccountClass class, the AccountClass class is coded in two files:

account.h

```
/* Implements a bank account class which maintains and
   can display a list of all transactions on the account      */

#include <iostream.h>
#include <lvp\bool.h>
#include <lvp\string.h>
#include <lvp\vector.h>

class AccountClass {
public:
  // Constructor
  AccountClass(String AcctName, String AcctOpenDate);
  /* Opens AcctName account on AcctOpenDate.
     Post: AcctName balance is zero, and transaction recorded */

  void Deposit(double Amt, String Date);
  /* Adds deposit to Acct and records transaction
     Post: Amt added to account, and transaction recorded */

  bool Withdrawal(double Amt, String Date);
  /* Subtracts withdrawal from account and records transaction
     Post: if Amt<=Balance, Amt deleted from account,
     transaction recorded, and true returned. Otherwise, false returned,
     attempt recorded, and balance unchanged.                 */

  double GetBalance() const;
  /* Determines current balance
     Post: Current balance returned */

  void WriteTransactions(ostream & OutFile) const;
  /* Writes transactions to OutFile
     Post: All information about the account written to OutFile,
     including a list of all transactions.                    */

private:
  String Name;
  String OpenDate;
  double Balance;
  vector<String> TransDates, TransKinds;
  vector<double> TransAmts;
};

#include "account.cpp"
```

To inform the compiler that account.h requires the code in account.cpp it ends with the statement:

```
#include "account.cpp"
```

The .cpp file must be included at the end so that the implementations are compiled after the declaration of the class. Double-quotation marks are used rather than angle brackets to indicate that the #include file is in the current directory rather than in the standard include directory.

account.cpp

```cpp
/* AccountClass class implementation */

#include <iostream.h>
#include <lvp\vector.h>
#include <lvp\string.h>

//-------------------------------------------------------------------
AccountClass::AccountClass(String AcctName, String AcctOpenDate)
  : Name(AcctName), OpenDate(AcctOpenDate), Balance(0),
    TransDates(0), TransKinds(0), TransAmts(0)
/* Opens AcctName account on AcctOpenDate.
   Post: AcctName balance is zero, and transaction recorded */
{
}
//-------------------------------------------------------------------
void AccountClass::Deposit(double Amt, String Date)
/* Adds deposit to Acct and records transaction
   Post: Amt added to account, and transaction recorded */
{
  Balance += Amt;
  TransDates.resize(TransDates.length() + 1);
  TransDates[TransDates.length()-1] = Date;

  TransKinds.resize(TransKinds.length() + 1);
  TransKinds[TransKinds.length()-1] = "Deposit";

  TransAmts.resize(TransAmts.length() + 1);
  TransAmts[TransAmts.length()-1] = Amt;
}
//-------------------------------------------------------------------
bool AccountClass::Withdrawal(double Amt, String Date)
/* Subtracts withdrawal from account and records transaction
   Post: if Amt<=Balance, Amt deleted from account, transaction recorded,
   and true returned. Otherwise, false returned, attempt recorded,
   and balance unchanged.                                          */
{
  TransDates.resize(TransDates.length() + 1);
  TransDates[TransDates.length()-1] = Date;
  TransKinds.resize(TransKinds.length() + 1);
  TransAmts.resize(TransAmts.length() + 1);
  TransAmts[TransAmts.length()-1] = Amt;
  if (Amt <= Balance) {
    Balance -= Amt;
    TransKinds[TransKinds.length()-1] = "Withdrawal";
    return(true);
  }
  else {
    TransKinds[TransKinds.length()-1] = "Withdrawal/Failed";
    return(false);
  }
}
```

```
//----------------------------------------------------------------------------
double AccountClass::GetBalance() const
/*Determines current balance
   Post: Current balance returned */
{
  return (Balance);
}
//----------------------------------------------------------------------------
void AccountClass::WriteTransactions(ostream & OutFile) const
/*Writes transactions to OutFile
   Post: All information about the account written to OutFile,
   including a list of all transactions.                        */
{
  OutFile.setf(ios::fixed);
  OutFile.precision(2);
  OutFile << Name << endl;
  OutFile << "Acct opened on " << OpenDate << " Balance: "
  << Balance << endl;
  OutFile << "Transactions" << endl;
  for (int i=0; i<TransDates.length(); i++) {
    OutFile.width(12); OutFile << TransDates[i];
    OutFile.width(22); OutFile << TransKinds[i];
    OutFile.width(12); OutFile << TransAmts[i] << endl;
  }
}
```

The account library can now be included in a program to use the
AccountClass class. A program that uses a class is often called the *client
program*. The following client program demonstrates AccountClass:

client program

```
/*AccountClass class demonstration program */

#include "account.h"
#include <iostream.h>

int main()
{
  AccountClass Storer("Ms. Tomacina Storer", "1/2/98");
  Storer.Deposit(100,"1/2/98");
  Storer.Withdrawal(10,"1/7/98");
  Storer.Withdrawal(15,"1/9/98");
  Storer.Withdrawal(95,"1/19/98");
  Storer.WriteTransactions(cout);
  return(0);
}
```

When run, the program output is:

```
Ms. Tomacina Storer
Acct opened on 1/2/98 Balance: 75.00
Transactions
        1/2/98               Deposit        100.00
        1/7/98            Withdrawal         10.00
        1/9/98            Withdrawal         15.00
       1/19/98     Withdrawal/Failed         95.00
```

It is usually necessary to compile only the client program because most
compilers automatically compile and link any libraries used by the client
program.

A program that uses a class cannot access the private members of the class. For example, if the main() function above contained the statement

```
cout << Storer.Balance << endl;
```

a compiler error would be generated indicating that Balance is "not accessible." Designating Balance as private in the AccountClass class guarantees that its value cannot be modified without the change being recorded in the transaction list.

Review 3

Write a program that tests a function TransFunds(). Use the following header for TransFunds():

```
bool TransFunds(AccountClass &Source, AccountClass &Dest,
    double Amount)
/*Transfers funds from Source account to Dest account.
    Post: If Source >=Amount, true returned, Amount subtracted from
    Source account, and Amount added to Dest account. If Source<Amount,
    false returned, Source and Dest unchanged.                  */
```

Review 4

Write a function GiveInterest() that adds interest to an AccountClass object using the Deposit() member function. The account and interest rate should be passed as arguments.

Review 5

The Withdrawal() function returns a bool value indicating whether the withdrawal was successful or not. Modify the AccountClass Class Demonstration program to examine this returned value. Have the program display an appropriate message depending on the return value.

10.5 Default Constructors

A *default constructor* requires no parameters to instantiate an object. For example, the following statement creates an array of 100 accounts:

```
vector<AccountClass> Bank(100);
```

When a default constructor is used to instantiate an object, the class must include member functions to initialize the object.

The AccountClass class is modified to include a default constructor by first adding the default constructor prototype to the class declaration in account.h:

```
class AccountClass {
public:
    AccountClass();
    /*Default constructor */

    AccountClass(String AcctName, String AcctOpenDate);
    /*Opens AcctName account on AcctOpenDate.
        Post: AcctName balance is zero, and transaction recorded */
    . . .
    Remainder of AccountClass class declaration
```

Next, data members and member functions for initializing an object must be added to the class. Good programming style dictates that access to data be restricted so that the integrity and consistency of the data can be maintained. Therefore, when modifying AccountClass:

- No transactions may be made on an account until a name and date have been specified.

- The name and date may be specified only once on a given account.

The AccountClass class declaration in account.h is modified to contain three more additional members. Two public member functions:

```
void SpecifyAccount(String AcctName, String AcctOpenDate);
/* Assigns AcctName and AcctOpenDate to account if account not initialized
   Post: AcctName assigned to Name and AcctOpenDate assigned to
   OpenDate if account was not already initialized. IsOpen is true.         */

String GetName() const;
/* Determines account name
   Post: Name returned         */
```

and a private data member:

```
bool IsOpen;
```

The new data member, IsOpen, keeps track of the state of the account, and is initialized to false in the default constructor and true in the constructor with parameters. GetName() is useful when there is an array of accounts.

Other AccountClass member functions will need to be modified. The Deposit() and Withdrawal() functions should check IsOpen before proceeding, and return false if the operation failed because the account was not open. This will require changing the Deposit() function to return a bool value rather than void. Since the WriteTransactions() and GetBalance() functions do not modify the account in any way, they remain unchanged.

Finally, the new member function definitions are added to account.cpp. The default constructor, SpecifyAccount(), and GetName() member function definitions are:

```
AccountClass::AccountClass()
 : Balance(0), TransDates(0), TransKinds(0), TransAmts(0), IsOpen(false)
/* default constructor */
{
}
//----------------------------------------------------------------------------
void AccountClass::SpecifyAccount(String AcctName,
  String AcctOpenDate)
/* Assigns AcctName and AcctOpenDate to account if account not initialized
   Post: AcctName assigned to Name and AcctOpenDate assigned to
   OpenDate if account was not already initialized. IsOpen is true.         */
{
  if (!IsOpen) {
    Name = AcctName;
    OpenDate = AcctOpenDate;
    IsOpen = true;
  }
}
```

```
//-------------------------------------------------------------------------
String AccountClass::GetName() const
/* Determines account name
   Post: Name returned        */
{
  return(Name);
}
```

Also in account.cpp, the Deposit() and Withdrawal() member functions are modified to check the status of IsOpen.

For demonstration purposes, the modified AccountClass class is saved in account2.h and account2.cpp. The program below demonstrates the modified AccountClass class:

```
/* AccountClass class with default constructor program */

#include "account2.h"
#include <iostream.h>
#include <lvp\vector.h>

int main()
{
  vector<AccountClass> Bank(100);
  int NumAccounts = 0;
  int i;
  const int NumToTest = 3;
  String Name, Date;
  double InitialDeposit;

  // Enter account data
  for (i=0; i<NumToTest; i++) {
    cout << "Enter name #" << (i+1) << ": " ;
    getline(cin, Name);
    cout << "Enter date #" << (i+1) << ": " ;
    getline(cin, Date);
    cout << "Enter initial deposit for #" << (i+1) << ": " ;
    cin >> InitialDeposit;
    cin.ignore(80,'\n');

    Bank[i].SpecifyAccount(Name, Date);
    Bank[i].Deposit(InitialDeposit, Date);
    NumAccounts++;
  }

  // Display a list of accounts
  for (i=0; i<NumAccounts; i++) {
    cout.width(25);
    cout.setf(ios::left);
    cout << Bank[i].GetName() << Bank[i].GetBalance() << endl;
  }
  return(0);
}
```

When run, the program displays:

```
Enter name #1: Samantha Jones
Enter date #1: 3/10/97
Enter initial deposit for #1: 100
Enter name #2: Daniel Adams
Enter date #2: 3/21/97
Enter initial deposit for #2: 345
```

```
Enter name #3: Matthew Curry
Enter date #3: 2/16/97
Enter initial deposit for #3: 260
Samantha Jones      100
Daniel Adams        345
Matthew Curry       260
```

Review 6

Will the AccountClass class demonstration program in Section 10.4 work as expected with the modified AccountClass class (account2.h)? Explain your reasoning, and then test it.

Review 7

Modify the demonstration program in Section 10.5 to use a function AddAccount() that has the following header:

```
void AddAccount(vector<AccountClass> &Bank, int &NumAccounts,
    String NameOfAcct, String DateOfAcct)
/*Adds NameOfAcct account to Bank
   Pre: NumAccounts < Bank.length()
   Post: NameOfAcct account added to Bank array and
   NumAccounts incremented.                              */
```

Review 8

Use function GiveInterest() from Review 4 to write a function AddInterest() that adds interest to all accounts numbered 0 to NumAccount–1 in the bank array used in Section 10.5. The function should take the interest rate, the Bank array, and NumAccounts as arguments.

10.6 Building Utility Classes

DateClass class

The AccountClass class is *application specific*, meaning that it is primarily useful only in the single application for which it is designed. However, classes can add a code-reusability feature to object-oriented programming. The string, TopClass, and iostream classes are examples of classes that are reusable for many different applications. This type of class is called a *utility class*. In the next several sections, a utility class, DateClass, will be created.

specification

The DateClass class is to be used by programs manipulating dates. The member functions of a utility class are usually very general in application. The public member functions of DateClass are operations that can be performed on a date:

```
DateClass();
/*Default constructor */

DateClass(int M, int D, int Y);
/*Constructor */

void SetDate(int M, int D, int Y);
/*M, D, Y assigned to Month, Day, and Year
   Pre: M, D, and Y are valid a valid month, day, and year
   Post: Month=M, Day=D, and Year=Y                       */

void Write(ostream & OutFile) const;
/*Writes the date to OutFile
   Post: Date written to OutFile */
```

```
bool Read(istream & InFile);
/*Reads a date from InFile. Input is assumed to be in mm/dd/yy form.
   If read fails, returns false.
   Post: Date read from InFile. true returned for successful read,
   false returned otherwise.*/

bool IsEqualTo(const DateClass Date2) const;
/*Determines if date is equal to Date2
   Post: true returned if date=date2, false returned otherwise */

bool IsEarlierThan(const DateClass Date2) const;
/*Determines if date is less than Date2
   Post: true returned if date<date2, false returned otherwise */

bool IsLaterThan(const DateClass Date2) const;
/*Determines if date is greater than Date2
   Post: true returned if date>date2, false returned otherwise */
```

programming style

Good programming style dictates that a default constructor be included. Including the default constructor requires that a SetDate function be included. Write() is designated as const since it does not change the value of its object. The Read() function returns a bool to indicate whether the read was successful. The last three functions are for comparing dates.

design

The data members for DateClass need to store int values for the month, day, and year. Therefore, the private section of the class declaration is:

```
private:
    int Month;
    int Day;
    int Year;
```

coding

Most of the member function definitions are straightforward, and are shown later in the chapter. The Read() function has to parse (cut up and analyze) the input to determine the parts of the date. The Read() algorithm uses getline() to read an entire line of input into a string. The find() string function can then be used to find the / characters, and the atoi() function from the stdlib library used to convert the numeric portions into integer values:

```
bool DateClass::Read(istream & InFile)
/*Reads a date from InFile. Input is assumed to be in mm/dd/yy form.
   true returned if date not 0/0/0.
   Post: String read from InFile and parsed into Month, Day, and Year.
   true returned if date not 0/0/0. false returned otherwise.        */
{
  String S, MonthStr, DayStr, YearStr;
  getline(InFile,S);

  MonthStr = S.substr(0,S.find('/'));
  S = S.substr(S.find('/')+1,S.length()-S.find('/')-1);
  DayStr = S.substr(0, S.find('/'));
  YearStr = S.substr(S.find('/')+1, S.length()-S.find('/')-1);

  Month = atoi(MonthStr.c_str());
  Day = atoi(DayStr.c_str());
  Year = atoi(YearStr.c_str());

  return ((Month!=0) && (Day!=0) && (Year!=0));
}
```

A Guide to Programming in C++

Read() needs to be tested carefully with various kinds of input. If the input is not in the correct format, atoi() will try to convert at least one string that is not an integer quantity and will therefore return zero. This is used to determine the value to be returned from the function.

Review 9

Write a program that tests the DateClass class member functions. main() should call each function at least once, and display output indicating whether each function has worked correctly.

Review 10

Write the code for the DateClass class comparison member functions. (Hint: Write IsLaterThan() using only IsEqualTo() and IsEarlierThan() and boolean operators for and, or, not.)

10.7 Overloading Operators

Member functions can be written to overload the built-in operators (<, >, <=, >=, ==, !=, *, +, –, /). For example, instead of the statement:

```
if (Date1.IsEqualTo(Date2))
    cout << "Equal! " << endl;
```

the == operator could be overloaded so that the following statement could be used:

```
if (Date1 == Date2)
    cout << "Equal! " << endl;
```

operator member function

An *operator member function* has the name operator followed by the operator to overload. For example, the DateClass member function IsEqual() could be replaced with:

```
bool DateClass::operator ==(const DateClass Date2) const
{
    return ((Day == Date2.Day) && (Month == Date2.Month) &&
      (Year == Date2.Year));
}
```

Whenever the compiler encounters an operator, the types in the expression are used to determine which operator is used. In this case, the overloaded == operator in DateClass is automatically called when two DateClass objects are compared using ==.

programming style

It is good programming style to overload all similar operators for a utility class, or not overload them at all. For example, if the < operator is overloaded to mean IsEarlierThan() for DateClass, then the <= operator should also be overloaded to mean "is the same or earlier than." When one relational operator is overloaded, then all relational operators should be overloaded.

To use an overloaded operator from another member function, the function name must be used. For example, the following DateClass member function overloads the != operator:

```
bool DateClass::operator !=(const DateClass Date2) const
{
  return !(operator==(Date2));
}
```

The not symbol (!) must appear outside the parentheses.

It is important to understand that overloaded operators implicitly use the left object in an expression as the object whose member function is to be used. For example, the code:

```
if (OneDay == AnotherDay)
```

is automatically translated into:

```
if (OneDay.operator==(AnotherDay))
```

10.8 Overloading Stream Operators

Stream operators (<<, >>) can also be overloaded. For example, overloading the << operator in DateClass enables the following statement to display the Today object to the screen (the cout stream):

```
cout << Today << endl;
```

Overloaded stream operator member functions have the same form as other overloaded operator member functions. However, for DateClass, the simplest way to overload the << operator is with a nonmember function that uses the member function Write():

```
ostream & operator <<(ostream &OutFile, const DateClass &D)
/*Writes D to the output stream
   Post: D written to OutFile          */
{
  D.Write(OutFile);
  return (OutFile);
}
```

The first argument is the stream (on the left of the << expression), and the second is the DateClass object (on the right of the expression). The function returns a stream reference, which is good programming style with stream operations.

free functions

The overloaded << function can be added to the end of the date library implementation file (date.cpp). Since it is not a member function of DateClass, the << function does not need to be added to the class interface in the header file (date.h). Library functions that are not member functions of a class are called *free functions*.

Since the << operator is overloaded for DateClass, the >> operator should be overloaded as well. For the overloaded >> function, the Read() member function will be used:

```
istream & operator >>(istream &InFile, DateClass &D)
/*Reads from InFile to D
   Post: D is read from Infile */
{
   D.Read(InFile);
   return (InFile);
}
```

The program below demonstrates the overloaded DateClass operators:

```
/* DateClass overloaded operator functions demonstration program */

#include <iostream.h>
#include "date.h"

int main()
{
   DateClass Today, MyBirthday(1,3,98);
   cout << "Enter today's date: ";
   cin >> Today;

   if (Today == MyBirthday)
      cout << "Hooray! " << Today << " is my birthday! " << endl;
   else
      cout << "Hooray! " << Today << " is my un-birthday! " << endl;

   return(0);
}
```

When run, the program displays:

```
Enter today's date: 3/14/98
Hooray! 3/14/98 is my un-birthday!
```

Review 11

Write a program that asks the user for the birthdays of two people, and then displays which person is older. The program output should be similar to:

```
Enter first person's birthdate: 1/3/76
Enter second person's birthdate: 5/14/76
The first person is older.
```

Review 12

If a user enters two dates, one as 1/5/98 and the other as 01/05/98, will the two dates be considered equal by the DateClass equality comparison? Explain your answer, and indicate why you think this is or is not a good behavior for the class.

10.9 Compiler Directives

#include

Strictly speaking, #include is not really part of the C++ language. It is a *compiler directive*. A compiler directive tells the compiler to take a special step in compiling a program. The #include directive tells the compiler to load and compile additional files.

Other compiler directives are #ifndef, #endif, and #define. These directives are used to prevent a program from including a library more than once. For example, the date library should be included in account.h to handle dates. However, unless these compiler directives are used, a program that includes both the date and account libraries will generate an error message because the compiler encounters date.h twice.

#ifndef

The #ifndef directive (<u>If</u> <u>n</u>ot <u>def</u>ined) has the form

    #ifndef *identifier*

and tests to see if *identifier* has been defined. If it has not, then compilation proceeds to the next line. If it has been defined, code is skipped until the #endif directive is encountered.

#endif

#define

The #define directive has the form

    #define *identifier*
    statements associated with identifier

and associates the statements following the directive with *identifier*.

programming style

It is good programming style to use compiler directives in a library. For example, the date.h file should use the following directives:

    #ifndef _DATECLASS_
    #define _DATECLASS_

    DateClass class declaration

    #include "date.cpp"
    #endif

When the compiler first encounters date.h, the identifier _DATECLASS_ has not yet been defined. Therefore, _DATECLASS_ is defined, the class declaration compiled, and date.cpp compiled. The second time date.h is encountered, _DATECLASS_ has already been defined. Therefore, the compiler skips all the code to the #endif.

programming style

It is considered good programming style to choose a #define *identifier* that begins and ends with underscore characters (_) and is in all uppercase. This helps avoid conflict with identifiers in program code.

10.10 The date Library

The DateClass class needs to be modified to include overloaded operators, including stream operators, and compiler directives. The final coding of date.h and date.cpp is shown below:

date.h

```
/*Implements a DateClass class that stores month, day, and year.
  Two free functions are included: operator << and operator >>    */

#ifndef _DATECLASS_
#define _DATECLASS_

#include <iostream.h>
#include <lvp\string.h>
#include <lvp\bool.h>
#include <stdlib.h>  // for atoi()

class DateClass {
public:
  DateClass();
  DateClass(int MonthArg, int DayArg, int YearArg);

  bool Read(istream & InFile);
  void SetDate(int MonthArg, int DayArg, int YearArg);
  void Write(ostream & OutFile) const;

  bool operator ==(const DateClass Date2) const;
  bool operator !=(const DateClass Date2) const;
  bool operator <(const DateClass Date2) const;
  bool operator <=(const DateClass Date2) const;
  bool operator >(const DateClass Date2) const;
  bool operator >=(const DateClass Date2) const;

private:
  int Month;
  int Day;
  int Year;
};

#include "date.cpp"
#endif
```

date.cpp

```
/*Implementation of a DateClass class that stores month, day, and year.
  Two free functions are included: operator << and operator >>       */

DateClass::DateClass()
  : Month(0), Day(0), Year(0)
{
}
//-------------------------------------------------------------------------
DateClass::DateClass(int MonthArg, int DayArg, int YearArg)
  : Month(MonthArg), Day(DayArg), Year(YearArg)
{
}
```

```
//---------------------------------------------------------------
bool DateClass::Read(istream & InFile)
/*Reads a date from InFile. Input is assumed to be in mm/dd/yy form.
    true returned if date not 0/0/0.
    Post: String read from InFile and parsed into Month, Day, and Year.
    true returned if date not 0/0/0. false returned otherwise.         */
{
    String S, MonthStr, DayStr, YearStr;
    getline(InFile,S);

    MonthStr = S.substr(0,S.find('/'));
    S = S.substr(S.find('/')+1,S.length()-S.find('/')-1);
    DayStr = S.substr(0,S.find('/'));
    YearStr = S.substr(S.find('/')+1,S.length()-S.find('/')-1);

    Month = atoi(MonthStr.c_str());
    Day = atoi(DayStr.c_str());
    Year = atoi(YearStr.c_str());

    return ((Month!=0) && (Day!=0) && (Year!=0));
}
//---------------------------------------------------------------
void DateClass::SetDate(int MonthArg, int DayArg, int YearArg)
{
    Month = MonthArg;
    Day = DayArg;
    Year = YearArg;
}
//---------------------------------------------------------------
void DateClass::Write(ostream & OutFile) const
/*Writes D to the output stream
    Post: D written to OutFile          */
{
    OutFile.width(2); OutFile << Month << '/';
    OutFile.width(2); OutFile << Day << '/';
    OutFile.width(2); OutFile << Year;
}
//---------------------------------------------------------------
bool DateClass::operator <(const DateClass Date2) const
{
    if (Year < Date2.Year)
        return (true);
    else if (Year > Date2.Year)
        return (false);
    else if (Month < Date2.Month)
        return (true);
    else if (Month > Date2.Month)
        return (false);
    else
        return (Day < Date2.Day);
}
//---------------------------------------------------------------
bool DateClass::operator > (const DateClass Date2) const
{
    return (!(operator==(Date2)) && !(operator<(Date2)));
}
//---------------------------------------------------------------
bool DateClass::operator == (const DateClass Date2) const
{
    return ((Day == Date2.Day) && (Month == Date2.Month) &&
        (Year == Date2.Year));
}
```

A Guide to Programming in C++

```
//-------------------------------------------------------------
bool DateClass::operator != (const DateClass Date2) const
{
    return !(operator==(Date2));
}
//-------------------------------------------------------------
bool DateClass::operator >= (const DateClass Date2) const
{
    return ((operator==(Date2)) || (operator>(Date2)));
}
//-------------------------------------------------------------
bool DateClass::operator <= (const DateClass Date2) const
{
    return ((operator==(Date2)) || (operator<(Date2)));
}


//-------------------------------------------------------------
ostream& operator << (ostream & OutFile, const DateClass &D)
{
    D.Write(OutFile);
    return (OutFile);
}
//-------------------------------------------------------------
istream & operator >>(istream &InFile, DateClass &D)
/*Reads from InFile to D
    Post: D is read from Infile */
{
    D.Read(InFile);
    return (InFile);
}
```

Review 13

Add to the date library an operator function that overloads the subtraction operator (–) so that when two dates are subtracted, it gives the approximate number of days between the two dates. Assume each month has 30 days and each year has 365 days. Use the header:

```
long DateClass::operator – (const DateClass &Date2)
```

Write a short test program.

Review 14

Write a function MaxDate() that returns the latest date in an array of dates passed as an argument. Use the header:

```
DateClass MaxDate(const vector<DateClass> &DateList)
/*Returns the value of the latest date in DateList
    Pre: DateList contains 1 or more dates
    Post: The value of the latest date in DateList is returned */
```

Write a short test program.

10.11 Special Member Functions

Some member functions are automatically created by the compiler if not declared in a class, and are automatically called without a program explicitly calling them. These special member functions are:

- The *default constructor*, which is called whenever a new object is instantiated.

- The *destructor*, which is called whenever an object goes out of scope. An object goes out of scope at the end of a program, function, or compound statement in which the object is instantiated.

- The *copy constructor*, which is called whenever an object is copied. For example, when an object is passed as a value parameter, or an object is initialized as in the statements:

```
DateClass Today(1/1/99);
DateClass Another = Today;  //copy constructor called
```

- The *assignment operator*, which is called whenever one object is copied to another in an assignment statement.

When an object is somehow connected to data or a device outside the object itself, these special member functions need to be explicitly declared and defined in a class. For example, a TopListClass object uses files that need to be opened, read from, and closed. Therefore, the TopListClass class must include constructor, destructor, and assignment operator member functions that handle files. PegClass, which draws to the screen, also needs to explicitly include these special member functions.

Default constructor member functions have been covered in detail in Section 10.5.

destructor

The destructor member function cannot have parameters, and must be given the name of the class preceded by the tilde symbol, ~. For example, the TopListClass class is used to create and maintain a file of scores. The TopListClass destructor declaration appears in toplist.h like:

```
class TopListClass {
public:
    TopListClass(String Filename, int MaxItemsArg=10);
    ~TopListClass();  // Destructor

    ...
    // Other member functions

private:
    vector<String> NameList;
    vector<long> ScoreList;
    String FN;    // Filename to store data
    int MaxItems;
};
```

The TopListClass constructor loads data from a specified file on disk into the arrays shown in the private section of the declaration. Changes to a TopListClass object are maintained only in memory in arrays NameList and ScoreList. When the object goes out of scope, the destructor is called. The TopListClass destructor writes the data stored in NameList and ScoreList to the file associated with the TopListClass object.

The TopListClass destructor definition appears in toplist.cpp like:

```
TopListClass::~TopListClass()
/*Pre: TopListClass object exists
   Post: Object destroyed, and data stored */
{
   fstream File(FN.c_str(), ios::out);

   if (File.fail()) {
      cout << "Error opening file to save!" << FN << endl;
   }
   else {
      for (int i=0; i<MyMaxItems; i++) {
         File << NameList[i] << endl;
         File << ScoreList[i] << endl;
      }
      File.close();
   }
}
```

The copy constructor and assignment operator functions are discussed in the next section.

10.12 The Copy Constructor and Assignment Operator Functions

Copy constructor and assignment operator functions are not always desirable. For example, consider the following statements:

```
TopListClass T1("toplist1.dat", 10), T2("toplist2.dat", 20);
T2 = T1;
```

What should the effect be? Should T2 now store T1's data? Should T2 store data in toplist1.dat or toplist2.dat? There is no clear answer. Similar questions arise when a TopListClass object is passed by value.

The compiler automatically generates copy constructor and assignment operator functions unless they are declared in the class. In the case of TopListClass, copying and assignment is to be prevented. Therefore, the copy constructor and assignment operator functions are declared in the private section of the class where they will not be accessible to a client program:

```
class TopListClass {
   public:
   TopListClass(String Filename, int MaxItemsArg=10);
   ~TopListClass();  // Destructor

      ...
   // Other member functions
```

```
private:
   vector<String> NameList;
   vector<long> ScoreList;
   String FN;  // File name to store data
   int MaxItems;

   // Private functions to prevent copying of objects
   TopListClass(const TopListClass &T);   // Copy constructor
   operator=(const TopListClass &T);   // Assignment operator
};
```

A copy constructor takes the class as a const reference parameter. The definitions of the copy constructor and assignment operator functions do not need to exist at all. Therefore, the TopListClass implementation file does not contain the private member function definitions.

If an attempt is made to assign or pass an object as a value parameter, the compiler generates an error message. For example, attempting to copy an object, as in the statements

```
TopListClass TopList("Toplist.dat");
TopListClass Foo = TopList;
```

generates a compiler error indicating that the copy constructor is not accessible. Similarly, attempting assignment, as in the statements

```
TopListClass TopList("Toplist.dat");
TopListClass Foo;
Foo = TopList;
```

generates a compiler error indicating that the assignment member function is not accessible.

10.13 Object-Oriented Programming

The concepts of object-oriented programming (OOP) and object-oriented design (OOD) are being used in all major software development efforts. OOD and OOP change the program design process so that once the specification for a program has been created, the next step is to carefully consider all the objects required to satisfy the specification, and to define their behavior. The objects are then coded and used to write the program. This differs in approach and style from the "top-down" approach where one begins with the code for the main() function, and works down to lower-level functions.

The OOP/OOD approach has the following advantages:

- *Reusability*: Well-designed classes can be used in many applications. This means that code can be reused, saving programming effort. The CollegeListClass, PegClass, string, and vector are examples of reusable classes.

- *Reliability*: Programs using classes that are written for many applications are more reliable because the classes have usually been fully tested and debugged.

- *Reduction of complexity*: As software becomes more and more complex, it becomes more and more difficult to manage. The object-oriented approach helps divide the total programming task so that programmers can work on well-defined, smaller tasks. This is especially important since most software is now written by teams of programmers.

Review 15

Write a class called PermanentStringClass that has the following member functions:

A constructor that reads a string from the first line of the file onestr.dat.

A destructor that writes a string to the file onestr.dat.

A function Display() that displays the string on the screen.

A function Replace() that replaces the string with one given as an argument.

Write a program to test PermanentStringClass that includes the code:

```
PermanentStringClass Test;
String NewString;
Test.Display();
cout << "Enter a new string: ";
getline(cout,NewString);
Test.Replace(NewString);
Test.Display();
```

Case Study

In this Case Study, AccountClass will be improved. One improvement will be incorporating DateClass in AccountClass.

specification

Improve AccountClass by incorporating DateClass and making the following enhancements:

1. Transactions are to be displayed in order by date.

2. Add member functions Store() and Retrieve() to allow an entire account to be stored in a file stream and retrieved.

3. Add the following member functions so that a client program can obtain all information about the account, including the individual transactions:

```
DateClass GetOpenDate() const;
String GetName() const;

int GetTransCount() const; //returns the number of transactions
DateClass GetTransDate(int TransNum) const;
String GetTransKind(int TransNum) const;
double GetTransAmt(int TransNum) const;
```

To complete Task 1 in the specification, transactions (deposits and withdrawals) will be stored in the transaction arrays in order by date. To store transaction data in the appropriate position of the arrays, a private member function AddTransaction() will be added to AccountClass, and called by both Deposit() and Withdrawal().

To complete Task 2 in the specification, a file with the following format will be implemented:

> *Line 1*: Account name
> *Line 2*: Opening date
> *Line 3*: Balance
> *Line 4*: Number of transactions
> *Line 5*: First transaction date
> *Line 6*: First transaction kind
> *Line 7*: First transaction amount
> Lines 5 through 7 repeat for remaining transactions.
> Entire structure repeats for remaining accounts.

By storing the number of transactions, a for loop can be used to retrieve an account's transactions without inadvertently reading into the next account in the file.

To complete Task 3 in the specification, new member functions will be added to AccountClass.

Modifications to the AccountClass interface include new member function declarations, and using DateClass to implement dates. Compiler directives will also be added. The new interface file is shown below:

```
account3.h

/* Improved bank account class which maintains and
   can display a list of all transaction on the account    */

#ifndef _ACCOUNTCLASS_
#define _ACCOUNTCLASS_

#include <fstream.h>
#include <iostream.h>
#include <lvp\bool.h>
#include <lvp\string.h>
#include <lvp\vector.h>
#include "date.h"

class AccountClass {
public:
    AccountClass();
    /* Default constructor */

    AccountClass(String AcctName, DateClass AcctOpenDate);
    /* Opens AcctName account on AcctOpenDate.
       Post: AcctName balance is zero, and transaction recorded */

    void SpecifyAccount(String AcctName, DateClass AcctOpenDate);
    /* Assigns AcctName and AcctOpenDate to account if account not initialized
       Post: AcctName assigned to Name and AcctOpenDate assigned to
       OpenDate if account was not already initialized. IsOpen is true.        */
```

```
bool Deposit(double Amt, DateClass Date);
/* Post: If account open, adds deposit to Acct, records transaction,
   and returns true; returns false otherwise.                        */

bool Withdrawal(double Amt, DateClass Date);
/* Post: if Amt<=Balance, Amt deleted from account,
   transaction recorded, and true returned. Otherwise, false returned,
   attempt recorded, and balance unchanged.                          */

//Access functions that return account information
DateClass GetOpenDate() const;
/* Post: Account open date returned. */

String GetName() const;
/* Post: Name returned       */

double GetBalance() const;
/* Post: Current balance returned */

//Access functions that return transaction information
int GetTransCount() const;
/* Post: Number of transactions returned */

DateClass GetTransDate(int TransNum) const;
/* Post: Date of transaction returned */

String GetTransKind(int TransNum) const;
/* Post: Type of transaction returned */

double GetTransAmt(int TransNum) const;
/* Post: Amount of transaction returned */

//Stream functions
void WriteTransactions(ostream & OutFile) const;
/* Writes transactions to OutFile
   Post: All information about the account written to OutFile,
   including all transactions in order by date.                      */

void Store(ostream & OutFile) const;
/* Pre: InFile is open
   Post: Account written in standard format to OutFile */

void Retrieve(istream & InFile);
/* Pre: InFile is open and positioned at a properly formatted account
   Post: Next account has been read from InFile into account         */

private:
   bool IsOpen;
   String Name;
   DateClass OpenDate;
   double Balance;
   vector<DateClass> TransDates;
   vector<String> TransKinds;
   vector<double> TransAmts;

   void AddTransaction(String Kind, DateClass Date, double Amt);
   /* Post: Transaction recorded at appropriate position by date. */
};

#include "account3.cpp"
#endif
```

design—level 2

In the next level of design, the new member functions are refined. The new member functions for accessing account information simply return the value of a data member. With the simplicity of these functions, it is fair to ask why the data members should not be made public so that they can be accessed directly. By using private data members:

- The writer of the class has full control over the way data members can be manipulated. By allowing manipulation only through calls to member functions, the integrity and consistency of objects is maintained.

- The writer of the class has complete freedom in designing the class code. The author may change the names or types of the date members, modify the way they are implemented, etc., without needing to change the interface.

These are clear benefits of the OOP approach.

The Store() function sends all the data in the three transaction arrays into the file stream for writing to a file. Similarly, the Retrieve() function reads all information into the three transaction arrays from a file.

The AddTransaction() function is used to maintain the transactions in order by date. This means that when a new transaction is to be added, it must be inserted in the correct location in the array. An algorithm for doing this is to move all items with later dates than the one to be inserted up by one place in the array, and then to insert the new item in the open space. This can be illustrated as:

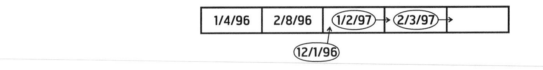

The AddTransaction() algorithm is implemented by moving all items which have later dates one position later in the array, making room for the new data in its correct spot. The AddTransaction() pseudocode is:

```
increase by one the array size
start with the last item in the array as the last item
while (current item date > new date)
    move current item to the next position in the array
    go to previous item in the array
put the new data in the current spot
```

The transaction kind and amount arrays are handled the same way.

coding—level 2

The next step is to write the code to implement the new member functions. The new access functions (GetName(), GetOpenDate(), etc.) can each be implemented in a single line. For example:

```
String AccountClass::GetName() const
/*Post: Account name returned */
{
    return (Name);
}
```

A Guide to Programming in C++

10

```
int AccountClass::GetTransCount() const
/*Post: Date of transaction returned */
{
  return (TransDates.length());
}

DateClass AccountClass::GetTransDate(int TransNum) const
/*Post: Date of transaction returned */
{
  return (TransDates[TransNum]);
}
```

The AddTransaction() pseudocode is implemented as:

```
void AccountClass::AddTransaction(String Kind, DateClass Date,
  double Amt)
/*Records transaction in appropriate position of arrays by date
  Post: Transaction recorded in appropriate position by date     */
{
  int NewSize = TransDates.length() + 1;
  TransDates.resize(NewSize);
  TransKinds.resize(NewSize);
  TransAmts.resize(NewSize);
  int NewSpot = NewSize - 2;
  while ((NewSpot >= 0) && (TransDates[NewSpot] > Date)) {
    TransDates[NewSpot+1] = TransDates[NewSpot];
    TransKinds[NewSpot+1] = TransKinds[NewSpot];
    TransAmts[NewSpot+1] = TransAmts[NewSpot];
    NewSpot--;
  }
  TransDates[NewSpot+1] = Date;
  TransKinds[NewSpot+1] = Kind;
  TransAmts[NewSpot+1] = Amt;
}
```

The Deposit() and Withdrawal() functions must be modified to use AddTransaction(). For example, Withdrawal() becomes:

```
bool AccountClass::Withdrawal(double Amt, DateClass Date);
/*Post: if Amt<=Balance, Amt deleted from account,
  transaction recorded, and true returned. Otherwise, false returned,
  attempt recorded, and balance unchanged.                      */
{
  if (Amt <= Balance) {
    Balance -= Amt;
    AddTransaction("Withdrawal", Date, Amt);
    return(true);
  }
  else {
    AddTransaction("Withdrawal/Failed", Date, Amt);
    return(false);
  }
}
```

The Store() and Retrieve() functions are written based on the file structure in the design. For example, Store() sends data to the file stream:

```
void AccountClass::Store(ostream & OutFile) const;
/* Pre: InFile is open
   Post: Account written in standard format to OutFile */
{
  OutFile << Name << endl;
  OutFile << OpenDate << endl;
  OutFile << Balance << endl;
  OutFile << TransDates.length() << endl;
  for (int TransNum = 0; TransNum < TransDates.length(); TransNum++) {
    OutFile << TransDates[TransNum] << endl;
    OutFile << TransKinds[TransNum] << endl;
    OutFile << TransAmts[TransNum] << endl;
  }
}
```

Similar to Store(), Retrieve() is coded using getline() to retrieve strings, the >> operator combined with ignore() to obtain numbers, and the DateClass overloaded >> operator to retrieve dates. Retrieve() should also include the statement:

```
IsOpen = true;
```

so that it may be used to initialize an account opened with the default constructor.

The complete AccountClass implementation is shown below:

account3.cpp

```
/* AccountClass class implementation */

#include <iostream.h>
#include <lvp\vector.h>
#include <lvp\string.h>

//----------------------------------------------------------------------
AccountClass::AccountClass()
  : Balance(0), TransDates(0), TransKinds(0), TransAmts(0), IsOpen(false)
{
}
//----------------------------------------------------------------------
AccountClass::AccountClass(String AcctName, DateClass AcctOpenDate)
  : Name(AcctName), OpenDate(AcctOpenDate), Balance(0),
    TransDates(0), TransKinds(0), TransAmts(0), IsOpen(true)
/* Opens AcctName account on AcctOpenDate with 0 balance */
{
}
//----------------------------------------------------------------------
void AccountClass::SpecifyAccount(String AcctName,
    DateClass AcctOpenDate)
/* Assigns AcctName and AcctOpenDate to account if account not initialized
   Post: AcctName assigned to Name and AcctOpenDate assigned to
   OpenDate if account was not already initialized. IsOpen is true.      */
{
  if (!IsOpen) {
    Name = AcctName;
    OpenDate = AcctOpenDate;
    IsOpen = true;
  }
}
```

```
//------------------------------------------------------------------
bool AccountClass::Deposit(double Amt, DateClass Date)
/*Post: If account open, adds Amt to Acct, records transaction,
  and returns true; returns false otherwise.                    */
{
  if (IsOpen) {
    Balance += Amt;
    AddTransaction("Deposit", Date, Amt);
    return(true);
  }
  else
    return(false);
}
//------------------------------------------------------------------
bool AccountClass::Withdrawal(double Amt, DateClass Date)
/*Post: if Amt<=Balance, Amt deleted from account,
  transaction recorded, and true returned. Otherwise, false returned,
  attempt recorded, and balance unchanged.                      */
{
  if (Amt <= Balance) {
    Balance -= Amt;
    AddTransaction("Withdrawal", Date, Amt);
    return(true);
  }
  else {
    AddTransaction("Withdrawal/Failed", Date, Amt);
    return(false);
  }
}
//------------------ACCESS FUNCTIONS------------------------------
double AccountClass::GetBalance() const //Returns current balance
{ return (Balance); }
String AccountClass::GetName() const
{ return (Name); }
DateClass AccountClass::GetOpenDate() const
{ return (OpenDate); }
int AccountClass::GetTransCount() const //Returns number of trans
{ return (TransDates.length()); }
DateClass AccountClass::GetTransDate(int TransNum) const
{ return (TransDates[TransNum]); }
String AccountClass::GetTransKind(int TransNum) const
{ return (TransKinds[TransNum]); }
double AccountClass::GetTransAmt(int TransNum) const
{ return (TransAmts[TransNum]); }
//------------------------------------------------------------------
void AccountClass::WriteTransactions(ostream & OutFile) const
/*Writes transactions to OutFile
  Post: All information about the account written to OutFile,
  including a list of all transactions.                         */
{
  OutFile.setf(ios::fixed);
  OutFile.precision(2);
  OutFile << Name << endl;
  OutFile << "Acct opened on " << OpenDate << " Balance: "
  << Balance << endl;
  OutFile << "Transactions" << endl;
  for (int i=0; i<TransDates.length(); i++) {
    OutFile.width(12); OutFile << TransDates[i];
    OutFile.width(22); OutFile << TransKinds[i];
    OutFile.width(12); OutFile << TransAmts[i] << endl;
  }
}
```

```
//-------------------------------------------------------------------------
void AccountClass::AddTransaction(String Kind, DateClass Date,
    double Amt)
/* Records transaction in appropriate position of arrays by date
   Post: Transaction recorded in appropriate position by date     */
{
  int NewSize = TransDates.length() + 1;
  TransDates.resize(NewSize);
  TransKinds.resize(NewSize);
  TransAmts.resize(NewSize);
  int NewSpot = NewSize – 2;
  while ((NewSpot >= 0) && (TransDates[NewSpot] > Date)) {
    TransDates[NewSpot+1] = TransDates[NewSpot];
    TransKinds[NewSpot+1] = TransKinds[NewSpot];
    TransAmts[NewSpot+1] = TransAmts[NewSpot];
    NewSpot--;
  }
  TransDates[NewSpot+1] = Date;
  TransKinds[NewSpot+1] = Kind;
  TransAmts[NewSpot+1] = Amt;
}
//-------------------------------------------------------------------------
void AccountClass::Store(ostream & OutFile) const
/* Pre: InFile is open
   Post: Account written in standard format to OutFile */
{
  OutFile << Name << endl;
  OutFile << OpenDate << endl;
  OutFile << Balance << endl;
  OutFile << TransDates.length() << endl;
  for (int TransNum = 0; TransNum < TransDates.length(); TransNum++) {
    OutFile << TransDates[TransNum] << endl;
    OutFile << TransKinds[TransNum] << endl;
    OutFile << TransAmts[TransNum] << endl;
  }
}
//-------------------------------------------------------------------------
void AccountClass::Retrieve(istream & InFile)
/* Pre: InFile is open and positioned at a properly formatted account
   Post: Next account has been read from InFile into account       */
{
  getline(InFile, Name);
  OpenDate.Read(InFile);
  InFile >> Balance; InFile.ignore(80,'\n');
  int TransCount;
  InFile >> TransCount; InFile.ignore(80,'\n');
  TransDates.resize(TransCount);
  TransKinds.resize(TransCount);
  TransAmts.resize(TransCount);
  for (int TransNum = 0; TransNum < TransCount; TransNum++) {
    InFile >> TransDates[TransNum];
    getline(InFile, TransKinds[TransNum]);
    InFile >> TransAmts[TransNum]; InFile.ignore(80,'\n');
  }
  IsOpen = true;
}
```

testing and debugging

Testing such a large and complex class is a formidable task. Testing must include verifying that the store/retrieve sequence works properly for all sizes of accounts, and transactions are properly added at the end, beginning, and middle of the transaction list.

The AccountClass library is tested with a menu-driven program that reads a file of accounts into an array of accounts, allows the user to add accounts and transactions, and stores all accounts at the end of the program. When run, the client program displays output similar to:

```
AddAccount/Deposit/Withdrawal/disPlay/Quit:  P
John Nicola
Acct opened on   2/ 3/97  Balance: 60123.45
Transactions
  2/ 3/97                    Deposit    10000.00
  2/ 5/97                    Deposit    20000.00
  2/ 10/97                   Deposit      123.45
  2/ 15/97                   Deposit    30000.00
Craig Mackay
Acct opened on   2/ 5/97  Balance: 1109.00
Transactions
12/23/97                     Deposit      100.00
  2/ 4/98          Withdrawal/Fail       1000.00
  2/ 5/98                     Deposit     1009.00
AddAccount/Deposit/Withdrawal/disPlay/Quit:  A
Enter name: Alex Rhett
Enter date: 2/6/98
Enter initial deposit: 300
AddAccount/Deposit/Withdrawal/disPlay/Quit:  D
Enter account number: 1
Enter amount: 200
Enter date: 1/3/98
AddAccount/Deposit/Withdrawal/disPlay/Quit:  q
```

For the sake of brevity, the test program is written in a single main() function. However, it would be better programming style to divide the tasks of the program into functions. The file of accounts used by the program has the format:

> *Line 1*: Number of accounts in the file
> *remaining lines*: Accounts formatted as expected by the
>   AccountClass Store() function.

The client program is shown below:

```
/* Improved AccountClass demonstration program */

#include "account3.h"
#include "date.h"
#include <iostream.h>
#include <lvp\vector.h>
#include <conio.h>  // for getche()

int main()
{
    vector<AccountClass> Bank(100);
    fstream BankData;
    int NumAccounts = 0;
    int AcctNum;
```

```cpp
// Retrieve accounts from file
BankData.open("bankdata.dat", ios::in);
BankData >> NumAccounts; BankData.ignore(80,'\n');
for (AcctNum=0; AcctNum < NumAccounts; AcctNum++) {
  Bank[AcctNum].Retrieve(BankData);
}
BankData.close();

//Test AccountClass
char Choice;
String Name;
DateClass Date;
double Amount;
while (true) {
  cout << "AddAccount/Deposit/Withdrawal/disPlay/Quit: ";
  Choice = getche();
  cout << endl;
  if (Choice == 'Q' || Choice == 'q')
    break;
  switch (Choice) {
    case 'A':
    case 'a':   //Add an account
      cout << "Enter name: ";
      getline(cin, Name);
      cout << "Enter date: ";
      Date.Read(cin);
      cout << "Enter initial deposit: ";
      cin >> Amount; cin.ignore(80,'\n');
      Bank[NumAccounts].SpecifyAccount(Name, Date);
      Bank[NumAccounts].Deposit(Amount, Date);
      NumAccounts++;
      break;
    case 'D':
    case 'd':   //Deposit
      cout << "Enter account number: ";
      cin >> AcctNum;
      cout << "Enter amount: ";
      cin >> Amount; cin.ignore(80,'\n');
      cout << "Enter date: ";
      Date.Read(cin);
      Bank[AcctNum].Deposit(Amount, Date);
      break;
    case 'W':
    case 'w':   //Withdrawal
      cout << "Enter account number: ";
      cin >> AcctNum;
      cout << "Enter amount: ";
      cin >> Amount; cin.ignore(80,'\n');
      cout << "Enter date: ";
      Date.Read(cin);
      Bank[AcctNum].Withdrawal(Amount, Date);
      break;
    case 'P':
    case 'p':   //Display accounts
      for (AcctNum=0; AcctNum < NumAccounts; AcctNum++) {
          Bank[AcctNum].WriteTransactions(cout);
      }
      break;
  }
}
```

```
// Save accounts in file
BankData.open("bankdata.dat", ios::out);
BankData << NumAccounts << endl;
for (AcctNum=0; AcctNum < NumAccounts; AcctNum++) {
    Bank[AcctNum].Store(BankData);
}
BankData.close();
return (0);
}
```

All three transactions performed in the switch statement require a date entered by the user. To get the date typed by the user, the DateClass member function Read() was passed cin as the InFile parameter.

Review 16

Can the Case Study client program add a transaction directly? For example, explain why or why not the following statement is legal:

Bank[1].AddTransaction("Special",Today, 1000);

Review 17

A weakness of the Case Study client program is that accounts must be accessed by number. Write a function FindAccount() that finds the account number for the name given as an argument:

```
int FindAccount(const vector<AccountClass> &Bank,
        const int NumAccounts, const String &Name)
/*Post: Account number of Name account returned,
    or –1 returned if Name account not found.         */
```

Review 18

The access functions of the account3 library do not determine if an account is open before trying to return information about the account. This causes a runtime error in a program that tries to access an account that is not open. Modify the access functions (declarations and definitions) to first check for an open account.

Chapter Summary

The methodology for creating a class is specification, design, coding, and testing and debugging. The specification of a class defines how an object may be accessed by a program, and is called the public section of a class. The private part of a class is the functions and data members not accessible to code outside the class, and is part of the design of a class.

A library is coded in two files and often contains classes. The header file, also called the interface file, contains the class declaration. The declaration of a class has the form:

```
class classname {
  public:
    // public members listed here
  private:
    // private members listed here
```

The implementation file contains class member function definitions. The compiler is informed that the implementation file requires the code in the header file with an #include directive at the end of the header file.

Member functions may be public or private. Public member functions are accessible to the client code. Private member functions are accessible only within the class. Member functions that do not change their calling object in any way include the keyword const in the header to reinforce this. Member functions that overload built-in operators are called operator member functions.

Special member functions are the default constructor, copy constructor, assignment operator, and destructor. Each of these functions are automatically created by the compiler if a declaration does not exist in the class. The copy constructor and assignment operator member functions are not always desirable, and can be made inaccessible to a client program by including their declarations in the private section of a class.

A library may also contain free functions that are not member functions of a class, but may be useful to class object operations.

Compiler directives tell the compiler to take a special step in compiling a program. The #include directive tells the compiler to load in and compile additional files. The #ifndef, #endif, and #define directives are used to prevent a program from including a library more than once. The #ifndef directive tests to see if an identifier has been defined. If the identifier has been defined, the code after the #ifndef is skipped until an #endif is encountered. The #define directive defines an identifier.

The object-oriented approach to programming offers reusable, reliable code that can reduce the complexity of a program.

Vocabulary

Application Specific Term applied to a class that is primarily useful only in the single application for which it was designed.

Assignment Operator Member Function Member function that is automatically called when an object copied through assignment. Automatically created by the compiler if not declared in the class.

Class Declaration Member function and data member declarations of a class.

Client Program A program that uses a class.

Compiler Directive Used to tell the compiler to take a special step in compiling a program.

Copy Constructor Member function that is automatically called when an object is copied. Automatically created by the compiler if not declared in the class.

Data Hiding The property of object-oriented programming in which classes can be used without regard to how they are implemented.

Default Constructor Member function that is automatically called when an object is instantiated with no parameters. Automatically created by the compiler if not declared in the class.

Destructor Member function that is automatically called when an object goes out of scope. Automatically created by the compiler if not declared in the class.

Encapsulation   The property of object-oriented programming in which code is self-contained in a separate unit

Free Function   Library functions that are not member functions of a class.

Header File   The class declaration file that is saved with a .h extension.

Implementation File   The file containing class member function definitions and free functions.

Interface File   A header file.

Library   Files that contain classes and functions for use in client programs.

Operator Member Function   Member function that overloads a built-in operator or stream operator.

Private   The section of a class declaration that is not accessible to a client program.

Public   The section of a class declaration that is accessible to a client program.

Reduction of Complexity   An advantage of OOP/OOD in which the total programming task can be divided into well-defined, smaller tasks, which reduces the overall complexity.

Reliability   An advantage of OOP/OOD in which classes that are written for many applications have been fully tested, making them more reliable.

Reusability   An advantage of OOP/OOD in which a well-designed class can be reused, saving programming effort.

C++

:: Used to separate a class name and function name in a member function definition.

~ Used to indicate a destructor member function.

#define Compiler directive that defines an identifier. Used in conjunction with #ifndef and #endif to prevent a program from including a library more than once.

#endif Compiler directive that is used to signify the end of the #ifndef directive.

#ifndef Compiler directive that tests to see if an identifier has been defined. If the identifier has been defined, the code after the #ifndef is skipped until an #endif directive is encountered.

#include Compiler directive that tells the compiler to load in and compile additional files.

operator Keyword used to indicate a member function is written to overload a built-in operator.

public The section of a class declaration that contains the data members and member functions that are not accessible to a client program.

private The section of a class declaration that contains the member functions accessible to a client program.

Exercises

Exercise 1

Modify the Student Records program on page 8-24 to use a class, StudentClass that has member functions Read() and Write().

Exercise 2

a) Write a class called BookClass to replace the BookType structure used in the Case Study of Chapter Nine. Include member functions Read(), Write(), AddACopy(), and SubtractACopy() and any other functions needed.

b) Modify the Chapter Nine Case Study to use the BookClass library.

Exercise 3

In Chapter Eight, a Tic-Tac-Toe program was written. Write this program by designing and implementing a TTTClass. A TTTClass object should display the board on the screen, and have member functions Move() that get a move and update the screen, and Winner() that returns a code indicating who has won, if anyone. To simplify the class code, an enumerated type should be specified in TTTClass.h:

```
enum PlayerCode {XCode, OCode, BlankCode};
```

Exercise 4

Chapter Five Exercise 18 gave the specification of a "Horse Race" simulation. Write this program by designing and implementing a HorseClass. A HorseClass object should display its horse and track on the screen, and update the display when the horse moves.

Exercise 5

a) Design and implement a FractionClass utility class. It should allow reading and writing numbers in fractional form, and arithmetic operations on fractions. Overload the <<, >>, +, –, *, and / operators to work on fractions.

b) Write a client program that uses FractionClass to simulate a fraction-based calculator. The program output should look similar to:

```
Enter a fraction: 1/3
Enter an operator (= to quit): +
Enter a fraction: 1/4
Result: 7/12
Enter an operator (= to quit): *
Enter a fraction: 4/1
Result: 7/3
Enter an operator (= to quit): =
```

Exercise 6

a) Design and implement an ElapsedTimeClass utility. It should allow reading and writing of times in the form: 15:13:27 (fifteen hours, thirteen minutes, and 27 seconds). Member functions should include operator functions that overload <<, >>, +, and –.

b) Write a client program that fully tests the library.

Exercise 7

A weakness of DateClass is that output is in the form mm/dd/yy. Add a member function SetFormat() that sets the format for the output of the date to one of several possible formats:

Format command	Style	Example
Standard	mm/dd/yy	11/ 4/97
Standard4	mm/dd/yyyy	11/ 4/1997
Fullmonthtext	m dd, yyyy	November 4, 1997

For example, the statements:

```
DateClass Date(11,4,97);
Date.SetFormat("Fullmonthtext");
cout << Date;
```

display

```
November 4, 1997
```

Exercise 8

The "Millennium bug" is the difficulty many computer programs will have in the year 2000 because they store dates as two-digit numbers. For example, an afflicted computer will consider the date 1/3/00 (i.e., January 3, 2000) to be before 1/3/99 in a comparison.

The DateClass class suffers from exactly this problem. Modify the class so that it stores four digit years (e.g., 1999 or 2000). When a date is read, it should allow four or two digit years to be entered. If only two digits are entered, the class should assume it is in the 1900s.

Exercise 9

a) Write a DateClass operator member function that overloads the ++ operator to add one day to a date. Use the following header:

```
DateClass DateClass::operator++()
```

Be sure that the function correctly handles leap years. The rule is that leap years occur in any year divisible by four, unless the year ends in 00, in which case only if the year is also divisible by 400.

b) Write a DateClass operator member function that overloads the -- operator to subtract one day from a date.

c) Modify the date library to include the overloaded increment and decrement operators, and write a test program.

Exercise 10

a) Using the information in Exercise 9, modify the subtraction operator member function created in Review 13 to return the correct number of days between two dates (a long value). Use the header:

long DateClass::operator – (const DateClass &Date2)

b) Modify the date library to include the modified operator function, and write a test program.

Exercise 11

Use the DateClass library to implement a database of historical events. The client program should allow events to be stored using the date and a description (a string), and allow the events to be displayed in chronological order. The program output should be similar to:

```
. . .
Add, Display, Quit: A
Enter date: 1/28/97
Enter Description: Clinton inaugurated for second term
Add, Display, Quit: D
11/ 5/96 Clinton wins election
1/28/97 Clinton inaugurated for second term
```

Exercise 12

a) Write a class called DumbbellClass that uses conio library functions to animate a dumbbell figure on the screen. The dumbbell is displayed with characters O=O. DumbbellClass should have three member functions:

• A constructor that draws the dumbbell at location 40, 10.

• The Move() member function that erases the dumbbell from its current position by overwriting it with blanks, and redraws it one position to the left or right, depending upon which way it is moving. Initially, the dumbbell moves right until the right side of the screen (position 80) is reached, and then it changes direction.

• A destructor that erases the dumbbell by overwriting with blanks.

b) Write a program that moves the dumbbell 500 times.

c) Modify the dumbbell class created in Review 15 so that the dumbbell can move in eight directions (up, down, left, right, and the four diagonal directions). When the dumbbell reaches the edge of the screen, it should pick a new direction at random and keep moving.

Exercise 13

Improve the Case Study client program so that it implements a BankClass class. The BankClass class should store the accounts and the NumAccounts value, and contain member functions to perform all operations needed by the program. The constructor should load the data from disk, and the destructor should save data back to disk.

Chapter Eleven
Graphics and Event-Driven Programming

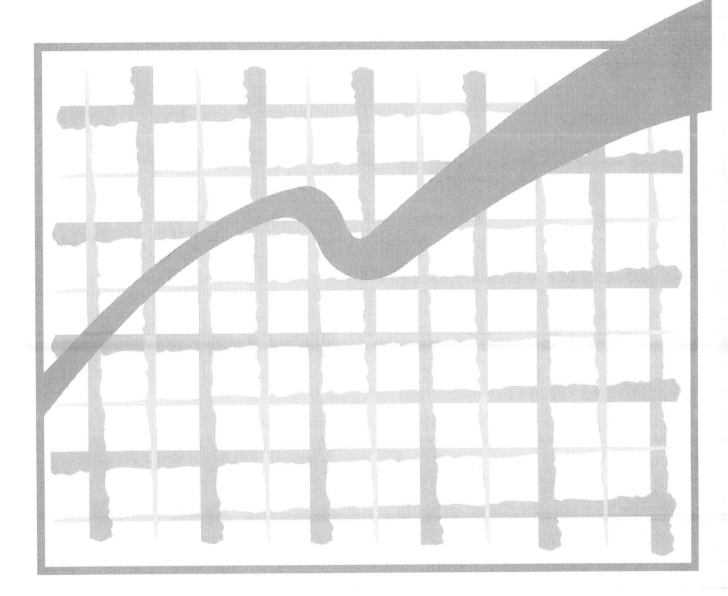

Objectives

After completing this chapter you will be able to:

1. Understand event-driven programming.

2. Use a minimal GUI program to write event-driven programs.

3. Write programs that display message boxes using the GUI libraries.

4. Write programs that display graphics using the GUI libraries.

11

In this chapter you will learn how to write programs that use some of the basic graphical user interface features of Windows (the GUI). While a full treatment of Windows programming is beyond the scope of this text, you will gain the ability to create GUI-based programs in a style similar to that used by professional programmers.

11.1 Event-Driven Programming

console based programs

A *console based program* interacts with the user through text displayed on the screen, and keystrokes from the user. Up to now all the programs in the text have been console based.

GUI based programs

A *GUI based program* waits for the user to tell the computer what to do. For example, clicking on a menu or dragging an object is how a user interacts with a typical Windows program. This is in sharp contrast to the console-based programs in which the user often has only one option available (entering data, choosing from a menu, etc.) and the computer is telling the user what to do.

Programming in the GUI environment requires writing *event-driven* code. In an event-driven program, the program becomes a set of instructions indicating what is to be done for each possible *event*. An event is something to which the program must respond. For example, a left-button mouse click is a mouse-click event. Each time a window is resized or moved, it must be redrawn on the screen. This is an event. In the simplified approach to event-driven programming used in this chapter, these are the only two events to which our code will respond.

11.2 Object-Oriented Programming

In Windows programs, the system supplies a main() program loop that processes events by dispatching them to the appropriate function. A simple, event-driven program can be written by creating an object that responds to events, and adding this object to the system. The gui_top and gui_bot libraries, supplied with this text, allow this. The structure of a simplified event-driven program will be as follows:

```
#include <lvp\gui_top.h>
// class GuiClass definitions
#include <lvp\gui_bot.h>
```

GuiClass is a special class that is used by the gui_top library to instantiate an object. The programs in this chapter will be written by modifying the GuiClass class. With this approach, a minimal GUI program is:

```
/* Minimal GUI program */

#include <lvp\gui_top.h>

class GuiClass {
  public:
  GuiClass();
  void GuiMouseClick(int x, int y); // Action if mouse click
  void GuiPaint();  // Repaint the entire window
  String Title(); // Return the title for the Window
  private:
};
//------------------------------------------------------------------------
GuiClass::GuiClass()
{
}
//------------------------------------------------------------------------
String GuiClass::Title()
{
    return ("A minimal GUI program");
}
//------------------------------------------------------------------------
void GuiClass::GuiMouseClick(int x, int y)
{
}
//------------------------------------------------------------------------
void GuiClass::GuiPaint()
{
}
//------------------------------------------------------------------------
#include <lvp\gui_bot.h>
```

In order to work correctly, GuiClass must be declared with a default constructor and three public member functions: GuiMouseClick(), GuiPaint(), and Title(). As it stands, this program displays nothing (because the GuiPaint() function is empty) and does not respond to mouse clicks (because the GuiMouseClick() function is empty), but it does compile and create a window with the title provided by the Title() function. Note that the empty functions may generate warning messages that can be safely ignored for now.

11.3 Graphic Functions

Windows provides a wealth of functions for creating graphic images. The simplified GUI system in this chapter includes a subset of these:

```
void Circle(int xc, int yc, int r);
/* Draws a circle with the given center and radius */

void FilledCircle(int xc, int yc, int r);
/* Draws a filled circle with the given center and radius */

void Line(int x1, int y1, int x2, int y2);
/* Draws a line from the point x1, y1 to x2, y2 */
```

```
void Rectangle(int x1, int y1, int x2, int y2);
/*Draws a rectangle with upper-left corner at x1, y1 and
  lower-right corner at x2, y2 */

void FilledRectangle(int x1, int y1, int x2, int y2);
/*Draws a filled rectangle with upper-left corner at x1, y1
  and lower-right corner at x2, y2 */

void SetPixel(int x, int y);
/* Plots the indicated pixel using the current pen color */
```

pixel

The parameters of the functions correspond to pixel units. A *pixel* is a single dot, or *picture element* on the screen. Position (0, 0) is in the upper-left of the window, with y-values increasing downward and x-values increasing toward the right.

The program below uses Circle() to produce the Olympic symbol:

```
/*Olympic Symbol program */

#include <lvp\gui_top.h>

class GuiClass {
  public:
  GuiClass();
  void GuiMouseClick(int x, int y); // Action if mouse click
  void GuiPaint();  // Repaint the entire window
  String Title(); // Return the title for the Window
  private:
};
//-----------------------------------------------------------------
GuiClass::GuiClass()
{
}
//-----------------------------------------------------------------
String GuiClass::Title()
{
   return "The Olympic Symbol!";
}
//-----------------------------------------------------------------
void GuiClass::GuiMouseClick(int x, int y)
{
}
//-----------------------------------------------------------------
void GuiClass::GuiPaint()
{
   Circle(180,200,50);
   Circle(250,200,50);
   Circle(320,200,50);
   Circle(215,270,50);
   Circle(285,270,50);
}
//-----------------------------------------------------------------
#include <lvp\gui_bot.h>
```

The program output is similar to:

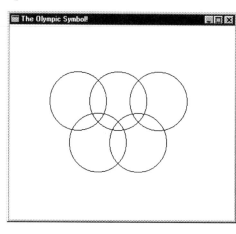

Review 1 ───

Add a line of code to the Olympic symbol program that will put a large circle around the entire symbol. Modify the program to title the display window "Olympics Logo."

Review 2 ───

Write a GUI program that produces a window titled "Wheels!" with a display similar to:

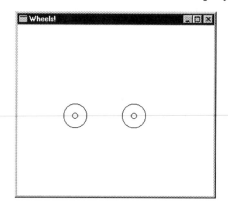

11.4 Controlling Colors and Line Thickness

non-filled objects

In addition to the drawing functions, there are functions that control the colors of the objects drawn. When drawing non-filled objects, the color of the "pen" is specified using the SetColor() function. The GUI library includes color constants BLACK, RED, GREEN, BLUE, GRAY, YELLOW, VIOLET, ORANGE, and WHITE, with BLACK being the default. For example, the pen color is set to red in the following statement:

```
SetColor(RED);
```

SetColor() remains in effect until the next use of SetColor().

The color constants are a Windows-defined type, COLORREF, that can be used to store colors and allow them to be used as parameters, as in the following function:

```
void ColoredCircle(COLORREF Color, int x, int y, int r)
/*Post: Circle drawn of color Color at (x, y) with radius r */
{
  SetColor(Color);
  Circle(x, y, r);
}
```

filled objects

For filled objects, the outline of the object is specified with SetColor(), and the inside, or fill, is specified with SetFillColor(). This uses the same color constants as SetColor(). For example, the following statements draw a gray box with a black outline:

```
SetFillColor(GRAY);
SetColor(BLACK);
FilledRectangle(120, 120, 140, 140);
```

line thickness

The line thickness of the pen used to draw figures and to outline filled figures is specified with SetThickness(), where the thickness is specified in pixels. For example, the following statements draw a box with lines that are two pixels thick:

```
SetThickness(2);
Rectangle(100,100,200,200);
```

The following program demonstrates the "pen" functions:

```
/*Sunny Day program */

#include <lvp\gui_top.h>

class GuiClass {
  public:
  GuiClass();
  void GuiMouseClick(int x, int y); // Action if mouse click
  void GuiPaint();  // Repaint the entire window
  String Title();
  private:
};
//--------------------------------------------------------------------------
GuiClass::GuiClass()
{
}
//--------------------------------------------------------------------------
String GuiClass::Title()
{
  return ("Sunny day!");
}
//--------------------------------------------------------------------------
void GuiClass::GuiMouseClick(int x, int y)
{
}
//--------------------------------------------------------------------------
void GuiClass::GuiPaint()
{
  // House
  SetColor(BLACK);
  SetThickness(2);
  Rectangle(100,100,200,200);
  Line(100,100,150,50);
  Line(150,50,200,100);
```

```
// Windows and door
SetColor(BLACK);
SetThickness(1);
SetFillColor(GRAY);
FilledRectangle(120,120,140,140);
FilledRectangle(160,120,180,140);
FilledRectangle(135,160,165,200);
SetColor(WHITE);
SetPixel(160,180);    // Doorknob!

// Sun
SetFillColor(YELLOW);
SetColor(YELLOW);
FilledCircle(280,50,30);
}
//--------------------------------------------------------------------------------

#include <lvp\gui_bot.h>
```

The program output displays a bright yellow sun, and looks similar to:

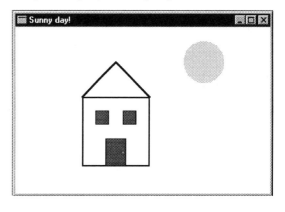

11.5 Floodfill

The FloodFill() function is used to color in a region that is irregularly shaped. For example, in the Sunny Day program, FloodFill() could be used to color the house red and the roof gray.

To identify the region to be filled, FloodFill() requires a starting point within the region. It then "floods" the region with the current fill color. The FloodFill() prototype is:

```
void FloodFill(int x, int y);
/* Post: All pixels connected to (x, y) with the same color
   are changed to the fill color                          */
```

FloodFill() considers any pixel which differs in color from the first pixel to be the border of the region and does not color it or go beyond it. Therefore, the following statements color the house and roof:

```
SetFillColor(RED);    // Paint house red
FloodFill(150, 110);
SetFillColor(GRAY);      // Paint roof gray
FloodFill(150, 90);
```

The x, y parameters passed to FloodFill() are not important so long as the points are in the region to be colored.

A Guide to Programming in C++

Review 3

Modify the Sunny Day program to display a small orange dog house next to the house.

Review 4

Modify Review 2 to display a yellow car using FilledRectangle().

Review 5

Modify Review 4 to display gray wheels on the car using FloodFill().

11.6 Text Functions

A GUI-based program window displays only graphics. Therefore, cout and cin cannot be used to display text. For displaying text, the simplified GUI system in this chapter includes the functions:

```
// The following function draw their arguments as text on the graphics display
// starting at the "output cursor" position.
void DrawText(String &S);
void DrawText(int N);
void DrawText(long N);
void DrawText(double N);
// The following functions draws their arguments as text on the graphics
// display centered at the "output cursor" position.
void DrawCenteredText(String &S);
void DrawCenteredText(int N);
void DrawCenteredText(long N);
void DrawCenteredText(double N);
```

The system keeps track of the last graphics operation, and starts the text output at this position. For example, if a line is drawn from 10,10 to 100,100, text output starts at 100,100.

To start text output at a position other than where the last graphics operation ended, the following functions may be used:

```
void gotoxy(int x, int y);
/*Moves the "output cursor" to the indicated position for
    subsequent text output                                    */
int Wherex();
/*Returns the current x-coordinate of the output cursor */
int Wherey();
/*Returns the current y-coordinate of the output cursor */
```

For example, adding the following statements to the Sunny Day program

```
// Label
gotoxy(90, 220);
DrawText("Home, Sweet, Home!");
```

displays a label below the house.

11.7 Text Formatting

The default style for text output is called "System" and is the same style and size used by Windows for the title in an output window. The following functions control fonts, colors, and sizes of text to enhance text output:

```
void SetTextFont(String FontName);
/* Controls the output of text. Valid fonts are:
   Arial
   System
   Times New Roman
   If names other than these are sent, the font is left unchanged. */
void SetTextColor(COLORREF NewColor);
void SetTextSize(int NewFontSize);
/* Font size specified in points. A point size of 72 is one inch.
   "System" font size cannot be changed from its default 10-point */
```

For example, the following statements display "Lawrenceville Press" in RED, Times New Roman, 20 point:

```
SetTextFont("Times New Roman");
SetTextColor(RED);
SetTextSize(20);
DrawText("Lawrenceville Press");
```

When included in a program, these statements display the window:

```
┌─────────────────────────────────────────┐
│ ▣ Text Formatting!              �au_ □ ×  │
├─────────────────────────────────────────┤
│                                          │
│            Lawrenceville Press           │
│                                          │
│                                          │
└─────────────────────────────────────────┘
```

11.8 Screen Sizes

resolution

Windows makes it possible to specify a screen size, or *resolution*, depending upon the display type and drivers. Common sizes are 640x480, meaning 640 pixels across and 480 pixels down, and 800x600. To write programs that center an object, it is important to know if the object should be at x = 320 (i.e. half of 640), x = 400 (half of 800), or some other x. The following two functions return the size of the current screen:

```
GetMaxX();
GetMaxY();
/* Returns the x and y dimensions of the entire screen */
```

Note that these functions return the sizes of the entire screen, not the program window. For example, the following statement draws a circle in the center of the screen, regardless of the screen size, and makes it approximately half the height of the display:

```
Circle(GetMaxX()/2, GetMaxY()/2, GetMaxY()/4);
```

11.9 Generalizing Object Locations

It is usually desirable to use named constants or variables to identify the location of an object on the screen so that changing a single value is all that is required to move the object to a different location or create another copy of the object. For example, the following statements can be used in the Sunny Day program to add grass to the picture:

```
const int x = 60;
const int y = 200;
SetColor(GREEN);
SetThickness(1);
Line(x, y, x+10, y-20);
Line(x, y, x-10, y-20);
Line(x-5, y, x+15, y-15);
```

A sprig of grass is displayed at base location 60,200. To change the location, only the values of the constants need to be changed.

Implementing a Grass() function adds more versatility to the Sunny Day program:

```
void Grass(int x, int y)
/*Draws a sprig of grass with base at x, y */
{
   SetColor(GREEN);
   SetThickness(1);
   Line(x, y, x+10, y-20);
   Line(x, y, x–10, y–20);
   Line(x–5,y,x+15,y–15);
}
```

The function could be made a "standalone" function outside of our GuiClass, or it could be made a member function of GuiClass. The modified Sunny Day program below implements Grass() as a standalone function.

```
/*Sunny Day with Grass() program */

#include <lvp\gui_top.h>

void Grass(int x, int y)
/*Draws a sprig of grass with base at x, y */
{
   SetColor(GREEN);
   SetThickness(1);
   Line(x, y, x+10, y–20);
   Line(x, y, x–10, y–20);
   Line(x–5, y, x+15, y–15);
}
//------------------------------------------------------------------------
class GuiClass {
   public:
   GuiClass();
   void GuiMouseClick(int x, int y); // Action if mouse click
   void GuiPaint();  // Repaint the entire window
   String Title();
   private:
   };
```

```
//--------------------------------------------------------------
GuiClass::GuiClass()
{
}
//--------------------------------------------------------------
String GuiClass::Title()
{
   return ("Grassy Sunny day!");
}
//--------------------------------------------------------------
void GuiClass::GuiMouseClick(int x, int y)
{
}
//--------------------------------------------------------------
void GuiClass::GuiPaint()
{
  // House
  SetColor(BLACK);
  SetThickness(2);
  Rectangle(100, 100, 200, 200);
  Line(100, 100, 150, 50);
  Line(150, 50, 200, 100);
  SetFillColor(RED);    // Paint house red
  FloodFill(150,110);
  SetFillColor(GRAY);    // Paint roof gray
  FloodFill(150,90);

  // Lawn
  for (int x = 30; x <= 300; x += 12)
    Grass(x, 215);

  // Windows and door
  SetColor(BLACK);
  SetThickness(1);
  SetFillColor(GRAY);
  FilledRectangle(120, 120, 140, 140);
  FilledRectangle(160, 120, 180, 140);
  FilledRectangle(135, 160, 165, 200);
  SetColor(WHITE);
  SetPixel(160, 180);    // Doorknob!

  // Sun
  SetFillColor(YELLOW);
  SetColor(YELLOW);
  FilledCircle(280, 50, 30);

  // Label
  gotoxy(150, 230);
  SetTextColor(RED);
  SetTextFont("Times New Roman");
  SetTextSize(26);
  DrawCenteredText("Home, Sweet, Home");
}
//--------------------------------------------------------------
#include <lvp\gui_bot.h>
```

A Guide to Programming in C++

The program output shows a field of green grass in front of the house:

Review 6

Modify Review 5 to display a taxi, as shown below:

Review 7

Modify the Sunny Day program to display an additional row of grass in front of the existing grass, increasing the size of the "lawn."

Review 8

Write a GUI program with a standalone function DrawCar() that draws a car at the location given by the x and y coordinate parameters. Have the program draw several cars at different locations.

Review 9

Write a GUI program with a standalone function DrawBorder() that puts a green border four pixels thick in the output window, where each side of the border is 20 pixels from the edge of the window. Be sure the program is designed to work regardless of the screen resolution.

11.10 Handling Mouse Click Events

Mouse click events are handled by adding code to the GuiMouseClick() function. When a mouse click event occurs, the system passes arguments to the function indicating the x and y coordinates of the location clicked. The GuiMouseClick() function can be coded to register this event in some way (generally though private data members) and the GuiPaint() function can be coded to use this information to update the display. In programming with GUI library, the GuiMouseClick() function never displays graphics output directly.

To illustrate handling mouse click events, a program will be written in this section to keep track of the last location clicked, put a circle wherever the user clicks, and display the coordinates of the last click and the number of clicks made. For this program, private data members are added to store the last coordinates, and the number of clicks so far:

```
class GuiClass {
  public:
  GuiClass();
  void GuiMouseClick(int x, int y);   // Action if mouse click
  void GuiPaint();   // Repaint the entire window
  String Title();
  private:
  int LastX;   // Last location clicked
  int LastY;
  int NumClicks;
};
```

GuiMouseClick() updates the values of these variables when a mouse click occurs:

```
void GuiClass::GuiMouseClick(int x, int y)
{
  LastX = x;
  LastY = y;
  NumClicks++;
}
```

The data members are initialized in the constructor:

```
GuiClass::GuiClass():
LastX(100), LastY(100), NumClicks(0)
{
}
```

LastX and LastY are initialized to 100 so that at least one circle appears in the window.

Finally, the GuiPaint() function is modified to update the window:

```
GuiClass::GuiPaint()
{
  FilledCircle(LastX, LastY, 10);
  gotoxy(10, 20);
  DrawText("Clicked at (");
  DrawText(LastX);
  DrawText(",");
  DrawText(LastY);
  DrawText(")   Number of clicks: ");
  DrawText(NumClicks);
}
```

The private data members are used in producing a filled circle at the location last clicked, and displaying near the top of the screen the coordinates and the number of clicks.

The complete program for handling mouse click events is:

```
/* Click Tracker program */

#include <lvp\gui_top.h>

class GuiClass {
  public:
  GuiClass();
  void GuiMouseClick(int x, int y);    // Action if mouse click
  int GuiPaint();    // Repaint the entire window
  String Title();    // Return the title for the Window
  private:
  int LastX;    // Last location clicked
  int LastY;
  int NumClicks;
};
//-----------------------------------------------------------------------
GuiClass::GuiClass():
LastX(100),LastY(100),NumClicks(0)
{
}
//-----------------------------------------------------------------------
String GuiClass::Title()
{
  return ("Click tracker!");
}
//-----------------------------------------------------------------------
void GuiClass::GuiMouseClick(int x, int y)
{
  LastX = x;
  LastY = y;
  NumClicks++;
}
```

```
//-----------------------------------------------------------
GuiClass::GuiPaint()
{
    FilledCircle(LastX,  LastY, 10);
    gotoxy(10, 20);
    DrawText("Clicked at (");
    DrawText(LastX);
    DrawText(",");
    DrawText(LastY);
    DrawText(")    Number of clicks: ");
    DrawText(NumClicks);
}
//-----------------------------------------------------------
#include <lvp\gui_bot.h>
```

The program output after two mouse clicks looks similar to:

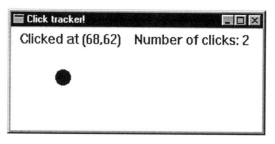

Review 10

Modify the Click Tracker program so that the last two clicks are recorded and circles displayed for each, with a red circle for the most recent, and a black circle for the previous one. (The message can continue to display the coordinates of just the last click.)

Review 11

Modify the Click Tracker program so that it maintains a list (using an array) of all previous click locations. Have the GuiPaint() function draw circles for all the locations on the list. You need not print information across the top of the window.

11.11 Hit Detection

The next step in developing a GUI application is to have items in a window that can be clicked on to perform certain actions. For example, a game board that allows clicking on a square to place a game piece on that square, or a button that indicates that the user wishes to stop the program. The process of determining what window object has been clicked is called *hit detection*.

Treasure Hunt game   To illustrate hit detection, a game program called Treasure Hunt will be written in this section. In this game, the user is presented with an empty grid. In one box of the grid, a treasure is hidden. The user must guess boxes by clicking on them. When a box is clicked and found empty, it changes to gray. When a box is clicked and the treasure is found, it changes to red and the game ends, and the number of clicks is reported. Program output looks similar to that shown at the top of the next page:

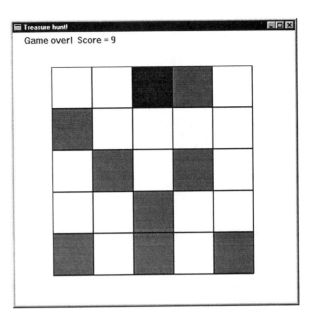

Rather than modifying the minimal GUI program, a new class GridClass will be created to encapsulate the game actions. GridClass will have Paint() and MouseClick() member functions that will handle these events.

Private to GridClass are data members and functions that will support the game. The grid can be represented using a matrix structure with each item in the matrix storing a value that indicates the status of the box. This status may be empty-and-unpicked, empty-and-already-picked, treasure-and-unpicked, and treasure-and-already-picked. These four cases can be represented with four constants. The data member declarations are:

```
// Constants for board; must all differ
const int Empty, EmptyPicked, Treasure, TreasurePicked;
matrix<int> Board;   // Uses above constants
int GridDimension;   // # of rows and columns in grid
```

Other data members will track how many boxes the user has clicked on, and whether or not the treasure has been found.

To display the grid in the most general way possible, constants which describe the location in the window will be used:

```
int BoxSize;    // Pixels per box
int LeftMargin;    // Pixels from left
int TopMargin;    // Pixels from top
```

These constants can be initialized in the constructor using GetMaxX() and GetMaxY() so that the display looks roughly the same regardless of the screen resolution:

```
BoxSize(GetMaxY()/2/GridDimension),    // Fill half of y-dimension
LeftMargin((GetMaxX()–BoxSize*GridDimension)/2),
TopMargin(GetMaxY()/4)
```

The box size is computed so that the grid fills half of the vertical dimension. The margins center the grid on the screen. The appearance will be nearly the same on an 800x600 screen as on a 640x480 or any other screen.

The grid is drawn using two loops. The first loop draws the lines for the columns:

```
for (Col=0; Col<=GridDimension; Col++)
    Line(LeftMargin+Col*BoxSize, TopMargin,
        LeftMargin+Col*BoxSize, TopMargin+GridDimension*BoxSize);
```

Note how the constants are used to position and size the lines. If the grid is five boxes across, this loop draws six lines, thus including lines for the left and right side. A similar loop is needed for the rows.

The boxes must be colored according to their contents. To do this, a private member function MarkBox() is called for each item in the grid. MarkBox() calculates the screen coordinates corresponding to the row and column, and then draws a rectangle of the appropriate color using these coordinates:

```
void GridClass::MarkBox(int Row, int Col, int BoxContents)
/* Post: Row, Col box in appropriate color */
{
    SetColor(BLACK);    // For outline
    SetFillColor(WHITE);
    if (BoxContents==EmptyPicked)
        SetFillColor(GRAY);
    else if (BoxContents==TreasurePicked)
        SetFillColor(RED);
    FilledRectangle(Col*BoxSize+LeftMargin, Row*BoxSize+TopMargin,
            (Col+1)*BoxSize+LeftMargin, (Row+1)*BoxSize+TopMargin);
}
```

The constants are used with the rows and columns multiplied by the BoxSize in order to find the correct screen position.

To manage hit detection the coordinates of a mouse click must be translated to the grid coordinates. This is the opposite of the problem MarkBox() solves. Private member function XYToRowCol() does the translation:

```
void GridClass::XYToRowCol(int x, int y, int &Row, int &Col)
/* Post: Row and Column corresponding to x, y returned,
    or -1 returned if x, y is not on the board         */
{
    int DistFromLeft = x - LeftMargin;
    Col = (DistFromLeft+BoxSize)/BoxSize-1;
    int DistFromTop = y - TopMargin;
    Row = (DistFromTop+BoxSize)/BoxSize-1;
    if (Col < 0 || Col >= GridDimension ||
        Row < 0 || Row >= GridDimension) {
        Row = -1;
        Col = -1;
    }
}
```

The Treasure Hunt program follows:

```
/*Treasure Hunt program */

#include <lvp\gui_top.h>
#include <lvp\matrix.h>
#include <lvp\string.h>
#include <lvp\bool.h>
#include <lvp\random.h>

class GridClass {
  public:
  GridClass();
  void Paint();
  void MouseClick(int x, int y);
  private:
  const int GridDimension;    // # of rows and columns in grid
  // Constants for board; must all differ
  const int Empty, EmptyPicked, Treasure, TreasurePicked;
  matrix<int> Board;    // Uses above constants
  bool GameOver;
  int NumClicks;
  int BoxSize;    // Pixels per box
  int LeftMargin;    // Pixels from left
  int TopMargin;    // Pixels from top
  void XYToRowCol(int x, int y, int &Row, int &Col);
  void MarkBox(int Row, int Col, int BoxContents);
};

GridClass::GridClass()
  : GridDimension(5),
  Empty(0), EmptyPicked(-1), Treasure(1), TreasurePicked(2),
  Board(GridDimension, GridDimension,0),
  NumClicks(0), GameOver(false),
  BoxSize(GetMaxY()/2/GridDimension),    // Fill half of y
  LeftMargin((GetMaxX()-BoxSize*GridDimension)/2),
  TopMargin(GetMaxY()/4)
{
  randomize();
  Board[random(GridDimension)][random(GridDimension)] = Treasure;
}
//----------------------------------------------------------------------
void GridClass::XYToRowCol(int x, int y, int &Row, int &Col)
/*Post: Row and Column corresponding to x, y returned,
  or -1 returned if x, y is not on the board            */
{
  int DistFromLeft = x - LeftMargin;
  Col = (DistFromLeft+BoxSize)/BoxSize-1;
  int DistFromTop = y - TopMargin;
  Row = (DistFromTop+BoxSize)/BoxSize-1;
  if (Col < 0 || Col >= GridDimension ||
    Row < 0 || Row >= GridDimension) {
    Row = -1;
    Col = -1;
  }
}
```

```
//--------------------------------------------------------------------
void GridClass::MarkBox(int Row, int Col, int BoxContents)
/*Post: Row, Col box in appropriate color */
{
  SetColor(BLACK);   // For outline
  SetFillColor(WHITE);
  if (BoxContents==EmptyPicked)
    SetFillColor(GRAY);
  else if (BoxContents==TreasurePicked)
    SetFillColor(RED);
  FilledRectangle(Col*BoxSize+LeftMargin, Row*BoxSize+TopMargin,
    (Col+1)*BoxSize+LeftMargin, (Row+1)*BoxSize+TopMargin);
}
//--------------------------------------------------------------------
void GridClass::MouseClick(int x, int y)
{
  int Row, Col;
  XYToRowCol(x, y, Row, Col);
  if (Row != -1 && Col != -1 && Board[Row][Col] != EmptyPicked) {
    if (Board[Row][Col] == Empty)
      Board[Row][Col] = EmptyPicked;
    else if (Board[Row][Col] == Treasure) {
      Board[Row][Col] = TreasurePicked;
      GameOver = true;
    }
    NumClicks++;
  }
}
//--------------------------------------------------------------------
void GridClass::Paint()
{
  SetColor(BLACK);
  int Row,Col;
  // Draw lines
  for (Col = 0; Col <= GridDimension; Col++)
    Line(LeftMargin+Col*BoxSize, TopMargin,
      LeftMargin+Col*BoxSize, TopMargin+GridDimension*BoxSize);
  for (Row = 0; Row <= GridDimension; Row++)
    Line(LeftMargin, TopMargin+Row*BoxSize,
      LeftMargin+GridDimension*BoxSize, TopMargin+Row*BoxSize);
  // Color in boxes
  for (Row=0; Row < GridDimension; Row++)
    for (Col=0; Col < GridDimension; Col++)
      MarkBox(Row, Col, Board[Row][Col]);
  // Display results
  if (GameOver==true) {
    gotoxy(20, 20);
    DrawText("Game over!  Score = ");
    DrawText(NumClicks);
  }
}
//--------------------------------------------------------------------
//--------------------------------------------------------------------
class GuiClass {
public:
  GuiClass();
  void GuiMouseClick(int x, int y);   // Action if mouse click
  void GuiPaint();   // Repaint the entire window
  String Title();   // Title to display
private:
  GridClass Game;
};
```

```
//-------------------------------------------------------------------------
GuiClass::GuiClass()
{
}
//-------------------------------------------------------------------------
String GuiClass::Title()
{
    return ("Treasure hunt!");
}
//-------------------------------------------------------------------------
void GuiClass::GuiMouseClick(int x, int y)
{
    Game.MouseClick(x, y);
}
//-------------------------------------------------------------------------
void GuiClass::GuiPaint()
{
    Game.Paint();
}
//-------------------------------------------------------------------------
#include <lvp\gui_bot.h>
```

Notice that all the application-specific code is stored in the new class, GridClass. This allows the GuiClass code to be kept simple, and makes it possible to have a single program perform a number of different tasks.

Review 12

The Treasure Hunt program has the odd behavior that after the treasure is found, it keeps counting clicks made to the red treasure box (but not to gray boxes) and also continues to allow the user to click on empty boxes. Determine why this is so, and modify the program to prevent this.

Review 13

Modify the Treasure Hunt program so that clicks off the side of the board cause an error message to be displayed at the top of the screen.

11.12 Message Boxes and PostQuitMessage()

In communicating with the user, Windows programs often create "message boxes" which give an important message, or ask for specific information. For example, a message box might ask if the user wants to play a game again, or confirm that the user really wants to delete some text, and so on. The GUI library used in this chapter provides a few simple message box functions based on standard Windows message boxes. More complex message boxes including those that ask the user for strings or numbers are beyond the scope of this text.

The simplest message box function is not really a box at all:

void MessageBeep(**int** BeepSound);

This function generates a system beep sound. The arguments used with this function are the constants listed below:

Argument	Sound
-1	Standard beep using the computer speaker.
MB_ICONASTERISK	Plays the sound identified by the SystemAsterisk entry in the [sounds] section of WIN.INI.
MB_ICONEXCLAMATION	Plays the sound identified by the SystemExclamation entry
MB_ICONHAND	Plays the sound identified by the SystemHand entry.
MB_ICONQUESTION	Plays the sound identified by the SystemQuestion entry.
MB_OK	Plays the sound identified by the SystemDefault entry.

Messages are displayed with the following functions:

```
int MessageBox(String Text, String Title);
/* Post: A message box with an OK button displayed */
int MessageBoxYN(String Text, String Title);
/* Post: A message box with YES and NO buttons displayed.
   Returns 1 if user hits YES button; 0 if hits NO button     */
```

Each of these functions stop program execution, and wait for the user to click on a button. For example, the following statements:

```
MessageBox("Box Text",  "Box Title");
MessageBoxYN("Box Text",  "Box Title");
```

Produce the two boxes:

 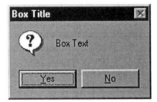

These boxes, like other windows, can be dragged to reveal information behind them. It is very important that these functions <u>not</u> be called by the Paint() function because this will cause the boxes to be generated whenever the window is moved, resized, or otherwise repainted. Typically, these functions are called in response to other events; for example, mouse click events.

The PostQuitMessage() function immediately terminates the program and closes the window. This function behaves like a return statement, and is usually given an argument of 0 to indicate normal termination, as in the statement

```
PostQuitMessage(0);
```

which immediately ends the running program.

11.13 GUI Programming without the GUI Library

The GUI library provided with this text makes it easier to program a graphical user interface under Windows. In particular, it allows the programmer access to a number of Windows functions without knowledge of two difficult topics: pointers and inheritance. However, the style of programming, and even many of the function names, are identical to those used in programming without the library. If you have experience using the GUI library, you will be well poised to take the next step after you finish your study of this text.

Case Study

In this Case Study, the Treasure Hunt game will be improved. In addition, a ButtonClass will be written to serve as a utility in other GUI programs.

specification

The Treasure Hunt should contain the following improvements:

- The program beeps when an illegal click is made

- When the player wins, the program asks if another game is to be played.

- The screen contains a "I give up!" button that when clicked stops the program after giving a simple message and showing the location of the treasure.

Program output should look similar to:

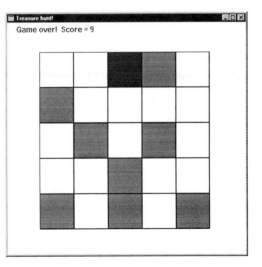

Creating beeps and querying the user when the game is over can be done with modifications to MouseClick().

Creating a button is a harder task, but one which could be useful in many programs. Therefore, a new ButtonClass class will be created. ButtonClass will have the following specifications:

```
class ButtonClass {
public:
    ButtonClass(String Text, int X1,int Y1, int X2, int Y2);
    /* Post: A button created with upper-left corner at X1,Y1 and
       lower-right corner at X2,Y2 with Text centered in box        */
    void Paint();
    bool IsHit(int x, int y);
    /* Post: true returned if and only if (x,y) is on the button */
private:
    int MyX1, MyY1, MyX2, MyY2;
    String MyText;
};
```

The GridClass functions can call the Paint() and IsHit() functions of the ButtonClass object. Private data members keep track of the location of the button, and the text of the button.

The ButtonClass Paint() uses the private data members:

```
void ButtonClass::Paint()
{
    SetColor(BLACK);
    Rectangle(MyX1, MyY1, MyX2, MyY2);
    gotoxy((MyX1+MyX2)/2, 5+(MyY1+MyY2)/2);
    DrawCenteredText(MyText);
}
```

The text is centered by calculating the middle of the button, and using the DrawCenteredText() function. The value 5 is used to roughly center the text vertically in the button.

The IsHit() function is coded as:

```
bool ButtonClass::IsHit(int x, int y)
/* Post: true returned if and only if point (x, y) is on the button */
{
    return (x >= MyX1 && x <= MyX2 && y >= MyY1 && y <= MyY2);
}
```

The button object is defined by GridClass as a private data member. The GridClass Paint() function calls the button object's Paint() function. The GridClass MouseClick() function calls the button object's IsHit() function:

```
void GridClass::MouseClick(int x, int y)
{
  int Row, Col;
  if (QuitButton.IsHit(x,y)) {
    GameOver = true;
    Board[TreasureRow][TreasureCol] = TreasurePicked;
    Paint();    // To show the treasure square
    MessageBox("Come back again!", "Quit button clicked");
    PostQuitMessage(0);
  }
  else {
    XYToRowCol(x, y, Row, Col);
    if (Row != -1 && Col != -1 && Board[Row][Col] != EmptyPicked) {
      if (Board[Row][Col] == Empty)
        Board[Row][Col] = EmptyPicked;
      else if (Board[Row][Col] == Treasure) {
        Board[Row][Col] = TreasurePicked;
        GameOver = true;
        Paint();    // To show treasure square
        if (MessageBoxYN("Play again?", "Game over")==1)
            InitGrid();
        else
            PostQuitMessage(0);
      }
      NumClicks++;
    }
    else
      MessageBeep(-1);
  }
}
```

The GridClass Paint() function is called each time a message box is displayed. This is so the user can see the effects of the last mouse click before the message box is displayed. An InitGrid() function is needed to reinitialize the grid before playing for a second time. This function will be added to the GridClass declaration.

The improved version of the Treasure Hunt is as follows:

```
/* Improved Treasure Hunt game */

#include <lvp\gui_top.h>
#include <lvp\matrix.h>
#include <lvp\string.h>
#include <lvp\bool.h>
#include <lvp\random.h>

//-------------------------------------------------------------------------
class ButtonClass {
public:
  ButtonClass(String Text, int X1,int Y1, int X2, int Y2);
  /* Post: A button created with upper-left corner at X1,Y1 and
     lower-right corner at X2,Y2 with Text centered in box        */
  void Paint();
  bool IsHit(int x, int y);
  /* Post: true returned if and only if (x,y) is on the button */
private:
  int MyX1, MyY1, MyX2, MyY2;
  String MyText;
};
```

```
//--------------------------------------------------------------------------
ButtonClass::ButtonClass(String Text, int X1, int Y1, int X2, int Y2)
   : MyText(Text), MyX1(X1), MyY1(Y1), MyX2(X2), MyY2(Y2)
/* Post: Button created with upper-left corner at X1, Y1 and
   lower right corner at X2,Y2 with Text centered in box */
{
}
//--------------------------------------------------------------------------
void ButtonClass::Paint()
{
  SetColor(BLACK);
  Rectangle(MyX1, MyY1, MyX2, MyY2);
  gotoxy((MyX1+MyX2)/2, 5+(MyY1+MyY2)/2);
  DrawCenteredText(MyText);
}
//--------------------------------------------------------------------------
bool ButtonClass::IsHit(int x, int y)
/* Post: true returned if and only if point (x, y) is on the button */
{
  return (x >= MyX1 && x <= MyX2 && y >= MyY1 && y <= MyY2);
}
//--------------------------------------------------------------------------
//--------------------------------------------------------------------------
class GridClass {
public:
  GridClass();
  void Paint();
  void MouseClick(int x, int y);
  void InitGrid();
private:
  const int GridDimension;    // # of Rows/columns in grid
  // Constants for board; must all differ
  const int Empty, EmptyPicked, Treasure, TreasurePicked;
  matrix<int> Board;    // Uses above constants
  int TreasureRow, TreasureCol;
  bool GameOver;
  int NumClicks;
  int BoxSize;       // Pixels per box
  int LeftMargin;    // Pixels from left
  int TopMargin;     // Pixels from top
  void XYToRowCol(int x, int y, int &Row, int &Col);
  void MarkBox(int Row, int Col, int BoxContents);
  ButtonClass QuitButton;
};
//--------------------------------------------------------------------------
GridClass::GridClass()
   : GridDimension(5),
   Empty(0), EmptyPicked(-1), Treasure(1), TreasurePicked(2),
   Board(GridDimension,GridDimension,0),
   NumClicks(0), GameOver(false),
   BoxSize(GetMaxY()/2/GridDimension),    // Fill half of y-dimension
   LeftMargin((GetMaxX()-BoxSize*GridDimension)/2),
   TopMargin(GetMaxY()/4),
   QuitButton("I give up!",10,10,100,40)
{
  randomize();
  TreasureRow = random(GridDimension);
  TreasureCol = random(GridDimension);
  Board[TreasureRow][TreasureCol] = Treasure;
}
```

```
//--------------------------------------------------------------------
void GridClass::InitGrid()
/*Post: Grid initialized for a new game */
{
  NumClicks = 0;
  GameOver = false;
  for (int Row=0; Row < GridDimension; Row++)
    for (int Col=0; Col < GridDimension; Col++)
      Board[Row][Col] = Empty;
  TreasureRow = random(GridDimension);
  TreasureCol = random(GridDimension);
  Board[TreasureRow][TreasureCol] = Treasure;
}
//--------------------------------------------------------------------
void GridClass::XYToRowCol(int x, int y, int &Row, int &Col)
/*Post: Row and Column corresponding to x, y returned,
  or -1 for if x, y is not on the board                  */
{
  int DistFromLeft = x - LeftMargin;
  Col = (DistFromLeft+BoxSize)/BoxSize -1;
  int DistFromTop = y - TopMargin;
  Row = (DistFromTop+BoxSize)/BoxSize -1;
  if (Col < 0 || Col >= GridDimension ||
    Row < 0 || Row >= GridDimension) {
    Row = -1;
    Col = -1;
  }
}
//--------------------------------------------------------------------
void GridClass::MarkBox(int Row, int Col, int BoxContents)
/*Post: Row, Col box in appropriate color */
{
  SetColor(BLACK);    // For outline
  SetFillColor(WHITE);
  if (BoxContents==EmptyPicked)
    SetFillColor(GRAY);
  else if (BoxContents==TreasurePicked)
    SetFillColor(RED);
  FilledRectangle(Col*BoxSize+LeftMargin, Row*BoxSize+TopMargin,
  (Col+1)*BoxSize+LeftMargin,
  (Row+1)*BoxSize+TopMargin);
}
```

```
//-------------------------------------------------------------------------
void GridClass::MouseClick(int x, int y)
{
  int Row, Col;
  if (QuitButton.IsHit(x,y)) {
    GameOver = true;
    Board[TreasureRow][TreasureCol] = TreasurePicked;
    Paint();    // To show the treasure square
    MessageBox("Come back again!", "Quit button clicked");
    PostQuitMessage(0);
  }
  else {
    XYToRowCol(x, y, Row, Col);
    if (Row != -1 && Col != -1 && Board[Row][Col] != EmptyPicked) {
      if (Board[Row][Col] == Empty)
        Board[Row][Col] = EmptyPicked;
      else if (Board[Row][Col] == Treasure) {
        Board[Row][Col] = TreasurePicked;
        GameOver = true;
        Paint();    // To show treasure square
        if (MessageBoxYN("Play again?", "Game over")==1)
            InitGrid();
        else
            PostQuitMessage(0);
      }
      NumClicks++;
    }
    else
      MessageBeep(-1);
  }
}
//-------------------------------------------------------------------------
void GridClass::Paint()
{
  QuitButton.Paint();
  SetColor(BLACK);

  int Row, Col;
  // Draw lines
  for (Col = 0; Col <= GridDimension; Col++)
    Line(LeftMargin+Col*BoxSize, TopMargin,
    LeftMargin+Col*BoxSize,
    TopMargin+GridDimension*BoxSize);
  for (Row = 0; Row <= GridDimension; Row++)
    Line(LeftMargin, TopMargin+Row*BoxSize,
    LeftMargin+GridDimension*BoxSize,
    TopMargin+Row*BoxSize);
  // Color in boxes
  for (Row=0; Row < GridDimension; Row++)
    for (Col=0; Col < GridDimension; Col++)
      MarkBox(Row,Col,Board[Row][Col]);
  // Display results
  if (GameOver==true) {
    gotoxy(20,GetMaxY()-60);
    DrawText("Game over!  Score = ");
    DrawText(NumClicks);
  }
}
```

```
//-----------------------------------------------------------------
//-----------------------------------------------------------------
class GuiClass {
public:
  GuiClass();
  void GuiMouseClick(int x, int y);    //Action if mouse click
  void GuiPaint();    // Repaint the entire window
  String Title();    // Title to display
private:
  GridClass Game;
};
//-----------------------------------------------------------------
GuiClass::GuiClass()
{
}
//-----------------------------------------------------------------
String GuiClass::Title()
{
  return ("Treasure hunt!");
}
//-----------------------------------------------------------------
void GuiClass::GuiMouseClick(int x, int y)
{
  Game.MouseClick(x, y);
}
//-----------------------------------------------------------------
void GuiClass::GuiPaint()
{
  Game.Paint();
}
//-----------------------------------------------------------------
#include <lvp\gui_bot.h>
```

The ButtonClass may be useful in other programs as well. To make it easily accessible to other programs, it would be best to create a library with ButtonClass. For this reason, it is included with this text, and may be used in your programs that have the statement:

```
#include <lvp\button.h>
```

Review 14

Modify the Case Study program to include a "Trap Door" placed randomly. If the user clicks on the trap door before finding the treasure, he loses. To win, the user must find the treasure first.

Review 15

Use button.h to create a program with three buttons labeled Circle, Square, and Quit. Show a square if the Square button is clicked, a circle if the Circle button is clicked, and terminate the program if the Quit button is clicked.

Chapter Summary

Event-driven programming is used to program in a GUI environment. The event-driven program is a set of instructions indicating what is to be done for each possible event. This type of programming differs from console based programming because the program waits for the user to tell the computer what to do.

The gui_top and gui_bot libraries included with this text allow event-driven programs to be written by creating an object that responds to events, and adding this object to the system.

Functions introduced in this chapter to create graphic images include Circle(), FilledCircle(), Line(), Rectangle(), FilledRectangle(), and SetPixel(). The parameters of these functions refer to pixel units which are single dots on the screen. The upper-left corner of the screen is position (0,0).

The outline color and fill color of a graphic image can be specified using SetColor() and SetFillColor() respectively. The line thickness of the outline can be specified with SetThickness(). The color and thickness specified when using these functions stay in effect until the color or thickness is changed again.

To color in a region that is irregularly shaped, the FloodFill() function is used. The parameters passed to FloodFill() need to be a single point within the region to be colored. FloodFill() colors any pixel which differs in color from the passed pixel with the current fill color.

Because a GUI-based program displays only graphics, cout and cin cannot be used to display text. To display text, the DrawText() and DrawCenteredText() functions are used. Text output is displayed after the last graphics operation. To specify the position of text output, the gotoxy(), wherex(), and wherey() functions are used. Text can also be formatted for font, color, and size using SetTextFont(), SetTextColor(), and SetTextSize().

Because screen resolution can differ from computer to computer, it is useful for a program to know the size of the current screen. The GetMaxX() and GetMaxY() functions are used to return the size of the current screen. Having named constants or variables to identify the location of an object on the screen is useful so that changing a single value is all that is required to modify the object.

Mouse click events are handled by the system passing arguments to GuiMouseClick() indicating the x and y coordinates of the location clicked. Code can be added to the GuiMouseClick() function to register the event and the GuiPaint() function can be coded to use this information to update the display.

Hit detection is the process of determining what window object has been clicked. This enables a program to have items in a window that can be clicked on to perform certain actions.

Message boxes are used to communicate with the user. Message box functions include MessageBeep(), MessageBox(), and MessageBoxYN().

Vocabulary

Console Based Program Program that interacts with the user through text displayed on the screen, and keystrokes from the user.

Event Something to which a program must respond.

Event-driven A program that becomes a set of instructions indicating what is to be done for each event possible.

A Guide to Programming in C++

GUI Based Program A program that waits for the user to tell the computer what to do, usually using graphics and mouse input.

Hit Detection The Process of determining what window object has been clicked.

Message Box Used to display an important message or ask for specific information.

Picture Element A single dot on the screen.

Pixel A picture element on the screen.

Resolution The fineness of detail that can be displayed on the screen; it depends upon the display and hardware and software.

C++

gui_bot.h A library that creates an object that responds to an event, and adds this object to the system.

gui_top.h A library that implements the GuiClass class.

GUI Library Functions

```
void Circle(int xc, int yc, int r);
void FilledCircle(int xc, int yc, int r);
void Line(int x1, int y1, int x2, int y2);
void Rectangle(int x1, int y1, int x2, int y2);
void FilledRectangle(int x1, int y1, int x2, int y2);
void SetPixel(int x, int y);
SetFillColor(COLORREF Color);
SetColor(COLORREF Color);
void FloodFill(int x, int y);
void DrawText(String &S);
void DrawText(int N);
void DrawText(long N);
void DrawText(double N);
void DrawCenteredText(String &S);
void DrawCenteredText(int N);
void DrawCenteredText(long N);
void DrawCenteredText(double N);
void gotoxy(int x, int y);
int wherex();
int wherey();
void SetTextFont(String FontName);
void SetTextColor(COLORREF NewColor);
void SetTextSize(int NewFontSize);
GetMaxX();
GetMaxY();
int MessageBox(String Text, String Title);
int MessageBoxYN(String Text, String Title);
PostQuitMessage(0);
```

Exercises

Exercise 1

Write a program that draws the Lawrenceville Press symbol (shown below) roughly in the middle of a window. Use GetMaxX() and GetMaxY() so that it appears in the middle regardless of the screen resolution.

Exercise 2

Write a program that draws 10 rectangles with random coordinates.

Exercise 3

Modify Review 11 so that every time a circle is drawn, matching circles are drawn in the other three quarters of the screen. A sample display is shown below:

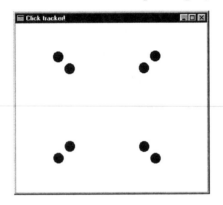

Exercise 4

Modify Review 11 to add buttons for blue, red, and green. When a button is clicked, the drawing "pen" is changed to that color so that subsequent circles are drawn in the color clicked.

Exercise 5

Modify Review 11 so that a sprig of grass is placed wherever the user clicks.

Exercise 6

Write a program that allows two people to play Tic-Tac-Toe. The program should let X play first, and then have the players alternate turns. Moves off the board should generate a beep. When a player wins, the program should detect this, give a message, and end the program.

Exercise 7

Modify Exercise 6 to play a 4 x 4 game of Tic-Tac-Toe.

Exercise 8

Write a program that allows a person to play the "15" solitaire game. In this game, the numbers 1 through 15 are randomly distributed around a 4 x 4 grid. Moves are made by sliding numbers into the empty slot. The game is won by getting all the numbers in order with the empty slot in the lower-right corner.

In the computer version, the user clicks on a number to slide it into the empty spot. For example, clicking on the 12 below:

13	8	12	7
6		15	11
14	4	5	1
10	2	3	9

produces the board:

13	8	12	7
6	15		11
14	4	5	1
10	2	3	9

Note that not every random board has a solution! To make sure there is a solution, the program must randomly push the numbers around, starting with a correct layout.

Exercise 9

Write a program that plays the game "Concentration" with the user. A 6 x 6 grid forms a board with all squares initially shown as blank. "Behind" each square is a number from 1 to 18, in pairs. On each turn, the user clicks on a square, sees what is behind it, then tries to click on the box containing a match. If a match is hit, then the boxes are colored gray, and the player gets another turn. Have the program display which player's (computer or user) turn it is, and keep score by counting the number of matches found by each player.

Exercise 10

Write a program to play "Connect-Four." This game is played on a grid that contains 7 columns each 5 squares tall. On each turn, the player drops a disk of his or her color into a column, and it falls until it hits the bottom or a previous disk. The game is won by forming a sequence of four disks diagonally, horizontally, or vertically all of one color.

Exercise 11

Write a program that allows the user to play a game of "Battleship" against the computer. The program randomly places 4 "ships" under the water in a 10 x 10 grid. The ships are placed horizontally or vertically, and occupy 2, 3, 4, and 5 squares respectively. The user then clicks on squares in the grid, trying to sink the ships by clicking on all of the squares each occupies. Keep score by showing the number of ships sunk and the number of clicks taken.

Exercise 12

Create a DieClass that implements a die with Paint(), GetValue(), and Roll() functions that could be used in a dice-based game.

Exercise 13

Write a program to play "Clacker." In Clacker, the numbers 1 through 12 are initially uncovered. The player throws two dice, and may cover the number representing either the total, or the two numbers on the individual dice. For a throw of 3 and 5, for example, the player may cover the 3 and the 5, or just the 8. Play continues until all numbers are covered. The goal is to have the lowest number of rolls. You may wish to use a DieClass as described in the previous exercise.

Exercise 14

Write a program that allows the game Nim to be played with the mouse. Nim is described in Chapter 5 Exercise 12. When a circle is clicked, it becomes highlighted, and all circles in other groups are de-highlighted. When a player has made a selection, a button labeled "Take Stones" can be clicked and the stones will be removed from the board. You may wish to devise a StoneClass to assist in implementing this game.

Exercise 15

Write a program that allows the Hanoi puzzle to be played on the computer screen. Clicking on a column highlights (or de-highlights) the top ring on the peg. Clicking on another peg causes the ring to be moved. You may want to devise a new PegClass to implement the pegs in this game.

Exercise 16

Write a program that implements a simple flash card system with pairs of items from a file. Initially a word is displayed on the "card." When a button labeled "Flip Card" is clicked, the corresponding word is displayed. When the "Flip Card" button is clicked again, the original word is displayed. Another button labeled "Next Card" brings up the next card, and so on.

Exercise 17

Write a class RadioClass the implements "radio buttons." In a set of radio buttons, only one button is selected at a time. If the user clicks on another button, it becomes the selected button and the others are deselected. The declaration for the class should be:

```
class RadioClass {
public:
    RadioClass(int xLoc, int yLoc);
    // location of top left of first button
    void AddButton(String Text);
    void Paint();
    bool MouseClick(int x, int y);
    // returns true if click was on a button
    String NowSelected();
    // returns text of currently selected button
private:
};
```

A typical set of buttons would be similar to:

⦿ Freshman
◯ Sophomore
◯ Junior
◯ Senior

Exercise 18

Write a program to display the graph of a function on the screen, complete with axes, etc. Use constants to specify the maximum x and y values on the graph. Use the function $y = x^2$ to test your program. Note that since you may wish to graph the function from 0 to 4 on the x-axis and from 0 to 16 on the y-axis, but the screen measures in pixels from 0 to the size of the screen, you will want to write a function to convert pixel location values to x and y values for your graph.

Exercise 19

Write a program that simulates a game of Life as described in Chapter Eight Exercise 13 but which obtains the starting grid by allowing the user to use mouse clicks to add and remove cells. Have the program display buttons at the bottom of the screen to quit and go to the next generation.

Exercise 20

An important area of current mathematical research concerns the topic of *iteration*. Iteration is the repetition of a mathematical process, and the research concerns how values behave after many iterations. Because of the need for large amounts of computation, this research is possible only because of the computer. Mathematicians have found that many processes behave "chaotically" meaning that small variations in starting values lead to dramatic variations in results.

A famous example of this is the Mandelbrot Set. This is a diagram showing the results of iterating a certain operation on points in the x, y plane. If the iteration leads to values that grow very large, the point is colored black. If the iteration leads to values that do not grow, the point is colored white. A graph of the most interesting region of the Mandelbrot Set is shown below:

1.50

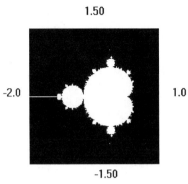

-2.0   1.0

-1.50

The test for black or white is performed by the following function:

```
int Test(double x, double y)
/* Post: Returns 0 if the point x,y does not grow large;
   non-zero if the point grows                    */
{
   const int MaxIter = 100;   // Times to iterate
   double a = 0;   // Seed value
   double b = 0;
   double newa, newb;
   for (int i=0; i<MaxIter; i++) {
      newa = a*a - b*b + x;   // Equations of iteration
      newb = 2*a*b + y;
      a = newa;
      b = newb;
      if (a > 2 || b > 2)   // if grows large, break
         break;
   }
   if (i == MaxIter)   // i.e., did not break out of loop
      return 0;
   else
      return i;
}
```

Use this function in a program to display the Mandelbrot Set. Experiment with different ranges of x and y for the picture.

Chapter Twelve
Advanced Algorithms and Recursion

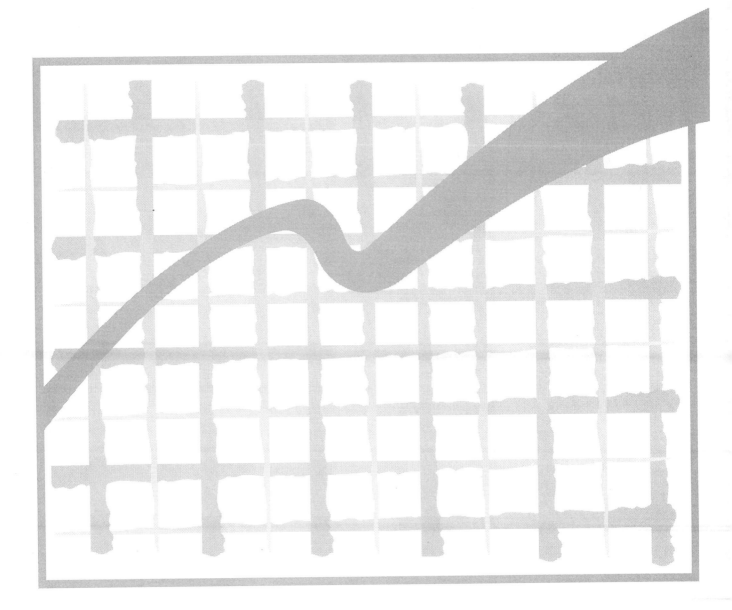

Objectives

After completing this chapter you will be able to:

1. Implement the selection sort and merge sort algorithms.

2. Implement a binary search algorithm.

3. Implement the depth-first search algorithm.

12

$\mathbf{I}$n this chapter you will learn advanced algorithms for manipulating and analyzing information.

12.1 Selection Sort

Sorting is the process of putting items in a designated order, either from low to high or high to low. One algorithm for sorting is *selection sort*.

The basic idea of selection sort is similar to how one might sort a short list of numbers. The list is first scanned for the lowest item. This item is then copied to a new list, and removed from the old list. The process is repeated until all the items on the list have been moved to the new list. The new list contains all the numbers of the original list sorted in order from low to high.

For numbers stored in an array, the SelectionSort() pseuodocode is:

```
while (elements in array > 1)
    Find lowest number in array
    Remove element from original array
    Add number to new array
copy new array to original array
```

The SelectionSort() subtasks may look familiar. Functions that achieved similar tasks were presented in Chapter Eight (p. 8-7). The coded SelectionSort(), with a **typedef** to simplify the definition is:

```
typedef vector<int> ArrayType;

void SelectionSort(ArrayType &A)
/*Sorts A from low to high
   Post: Elements of A in order from low to high */
{
  ArrayType Temp(0);
  while (A.length() != 0) {
    int LowSpot = FindLowest(A);
    AddToArray(Temp, A[LowSpot]);
    RemoveFromArray(A, LowSpot);
  }
  A = Temp;
}
```

The program below demonstrates the selection sort:

```
/* Selection Sort program */

#include <stdlib.h>
#include <iostream.h>
#include <lvp\vector.h>
#include <lvp\random.h>

typedef vector<int> ArrayType;

//----------------------------------------------------------------
int FindLowest(const ArrayType &A)
/* Returns the index of the lowest value in the array.
   Post: Index of lowest value in array returned      */
{
  int LowSpotSoFar = 0;
  for (int i=1; i<A.length(); i++) {
    if (A[i] < A[LowSpotSoFar])
      LowSpotSoFar = i;
  }
  return(LowSpotSoFar);
}
//----------------------------------------------------------------
void AddToArray(ArrayType &A, const int NewItem)
/* Increases size of A by 1 and adds NewItem to A
   Post: Size of A increased by 1, NewItem last element in A */
{
  A.resize(A.length()+1);
  A[A.length()-1] = NewItem;
}
//----------------------------------------------------------------
void RemoveFromArray(ArrayType &A, const int Index)
/* Removes element A[Index] by sliding later elements back.
   Assumes 0 <= Index < A.length()-1
   Post: A[Index] deleted, size of A decreased by 1      */
{
  for (int i=Index; i<A.length()-1; i++)
    A[i] = A[i+1];
  A.resize(A.length()-1);
}
//----------------------------------------------------------------
void SelectionSort(ArrayType &A)
/* Sorts A from low to high
   Post: Elements of A in order from low to high */
{
  ArrayType Temp(0);
  while (A.length() != 0) {
    int LowSpot = FindLowest(A);
    AddToArray(Temp, A[LowSpot]);
    RemoveFromArray(A, LowSpot);
  }
  A = Temp;
}
//----------------------------------------------------------------
void LoadRandomArray(ArrayType &A, int Size)
/* Fills array A with Size random values in the range 0..999 */
{
  const int MaxValue = 999;
  A.resize(Size);
  for (int i=0; i<Size; i++)
    A[i] = random(MaxValue+1);
}
```

```
//------------------------------------------------------------
void DisplayArray(const ArrayType &A)
/*Displays the items of A, with field width of 5, 10 per line */
{
  for (int i=0; i<A.length(); i++) {
    cout.width(5); cout << A[i];
    if ((i+1)%10 == 0)
      cout << endl;
  }
  cout << endl;
}
//------------------------------------------------------------
void Sort (ArrayType &A)
/*Sorts array A from low to high */
{
  SelectionSort(A);
}
//------------------------------------------------------------
int main()
{
  randomize();
  ArrayType Sample;
  const int SampleSize = 20;
  LoadRandomArray(Sample, SampleSize);
  DisplayArray(Sample);
  Sort(Sample);
  DisplayArray(Sample);
  return(0);
}
```

The Sort() function is not necessary, but hides the details of the sort from the programmer coding main(). The program output is similar to:

```
915   629    19   712    86   712   442   365   848   867
 30   902   774   798   564   800   405   198    16    96


 16    19    30    86    96   198   365   405   442   564
629   712   712   774   798   800   848   867   902   915
```

When testing such a complex program, it is important to use several different sample sizes, arrays that are already in order, arrays in reverse order, arrays with many duplicates, etc.

12.2 Timing Code

When choosing a sorting algorithm, one consideration is its efficiency. One measure of the *efficiency* of a sorting algorithm is the speed at which it can complete a sort. The stopwat library, provided with this text, contains the StopWatchClass to measure the time required for designated code to execute.

stopwat.h

The StopWatchClass documentation is as follows:

StopWatchClass (stopwat.h)

Functions
```
StopWatchClass();   // Creates and resets watch
void Reset();   // Resets watch to 0.00
double Reading();   // Returns current reading in seconds
```

To time SelectionSort() in the Selection Sort program, the stopwat library is included in the program, and main() is modified as follows:

```
int main()
{
    ...
    StopWatchClass S;
    S.Reset();
    Sort(Sample);
    cout << S.Reading() << endl;
    ...
}
```

In this case, the call to Reset() is unnecessary since the constructor automatically resets the stopwatch to 0.0.

Review 1

Modify the Selection Sort program to display the time required for Sort() to execute, and to allow the user to enter the sample size. Run the program using sample sizes of 1000, 2000, 3000, and 4000. Sketch a graph of sample size vs. time required. Be sure to time just Sort().

Review 2

The SelectionSort() uses a temporary array, which takes extra storage space, and makes frequent calls to resize(), increasing execution time. A different version of the selection sort algorithm orders elements by swapping values within the original array, which does not require a second array. This selection sort algorithm requires FindLowest() to find the lowest item in a range:

```
int FindLowest(const ArrayType &A, int Start, int End)
/*Returns the index of the lowest value in A[Start]..A[End]
    Post: Index of lowest value in A[Start]..A[End] returned  */
```

and is coded as:

```
void SelectionSort (ArrayType &A)
{
    for (int i=0; i<A.length(); i++) {
      int LowSpot = FindLowest(A, i, A.length()-1);

      // Swap lowest with next spot in array
      int T = A[LowSpot];
      A[LowSpot] = A[i];
      A[i] = T;
    }
}
```

Modify the Selection Sort program to implement the algorithm above. Include the timing code as done in Review 1, and perform time trials on sample sizes of 1000, 2000, 3000, and 4000. Compare the results with those in Review 1.

12.3 Writing Generic Code

Sorting algorithms are used for many data types, not just an array of int values as in the Selection Sort program. Code written as generically as possible can be easily implemented for any data type, saving a lot of time and extra effort. One approach to generic code is to use **typedefs**, as in the statements:

```
typedef int ItemType;
typedef vector<ItemType> ArrayType;
```

Sorting code can then be defined in terms of ItemType, rather than a specific type. For example:

```
void AddToArray(ArrayType &A, const ItemType NewItem)
/*Increases size of A by 1 and adds NewItem to A
   Post: Size of A increased by 1, NewItem last element in A */
```

If the items to be sorted are a **struct** or an object for which the comparison operators (<, >, <=, >=) are not defined, the comparison between elements must be changed accordingly. For example, if the items are **structs** containing both Name and Age fields, and it is desired to sort by Age, then the FindLowest() statement

```
if (A[i] < A[LowSpotSoFar])
   LowSpotSoFar = i;
```

would need to be changed to:

```
if (A[i].Age < A[LowSpotSoFar].Age)
   LowSpotSoFar = i;
```

12.4 Merge Sort

The selection sort is simple, but inefficient, especially for large arrays. Imagine using the selection sort process by hand for a pile of 1000 index cards. Searching through the cards for the lowest item would take a long time, but more importantly, after each search the remaining cards must be searched again! Each card ends up being examined about 500 times.

The *merge sort* algorithm takes a "divide-and-conquer" approach to sorting. Imagine the 1000 cards being divided into two piles of 500. Each pile could then be sorted (a simpler problem) and the two sorted piles could be combined (merged) into a single ordered pile. To further simplify the sorting, each subpile could be divided and sorted, and so on. This algorithm is best implemented recursively.

The MergeSort() pseudocode is:

```
if there are items remaining
   merge sort the left half of the items
   merge sort the right half of the items
   merge the two halves into a completely sorted list
```

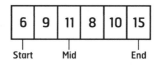

The MergeSort() subtasks are recursive calls to MergeSort() and a call to Merge(). Thus MergeSort() will need arguments indicating which portion of the array is to be sorted:

void MergeSort(ArrayType &A, **int** Start, **int** End)
/* Sorts A[Start..End] elements from low to high
   Pre: Start, End >= 0
   Post: Elements A[Start..End] are sorted from low to high */

Similarly, Merge() implements the merging of two halves and needs arguments indicating which portion of the array is to be merged:

void Merge(ArrayType &A, **int** Start, **int** Mid, **int** End)
/* Merges two sorted portions of A
   Pre: A[Start..Mid] is sorted, A[Mid+1..End] is sorted
   Start <= Mid <= End
   Post: A[Start..End] is sorted   */

The coded MergeSort is:

```
void MergeSort(ArrayType &A, int Start, int End)
/* Sorts A[Start..End] elements from low to high
   Pre: Start, End >= 0
   Post: Elements A[Start..End] are sorted from low to high */
{
  if (Start < End) {
    int Mid = (Start+End)/2;
    MergeSort(A, Start, Mid);
    MergeSort(A, Mid+1, End);
    Merge(A, Start, Mid, End);
  }
}
```

The stopping condition for the recursive function is determined by comparing Start and End. The middle of the array is calculated using integer division, which automatically truncates the decimal portion of division.

Merge() uses a temporary array to store items moved from two sorted portions of A. The items are moved so that the temporary array is sorted. To illustrate the Merge() algorithm, suppose at entry to Merge() the array looks like:

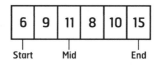

The array is sorted from Start to Mid and from Mid+1 to End. Merge() starts by examining the first element of each sorted portion, Start and Mid+1, as indicated by P1 and P2:

Since A[P1] < A[P2], the element A[P1] is moved to the new array, and P1 is incremented:

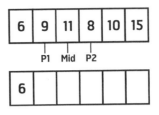

In this case, A[P1] > A[P2], so the the element A[P2] is moved to the new array and P2 incremented:

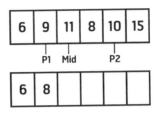

This process is repeated until all items have been moved. Since it is likely that one array portion will be exhausted before the other, Merge() tests for this case and just moves items from the remaining list. Finally, Merge() copies the merged items in the temporary array to the original array.

The Merge() code is:

```
void Merge(ArrayType &A, int Start, int Mid, int End)
/*Merges two sorted portions of A
    Pre: A[Start..Mid] is sorted, A[Mid+1..End] is sorted
    Start <= Mid <= End
    Post: A[Start..End] is sorted                        */
{
    ArrayType Temp(A.length());

    int P1 = Start; int P2 = Mid+1;    // Indexes of current item in each sublist
    int Spot = Start;    // Present location in Temp
    while (!(P1>Mid && P2>End)) {
        if ((P1>Mid) || ((P2<=End) && (A[P2]<A[P1]))) {
            Temp[Spot] = A[P2];
            P2++;
        }
        else {
            Temp[Spot] = A[P1];
            P1++;
        }
        Spot++;
    }
    // Copy values from Temp back to A
    for (int i=Start; i<=End; i++)
        A[i] = Temp[i];
}
```

The if says that if the P1 (left) sublist is exhausted, or if the P2 (right) sublist is not exhausted and the P2 element is less than the P1 element, then move an item from the P2 sublist to the Temp array, otherwise move an item from the P1 sublist. The process continues until both sublists are exhausted.

The Merge Sort program includes all the code for the sort and tests the merge sort:

```
/* Merge Sort program */

#include <stdlib.h>
#include <iostream.h>
#include <lvp\vector.h>
#include <lvp\random.h>

typedef int ItemType;
typedef vector<ItemType> ArrayType;

//--------------------------------------------------------------------------
void Merge(ArrayType &A, int Start, int Mid, int End)
/* Merges two sorted portions of A
   Pre: A[Start..Mid] is sorted, A[Mid+1..End] is sorted
   Start <= Mid <= End
   Post: A[Start..End] is sorted                        */
{
   ArrayType Temp(A.length());

   int P1 = Start; int P2 = Mid+1;   // Indexes of current item in each sublist
   int Spot = Start;   // Present location in Temp
   while (!(P1>Mid && P2>End)) {
     if ((P1>Mid) || ((P2<=End) && (A[P2]<A[P1]))) {
       Temp[Spot] = A[P2];
       P2++;
     }
     else {
       Temp[Spot] = A[P1];
       P1++;
     }
     Spot++;
   }
   // Copy values from Temp back to A
   for (int i=Start; i<=End; i++)
     A[i] = Temp[i];
}
//--------------------------------------------------------------------------
void MergeSort(ArrayType &A, int Start, int End)
/* Sorts A[Start..End] elements from low to high
   Pre: Start, End >= 0
   Post: Elements A[Start..End] are sorted from low to high */
{
   if (Start < End) {
     int Mid = (Start+End)/2;
     MergeSort(A, Start, Mid);
     MergeSort(A, Mid+1, End);
     Merge(A, Start, Mid, End);
   }
}
//--------------------------------------------------------------------------
void LoadRandomArray(ArrayType &A, int Size)
/* Fills array A with Size random values in the range 0..999 */
{
   const int MaxValue = 999;
   A.resize(Size);
   for (int i=0; i<Size; i++)
     A[i] = random(MaxValue+1);
}
```

```
//------------------------------------------------------------------------
void DisplayArray(const ArrayType &A)
/*Displays the items of A, with field width of 5, 10 per line */
{
  for (int i=0; i<A.length(); i++) {
    cout.width(5); cout << A[i];
    if ((i+1)%10 == 0)
      cout << endl;
  }
  cout << endl;
}
//------------------------------------------------------------------------
void Sort (ArrayType &A)
/*Sorts array A from low to high */
{
  MergeSort(A, 0, A.length()-1);
}
//------------------------------------------------------------------------
int main()
{
  randomize();
  ArrayType Sample;
  const int SampleSize = 20;
  LoadRandomArray(Sample, SampleSize);
  DisplayArray(Sample);
  Sort(Sample);
  DisplayArray(Sample);
  return(0);
}
```

A merge sort is *much* faster than a selection sort. For example, on a Pentium PC, a sample size of 10,000 took almost 4 minutes to sort using the Selection Sort program. The Merge Sort program sorted the same size array in only 4 seconds!

Review 3

Modify the Merge Sort program to perform time trials on MergeSort() for 1000, 2000, 3000, and 4000 items, and compare the results to those for SelectionSort() in Review 1.

Review 4

Draw a recursive call tree for MergeSort() for an array with seven elements. Refer to Chapter Seven (p. 7-9) for more on recursive call trees.

12.5 Binary Search

Another algorithm that uses recursion to achieve efficiency is the binary search. A *binary search* is applied to ordered arrays to quickly find the location of a value. The algorithm works by examining the middle item of an array sorted from low to high, and determining if this item is above or below the item sought. If the item sought is below the middle item, then a binary search is applied to the lower-half of the array; if above the middle item, a binary search is applied to the upper-half of the array, and so on.

The BinarySearch() pseudocode is:

```
if (goal == A[middle point])
  return (middle point)
else if (goal < A[middle point])
  return (BinarySearch(lower-half))
else
  return (BinarySearch(upper-half))
```

The coded BinarySearch() is:

```
int BinarySearch(const ArrayType &A, int Start, int End, int Goal)
/* Returns position of Goal, or –1 if Goal not found
   Pre: Array A[Start..End] is sorted from low to high
   Post: Position of Goal in A[Start..End] returned, or –1 if Goal not found */
{
  if (Start > End)
    return (–1);
  else {
    int Mid = (Start+End)/2;
    if (Goal == A[Mid])
      return (Mid);
    else if (Goal < A[Mid])
      return (BinarySearch(A, Start, Mid-1, Goal));
    else
      return (BinarySearch(A, Mid+1, End, Goal));
  }
}
```

The recursive calls are made from **return** statements. This compact nota-tion passes the result of the recursive call back to the calling function. The stopping condition for the recursive function is when the Start index is greater than the End index, which indicates the item is not in the array.

The Binary Search program implements the binary search code:

```
#include <lvp\bool.h>

// Merge sort functions here
//-------------------------------------------------------------------------------
int BinarySearch(const ArrayType &A, int Start, int End, int Goal)
/* Returns position of Goal, or –1 if Goal not found
   Pre: Array A[Start..End] is sorted from low to high
   Post: Position of Goal in A[Start..End] returned, or –1 if Goal not found */
{
  if (Start > End)
    return (–1);
  else {
    int Mid = (Start+End)/2;
    if (Goal == A[Mid])
      return (Mid);
    else if (Goal < A[Mid])
      return (BinarySearch(A, Start, Mid-1, Goal));
    else
      return (BinarySearch(A, Mid+1, End, Goal));
  }
}
```

```
//--------------------------------------------------------------------------
int Search(ArrayType &A, int Goal)
/*Searches an array for position of Goal
   Pre: Array A is sorted from low to high
   Post: Position of Goal in A returned, or -1 returned if Goal not found */
{
  return(BinarySearch(A, 0, A.length()-1, Goal));
}
//--------------------------------------------------------------------------
int main()
{
  randomize();
  ArrayType Sample;
  const int SampleSize = 20;
  LoadRandomArray(Sample, SampleSize);
  Sort(Sample);
  DisplayArray(Sample);
  do {
    int Goal;
    cout << "Enter a number to search for (-1 = done): ";
    cin >> Goal;
    if (Goal == -1)
      break;
    cout << "Found at: " << Search(Sample,Goal) << endl;
  } while (true);
  return(0);
}
```

The Search() function is not necessary, but hides the details of the search from the programmer coding main(). When run, the program displays output similar to:

```
   45    48    86    99   207   209   230   246   293   319
  354   379   408   426   552   561   874   910   955   985

Enter a number to search for (-1 = done): 22
Found at: -1
Enter a number to search for (-1 = done): 319
Found at: 9
Enter a number to search for (-1 = done): 45
Found at: 0
Enter a number to search for (-1 = done): 985
Found at: 19
Enter a number to search for (-1 = done): 998
Found at: -1
Enter a number to search for (-1 = done): -1
```

The program was tested with values present and not present in the array, at and before the first element in the array, and at and after the last value in the array.

The efficiency of the binary search algorithm is remarkable. For example, in an array of 1,000,000 items, the search examines at most 20 elements. If a list of the entire world's inhabitants were to be searched using this algorithm, less than 40 items would need to be examined!

Review 5

Modify the BinarySearch() function so that it displays the locations examined in a search. For example:

```
        30    52    98   196   286   299   407   409   485   486
       516   571   585   605   668   720   779   780   868   966


       Enter a number to search for (-1 = done): 196
       Examining 9
       Examining 4
       Examining 1
       Examining 2
       Examining 3
       Found at: 3
       Enter a number to search for (-1 = done): -1
```

Determine at what position an item in the array requires the most examinations to find.

Review 6

The binary search algorithm can be implemented without recursion by the following steps:

- Enclose the function body with a do-while loop
- Replace the recursive calls with appropriate assignments to the values of Start or End.

Write and test a nonrecursive version of BinarySearch().

12.6 Depth-First Searching

Many programs generate and search through a series of possibilities, such as:

- different paths through a maze
- different possible ways of making change
- different possible plays in a game
- different schedules for a student in a school
- different pixels reachable from an initial pixel

All these tasks can be solved through the recursive technique called *depth-first searching*. The depth-first searching algorithm works by searching from a given starting position, processing that position, and then (recursively) searching from all adjacent positions.

Depth-first searching is illustrated in the following program that allows a researcher to determine the number and size of distinct colonies of bacteria on a large set of microscope slides. She has arranged to have the slides converted to digital form, where a * character represents a cell that is part of a colony, and a – character represents the background color of the slide. Each slide is stored in a file with the format:

First line: length of slide
Second line: width of slide
Remaining lines: characters representing cells.

For example, a slide file might contain:

```
7
9
_____
___*__*__
__***_**_
***___*__
**_**____
___****__
___*__*__
```

Cells are considered to be part of the same colony if they touch horizontally or vertically. This slide contains three colonies. Counting rows and columns starting from zero, one colony has a cell at (1, 3) and contains 9 elements. Another colony has four elements with a cell at (1, 6), and the third has eight elements with a cell at (4, 3). Note that the first and third colonies are considered separate because they touch across a diagonal but not horizontally or vertically.

The program output from the analysis of the above slide will be:

```
Colony at (1,3) with size 9
Colony at (1,6) with size 4
Colony at (4,3) with size 8
```

Depth-first search is appropriate here because once a colony cell is detected, all the possible directions for connected cells must be searched. If a connected cell is a colony cell, then all the possible directions for that cell must be searched, and so on. The basic idea is that, given a starting cell at (Row, Col) in a colony, the total number of connected cells in that colony can be found as:

> 1 for the starting cell
> + Count of connected cells starting with (Row+1, Col)
> + Count of connected cells starting with (Row–1, Col)
> + Count of connected cells starting with (Row, Col+1)
> + Count of connected cells starting with (Row, Col–1)

The latter four lines are recursive calls. To find all the starting cells, all the cells in the slide are tested with a nested for loop.

infinite recursion

When implementing a depth-first search algorithm, code must be included to avoid infinite recursion. For example, a starting cell of (1, 3) generates a recursive call with cell (2, 3), which generates a call with (1, 3) again, which generates a call with (2, 3), and so on. For this program, a cell will be changed to the background color once it has been examined. This makes counting colonies a destructive algorithm, so the original slide contents must be saved and then restored after counting.

A SlideClass class will be written to implement slide tasks (LoadSlide(), DisplaySlide(), and DisplayColonies()). To store the slide, an array data member S will be included in the class. Constants will be used to represent the characters * and – that are considered part of a colony (Colony) and not part of a colony (NonColony) so that these are easily recognized and easy to modify.

The key function, DisplayColonies() checks each cell of the entire slide, and whenever a colony cell is encountered, DisplayColonies() determines the colony size and displays data about the colony. To determine the size, DisplayColonies() calls a private member function with prototype:

```
int CollectCells(int Row, int Col);
/* Post: All Colony cells adjoining and including cell (Row,Col) have
   been changed to NonColony, and count of these cells is returned. */
```

DisplayColonies() is coded as:

```
void SlideClass::DisplayColonies()
/* Post: Displays a list of the colonies on the slide S, giving
   coordinates of a point in each colony and its size        */
{
   // Make copy since CollectCells destroys matrix
   matrix<char> Temp = S;

   for (int Row = 0; Row < S.numrows(); Row++)
     for (int Col = 0; Col < S.numcols(); Col++) {
       if (S[Row][Col] == Colony) {
         int Count = CollectCells(Row,Col);
         cout << "Colony at (" << Row << "," << Col << ") with size "
             << Count << endl;
       }
     }
   S = Temp; // Restore matrix
}
```

Note the use of a temporary matrix, Temp, to restore the contents of the matrix after CollectCells() has destroyed it.

The depth-first search algorithm is implemented in CollectCells():

```
int SlideClass::CollectCells(int Row, int Col)
/* Post: All Colony cells adjoining and including cell (Row,Col) have
   been changed to NonColony, and count of these cells is returned. */
{
   if ((Row<0) || (Row>=S.numrows()) || (Col<0) || (Col>=S.numcols())
     || (S[Row][Col] != Colony))
     return(0);
   else {
     S[Row][Col] = NonColony;  // Set to avoid multiple counting
     return(1+
             CollectCells(Row+1,Col)+
             CollectCells(Row-1,Col)+
             CollectCells(Row,Col+1)+
             CollectCells(Row,Col-1));
   }
}
```

The first if statement checks to see if the current position is on the board, and contains a colony cell. This eliminates the need to check before each recursive call. As good programming style, it is better to check data at the start of the recursive function rather than before each call.

The complete code, and a sample run, appears below.

```
/*Depth-First Search program for finding colonies */

#include <fstream.h>
#include <iostream.h>
#include <lvp\matrix.h>
#include <lvp\string.h>

class SlideClass {
public:
  SlideClass();
  void LoadSlide(const String &FileName);
  void DisplaySlide() const;
  void DisplayColonies();

private:
  matrix<char> S;
  int CollectCells(int Row, int Col);
  const char Colony, NonColony;
};
//--------------------------------------------------------------
SlideClass::SlideClass():
  Colony('*'), NonColony('-')

{
}
//--------------------------------------------------------------
int SlideClass::CollectCells(int Row, int Col)
/*Post: All Colony cells adjoining and including cell (Row,Col) have
  been changed to NonColony, and count of these cells is returned. */
{
  if ((Row<0) || (Row>=S.numrows()) || (Col<0) || (Col>=S.numcols())
    || (S[Row][Col] != Colony))
    return(0);
  else {
    S[Row][Col] = NonColony;
    return(1+
          CollectCells(Row+1,Col)+
          CollectCells(Row-1,Col)+
          CollectCells(Row,Col+1)+
          CollectCells(Row,Col-1));
  }
}
//--------------------------------------------------------------
void SlideClass::DisplayColonies()
/*Post: Displays a list of the colonies on the slide S, giving
  coordinates of a point in each colony and its size          */
{
  // Make copy since CollectCells destroys matrix
  matrix<char> Temp = S;

  for (int Row = 0; Row < S.numrows(); Row++)
    for (int Col = 0; Col < S.numcols(); Col++) {
      if (S[Row][Col] == Colony) {
        int Count = CollectCells(Row,Col);
        cout << "Colony at (" << Row << "," << Col << ") with size "
            << Count << endl;
      }
    }
  S = Temp; // Restore matrix
}
```

```
//-------------------------------------------------------------------
void SlideClass::LoadSlide(const String &FileName)
/* Pre: File FileName exists and is formatted as:
     First line: length of slide
     Second line: width of slide
     Remaining lines: characters representing cells.
   Post: S loaded from file                              */
{
   ifstream SlideData(FileName.c_str());
   int Length;
   int Width;
   SlideData >> Length;
   SlideData >> Width;
   S.resize(Length, Width);
   for (int Row = 0; Row < Length; Row++) {
     for (int Col = 0; Col < Width; Col++)
        SlideData >> S[Row][Col];
     }
}
//-------------------------------------------------------------------
void SlideClass::DisplaySlide() const
/* Post: Contents of the slide displayed in a compact format */
{
   for (int Row = 0; Row<S.numrows(); Row++) {
     for (int Col=0; Col<S.numcols(); Col++) {
        cout << S[Row][Col];
     }
     cout << endl;
   }
}
//-------------------------------------------------------------------
int main()
{
   SlideClass S;
   S.LoadSlide("slide.dat");
   S.DisplaySlide();
   S.DisplayColonies();
   return(0);
}
```

When run, program output is similar to:

```
_____
___*__*__
__***_**_
***___*__
**_**____
___****__
___*__*__
Colony at (1,3) with size 9
Colony at (1,6) with size 4
Colony at (4,3) with size 8
```

Review 7

How must the Depth-First Search program be modified if the definition of a colony allowed the colony to be connected across diagonals? What colonies would be reported by the Depth-First Search program for the sample slide?

Review 8

In the Depth-First Search program, suppose it is desired to display the slide colonies from largest to smallest. Briefly describe how the code would need to be modified to accomplish this, and then modify the code to implement this change.

Review 9

A programmer incorrectly saves and restores the matrix just before and after the call to CollectCells() in DisplayColonies(), as shown in the statements below:

```
if (S[Row][Col] == Colony) {
    Temp = S;
    int Count = CollectCells(Row,Col);
    S = Temp;
    cout << "Colony at (" << Row << "," << Col << ") with size "
            << Count << endl;
}
```

What would be the output? Explain.

Chapter Summary

Sorting is the process of putting items in a designated order, either from low to high or high to low. The selection sort and merge sort algorithms were presented in this chapter. The merge sort algorithm takes a divide-and-conquer approach to sorting. It is implemented recursively and is much faster than a selection sort.

One measure of the efficiency of a sorting algorithm is the time it takes. The StopWatchClass, included with this text, can be used to determine the time required for a function to execute.

A binary search algorithm can be used to find an element in a sorted array. Binary search is implemented recursively and is very efficient. The depth-first searching algorithm can be used to search through a series of possibilities. When implementing depth-first searching, code must be included to avoid infinite recursion.

Vocabulary

Sorting   The process of putting items in a designated order.

Selection Sort   A sorting algorithm that repeatedly selects the lowest item from a list and moves it to a new list until all the items are ordered from low to high in the new list.

Merge Sort   A sorting algorithm that recursively sorts a list by dividing the list in half, sorting the halves, and then merging the lists so that the items are in order.

Binary Search   A searching algorithm that recursively checks the middle of a sorted list for the item sought.

Depth-First Searching   A searching algorithm that recursively checks a given starting position, processes that position, and then searches adjacent positions.

Exercises

Exercise 1

Write a program that allows the user to enter any number of names in any order, and then displays the names in alphabetical order.

Exercise 2

a) Write a program that allows the user to enter any number of names of people and their ages in any order, and then displays the names in alphabetical order with their age.

b) Modify the program to allow the people's names and their ages to be displayed in order from lowest to highest age.

Exercise 3

Write a program to compare the efficiency of the linear and binary searches. Have the program load an array with random integers in order and then perform the binary search and linear search. For fairness, choose values to search for which are not in the array. Use StopWatchClass to compare the times taken. If a performance is so fast that StopWatch reports zero for the time, modify the program to perform 1000 trials, and then divide the total trial times by 1000 to find the time for one trial.

Have the program allow the user to specify the number of elements to place in the array. To avoid having to sort the array, generate the numbers like this:

```
A[0] = 1;
for (Index=1; Index<NumItems; Index++) {
A[Index] = A[Index–1] + random (3) + 1;
```

Compare the times with 10, 100, 1000, and 5000 elements.

Exercise 4

a) Perform time trials of the selection sort for different numbers of elements, and make a plot (either by hand or using the computer) of the time (y-axis) versus the number of elements (x-axis).

b) Perform time trials of the selection sort of Chapter Eight Exercise 10 for different numbers of elements, and make a plot (either by hand or using the computer) of the time (y-axis) versus the number of elements (x-axis).

c) Perform time trials of the merge sort for different numbers of elements, and make a plot (either by hand or using the computer) of the time (y-axis) versus the number of elements (x-axis).

d) Compare the results (a), (b), and (c). You may want to write the program output to a file, which can then be loaded into Excel or another spreadsheet for charting.

Exercise 5

Consider the following function prototype:

```
bool HasItemInCommon(const ArrayType &L1, const ArrayType &L2);
/*Returns true if and only if L1 and L2 have at least one value in common. */
```

Since it is not in the precondition, we cannot assume that the arrays are sorted. This function could be implemented in a number of ways, including:

a) Take each item from L1 and perform a linear search for it in L2.

b) Sort L2 via Merge Sort. Then take each item from L1 and perform a binary search for it in L2.

c) Sort L1 and L2 via Merge Sort. Then search for common values through an algorithm similar to merging.

Which algorithm do you think will be most efficient for large arrays? Write and test a program using one of these methods with arrays of 1000 integer values.

Exercise 6

Write a birthday database program that stores names and birthdays. Include DateClass from Chapter Ten in the database implementation. Have the program provide a menu similar to:

```
1. Create a new list
2. Display the list in date order
3. Display the list in alphabetical order by names
4. Find names with specified date
5. Quit
```

Note that there may be more than one name with a given birth date. Have the program save the information entered by the user in a file when the user quits.

Exercise 7

Write a program to merge two files containing integers. It should take two low-to-high ordered files and create a new file containing all of the elements from both files also in low-to-high order. Your program must not read the files into an array but instead should read from each file as they are being merged.

Exercise 8

Write a function TernarySearch(), similar to BinarySearch(), that divides the array into three pieces rather than two. TernarySearch() finds the points that divide the array into three roughly equal pieces, and then uses these points to determine where the goal should be searched for. Do time trials to determine if ternary search is faster than binary search.

Exercise 9

One variation of binary search is called the *interpolation search*. The idea is to look in a likely spot, not necessarily the middle of the array. For example, if the value sought is 967 in an array that holds items ranging from 3 to 1022, it would be intelligent to look nearly at the end of the array. Mathematically, because 967 is about 95% of the way from 3 to 1022, the position to start searching at is a position 95% of the way down the array. For example, if the array holds 500 elements, the first position to examine is 475 (95% of the way from 1 to 500). The search then proceeds to a portion of the array (either 1..474 or 476..500) depending upon whether 967 is greater or less than the 475th element.

a) Modify BinarySearch() to implement interpolation search for an array of integers. Perform time trials to determine if InterpolationSearch() is faster, with random numbers used for the array and also the items sought.

b) Can you determine a goal and an array that will produce poor results when the search used is an interpolation search.

Exercise 10

A sorting algorithm is said to be "stable" if two items in the original array that have the same "key value" (the value to be sorted on) maintain their relative position in the sorted version. For example, assume an array with the following data:

```
Kiki  Jon   Mel   Tom   Kim
 20    19    18    19    22
```

When the array is sorted by age, a stable sort would guarantee that Jon would stay ahead of Tom in the sorted array, as in:

```
Kim   Kiki  Jon   Tom   Mel
 22    20    19    19    18
```

and not:

```
Kim   Kiki  Tom   Jon   Mel
 22    20    19    19    18
```

Which of the sorts presented in this chapter (Selection, Merge) is stable? For each which is not stable, give an example of data to illustrate this.

Excerise 11

A *bubble sort* works as follows: A pass is made through the array in which each element is compared with the one following it, and the two are swapped if they are out of order. Thus A[1] is compared with A[2] and swapped if needed, then A[2] is compared with A[3], and so on. Passes like this are made repeatedly until a pass is completed with no swaps. Write a Sort() function to implement Bubble Sort().

12

Exercise 12

A researcher has a new digitizer that reports color codes instead of just black or white. For example, a slide file might contain:

```
6
8
00550000
00050000
00005500
01200000
01111000
00000030
```

The digits 1 through 9 represent various colors. The digit 0 represents black (background color).

Write a program that displays a listing of the size, location, and color value of each colony found on the slide. A colony is defined as a connected (horizontally or vertically) sequence of cells holding the same color value. For the above slide, the output would be:

Color	Size	Location
5	3	1,3
5	2	3,5
1	5	4,2
2	1	4,3
3	1	6,7

Exercise 13

A well-known problem in computer science is called the "knapsack" problem. A variation is as follows:

> Given a collection of objects of (possibly) different integral weights, is it possible to place some of the weights in a knapsack so as to fill it to some exact total weight?

> For example, if the weights are 3, 5, 6, and 9, then it is possible for such totals as 3, 8, 11, 14, 17, etc. to be made exactly, but 2, 4, 22, etc. are not possible.

Write a function IsPossible() to solve a given knapsack problem. Use the following header:

```
bool IsPossible(const ArrayType &A, int Goal)
/* Pre: All elements of A are > 0
   Post: true returned if and only if there exists a subset of the
   elements of A whose sum is exactly Goal                    */
```

Hint: This is a depth-first search problem which can be solved using recursion. Write a function Knapsack() using the following header:

```
bool KnapSack(const ArrayType &A, int Goal, int Start)
/* Pre: All elements of A[Start..A.length()] are > 0
   Post: true returned if and only if there exists a subset of the
   elements of A[Start..A.length()] that sums to exactly Goal    */
```

This handles the first item, and then recursively handles the remaining items in the array.

The algorithm is to determine if the goal can be found in all of the elements not including the first, or if it can be found by including the first in the subset. The pseudocode is:

```
if (simple case)
    handle simple cases
else
  if (KnapSack(A, Goal, Start+1))
    return(true);
  else if (KnapSack(A, Goal-A[Start], Start+1))
    return(true);
  else
    return(false);
```

Note that the simple cases will need to be determined and handled properly.

Exercise 14

A Maze can be defined in a file using X characters to represent walls, space characters to represent paths, and a $ character to represent the goal. For example:

```
8
10
XXXXXXXXXX
X        X
XX XXX XXX
XX   X   X
XXXX X X X
X      X XXX
X XXXX  $X
XXXXXXXXXX
```

The starting point is assumed to be location (1, 1) and the maze is assumed to have a border. Write a program that displays the sequence of positions in a path from the start to the goal, or indicate if no path is available. For example, for the maze above, the program displays:

```
Path:  (1,1)  (1,2)  (1,3)  (1,4)  (1,5)  (1,6)  (2,6)
       (3,6)  (4,6)  (5,6)  (6,6)  (6,7)  (6,8)
```

Advanced
Exercise 15

The game of Boggle is played on a square board with random letters. The object is to find words formed on the board by contiguous sequences of letters. Letters are considered to be touching if they are horizontally, vertically, or diagonally adjacent. For example, the board:

```
Q  W  E  R  T
A  S  D  F  G
Z  X  C  V  B
Y  U  A  O  P
G  H  J  K  L
```

contains the words WAS, WAXY, JOB, and others, but not the word BOX. Words can contain duplicate letters, but a single letter on the board may not appear twice in a single word, for example POP is not contained on this board.

Write a program that displays a random board, and allows the user to enter words found on the board. Have the program report if the word entered by the user is indeed on the board.

Hint: Search the board for the first letter of the word entered, and then recursively search around the found letter for the remaining letters of the word.

A Guide to Programming in C++

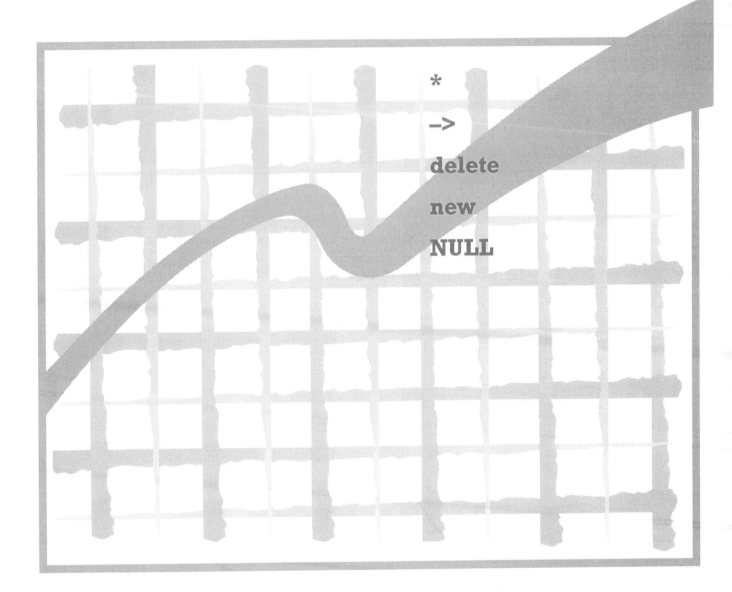

Objectives

After completing this chapter you will be able to:

1. Understand stack and queue data structures.

2. Use the stack and queue libraries to implement stacks and queues.

3. Implement linked lists in dynamic memory.

4. Understand pointers.

5. Implement a binary search tree.

13

Designing efficient data structures is of equal importance as designing algorithms in creating effective programs. In this chapter the stack and queue data structures will be explained. Linked lists will also be explained, and binary search trees will be implemented for efficiently searching linked lists.

13.1 The Stack Data Structure

top

A *stack* is a data structure that can contain many data items just as a vector can. One "end" of the stack is referred to as the *top* of the stack. For example, the stack shown below holds three items:

```
| 11 | top
| 34 |
| 12 |
```

pop

There are two standard operations that can be performed on a stack, and only the top item of a stack can be processed. One operation is the *pop* stack operation which removes the top item. For example, when a pop is executed on the stack above, the top value, 11, is removed:

```
| 34 | top
| 12 |
```

The next item, 34, is now at the top of the stack, and is the only item that can be accessed.

push

Another operation is the *push* stack operation which adds an item to the top of the stack. For example, if the value 27 is pushed onto the stack, the stack becomes:

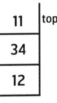

```
| 27 | top
| 34 |
| 12 |
```

Since the stack is designed so that the last item pushed on is the first item to be popped, it is sometimes referred to as a *last-in-first-out* (LIFO) data structure. There are a number of applications of stacks, particularly in writing compiler software. For example, each of the following is generally performed using a stack:

- Matching of braces, { and }. In C++ programs a close brace, }, always goes with the last open brace, }.

- Matching of else with if: An else always goes with the last if encountered.

- Matching of parentheses in an expression: A right parenthesis always goes with the last open parenthesis.

- Recursion: After completion of a recursive call, control returns to the last call that was executed. In fact, recursion is sometimes replaced with a stack.

13.2 The stack Library

stack type

The stack library supplied with this text contains the stack class to implement a stack type. The stack class is a class template that allows creation of stacks of any type. For example, the following statement instantiates a stack object:

stack<int> S;

More simply, this statement declares a stack S that can store integers.

The following is the stack class documentation:

stack (stack.h)

Constructor
stack();
/*Creates a stack
   Post: A stack with no elements created   */

Functions
const ItemType & top();
/*Returns top element without removing it from the stack
   Post: Value of top element of stack returned   */

bool empty();
/*Determines if stack is empty
   Post: true returned if stack empty, false otherwise */

int size();
/*Determines number of elements in stack
   Post: Number of elements in stack returned */

void pop();
/*Removes top element from the stack
   Post: Top element of stack removed   */

void pop(ItemType &Item);
/*Removes and returns top element from the stack
   Post: Top element of stack removed and returned */

void push(ItemType &Item);
/*Adds item to top of stack
  Post: Item added to top of stack */

void makeEmpty();
/*Removes all items from stack
  Post: Stack is empty */

Operators
=   Copies one stack to another

The following program demonstrates a stack:

```
/*Stack Demonstration program */

#include <iostream.h>
#include <lvp\stack.h>

int main()
{
  stack<int> S;
  S.push(12);
  S.push(34);
  S.push(11);
  int x;
  S.pop(x);
  cout << x << endl;
  cout << S.top() << endl;
  return(0);
}
```

When run, the program output is:

```
11
34
```

Review 1 ───────────────────────────────────

What is the output of the following program?

```
#include <iostream.h>
#include <lvp\stack.h>

int main()
{
  stack<int> S;
  int x, y;
  S.push (5);
  S.push (8);
  S.pop (x);
  S.push (x);
  S.push (12);
  S.push (13);
  S.pop(y);
  cout << x << "  " << y << endl;
  S.pop (y);
  x = S.top();
  cout << x << "  " << y << endl;
  return(0);
}
```

Review 2

Complete the function below, and write a program to test it.

```
bool BracketsMatch(const String &L)
/*Returns true if and only if L contains correctly
  matching and nonoverlapping brackets, []{}(). For instance:
  "[t(es)(ti)g]123"    returns true
  "[te(st]ing)"    returns false                    */
```

Hint: Push opening symbols onto a stack of char. When closing symbol is encountered, pop the stack and check to see if it is a match.

Review 3

Consider the "hot plate" problem: In a busy restaurant, fresh salad plates are brought out and added to the existing pile of plates. This means that, even though there may be plates that were washed long ago, the customer is frequently stuck with a warm plate for salad. Explain how this is analogous to a stack.

13.3 The Queue Data Structure

rear and front

A *queue* is a data structure similar to a stack in that it holds a number of data items. However, one end of the queue is referred to as the *rear* and the other end the *front*. For example, the queue shown below holds three items:

11	34	12
rear		front

All insertions are made at the rear and all removals are made at the front.

dequeue

There are two standard operations that can be performed on a queue. One operation is the *dequeue* operation which removes an item from the front. For example, when a dequeue is executed on the queue above, the value at the front, 12, is removed from the queue:

11	34
rear	front

enqueue

Another operation is the *enqueue* operation which adds an item to the rear of the queue. For example, if the value 27 is enqueued, the queue becomes:

27	11	34
rear		front

FIFO

A queue is analogous to a line at a ticket counter where "first come, first served," and is sometimes referred to as a *first in first out* (FIFO) data structure. There are a number of real-world situations that can be represented as a queue structure. For example:

• Lines at a toll booth or bank teller

- Waiting lists for tickets on planes
- Requests made for disk access to a central, shared server
- Pages of data queued up for a printer
- Performing *breadth-first-searching* where all items near the starting position are examined before looking at those farther away.

13.4 The queue Library

queue type

The queue library supplied with this text contains the queue class to implement a queue type. The queue class is a class template that allows creation of queues of any type. For example, the following statement instantiates a queue object:

queue<int> Q;

More simply, this statement declares a queue Q that can store integers.

The following is the queue class documentation:

queue (queue.h)

Constructor
queue();
/*Creates a queue
   Post: A queue with no elements created   */

Functions
const ItemType & front();
/*Returns front element without removing it from the queue
   Post: Value of front element of queue returned   */

bool empty();
/*Determines if queue is empty
   Post: true returned if queue empty, false otherwise */

int size();
/*Determines number of elements in queue
   Post: Number of elements in queue returned */

void dequeue();
/*Removes front element from the queue
   Post: Front element of queue removed */

void dequeue(ItemType &Item);
/*Removes and returns front element from the queue
   Post: Front element of queue removed and returned */

void enqueue(ItemType &Item);
/*Adds item to rear of queue
   Post: Item added to rear of queue */

void makeEmpty();
/*Removes all items from queue
   Post: Queue is empty */

Operators
=   Copies one queue to another

The following program demonstrates a queue:

```
/* Queue Demonstration program */

#include <iostream.h>
#include <lvp\queue.h>

int main()
{
  queue<int> Q;
  int x;
  Q.enqueue(12);
  Q.enqueue(34);
  Q.enqueue(11);
  Q.dequeue(x);
  cout << x << endl;
  cout << Q.front() << endl;
  return(0);
}
```

When run, program output is:

```
12
34
```

Review 4

What is the output of the following program?

```
#include <iostream.h>
#include <lvp\queue.h>

int main()
{
  queue<int> Q;
  int x, y;
  Q.enqueue (5);
  Q.enqueue (8);
  Q.dequeue (x);
  Q.enqueue (x);
  Q.enqueue (12);
  Q.enqueue (13);
  Q.dequeue(y);
  cout << x << " " << y << endl;
  Q.dequeue (y);
  x = Q.front();
  cout << x << " " << y << endl;
  return(0);
}
```

Compare this output to that in Review 1.

Review 5

Many bakeries have a "Take a Number" board where the customer takes a number from a hook containing numbers in numerical order, and the salesperson calls out the next number when she is ready for the next customer. Write a program that could replace this board. When a customer arrives, he enters his name in the computer. When the salesperson is ready, she presses a button and the program displays the name of the next customer. Program output should look similar to:

A Guide to Programming in C++

```
New-customer, Salesperson-ready, Quit: N
Enter your name: Bowen
New-customer, Salesperson-ready, Quit: N
Enter your name: Katie
New-customer, Salesperson-ready, Quit: B
Salesperson is ready for Bowen!
New-customer, Salesperson-ready, Quit: Q
```

13.5 Implementing Stacks and Queues

An important concept in object-oriented programming is making use of libraries written by other programmers. A well-designed library can be used without knowledge of its internals. This allows the library author to modify the library without affecting client programs.

stack implementation

However, as a programmer it is important to at least understand how a stack and a queue might be implemented. For both data structures, it seems natural that a vector be used to store data. In the case of a stack class, the private section could contain a vector to hold all the items on the stack, and an int variable indicating the index of the top of the stack. For example, the following depicts the structure of a stack:

An item is popped by reading the top item and decrementing the value of data member top. Once top is decremented, the contents of the array in location 2 no longer matter, as depicted:

Implementing the empty(), top(), size(), and makeEmpty() functions is a relatively simple matter.

queue implementation

In the case of the queue class, the private section could contain a vector to hold all the items on the queue, and an int variable indicating the index of the front of the queue. For example, the following depicts the structure of a queue:

When an item is dequeued, exactly the same steps are taken as when an item is popped from a stack:

When an item is enqueued, all the existing items must be moved up by one and the new item stored at index zero:

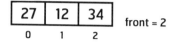

front = 2

Clearly enqueue is an inefficient, but effective, operation using this approach. The other functions, front(), empty(), size(), and makeEmpty() are straightforward to perform and can be efficiently done.

Review 6

Write a program that uses a class for implementing a stack of ItemType. Include member functions for the constructor, push(const ItemType &Item), pop(ItemType &Item), and top(ItemType &Item). Have the program use a typedef int ItemType, and test the class.

Review 7

Write a program that uses a class for implementing a queue of ItemType. Include member functions for the constructor, enqueue(const ItemType &Item), dequeue(ItemType &Item), and front(ItemType &Item). Have the program use a typedef int ItemType, and test the class.

13.6 Linked Lists

As presented in the previous section, the enqueue algorithm moves all existing items up by one and stores the new item at index zero. Items must be moved in an array because an array type places its elements *contiguously* in memory, which means each item is stored next to the previous item. Inserting a new item requires moving every later item down one. When implemented, the enqueue algorithm can result in a slow process, especially for large arrays.

pointers Another way of storing lists of data in memory requires each item to store a number that indicates where the next item is stored. These numbers are called *pointers* because they point to a data location. Rather than using an array of contiguous data, a list where each item points to the next item could be used. This kind of list is called a *linked list*. A linked list is illustrated like the following:

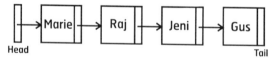

Head .... Tail

head, tail, and node The pointer to the first item in a linked list is called the *head*. The last item points to "nothing" and is called the *tail*. Each element of a linked list is called a *node*. Although the pointer number can be determined, this is usually not the way to determine the next data item in a linked list, as discussed in the next two sections.

The advantage of linked lists is that items can be inserted and deleted without moving other items. For example, to insert an item in the linked list, only pointers need to be changed:

13.7 Dynamic Memory Pointers

Linked lists are usually implemented in *dynamic memory*. Dynamic memory is memory that is allocated from a free area called the *heap* for use during execution of the program. The three fundamental operations needed to work with dynamic memory are declaring a pointer, allocating memory for storing data, and storing data in allocated memory.

declaring a pointer

The following statement declares a pointer to a dynamic memory location storing a string:

String *p;   // Declare a pointer to a string

The asterisk indicates that it is a pointer to a string, not a string variable. At this stage, p is a pointer, but does not yet have anything to point at.

allocating memory

The following statement allocates memory for the string:

p = **new** String;   // Allocate memory for the string

storing data

The pointer now points to an area in memory. To store data in memory allocated to p, the following statement is used:

(*p) = "Sandburg";   // Store data at the location pointed to by p

*p is thought of as "the location pointed to by p." To access the data at this location, a statement with the following notation is used:

cout << (*p) << endl;   // Display data at location pointed to by p *deallocating memory*   When the allocated memory is no longer needed, the following statement deallocates memory:

delete p;   // Deallocate the memory pointed to by p

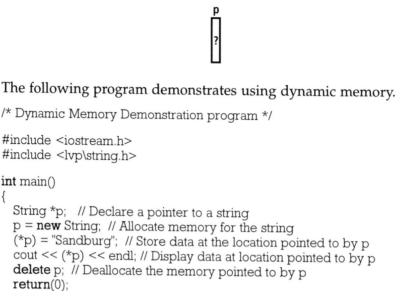

The following program demonstrates using dynamic memory.

```
/* Dynamic Memory Demonstration program */

#include <iostream.h>
#include <lvp\string.h>

int main()
{
    String *p;   // Declare a pointer to a string
    p = new String;  // Allocate memory for the string
    (*p) = "Sandburg";  // Store data at the location pointed to by p
    cout << (*p) << endl; // Display data at location pointed to by p
    delete p;  // Deallocate the memory pointed to by p
    return(0);
}
```

The program output is:

```
Sandburg
```

In this program, the use of delete is unnecessary since the computer automatically deallocates the memory when the program terminates.

Review 8

The output of the following code is 17. Explain how this can be true, in words or drawings.

```
int *p;
int *q;
p = new int;
q = new int;
(*p) = 12;
(*q) = 15;
p = q;
(*p) = 17;
cout << (*q) << endl;
```

13.8 Building Linked Lists in Dynamic Memory

The elements of a linked list are a structure that includes the data being stored and a pointer to the next element. A struct naturally represents an element in a linked list:

```
typedef String ItemType;
struct NodeType {
    ItemType Data;
    NodeType *Next;
};
```

ItemType is used to created a struct that is generic. Using this structure, each node can be depicted as:

The head of the linked list will simply be a NodeType with no data that points to the first element with data. The tail of the linked list must point to "nothing." To do this the C++ built-in constant NULL will be used.

NULL

ListClass class

Using this structure, a ListClass class can be implemented. The ListClass declaration is:

```
class ListClass {
public:
   ListClass();
   ~ListClass();
   void AddAtFront(const ItemType &Item);
   void Write(ostream &Output) const;
private:
   NodeType *First;
};
```

A destructor, ~ListClass() is necessary to delete the memory allocated with new. For private data, only a pointer to the first node on the list (or NULL if the list is empty) is needed. The constructor initializes the list:

ListClass()

```
ListClass::ListClass()
   : First(NULL)
{
}
```

Write()

The Write() pseudocode is:

        define a pointer Curr that points to the element
            pointed to by First
        While Curr points to a node
           Display the data in the node
           Advance Curr to the next node

Write() is coded as:

```
NodeType *Curr = First;
while (Curr != NULL) {
   Output << (*Curr).Data << endl;
   Curr = (*Curr).Next;
}
```

The notation, (*Curr).Data is used because Curr is a pointer; *Curr is the object pointed to, in this case a struct, and .Data refers to a field in the struct. The parentheses are needed because the rules of operator precedence require them.

The destructor code is similar to Write(). As the list is traversed, each node is deleted. It is illegal to use the data in a node that has already been deleted. Therefore, two pointers must be used:

```
NodeType *Curr = First;
NodeType *Previous;
while (Curr != NULL) {
   Previous = Curr;
   Curr = (*Curr).Next;
   delete Previous;
}
```

The pointer Previous points to the node behind the current node.

The AddAtFront() pseudocode is best described using a picture. For example, assume the following list:

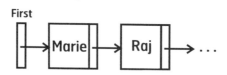

To add an element, the first step is to define a pointer:

```
NodeType *Temp;
```

Next, space must be allocated:

```
Temp = new NodeType;
```

Finally, the new data is stored in memory:

```
(*Temp).Data = "Gus";
```

At this point, the picture looks like this:

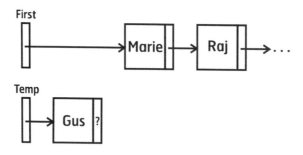

The new node must now be added to the list, using the statement:

```
(*Temp).Next = First;
```

which can be depicted as:

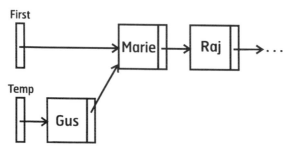

The following statement copies Temp to First, completing the insertion:

First = Temp;

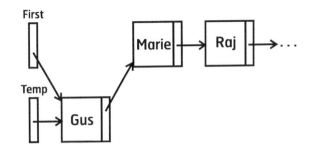

The program below demonstrates a linked list:

```
/*Linked List program */

#include <iostream.h>
#include <lvp\string.h>

typedef String ItemType;

// Nodetype is used by ListClass
struct NodeType {
  ItemType Data;
  NodeType *Next;
};

class ListClass {
public:
  ListClass();    // Instantiates an empty list
  ~ListClass();   // Deallocates memory used by list
  void AddAtFront(const ItemType &Item);    // Adds new node to front of list
  void Write(ostream &Output) const;    // Writes list data in order
private:
  NodeType *First;
};
//----------------------------------------------------------------------
ListClass::ListClass()
  : First(NULL)  // Sets list to empty
{
}
//----------------------------------------------------------------------
ListClass::~ListClass()
/*Post: Memory used by list deallocated */
{
  NodeType *Curr = First;
  NodeType *Previous;
  while (Curr != NULL) {
    Previous = Curr;
    Curr = (*Curr).Next;
    delete Previous;
  }
}
```

```
//------------------------------------------------------------------
void ListClass::AddAtFront(const ItemType &Item)
/*Post: New node containing Item added at front of list */
{
  NodeType *Temp;
  Temp = new NodeType;
  (*Temp).Data = Item;
  (*Temp).Next = First;
  First = Temp;
}
//------------------------------------------------------------------
void ListClass::Write(ostream &Output) const
/*Post: Write the data of nodes to Output */
{
  NodeType *Curr = First;
  while (Curr != NULL) {
    Output << (*Curr).Data << endl;
    Curr = (*Curr).Next;
  }
}
//------------------------------------------------------------------
int main()
{
  ListClass L;
  L.AddAtFront("Sandburg");
  L.AddAtFront("Strand");
  L.AddAtFront("Angelou");
  L.Write(cout);
  return(0);
}
```

The program output is:

```
Angelou
Strand
Sandburg
```

Since nodes were inserted with AddAtFront(), the list appears in the opposite order from which the items were inserted.

13.9 Avoiding Dynamic Memory Bugs

Research in the field of software engineering has shown that bugs in using dynamic memory are among the most common and most time-consuming. For example, errors occur if an attempt is made to follow a pointer that does not point to valid memory, or if memory is allocated but not deallocated. Windows traps some of these bugs, and gives a "General Protection Fault" error.

If constructed correctly, C++ classes can prevent many of these errors from occurring in the first place. The two keys to this are the copy constructor and the assignment operator. Whenever writing classes that use dynamic memory these two functions must be either inaccessible (as done in Chapter Ten) or correctly written. The default actions taken by the compiler do *not* work correctly on dynamic memory data.

13

For the purposes of this text, we suggest that the copy constructor and the assignment operator functions be hidden, or made inaccessible. As discussed in Chapter Ten, this requires declaring these member functions in the private section of the class declaration:

```
private:
    ListClass(const ListClass &L);    // Copy constructor
    operator=(const ListClass &L);    // Assignment operator
```

If there is a need to assign or make a copy of a linked list, then it may be done by copying each of the data items on the list individually, possibly using a Copy() member function.

13.10 Pointer Notation

Some rules and pointer notation variations are listed below.

If more than one pointer variable is to be declared in a single statement, then the asterisk must appear with each variable. For example:

```
NodeType *p, *q;
```

If the asterisk is omitted from the second variable, then q will be declared as a NodeType rather than as a pointer.

The notation (*pointer).fieldname can be replaced by the notation pointer–>fieldname. For example, the statement

```
(*Temp).Next = First;
```

can be replaced with:

```
Temp–>Next = First;
```

This is largely a matter of programmer preference.

When passing a pointer as a reference parameter, the declaration of the parameter must have the asterisk first, as in the prototype:

```
int Foo(NodeType *&p);
```

Review 9

Modify the ListClass class to include a member function Length() that returns the number of elements in the list.

Review 10

Modify the ListClass class to include a member function LastOnList() that returns the data value stored in the last node of the list.

13.11 Binary Search Trees

Linked lists have an advantage in that insertions and deletions are very fast. However, they are slow to search. An ordered array can be searched quickly using binary search, but a linked list must be searched sequentially even if it is ordered. The *binary search tree* data structure contains the best of both worlds: fast insertion and fast searching.

In a binary search tree, each node has two pointers. The left pointer points to a subtree containing only nodes with lower values in the data fields. The right pointer points to a subtree containing only nodes with higher values in the data fields. For example, a binary tree can be illustrated as:

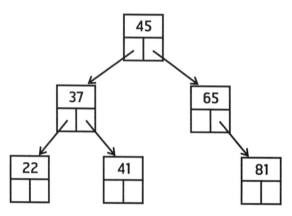

root, children, parents, leaves

The node at the top of the tree is called the *root*. In this tree the root stores 45. The nodes pointed to by any given node are called its *children*, and that node the *parent*. For example, the parent of 22 and 41 is 37. Nodes with no children, for example 81, are called *leaves*.

searching

The algorithm for searching is start at the root and if the value sought is less than the root, search the left subtree. If it is greater, search the right. For example, in a search for 41, the root is greater than 41 so the left subtree is searched. Since the left subtree is a tree, this search algorithm can be applied recursively. This proceeds until the data item is found, or an attempt is made to search an empty tree. Note how this approach is similar to binary search.

inserting data

New data is inserted in a binary search tree by following the appropriate left and right pointers until a NULL pointer is found. The new data is put in a node and the NULL pointer is set to point to the new node.

displaying data

Binary search trees are easily traversed, and therefore its data is easily displayed in order. Data stored in the nodes of a binary search tree are displayed by recursively displaying the data in the left subtree, then displaying the root, and then recursively displaying the right subtree.

13.12 Implementing Binary Search Trees

Trees can be implemented in arrays or other structures, but the most common approach is to implement them in dynamic memory using pointers. Similar to a linked list, a tree can be implemented by representing each node as a struct, and the entire tree with a class:

```
typedef String ItemType;
struct TreeNodeType {
  ItemType Data;
  TreeNodeType *Left;
  TreeNodeType *Right;
};
```

TreeClass class

```
class TreeClass {
  public:
    TreeClass();
    ~TreeClass();
    void Insert(const ItemType &Item);
    void Display(ostream &Output) const;
    bool InTree(const ItemType &Item);
  private:
    TreeNodeType *Root;
    TreeClass(const TreeClass &L);    // Copy constructor
    operator=(const TreeClass &L);    // Assignment operator
};
```

The private section holds a single pointer to the root of the tree, and hides the copy and assignment functions. The constructor sets the value of Root to NULL.

InTree()

The InTree() pseudocode is:

```
While (Tree not Null)
  If (goal == root)
    return true
  else if (goal < root)
    Search left subtree
  else
    Search right subtree
```

A public member function that requires only the goal as the parameter will be created. This function will call a private member function that implements the recursive search. This is similar to what was done in Chapter Twelve with the Binary Search program where a Sort() function was used to hide the sort details for the programmer coding main().

The private function is coded as:

```
bool TreeClass::MyInTree(TreeNodeType *T, const ItemType &Item)
{
  if (T == NULL)
    return (false);
  else if (Item == (*T).Data)
    return (true);
  else if (Item < (*T).Data)
    return MyInTree( (*T).Left, Item );
  else
    return MyInTree( (*T).Right, Item );
}
```

The public search function is coded as:

```
bool TreeClass::InTree(const ItemType &Item)
{
    return MyInTree(Root, Item);
}
```

Insert()

A similar approach can be taken with Insert(). In this case, the algorithm is to search for an empty subtree. When found, a new node is inserted. Since the tree will be modified, it is passed as a reference parameter to the private function:

```
void TreeClass::MyInsert(TreeNodeType* &T, const ItemType &Item)
{
    if (T == NULL) {    // Insert as root of subtree
        T = new TreeNodeType;
        (*T).Data = Item;
        (*T).Left = NULL;
        (*T).Right = NULL;
    }
    else if (Item < (*T).Data)    // Insert elsewhere
        MyInsert( (*T).Left, Item );
    else
        MyInsert( (*T).Right, Item );
}
```

Display()

Both MyInsert() and MyInTree() examine only one branch from any given node. The MyDisplay() function, on the other hand, must examine every node. Thus, instead of deciding which direction to follow, it must follow both directions, as shown below:

```
void TreeClass::MyDisplay(TreeNodeType* T, ostream &Output) const
{
    if (T != NULL) {
        MyDisplay( (*T).Left, Output );
        Output << (*T).Data << endl;
        MyDisplay( (*T).Right, Output);
    }
}
```

This simple code displays the data of an entire tree in order.

~TreeClass()

The destructor must examine every node and deallocate the memory it uses. Once again, the simplest approach is to use recursion with another function, MyDestructor():

```
void TreeClass::MyDestruct(TreeNodeType *&T)
{
    if (T != NULL) {
        MyDestruct( (*T).Left );
        MyDestruct( (*T).Right );
        delete T;
    }
}
```

Note, that the two subtrees are deleted before the root. Once the root node is deleted, the left and right subtrees are not accessible.

The program below demonstrates a binary search tree:

```
/*Binary Search tree program */

#include <iostream.h>
#include <lvp\string.h>
#include <lvp\bool.h>

typedef String ItemType;
struct TreeNodeType {
  ItemType Data;
  TreeNodeType *Left;
  TreeNodeType *Right;
};

class TreeClass {
  public:
    TreeClass();
    ~TreeClass();
    bool InTree(const ItemType &Item);
    void Insert(const ItemType &Item);
    void Display(ostream &Output) const;
  private:
    TreeNodeType *Root;
    void MyDestruct(TreeNodeType *&T);
    bool MyInTree(TreeNodeType *T, const ItemType &Item);
    void MyInsert(TreeNodeType *&T, const ItemType &Item);
    void MyDisplay(TreeNodeType *T, ostream &Output) const;
    TreeClass(const TreeClass &L); // Copy constructor
    operator=(const TreeClass &L); // Assignment operator
};
//------------------------------------------------------------------------
TreeClass::TreeClass()
  : Root(NULL)
{
}
//------------------------------------------------------------------------
void TreeClass::MyDestruct(TreeNodeType *&T)
{
  if (T != NULL) {
    MyDestruct( (*T).Left );
    MyDestruct( (*T).Right );
    delete T;
  }
}
//------------------------------------------------------------------------
TreeClass::~TreeClass()
{
  MyDestruct(Root);
}
//------------------------------------------------------------------------
bool TreeClass::MyInTree(TreeNodeType *T, const ItemType &Item)
{
  if (T == NULL)
    return false;
  else if (Item == (*T).Data)
    return true;
  else if (Item < (*T).Data)
    return MyInTree( (*T).Left, Item );
  else
    return MyInTree( (*T).Right, Item );
}
```

```
//-----------------------------------------------------------
bool TreeClass::InTree(const ItemType &Item)
{
   return MyInTree(Root, Item);
}
//-----------------------------------------------------------
void TreeClass::MyInsert(TreeNodeType* &T, const ItemType &Item)
{
  if (T == NULL) {
    T = new TreeNodeType;
    (*T).Data = Item;
    (*T).Left = NULL;
    (*T).Right = NULL;
  }
  else if (Item < (*T).Data)
    MyInsert( (*T).Left, Item );
  else
    MyInsert( (*T).Right, Item );
}
//-----------------------------------------------------------
void TreeClass::Insert(const ItemType &Item)
{
   MyInsert(Root, Item);
}
//-----------------------------------------------------------
void TreeClass::MyDisplay(TreeNodeType* T, ostream &Output) const
{
  if (T != NULL) {
    MyDisplay( (*T).Left, Output );
    Output << (*T).Data << endl;
    MyDisplay( (*T).Right, Output);
  }
}
//-----------------------------------------------------------
void TreeClass::Display(ostream &Output) const
{
   MyDisplay(Root, Output);
}
//-----------------------------------------------------------
int main()
{
   TreeClass T;
   T.Insert("Sandburg");
   T.Insert("Strand");
   T.Insert("Angelou");
   T.Display(cout);
   return (0);
}
```

When run, the program output is:

```
Angelou
Sandburg
Strand
```

Note that, without explicitly sorting, output is sorted. This is a very useful feature of the binary tree structure.

Review 11

Draw a binary tree that has 6 nodes with 3 leaves. Draw one with 6 nodes but only 2 leaves, and one with 6 nodes and only 1 leaf.

Review 12

Modify the TreeClass class to include member functions Length() and MyLength() that return the number of nodes in the tree.

Review 13

Assume that the items 45, 67, 34, 78, and 22 are placed in this sequence in an ordered binary tree of int values using the Insert() function of the TreeClass class. Draw the tree that would be formed. Draw the tree when same items are inserted but in the order 78, 67, 45, 34, 22.

13.13 Beyond this Book

This chapter has presented just a brief survey of the material covered in a more advanced computer science course. These topics typically are covered in an entire text devoted to data structures and algorithms.

As you proceed in computer science, you will study more sophisticated algorithms for solving searching and sorting problems, as well as algorithms which solve more complex problems. You will also learn how to formally evaluate the efficiency of these algorithms. In addition, you will study more complex ways of structuring data, including situations that take advantage of more pointers in each node.

You will also study the many ways that C++ permits the programmer to devise and reuse classes with great power. The topics of inheritance, templates, and polymorphism are taught in more advanced C++ courses, and are used heavily in programming for GUI interfaces.

On the immediately practical side, you may choose to delve more deeply into the details of programming the Windows interface, including pull down menus, dialog boxes, etc. This requires a knowledge of the functions provided by the Windows libraries. Class libraries have been devised to simplify this work, including Borland's Object Windows Library (OWL) and Microsoft's Foundation Classes (MFC).

In the final analysis, you have learned a great deal about programming and about the C++ language, but there is more to the study of computer science than this. It is our hope that this text will serve as a good beginning.

Chapter Summary

A stack is a data structure in which only the top element can be processed. The operations that can be performed on a stack are push and pop. The push operation places an element in the stack as the top element. The pop operation removes the top element of the stack. A stack is sometimes called a LIFO because the first element in is the first element out. The stack library contains a stack class that implements a stack type.

The queue is a data structure that has a rear and a front. The dequeue operation removes an element from the front. An enqueue operation adds an element to the rear. A queue is sometimes called a FIFO because the first element in is the first element out. The queue library contains a queue class that implements a queue type.

A linked list contains nodes where each node contains data and a pointer to the next node in the list. The first node is called the head, and the last the tail. Linked lists are usually implemented in dynamic memory with each element a struct and the entire list represented with a class.

The three fundamental operations needed to work in dynamic memory are declaring a pointer, allocating memory for storage, and storing data in allocated space.

A binary search tree is a structure that allows for fast insertion and fast searching. In a binary tree, each node has two pointers. The left pointer points to a subtree containing only nodes with lower values of data, and the right contains only nodes with higher values of data. A binary search tree can be quickly searched by using recursion. Inserting and displaying data are also done recursively. Binary search trees are usually implemented in dynamic memory with each element a struct and the entire tree represented with a class.

Vocabulary

Binary search tree   A data structure usually implemented in dynamic memory where each node contains two pointers.

Children   The nodes pointed to by a parent node.

Dequeue   The queue operation that removes an element from the front.

Dynamic memory   Memory allocated from a free area called the heap for use during program execution.

Enqueue   The queue operation that adds an element to the rear.

FIFO   First In First Out. Term used to refer to a queue.

Front   The position of the first element of a queue.

Head   The first node of a linked list.

Heap   An area of memory that can be used by a program during execution.

LIFO   Last In First Out. Term used to refer to a stack.

Leaves   A node that does not point to another node.

Linked list   A data structure usually implemented in dynamic memory in which each element points to the next element in a list.

Node   An element in a linked list or binary tree.

Parents   Nodes that point to other nodes.

Pointer   Used by an element of a linked list or binary tree to point to another element.

Pop   The stack operation that removes the top element.

Push   The stack operation that adds the top element.

Queue   A data structure that has a rear and a front.

Rear   The position of the last element of a queue.

Root   The top node of a binary search tree.

Stack   A data structure in which only the top element can be processed.

Tail   The last element of a linked list.

Top   The position of the element just added to a stack.

C++

*   Used to declare a pointer

–>   Symbol used to read the data pointed to in a struct.

delete   Keyword used to deallocate memory.

new   Keyword used to allocate memory

NULL   Built-in constant used to indicate "nothing."

Exercises

Exercise 1

The stack implementation presented in this chapter employs an array. A stack can also be implemented using a linked list. Write a stack class that uses a linked list. What are the advantages or disadvantages of using a linked list rather than an array?

Exercise 2

Write a program that uses a stack to reverse a set of integers entered by the user and terminated by 999. The program output should look similar to:

```
Enter an integer: 87
Enter an integer: 20
Enter an integer: 6
Enter an integer: 999

The list reversed: 6 20 87
```

Exercise 3

To analyze an expression with parentheses, the computer must be able to determine which left parenthesis any given right parenthesis matches.

a) Write a program that asks the user to enter an expression with parentheses, and then displays a list of the positions of pairs of parentheses. The program output should look similar to:

```
Enter an expression (3+4*(4-6))
Pair: 10 and 6
Pair: 11 and 1
```

You must store the positions of the left parentheses on a stack when they are found.

b) Modify the program to detect the two errors below and display appropriate error messages:

1. Attempt to pop an empty stack.
2. Stack not empty at the end of the program.

13

Exercise 4

The queue implementation presented in the text uses an array, with the rear at the 0th location growing upward, but other array and linked list approaches exist. For each approach described below, implement a class with the standard queue operations.

a) Store the queue in an array with the 0th element being the *front* of the queue. When a dequeue operation is performed, move all of the elements up one space to fill in the gap.

b) Store the queue in an array, keeping track of the front and the rear positions with the front towards the 0th element of the array, and the rear toward the end. When an element is dequeued, increment the front counter. When an element is enqueued, increment the rear counter. If the end of the array is reached, slide all the elements forward so that the front is in the 0th position.

c) Store the elements in a linked list, maintaining pointers to the first and last nodes on the list. Enqueue items by adding them to the end of the list, and dequeue items from the start of the list.

Exercise 5

Using diagrams as needed, determine the output of the following program:

```
int main()
{
   int *A, *B, *C;

   A = new int;
   (*A) = 10;
   B = A;
   C = new int;
   (*C) = (*A);
   cout << (*A) << " " << (*B) << " " << (*C) << endl;
   (*A) = 23;
   cout << (*A) << " " << (*B) << " " << (*C) << endl;
   return(0);
}
```

Exercise 6

Draw diagrams to illustrate the situation after each statement in the following program. Note that the program produces no output.

```
struct NodeType {
   int Data;
   NodeType *Next;
};
int main()
{
   NodeType *S, *T;
   S = new NodeType;
   S->Data = 12;
   T = new NodeType;
   T->Next = S;
   T->Data = 23;
   S->Next = T;
   return(0);
}
```

Exercise 7

a) Modify the ListClass to include a member function Sum() that returns the sum of the data fields of all nodes in the list. Note that this will restrict the use of the class to ItemTypes which can be added.

b) Modify the ListClass to include a member function Maximum() that returns the largest value found in any data field in the list. Note that this will restrict the use of the class to ItemTypes which can be compared.

Exercise 8

a) Modify the TreeClass to include a member function Sum() that returns the sum of the data fields of all nodes in the tree. Note that this will restrict the use of the class to ItemTypes which can be added.

b) Modify the TreeClass to include a member function Maximum() that returns the largest value found in any data field in the tree. Note that this will restrict the use of the class to ItemTypes which can be compared.

Exercise 9

Modify the ListClass to include a member function AddAtEnd() that adds new information at the end of the list rather than at the front. The function will need to search for the end of the list, and then add the information.

Exercise 10

A *doubly-linked list* has pointers to the next and previous nodes, and can be thought of as:

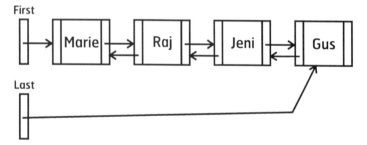

The node of the doubly-linked list may be represented as:

```
typedef String ItemType;
struct NodeType {
    ItemType Data;
    NodeType *Next;
    NodeType *Previous;
};
```

The previous field of the first node is set to NULL. The doubly-linked list may then be implemented with a class that has two pointers, First and Last, as private data members.

a) What advantages does this structure offer? What disadvantages?

b) Compare the doubly-linked list with the singly linked list. When would you choose to use one rather than the other?

c) Write a class that implements a doubly linked list. Include member functions Write() and WriteReverse().

d) Modify the class in (c) to include a member function Delete() that has the following prototype:

```
void Delete(const ItemType &ItemToDelete);
/*Deletes first node in the list with data field holding ItemToDelete */
```

Exercise 11

The height of a binary tree can be thought of as the number of levels in the tree. Below are three trees of height 3:

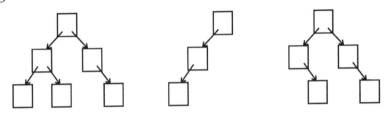

a) What is the least number of nodes in a tree of height 3? Of height 4? Of height 5? Of height N?

b) What is the most number of nodes in a tree of height 3? Of height 4? Of height 5? Of height N?

c) Modify TreeClass to include a member function that returns the height of the tree. Use recursion, and the idea that the height of a tree is one more than the height of the taller of its two subtrees. The height of an empty tree is zero.

Exercise 12

An ordered tree can be used to create sorted output, and is therefore the basis of a sort algorithm called TreeSort. The TreeSort algorithm involves adding all the items from an array one-by-one into a tree, and then recovering them back into an array by using a function similar to the Binary Search Tree Display() function. Write a Sort() function based on this idea, and perform timing tests for arrays of various sizes. Plot the results.

It is often useful to be able to analyze a text file and determine the number of different words it contains and how often they appear. A binary search tree can be especially helpful in solving this problem because it allows easy insertion and efficient searching.

Write a program that reads each word in a text file and then places it in an alphabetically ordered tree. Each node of the tree should contain a word and a counter which records the number of times the word has been read. Each time a new word is encountered the tree is searched to see if it contains the word, and if it does, its frequency counter is increased by 1. If it does not, the word is added to the tree.

You may assume that no word contains more than 15 characters, and may use a simple definition of a word as follows: a word is any sequence of letters terminated by nonletters. Thus "can't" is treated as a three-letter word followed by a one-letter word.

A | Appendix A - Turbo C++

Chapter Two introduced object-oriented programming with C++ and explained how a program is compiled before it can be run on the computer. This appendix introduces how to use the Turbo C++, version 4.5 for Windows 95 compiler.

A.1 Entering a Program in Turbo C++

When Turbo C++ is started, the *Integrated Development Environment* (IDE) is displayed. The IDE contains an edit window where a program is typed. In the edit window below, the Hello world program has been typed:

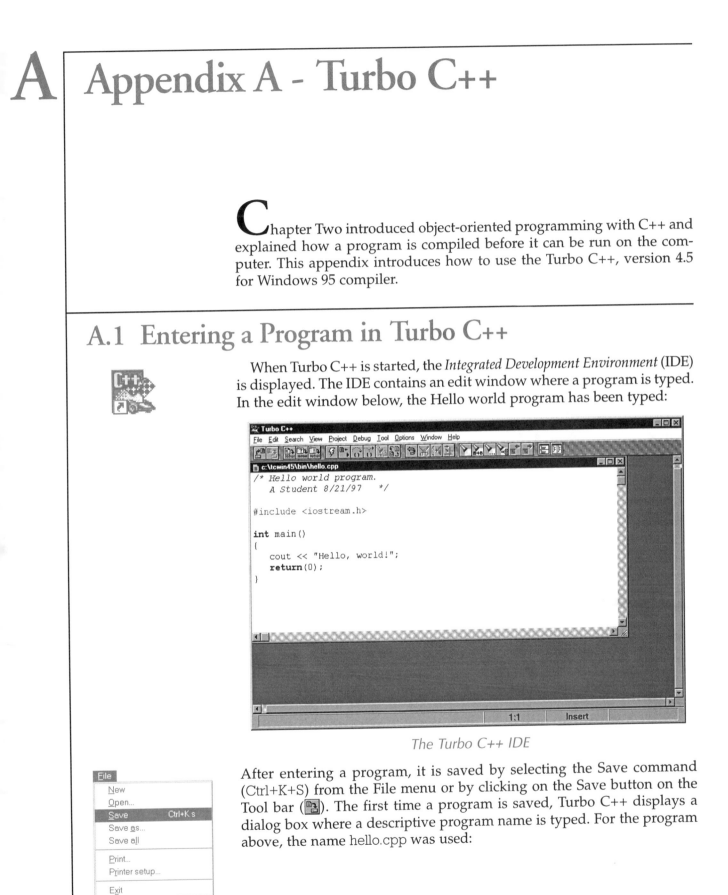

The Turbo C++ IDE

After entering a program, it is saved by selecting the Save command (Ctrl+K+S) from the File menu or by clicking on the Save button on the Tool bar (🖫). The first time a program is saved, Turbo C++ displays a dialog box where a descriptive program name is typed. For the program above, the name hello.cpp was used:

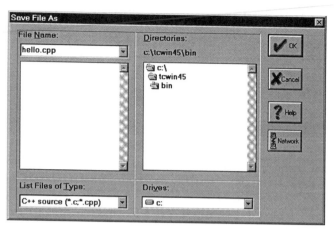

The Save File As dialog box

```
File
  New
  Open...
  Save           Ctrl+K s
  Save as...
  Save all

  Print...
  Printer setup...

  Exit
```

Selecting the OK button saves the program to disk. After a program is saved it can be run.

When finished working in Turbo C++, the Exit command from the File menu is selected to close any edit windows and remove the Turbo C++ IDE from the Desktop.

Review 1

In this review, you will enter the Hello world program.

1) ENTER A PROGRAM

    a. Start Turbo C++. The IDE is displayed with a blank edit window.

    b. In the edit window, type the following program

```
/*Hello world program.
  Your Name Date        */

#include <iostream.h>

int main()
{
  cout << "Hello, world!";
  return(0);
}
```

2) SAVE THE PROGRAM

    a. From the File menu, select the Save command. The Save File As dialog box is displayed.

    b. Type hello.cpp to replace the default file name.

    c. Select the OK button. The file name hello.cpp is now displayed at the top of the edit window.

3) EXIT TURBO C++

From the File menu, select the Exit command. The program's edit window is closed and the Turbo C++ IDE is removed from the screen.

A.2 Compiling

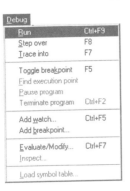

The Turbo C++ IDE automatically compiles the C++ source code into the object code and links the object code to create the executable file when the Run command (Ctrl+F9) from the Debug menu is selected or the Run button on the Tool bar (⚡) is clicked. The program, in linked object form, is then executed by the system. When a program is run, its output is displayed in a window. For example, when the Hello world program is run its output looks similar to:

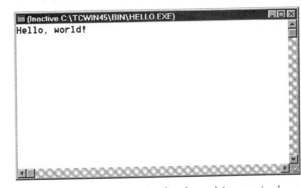

A program's output is displayed in a window

A.3 Errors

The Turbo C++ compiler will notify you of any syntax errors when the program is compiled:

Compile Status		
Status:	There are errors	
Files		
Main file:	hello.cpp	
Compiling:	hello.cpp	
Statistics	**Total**	**File**
Lines:	12	12
Warnings:	1	1
Errors:	1	1

✓ OK

The compiler notifies you if there are errors

Selecting OK in the Compiler Status dialog box removes it from the screen and a Message window listing possible causes for errors is displayed in the Turbo C++ IDE:

```
Message
Compiling HELLO.CPP:
Error HELLO.CPP 9: Statement missing ; in function main()
Warning HELLO.CPP 10: Function should return a value in function main()

                                                    9:9        Insert
```

The Message window lists probable causes for compilation errors

A.4 More on Using Turbo C++

opening a program

A program previously saved on disk can be opened for editing by selecting the Open command from the File menu or by clicking on the Open button on the Tool bar (🖫). When a file is opened for editing, it is placed in an edit window.

Save As

When an existing program is modified, it can be saved under a different name by selecting the Save as command from the File menu and typing a new name in the Save File As dialog box. When Save As is used to save a file under a new name, the previously saved file still exists under the original name.

creating a new program

To create a new program, the New command from the File menu is used to open an empty edit window where a program is typed.

printing a program

When the edit window is active, the Print command from the File menu is used to print a program. Before printing, it is important to save the program.

printing program output

When a program has just been run, clicking the Control-menu button in the upper-left corner of the output window displays a menu which contains a Print command:

Control-menu button

```
(Inactive C:\TCWIN45\BIN\HELLO.EXE)
Restore
Move
Size
Minimize
Maximize

Close     Alt+F4
Edit            ▸
Print
```

Selecting this Print command sends the output to the printer.

Review 2

In this review you will run the Hello world program.

1) OPEN HELLO.CPP

    a. From the File menu, select the Open command. The Open a File dialog box is displayed.

    b. Select hello.cpp from the list of file names.

    c. Select OK. The program is displayed in an edit window.

2) PRINT THE PROGRAM

    a. From the File menu, select the Print command. The Print Options dialog box is displayed.

    b. Select OK to accept the default options and print a copy of the program's source code.

3) RUN HELLO.CPP

From the Debug menu, select the Run command. The program is compiled. If there are no errors the program is also linked and then run, and the output from the program displayed in a window.

If the program has errors, they must be corrected and then the Run command selected again to compile, link, and run the program.

4) PRINT THE PROGRAM OUTPUT

a. In the upper-left corner of the output window, click on the Control-menu button. A menu is displayed.
b. Select the Print command. The Print dialog box is displayed.
c. Select OK to accept the default options and print a copy of the program's output.

5) CLOSE THE FILE

a. Click on the Close button in the upper-right corner of the output window to close it.
b. Click on the Close button in the upper-right corner of the edit window to close it.

A.5 Using Help

```
Help
  Contents
  Keyword search  F1
  Keyboard
  Using help

  Quick Tour
  Tips

  Windows API
  OWL API

  About...
```

The Help menu provides commands that can be selected to display online information. Selecting the Contents command displays a list of various help topics and buttons for searching for information on a specific topic.

The Quick Tour command is used to view the many features of Turbo C++ and the C++ language.

Pressing the F1 key brings up context sensitive online help. For example, when entering a program in an edit window, pressing the F1 key when the cursor is on a keyword displays a window with information about that keyword.

To learn more about online help, select the Using help command.

A.6 Debugging with Turbo C++

```
Debug
  Run                  Ctrl+F9
  Step over            F8
  Trace into           F7

  Toggle breakpoint    F5
  Find execution point
  Pause program
  Terminate program    Ctrl+F2

  Add watch...         Ctrl+F5
  Add breakpoint...

  Evaluate/Modify...   Ctrl+F7
  Inspect...

  Load symbol table...
```

The Turbo C++ IDE has tools that are useful for debugging and testing loops. The Step over command (F8) in the Debug menu is for watching and controlling program execution one statement at a time. The Add watch command (Ctrl+F5), also in the Debug menu, is for watching the values of variables as they change during program execution.

The Step over command can help detect errors in logic. To "step through" a program in the edit window, the F8 key is pressed to highlight the first executable statement. Pressing F8 again executes the highlighted statement and moves the highlight to the next executable statement. This process may be continued for the entire program, or the Run command from the Debug menu selected to finish program execution as usual.

Errors in a program can become more obvious if the values of variables are known throughout program execution. Highlighting a variable name in the edit window, selecting the Add watch command, and then selecting OK in the dialog box adds the variable name to a Watch window. The values of variables in the Watch window are updated as the statements in the program are executed. The watch window is most useful when stepping through a program.

A.7 Libraries

All C++ compilers include standard libraries that can be used in programs, such as the iostream library. However, each compiler may have additions to a library that are specific to that compiler. Below are notes about the libraries used in this text:

bool.h

Turbo C++ does not implement a bool type. Therefore, the bool library must be included in a program implementing this type.

random.h

The random() and randomize() functions may alternatively be implemented by including the stdlib library supplied by Borland.

Please refer to the Teacher's Resource Package and the README.TXT file supplied on disk for more information about libraries used in this text.

B | Appendix B - Microsoft Visual C++

Chapter Two introduced object-oriented programming with C++ and explained how a program is compiled before it can be run on the computer. This appendix introduces how to use the Microsoft Visual C++, version 4.0 for Windows compiler.

B.1 Entering a Program in Visual C++

When Visual C++ is started, the *Microsoft Developer Studio* (MDS) window is displayed. Before entering a program, a project workspace needs to be created. The *project workspace* stores the files associated with a program's executable file. To create a new project workspace, select the New command (Ctrl+N) from the File menu and then select Project Workspace in the New dialog box:

Select OK to display the New Project Workspace dialog box and then select Console Application in the Type options:

Typing a descriptive name in the Name entry box and then selecting the Create button will create the project workspace.

After the project workspace has been created, a program can be typed in an edit window. To display the edit window, select the New command from the File menu and then select Text File in the New dialog box. In the example below, a project workspace was created and then the Hello world program typed into the edit window:

The Visual C++ MDS window and edit window

After entering a program, it is saved by selecting the Save command (Ctrl+S) from the File menu or by clicking on the Save button on the Tool bar (■). The first time a program is saved, Visual C++ displays a dialog box where a descriptive program name is typed with the extension .cpp. For the program above, the name hello.cpp was used:

When finished working in Visual C++, the Exit command from the File menu is selected to close any edit windows and remove the Visual C++ MDS window from the Desktop.

A Guide to Programming in C++

Review 1

In this review, you will enter the Hello world program.

1) CREATE A PROGRAM WORKSPACE

   a. Start Visual C++. The MDS window is displayed.
   b. From the File menu, select the New command.
   c. Select Project Workspace in the New dialog box.
   d. Select OK. The New Project Workspace dialog box is displayed.
   e. Select Console Application in the Type options.
   f. Type hello in the Name entry box.
   g. Select the Create button to create a program workspace named hello.

2) ENTER A PROGRAM

   a. From the File menu, select New.
   b. Select Text File in the New dialog box.
   c. Select OK. A blank edit window is displayed.
   d. In the edit window, type the following program:

```
/*Hello world program.
    Your Name Date        */

#include <iostream.h>

int main()
{
   cout << "Hello, world!";
   return(0);
}
```

3) SAVE THE PROGRAM

   a. From the File menu, select the Save command. The Save As dialog box is displayed.
   b. Type hello.cpp to replace the default file name.
   c. Select the OK button. The file name hello.cpp is now displayed at the top of the edit window.

4) EXIT VISUAL C++

From the File menu, select the Exit command. The program's edit window is closed and the Visual C++ MDS window is removed from the screen.

B.2 Compiling

After the C++ source code has been saved, the file needs to be added to the project workspace before it can be compiled. To do this, select the Files into Project command from the Insert menu. Next, select the file name with the .cpp extension and select the Add button.

Visual C++ automatically compiles the C++ source code into the object code and links the object code to create the executable file when the Build *<project name>*.exe command from the Build menu is selected or the Build button on the Tool bar (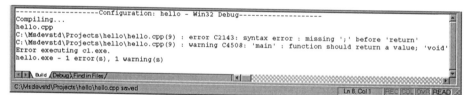) is clicked. The program, in linked object form, is then executed and the output displayed in a window by selecting the Execute *<project name>*.exe command from the Build menu. For example, when the Hello world program is run its output looks similar to:

A program's output is displayed in a window

At the end of the program output, the text `Press any key to continue` is automatically displayed. Pressing a key closes the output window.

B.3 Errors

The Visual C++ compiler will notify you of any syntax errors when the program is compiled. A message is displayed at the bottom of the Visual C++ MDS window listing possible causes for errors:

```
--------------------Configuration: hello - Win32 Debug--------------------
Compiling...
hello.cpp
C:\Msdevstd\Projects\hello\hello.cpp(9) : error C2143: syntax error : missing ';' before 'return'
C:\Msdevstd\Projects\hello\hello.cpp(9) : warning C4508: 'main' : function should return a value; 'void'
Error executing cl.exe.
hello.exe - 1 error(s), 1 warning(s)
```

The Message window lists probable causes for compilation errors

B.4 More on Using Visual C++

opening a program

To open a program previously saved on disk, its project workspace needs to be opened by selecting the Open Workspace command from the file menu. A project workspace file has the extension .mdp. The program stored in the workspace is automatically displayed in an edit window. If the program is not displayed, it can be opened by using the Open command from the File menu or the Open button on the Tool bar (🗁).

printing a program

When the edit window is active, the Print command from the File menu is used to print a program. Before printing, it is important to save the program.

B

Review 2

In this review you will run the Hello world program.

1) OPEN THE HELLO.MDB PROJECT WORKSPACE

   a. Start Visual C++.

   b. From the File menu, select the Open Workspace command. The Open Project Workspace dialog box is displayed.

   c. Double-click on the hello folder.

   d. Select hello.mdp.

   e. Select Open. The project workspace is opened and the hello.cpp program is displayed in an edit window.

2) PRINT THE PROGRAM

   a. From the File menu, select the Print command. The Print dialog box is displayed.

   b. Select OK to accept the default options and print a copy of the program's source code.

3) ADD THE PROGRAM TO THE WORKSPACE

   a. From the Insert menu, select the Files into Project command.

   b. Select hello.cpp and then the Add button.

4) RUN THE PROGRAM

   a. From the Build menu, select the Build hello.exe command. The program is compiled. If there are no errors the program is also linked.

       If the program has errors, they must be corrected and then the Build hello.cpp command selected again to compile and link the program.

   b. From the Build menu, select the Execute hello.exe command. The output from the program is displayed in a window.

5) CLOSE THE FILE AND EXIT VISUAL C++

   a. Press any key on the keyboard to close the output window.

   b. Click on the Close button in the upper-right corner of the edit window to close it.

   c. From the File menu, select Exit.

B.5 Using Help

```
Help
  Contents
  Search...
  Keyboard...

  Define Subset...
  Set Default Subsets...
  Open Information Title...   Ctrl+Shift+O

  Tip of the Day...

  Technical Support

  About Developer Studio...
```

The Help menu provides commands that can be selected to display online information. Selecting the Contents command displays a list of various help topics.

The Search command allows you to search on a specific topic that you enter.

Pressing the F1 key brings up context sensitive online help. For example, when entering a program in an edit window, pressing the F1 key when the cursor is on a keyword displays a window with information about that keyword.

B.6 Debugging with Visual C++

Visual C++ has tools that are useful for debugging and testing loops. The Step Into command (F11) in the Debug submenu from the Build menu is for watching and controlling program execution one statement at a time. The Watch window that is displayed while debugging is for watching the values of variables as they change during program execution.

The Step Into command can help detect errors in logic. To "step through" a program in the edit window, the F11 key is pressed to place an arrow next to the first executable statement. Pressing F11 again executes the statement and moves the arrow to the next executable statement. This process may be continued for the entire program, or the Stop Debugging command (Shirft+F5) from the Debug menu is selected to stop program execution.

Errors in a program can become more obvious if the values of variables are known throughout program execution. Highlighting a variable name in the edit window and dragging it to the Watch window at the bottom of the Visual C++ MDS window adds the variable name. The values of variables in the Watch window are updated as the statements in the program are executed. The Watch window is most useful when stepping through a program.

B.7 Libraries

All C++ compilers include standard libraries that can be used in programs, such as the iostream library. However, each compiler may have additions to a library that are specific to that compiler. Below are notes about the libraries used in this text:

iostream.h

To format output in a field, as done in Chapter Three, alignment can be changed from left to right by first unsetting the left alignment before setting the alignment to right. For example, to change a field's alignment from left to right, the following statements are required:

```
cout.unsetf(ios::left);
cout.setf(ios::right);
```

Please refer to the Teacher's Resource Package and the README.TXT file supplied on disk for more information about the libraries used in this text.

C Appendix C - Keywords in C++

Throughout this text C++ keywords were introduced. Keywords have special meanings in C++, therefore they may not be used as identifiers. The following is a list of the C++ keywords.

asm	double	new	switch
auto	else	operator	template
break	enum	private	this
case	extern	protected	throw
catch	float	public	try
char	for	register	typedef
class	friend	return	union
const	goto	short	unsigned
continue	if	signed	virtual
default	inline	sizeof	void
delete	int	static	volatile
do	long	struct	while

C

A Guide to Programming in C++

I | Program Index

Index

I

C

D

E

F

G

H

I

I